# Spokesman for Democracy

*Ambassador Claude G. Bowers*

PETER J. SEHLINGER

HOLMAN HAMILTON

# Spokesman for Democracy
# CLAUDE G. BOWERS
## 1878–1958

With a Foreword by Arthur Schlesinger, Jr.

Indiana Historical Society
Indianapolis 2000

Printed in the United States of America

The paper in this publication meets the minimum requirements of American National Standard for Information Sciences—Permanence of Paper for Printed Library Materials, ANSI Z39.48–1984. ∞

**Library of Congress Cataloging-in-Publication Data**

Sehlinger, Peter J.
    Spokesman for democracy: Claude G. Bowers, 1878–1958 / Peter J. Sehlinger, Holman Hamilton.
       p.   cm.
    Includes bibliographical references (p.   ) and index.
    ISBN 0-87195-145-2
    1. Bowers, Claude Gernade, 1879–1958. 2. Politicians–United States–Biography. 3. Diplomats–United States–Biography. 4. Journalists–United States–Biography. 5. United States–Politics and government–1901–1953. 6. United States–Foreign relations–20th century. I. Hamilton, Holman. II. Title.

E748.B724 S44 2000
973.91'092–dc21
[B]

                                         99-088011

*In Memoriam*

HOLMAN HAMILTON

*Fort Wayne, Indiana, 1910–Lexington, Kentucky, 1980*

# Contents

# Foreword

The reviewer declared the book "thrilling." At last, he wrote, Alexander Hamilton had been exposed as the arrogant champion of the regressive forces of wealth, birth, commerce, and the press. At last, Thomas Jefferson, rallying "the scattered raw material of the working masses, difficult to reach, difficult to organize," had been recognized as the savior of American democracy.

"I have a breathless feeling as I lay down this book," the reviewer concluded, "—a picture of escape after escape which this nation passed through in those first ten years, a picture of what might have been if the Republic had been finally organized as Alexander Hamilton sought. But I have a breathless feeling, too, as I wonder if, a century and a quarter later, the same contending forces are not again mobilizing. Hamiltons we have today. Is a Jefferson on the horizon?"

The year was 1925. The book was *Jefferson and Hamilton: The Struggle for Democracy in America*. The author was a forty-seven-year-old newspaperman named Claude G. Bowers. The reviewer was a forty-three-year-old politician named Franklin D. Roosevelt. There was indeed a Jefferson on the horizon (though, when FDR arrived in the White House seven years later, he turned out to be a Jefferson who freely employed Hamiltonian means to attain his ends).

Bowers's book, as Merrill D. Peterson observed in his fine study of *The Jeffersonian Image in the American Mind*, was "a major event in Jefferson's posthumous history." Nineteenth-century historians were mostly Republicans and had treated Jefferson with condescension and disdain. In 1925 *Jefferson and Hamilton* became a runaway best-seller; probably no book on Jefferson has ever sold so well. The book renewed the definition of American politics as a mortal struggle between the Hamiltonian vision (bad) and the Jeffersonian vision (good). Bowers's impassioned advocacy ushered in a grand revival of Jefferson's reputation.

Born in Westfield, Indiana, in 1878, Bowers could not afford college and was educated in newspaper offices. He was an insatiable reader, a famed orator (his keynote speech at the Democratic convention in 1928 stands with Alben Barkley's keynote in 1948 and Mario Cuomo's in 1984 as among the most effective political orations of the century), and a vivid and compelling writer.

Bowers liked to quote Hilaire Belloc: "Readable history is melodrama." That was his kind of history. He had prepared for *Jefferson and Hamilton* by writing the exciting *Party Battles of the Jackson Period* (1922). As he said in his introduction to the Jackson book, "The Drama—its motives—its actors—such is the theme of this history."

Bowers saw history as the theater of the past. He saw it also as an influence on the politics of the present. His cast of sharply defined heroes and villains and his mastery of pace, color, and anecdote gave his books uncommon narrative thrust. He combined this with enough in the way of citations and footnotes to suggest scholarly authority. Analysis was sketchy and simplistic; narrative was the thing. *Jefferson and Hamilton* was followed by *Jefferson in Power* (1936) and *The Young Jefferson* (1945). The three Jefferson books were lively reading but have long since been superseded as history.

Bowers's other notable best-seller, *The Tragic Era: The Revolution after Lincoln* (1929), seems out of character. He was in most matters a stalwart liberal, genial and tolerant, an unterrified champion of the "working masses." But Reconstruction roused in him racist emotions akin to those on display in D. W. Griffith's *The Birth of a Nation*. "The Southern people," he wrote, "literally were put to the torture" in "the dramatic struggle for the preservation of Southern civilization."

Also, as a loyal Democrat, he hoped that the book would be "the most powerful single factor in bringing the South back into line."

By attacking the Radical Republicans of the 1860s, those who sought a better break for the ex-slaves, he hoped to overcome resentments caused by the party's nomination of a Roman Catholic in 1928 and to remind the South what the Republican party was all about. "Never have American public men in responsible positions, directing the destiny of the Nation, been so brutal, hypocritical, and corrupt. . . . In this no American can take pride. The evil that they did lives after them."

Actually no American can take pride in *The Tragic Era*. But the book, it must be admitted, faithfully represented the professional scholarship of the day, dominated as it was by the school of William A. Dunning of Columbia. It also demonstrated the limitations of Jeffersonian liberalism. After all, Woodrow Wilson, another liberal Democrat, had resegregated Washington. As for Bowers's desire to recapture the South, FDR, without having read his book, wrote him from Warm Springs, Georgia, that it had "done much to bring back a great many erring members of our party."

Bowers was a hard worker and fluent writer. He produced book after book in the 1920s while writing editorials for the *New York World*. In the 1930s and 1940s he still wrote books even while changing careers. In 1933 President Roosevelt appointed him ambassador to the Spanish Republic. Bowers was strongly on the Loyalist side during the Spanish Civil War of 1936–39. When Franco triumphed, FDR sent him at once as ambassador to Chile, where he was a stout friend of Chilean democracy until he retired in 1953. In his new life as a diplomat, Bowers was an unrepentant champion, sometimes against his own State Department, of American democratic ideals.

Holman Hamilton and Peter J. Sehlinger deserve thanks for restoring this versatile and influential journalist, historian, and diplomat to his proper place in the annals of twentieth-century America.

Arthur Schlesinger, Jr.
15 August 1999

# Acknowledgments

This volume is the product of more than two authors, for many minds have helped to shape it. Spouses, friends, historians, archivists, librarians, and interviewees, in the United States and abroad, have contributed to the research, formulation, writing, and editing of this biography. Their suggestions, work at uncovering sources, stylistic and organizational aid, clues, and even disagreements proved of immeasurable help.

Several individuals offered their assistance to both writers. As in preparing his other books, Hamilton was indebted to his wife, Suzanne Bowerfind Hamilton, for her sacrifices and support as he dedicated his energies to the Bowers project. I, too, am grateful to her for her encouragement. Gayle Thornbrough, Hamilton's coeditor of *Indianapolis in the "Gay Nineties": High School Diaries of Claude G. Bowers*, devoted many hours while executive secretary of the Indiana Historical Society to uncovering sources and information about Bowers and his contemporaries. She was a good friend of Hamilton and a special person for me. While graduate students at the University of Kentucky, James C. Klotter and Thomas H. Appleton, Jr., labored as researchers for their professor in his quest for Bowers materials. They also provided me with valuable counsel and editorial advice from their posts at the Kentucky Historical Society. Klotter is now at Georgetown College.

Both authors also received essential assistance from the staffs of the Lilly Library at Indiana University, Bloomington, the National Archives and the Manuscript Division of the Library of Congress in Washington, D.C., the William Henry Smith Memorial Library at the Indiana Historical Society and the Indiana Division of the Indiana State Library in Indianapolis, the Houghton Library at Harvard University in Cambridge, Massachusetts, and the Franklin D. Roosevelt Library in Hyde Park, New York. Hamilton particularly valued the help of Caroline Dunn and Martha Hawkins Norman at the Smith Library. At the Lilly Library, Saundra B. Taylor's patience and her help in using the Bowers Manuscript Collection made research for me there profitable and always pleasant.

While researching and writing this biography, Hamilton benefited from the help of other librarians and students, as well as historians and friends of Bowers. Patricia Bowers gave the author access to her father's letters and other primary sources, and the staff at the Margaret I. King Library at the University of Kentucky helped locate secondary sources. Esther Cavanagh, the librarian at the former Shortridge High School in Indianapolis, furnished materials, and Jessie E. Moore, an Indianapolis friend of Sybil and Claude Bowers, gave Hamilton her correspondence with them. Dozens of Bowers's associates who knew him as a journalist, historian, political adviser, and diplomat graciously agreed to be interviewed by Hamilton in venues throughout the United States and in Mexico and Chile. At the University of Kentucky, fellow professors Thomas D. Clark, Charles P. Roland, and Carl B. Cone read drafts of his first chapters, while graduate student John David Smith researched secondary materials for the author. An important debt that Hamilton often mentioned was the financial support he received from the University of Kentucky while pursuing his research and writing.

I also am indebted to many for their contributions to this biography. At the General Archive and Library of the Ministry of Foreign Affairs in Madrid, María José Lazano Rincón helped me uncover significant sources relating to Bowers's diplomacy, as did Carmen Gloria Duhart de Vargas at the Historical Archive of the Ministry of Foreign Relations in Santiago. Martin Ridge's assistance and encouragement at the Henry E. Huntington Library in

San Marino, California, made researching the Bowers Collection there a marvelous experience. I would be remiss if I did not mention my thanks to the staffs of the Chilean National Archive, the French National Archives and the Quay d'Orsay archive at the Ministry of Foreign Affairs in Paris, the John F. Kennedy Library in Boston, Massachusetts, and the Columbia University Oral History Research Office in New York. Thanks are also due to James Baldwin and his colleagues at the University Library at Indiana University–Purdue University in Indianapolis for their help. Also deserving a special note of appreciation are those whom I interviewed in this country, Chile, Spain, and France.

I would like to express my gratitude for the financial assistance I received from several sources. Indiana University provided me with sabbatical leaves and funds to consult the Bowers Manuscripts at the Lilly Library and to travel to Spain and Chile, while the Indiana Historical Society awarded me a Director's Grant to visit the Roosevelt and Houghton Libraries. The National Endowment for the Humanities supported my research in Santiago, Chile, and I was an Andrew W. Mellon Fellow at the Huntington Library.

My greatest debts are to historians. Bernard Friedman and Ralph D. Gray, my colleagues at Indiana University, Indianapolis, read several chapters of the manuscript and offered insightful comments. Robert H. Whealey of Ohio University and Jon Kofas of Indiana University, Kokomo, offered valuable comments on the Spanish and Chilean chapters, respectively. Robert H. Ferrell of Indiana University, Bloomington, kindly read and reread every chapter of the biography. His counsel, editorial skill, and patience with me as I rewrote the manuscript were instrumental in bringing this work to publication. Like so many other authors, I am much in his debt.

At the Indiana Historical Society special thanks are due Thomas A. Mason, director of publications, Paula J. Corpuz, editor, and Kathleen M. Breen and George Hanlin, assistant editors, for their careful attention to this manuscript. Their encouragement and advice are much appreciated.

Most deserving of special thanks is my wife, Sabine Jessner. A European historian and retired colleague at Indiana University,

Indianapolis, she took careful notes during our research trips in the United States, France, and Spain, not to mention the hundreds of hours she spent at the computer typing and editing draft after draft. But more important than her historical skills as a researcher and astute critic were the support she afforded me and her enthusiasm for publishing Bowers's biography. Her aid, together with the help of so many others, means more to me than words on paper can express.

Peter J. Sehlinger
Indiana University, Indianapolis

# Introduction

"One of the most able public men of his generation" was Harry S. Truman's verdict on the life of Claude G. Bowers.[1] Indeed, from his modest origins in a small Indiana town, Bowers gained a national and international reputation as a spokesman for democracy. He was an outspoken proponent of the populist ideas of William Jennings Bryan, the progressivism of Woodrow Wilson, and the New Deal of Franklin D. Roosevelt. During the conservative Republican years of the 1920s—a discouraging decade for liberals—he encouraged the Democratic party to offer the nation an alternative to the GOP's complacent policy of "Normalcy." On the international stage he defended democracy in Spain and Chile against fascism in the 1930s and 1940s, and during the cold war he opposed communism, while also attacking the excesses of anti-democratic spokesmen in his own country.

The talented and versatile Bowers was widely known in the last half of the twentieth century as a journalist, orator, politician, historian, and diplomat, who advocated his democratic beliefs in each of these fields. As an editor in Indianapolis, Terre Haute, and Fort Wayne, his writings promoted the Democracy and sought to advance liberal reform. In New York his columns gained national prominence and were carried coast to coast by papers in the Hearst chain. An orator before and during the Radio Age, Bowers reached hundreds of thousands of people through innumerable speeches before Democratic audiences—campaign speeches, dinner talks, his memorable keynote address to the 1928 Democratic National Convention, and some of the first political broadcasts on a national hookup. As a writer of popular historical works, he praised what he considered the democratic and anti-oligarchical achievements of Andrew Jackson and Thomas Jefferson; indeed, the latter became his heroic model for the Democratic party. Likewise, he lambasted the deeds of the Radical Republicans during Reconstruction, while lauding their southern opponents. Presidents of the American Historical Association, as well as journalists, wrote glowing reviews of his works. His trilogy on Jefferson and his history of Reconstruction sold more copies than any other works on these subjects before or since. In the political arena he commanded the confidence of Democratic leaders from Bryan to Truman, while winning the friendship of some prominent Republicans. As an ambassador for twenty years, he was an important diplomatic figure, identified with the civil war in Spain and World War II and the cold war in Chile.

Repeatedly, Bowers was both observer and actor in the drama of domestic and diplomatic history. In Indiana he was closely associated with a series of Indiana senators and governors—including Samuel M. Ralston, Thomas R. Marshall, John W. Kern, Thomas Taggart, and Albert J. Beveridge. In New York he became a confidant of several influential leaders—Gov. Alfred E. Smith and Mayor Jimmy Walker, as well as Franklin and Eleanor Roosevelt. The versatile Hoosier also counted among his friends William G. McAdoo, Cordell Hull, James A. Farley, Eugene V. Debs, Theodore Dreiser, Edgar Lee Masters, John Dos Passos, and Ernest Hemingway. As ambassador in Madrid, Bowers befriended two of the Spanish Republic's most famous liberal reformers, President Manuel Azaña and Fernando de los Ríos, while as envoy to Chile he gained the respect of such important statesmen as former president Arturo Alessandri, Presidents Pedro Aguirre Cerda, Juan Antonio Ríos, and Gabriel González Videla, and future president Eduardo Frei Montalva.

Bowers's political activity spanned decades. In 1956 his last contribution to the party connected him with the second presidential campaign of Adlai E. Stevenson, whose grandfather Bowers had lauded editorially in 1900 when the first Adlai came to Indianapolis. As ambassador to Chile in 1941, Bowers chatted about world conditions during a three-hour tête-à-tête with twenty-four-year-old John F. Kennedy, whose grandfather John F. "Honey Fitz" Fitzgerald was an old friend.

Stars of the stage and screen, poets, painters, sculptors, behind-the-scenes wire-pullers like Col. Edward M. House, and influential legislators like Robert F. Wagner moved in and out of Bowers's days. A journalist and a historian, Bowers frequently took notes on who said what to whom and on the "How?" and "Why?" of history. He kept diaries of his high school days in the 1890s and from 1923 until his death, and he wrote hundreds of delightfully uninhibited letters to a score of friends, inspiring them to reply with regularity. More than his columns and editorials, more than his books, more than his orations or diplomacy, Bowers's private comments on contemporary men and women, issues, and events—a "hidden" history—are likely to arouse the reader's interest.

Although Bowers demonstrated his virtues as a proponent of democracy, he also had his faults. Convinced of the righteousness of his views, he was too self-assured on occasion, and this led to difficulties. Some of his celebrated problems with the State Department during his ambassadorial years were the result of his inability to consider opinions that conflicted with his own. At times Bowers proved unable to admit he was wrong—even when he realized he had made a mistake. Although he later became aware that Communists had exercised more influence in the Spanish Republic than he had realized, he never admitted this. For a modern audience, his most egregious flaw was his racism. In his writing—particularly in his history of Reconstruction—and in his personal feelings, he viewed African Americans with disdain. While many New Deal Democrats were advocating more rights for African Americans, Bowers remained an opponent of civil rights in the years after World War II.

Claude Bowers was a friend and mentor of the original author of this biography, Holman Hamilton. While Bowers was an editor at the *Fort Wayne Journal-Gazette,* his family lived next door to Hamilton's Aunt Mary Hoffman, and the Bowerses' daughter Patty was a playmate of Hamilton's cousin Billy. There Hamilton met

Bowers and became a favorite of the editor. In his teens the youth read Bowers's *The Party Battles of the Jackson Period* and *Jefferson and Hamilton: The Struggle for Democracy in America* and began his fascination with history.[2] The two became epistolary friends after the author left Fort Wayne in 1923.

In some ways the youth's path followed that of Bowers. Hamilton became an editor at the *Journal-Gazette* and then turned to history. While Hamilton was writing his two-volume biography of Zachary Taylor, Bowers offered advice, and he contributed the introduction when the first volume appeared in 1941. Hamilton later left journalism and in 1954 received his Ph.D. in history from the University of Kentucky, teaching history there from 1954 until his retirement in 1975. A well-respected author and professor, Hamilton was president of the Southern Historical Association in 1979. In his presidential address titled "Clio with Style," he insisted that historical works should be written with "such style that history glows, that leaders and followers of bygone eras spring to life, that spent forces are recharged and move again with their old momentum." Hamilton's admonition to historians, in effect, was to follow the same goal that Bowers earlier had told him was his goal: "I began the writing of history to make it readable to the general public."[3]

When Bowers was preparing to end his diplomatic service, Hamilton wrote him in 1952 asking his cooperation in writing a "full-dress biography." The subject not only agreed, he answered questions and prepared overviews on different periods of his life for his biographer. He also made available his voluminous diaries and correspondence.[4] After Bowers's death in 1958, Hamilton continued his research, collecting a tremendous amount of material. Over the next two decades he interviewed dozens of his subject's friends, acquaintances, and diplomatic associates, traveling throughout the United States and to Mexico and Chile. With Gayle Thornbrough of the Indiana Historical Society, Hamilton was the coeditor in 1964 of *Indianapolis in the "Gay Nineties": High School Diaries of Claude G. Bowers*. Not until the early 1970s did Hamilton find time to begin writing the biography.[5]

This book was unfinished when Hamilton died in 1980. He had completed drafts of chapters covering Bowers's life from 1878 until 1933—his childhood and his years in Washington, D.C., Indiana, and New York as an editor, orator, historian, and political adviser. Hamilton also had collected a great deal of primary and secondary sources on Bowers's twenty years as a diplomat to Spain and Chile.

In 1989 at the request of Hamilton's widow, Suzanne Bowerfind Hamilton, I agreed to become the coauthor and complete the Bowers biography. I have rewritten Hamilton's drafts that constitute the first six chapters of this work, covering Bowers's childhood through his years as a journalist in New York, and I have written the last five chapters of the biography. In composing these chapters and in rewriting Hamilton's unfinished manuscript, I have relied on the materials he collected, as well as my own research. While preparing this biography, I have come to share Hamilton's enthusiasm for his subject and respect for his accomplishments. This is Claude Bowers's story, and it is an important one.

# CHAPTER ONE

# "Bowers! Bowers! He Is Ours!"

No peaks. No valleys. Across the level land, the gray sky swept from Indianapolis north to Kokomo. The place: a cottage on the edge of a Quaker village—Westfield, Hamilton County, Indiana. The date: Wednesday, 20 November 1878.

As night came, rain came. An autumnal storm. Lewis Bowers, thirty-one-year-old proprietor of a small store in the village, hitched up the horse and set out in the family buggy for Jolietville five miles away. With "the moon and stars . . . hidden behind heavy clouds," the buggy slithered through the mud.[1] "I have often heard my father tell of that night," Claude Bowers was to write. The vehicle broke down and had to be fixed in the dark. Perhaps there was swearing, perhaps a prayer, before the wheels rolled again. An objective was reached: Dr. John N. Parr's large, comfortable house in the Jolietville hamlet. A shrewd and witty graduate of Indiana Asbury University, Parr doubled as physician and Methodist minister. The call was to deliver a baby, and fortunately, the doctor was at home. The buggy, with the doctor on board, returned to the village of Westfield, where in a cottage on the eastern edge, Julia Etta Bowers lay in labor. Before midnight a child was born, listed as "Claudius" in the 1880 census but otherwise known as Claude Gernade Bowers.[2]

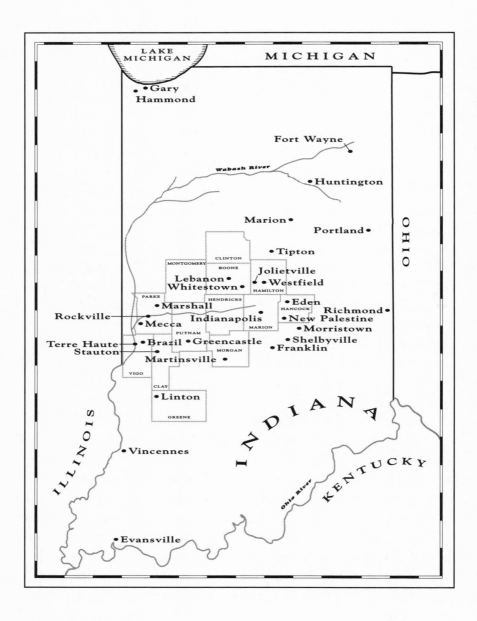

Claude's father, Lewis Bowers, was born in 1847. A slender man, he had blue-gray eyes, black hair, and a long black beard. He lived first in Westfield, next in Jolietville, and finally in Whitestown, twenty miles north of Indianapolis. The general store of Lew Bowers was a popular trading and social center. He had a fine voice, was an enthusiastic singer at the Lutheran and Methodist churches, and possessed a sense of humor. As the son recalled, his relations with the father were "very affectionate."[3]

What made a comparable impression on little Claude was Lew's adherence to the Democratic party. During the 1880 contest between the Republican James A. Garfield and the Democrat Winfield S. Hancock, Claude was not quite two years old. A Republican lounger in the store asked the child, "Are you for Garfield?" "Naw, naw, rah for Hancock!" was the treble answer.[4]

Lew Bowers's Democratic allegiance was a matter of inheritance as well as conviction. He was one of twelve children and two sons of Christian and Jemima Catron Bowers, settlers who helped carve Boone County out of Indiana swamps and woods. Born in Germany, Christian Bowers had come to America in the 1830s. Landing at Charleston, he lived for a time in East Tennessee, marrying a woman of Austrian extraction. She was related to John Catron, the Tennessee politician whom Martin Van Buren appointed to the Supreme Court. In the mid-1840s the family left for Indiana, where as a non-slave-owning farmer Christian believed his future would be brighter. The couple became leaders in a neighborhood of farmers and villagers and deeply ingrained Democrats.[5]

Christian built a house on his Worth Township farm on the periphery of Whitestown. It had a wide hall, stairs going up, and—as Claude Bowers wrote—on the banister the grandchildren "courted death." Here the boy came on Sundays and holidays. He was impressed by his grandmother, a "woman of grim determination and very strong character." Nor would he forget the dinner table with bustling aunts carrying trays of steaming dishes from the kitchen. When not beating on a drum or playing with the endless supply of cousins, he joined the elders in the living room and listened to political discussions.

Claude admired his Bowers grandfather—"respected for his honesty, fairness, sense of justice, toleration, even temper, and hospitality." The same height as his son Lew and just as thin, Christian Bowers belonged to the Lutheran Church and never rid himself of a German accent. He had supported Stephen A. Douglas against Abraham Lincoln in 1860, always insisting that the Democrat's election would have prevented the bloodshed that he ascribed to the "fanaticism of extremists."[6]

Julia Etta Tipton, Lewis Bowers's wife, was twenty-six when her son was born. She was a native Hoosier of English ancestry—five feet six, weighing 120 pounds, with brown hair and blue eyes. Eager for the advance of herself and family, she seemed stalked by tragedy. Her mother died at her birth, her father was killed when she was eleven, and her first child—four-year-old Gertrude—died of diphtheria a week before Claude was born. Julia Etta later changed her name to Juliet. Intimates knew her as Ett.[7] Restless, ambitious, making the best of things during a difficult life, she possessed energy, industry, and courage. It was she who would be closest to Claude.

Claude's maternal grandfather, James Tipton, influenced his grandson though the boy never knew him. A native of Maryland and so Whiggish that he named his eldest son for Winfield Scott, Tipton was a blacksmith and a farmer. His land in Hamilton County lay along the Boone County line. He possessed—in the words of a descendant—"forensic ability" or "the gift of gab." An original Republican, he identified as much virtue with the party of his choice as Christian Bowers saw in the Democratic cause. Tipton, too, was a patriot who enlisted in the Union army as a private at the age of forty. In November 1863 the blacksmith-turned-soldier lost his life in the assault on Missionary Ridge.[8]

Lewis and Julia Bowers's first move after Claude's birth came from two causes. Grief-stricken by their daughter's death, they wanted to leave Westfield. A store was available at Jolietville, and the family moved there in early 1879. While the tiny community offered no promise of expansion, it was near the Tipton farm where Julia could spend much time with her stepmother, half sister, and

half brothers. Claude and his parents stayed in Jolietville a year
and a half and proceeded on to Whitestown.[9]

Recollections of Whitestown were etched in Bowers's memory.
The puny lad often was sick, and twice his life was despaired of.
Susceptible to colds, he spent long winter days in bed at his
Whitestown home (now 101 Bowers Street). An only child, he
had parental concern hovering over him.[10]

When he was eight and nine and ten, Claude liked to read the
Indianapolis papers, especially the Democratic *Sentinel* with its partisan political news. Leaders, meetings, and conventions intrigued
the child. Propped up by pillows, he cut out the pictures of senators and governors. Mounting them on cardboard, he formed conventions of his own, with the counterpane as the convention hall
and a blanket or sheet as the speaker's platform. The boy acted as
a puppeteer or a deus ex machina. If he devised a Republican
assemblage, James G. Blaine or Robert G. Ingersoll might orate
through the medium of Claude's voice. If Democrats convened, the
eloquence of Daniel W. Voorhees would be imitated, or the red
bandana of Allen G. Thurman would be waved to signal an ovation. Now tactical motions are made and seconded. The chairman
raps for order. Resolutions are thrown out. At last a nominee
emerges, a running mate completes the ticket, and speeches of the
ensuing campaign come couched in the phrases of Claude.[11] Less
than half a century later the orator of the pillows would be delivering a keynote address at a Democratic national convention.

The boy was not always ill, and sickroom make-believe bore a
relation to the day-to-day world of which he had knowledge—
Whitestown of the 1880s. Among village personalities to whom
Claude liked to listen was the shoemaker J. S. Smith, a bearded
craftsman who smoked a corncob—its aroma mingling with the
smell of leather and wood burning in the shop's stove. Smith let
the child express a political opinion or two, listening with chuck-
les and injecting "pungent observations."

There was old "Colonel" Harrison Roberts, a veteran of the
Civil War, who went about in a faded uniform and, morose in daylight hours, became mellow after dark, when liquor worked a trans-

formation. Everyone was familiar with the colonel's tales of battle, and "young rowdies knew they could pull the bung out of the barrel of oratory by merely mentioning Shiloh." Roberts would launch into a description, eyes flashing, voice ringing, and eloquence flowing like a mountain torrent. When he seemed on the point of running down, a listener would murmur from the shadows, "Shiloh," and the orator was off.

D. O. (Dave) Trout, the harness maker who organized a debating society, interested young Bowers more than any other speaker. Claude's graphic vignette of the village life he knew was of a crowd listening while Trout, chair against the wall, "pulverized" those who challenged him. Trout's wit was biting, his tongue sarcastic. If "driven into a corner for want of mere facts, he opened his batteries of ridicule," while the crowd shouted and slapped one another on the shoulder.[12]

Bowers's absorption in speaking, evident so early, can be traced to his Grandfather Tipton, a natural orator, or it may have stemmed from Claude's attendance at Democratic rallies from the time he was five. The boy's interest in politics developed from the convictions of relatives and from conversations before he went to school.

Similarly, history caught and held his fancy. Minnie Booher Tomlinson, member of a Boone County farm family, often told her son that Claude loved to climb up on her lap and insist that she read American history. In the Whitestown grade school, *The Eclectic History of the United States* came into his hands. This illustrated book was political and presidential. Chapters ended with biographical notes. Thomas Jefferson and Alexander Hamilton received detailed treatment. Claude admired the chapter on John C. Calhoun. The Great Nullifier's appeal to the child may have related to the fact that Grandfather Bowers entered the New World at Charleston. The *Eclectic History* influenced Claude's acquisition, when eleven, of John S. Jenkins's biography of the Carolinian.[13] Knowledge of southern politics and an affinity for a southern leader thus were among the boy's interests before he entered high school.

Claude's eight years in Whitestown left a legacy of memories that brought confidence in the innate intelligence of the common man. Political debates, sleigh bells, and county fairs were but some of his Boone County recollections. "I think I learned more of the American mind from the villagers of Whitestown," he said, "than I ever learned afterwards."[14] Forged in rural Indiana, his respect for the sentiments of the people remained as he ascended the political ladder of importance and experienced the sophistication of cosmopolitan and diplomatic life.

While the youngster was forming convictions that would remain with him throughout his life, there was a cloud in his childhood that would affect him—financially at least. The trusting and optimistic Lewis Bowers, proving too generous for his own good, endorsed the IOUs of impecunious customers. When the notes came due, he was accountable, and his resources were unequal to the strain. The genial merchant took to drink, lost his Whitestown store, tried his hand at a restaurant, became a failure in his community, and fell into disagreement with his wife. The couple separated, and in October 1888 Julia was granted a divorce. By this time she was attempting to support Claude and herself by working as a milliner in Whitestown. Five months after the divorce, she took her ten year old to live in the town of Lebanon where she had relatives.[15]

In Lebanon, from 1889 until 1891, "Mrs. J. E. Bowers's millinery store" could "be found" first on the west side of the courthouse and then in the Bragg house "next door to M.E. church, near the depot." The public was informed that Mrs. Bowers "will keep a first-class stock of goods in all the latest styles." She thanked "her many customers for past favors and solicits the same in the future."[16]

But what of Claude? After the first weeks he and his mother ate and slept in the part of the two-story house not given to women's hats. The Methodist church occupied the lot next door, a saloon on the other side. Twelve of Lebanon's thirteen saloons had their swinging doors within two blocks.

Though the milieu may have been far from ideal, Lebanon was a pleasant place of 3,682 residents. Social gradations were less sharp than in larger cities, and Claude walked three blocks to the Central School. A bright lad, Harold Jones, later an Indianapolis friend, was one of his schoolmates. A pretty girl, Ruby Cross, seemed charming to Claude. With his ear for history, he may have learned that across the street from Central the poet Joaquin Miller lived with his mother's uncle before going west. A future Indiana governor and United States senator, Samuel M. Ralston, was Mrs. Bowers's lawyer and became her son's friend—their association lasting the rest of Ralston's life. When Claude wanted Jenkins's *Calhoun*, Julia bought the book on the advice of Ralston. In addition to playing with school chums, Claude did the unusual for a child. Reflecting his growing interest in the law, he attended trials in the Boone County courthouse.[17]

Mother and son moved again—this time to Indianapolis in 1891. The new location enabled Claude to attend the capital city's grade and high schools, which were among the best in America. He lived eleven years at 317 North Alabama Street, "a humble one-storied frame cottage," where Julia switched her vocation from millinery to dressmaking.[18]

Meanwhile, his father died at Whitestown under strange circumstances in the autumn of 1891. "Louis Bowers Dead," the *Lebanon Patriot* reported, misspelling Lew's first name. "His death is thought to be the result of injuries received at the hands of murderous robbers, who threw him from a railroad bridge near Morristown about two weeks ago." The court had ordered him to pay fifty dollars annually toward Claude's support, and the poor fellow had been trying the grocery business at Morristown.[19] Presumably, Lew had set out on the forty miles to Whitestown when the "murderous robbers" did him in.

How did the son react? "I have never known . . . a sweeter human being," Bowers was to write, "he was loved by all who knew him. His generosity was extreme, and not a few took advantage of it." Other accounts do not describe Lew "going sadly, yet smilingly through life," as the son wrote in 1897. There is no allusion to the alcohol problem in Claude's letters or memoirs. The youth refrained from blaming Lew for the family's hardships.[20]

Although Claude never mentioned or lamented the divorce, it left an impression. In an editorial years later, he defended drunkenness as cause for separation and disagreed with the "curious notion some people have that a child is better off in a home of two discordant parents than to live in peace with one of them."[21] No doubt his father's absence influenced Claude as an adult to display a great deal of caring concern toward his only child.

In the spring of 1891 Grandfather Bowers had been gored by a bull on his farm, ending an existence far happier than Lew's and removing a possible source of assistance. In 1892 Julia married for a second time. The new husband, William E. Johnson, clerked in an Indianapolis clothing store. Little is known of Johnson, and he is not mentioned by the stepson in his autobiography. By 1894 Julia was again a working widow, and she reassumed her former married name.[22]

Despite economic difficulties, Bowers kept on with his classes. His mother financed his secondary education through dressmaking and taking in an occasional boarder. Summers were spent at the farm of Julia's stepmother where the boy devoured tomes on Vice President Thomas A. Hendricks and leaders of the early Republic.

Influenced by his mother's family, the youthful Democrat became a Republican and remained one for six years—another fact omitted from his memoirs. So it logically followed that in 1892, when Benjamin Harrison and Grover Cleveland became rivals for the second time, Claude was a Republican. Not quite fourteen, he and his chum David Crawford won election to their first "political" posts, memberships on the executive committee of the Indianapolis Third Ward School's Grade 7A Students' Republican Club.[23]

And so the years passed, and the child of a village became the youth of a town and then, growing to adulthood, found himself in Indianapolis, a place rapidly becoming a metropolis. The census of 1890 counted a population of 128,000, and a decade later the city had 170,000 inhabitants. Industry was changing the face of urban America in startling ways. Tall chimneys ascended from factories, residential neighborhoods mushroomed, and a host of new appurtenances appeared—brick streets, electric lights, and water and sewage systems.

Like all emerging large cities, Indianapolis was an important rail center. The Pennsylvania System, the Monon, the Big Four, and other lines connected it with all parts of the country. Pork packers, commission merchants, and importers and jobbers of dry goods were among the business leaders. Flour-mill machinery was manufactured in Indianapolis. Breweries and lumberyards lent variety. The political center of the state, the city was also the financial center and almost precisely the geographical center. "In the heart of an agricultural region unsurpassed anywhere," a chronicler pointed out, Indianapolis lay within "easy reach of the great coal fields, of the gas belt, and of the stone quarries that have made Indiana famous."[24]

Bowers was attracted by the downtown and by public personalities as magnetic in flesh as in books. Horse-drawn streetcars, hansom cabs, victorias, and barouches were a part of the scene. The streetcar transfer corner, the City Market at Tomlinson Hall, farmers bringing in fresh produce, butchers at the stalls, actors and actresses at English's Opera House, drummers at the Denison and Grand Hotels, reporters hurrying into newspaper offices—all intrigued the newcomer.

The youth's gaze swept the Circle where the Soldiers and Sailors Monument was rising 284 feet. Exactly two blocks west loomed the domed-limestone Capitol. Construction on this building was started by Gov. James D. "Blue Jeans" Williams the year Bowers was born.[25]

A quarter of a mile north of the Circle on Meridian Street and to the left and the right lived national, state, and local celebrities. Already familiar with their careers and reputations, Bowers knew all of these men by sight after being in the city only a few months. At 674 North Delaware was Benjamin Harrison's red-brick house with its large bay windows and stone trim. There he returned, a widower and ex-president, from Washington in 1893.[26] Nearby were dwellings of other leading citizens: John M. Butler, Harrison's fellow Republican and rival at the bar; William H. H. Miller,

Harrison's law partner and attorney general; and Albert J. Beveridge, barely past thirty, who already showed promise as an orator, senator, and biographer.

On Meridian Street lived Addison C. Harris—wealthy, forbidding, privately kind—who would serve as minister to Austria-Hungary and offer Bowers a Princeton education. Pennsylvania Street was home to bewhiskered John W. Kern, future Democratic vice presidential nominee and later Bowers's Washington boss while majority leader of the Senate. Blocks to the west, on North Capitol, future senator Thomas Taggart and his Eva were rearing their young children, two of whom Claude knew. Not far from the business district was the Park Avenue residence of Charles W. Fairbanks, lawyer and owner of the *Indianapolis News*, who would precede Beveridge, Kern, and Taggart to the Senate and become vice president.[27]

Two governors of Indiana, whom he observed, were Albert G. Porter and Isaac P. Gray. Genial and handsome, the Republican Porter served both in Congress and as minister to Italy. Like Miller, he was Harrison's law partner. Gray, a Republican before Grant corruption disenchanted him, became a hero to the Democrats. Inheriting the governorship on Williams's death, he won a term in his own right and in 1888 was a vice presidential possibility. After Bowers came to Indianapolis, President Cleveland appointed Gray minister to Mexico. Gray and Porter wore silk hats and Prince Albert coats when they promenaded. Bowers was astonished when he saw Porter lift his hat to "a ragged Negro." Claude recalled with chagrin and amusement an episode at a soda fountain where Gray ordered a lemon phosphate and the fourteen year old a chocolate soda. The "near presence of the great man so confused me that when the clerk, by mistake, switched our drinks, I began to drink the phosphate before I could be stopped, and I remember the look of disgust in Gray's eyes."

Disgust was seldom a reaction of adults who encountered the youth. At the age of five, Claude wore a Cleveland-Hendricks cap when presented to Sen. Daniel W. Voorhees, "the Tall Sycamore of the Wabash." Appropriately, the lad felt "anointed" when the dignitary placed a hand on his head. Ralston befriended Bowers, who reciprocated. Bowers became acquainted with Beveridge while a high school student; they corresponded when both were established authors. Claude had a long conversation with seventy-year-old Gen. Lew Wallace, "a fine looking fellow yet—fine proportioned, of medium height, erect, dignified, military. . . . My boyish timidity faded instantly in the warmth of his amiability and humor."[28]

Bowers was not too timid to go twice to Harrison's house for interviews with the reputedly cold, unapproachable former president. The youth did not hesitate to call at the hotel room of William Campbell Preston Breckinridge when that flamboyant Bluegrass orator came to Indiana. Among other members of the older generation to whom he wrote were former Secretary of the Interior Carl Schurz, author-politician Ignatius Donnelly, and novelist Thomas Nelson Page.[29]

But of all these worthies—mostly political, but some literary—the most memorable was Robert Ingersoll, the adversary of the fundamentalist preachers of his time, whose numbers were legion. Ingersoll's ability at the podium, which even preachers admitted was formidable, charmed Bowers, aroused him from charm to paeans of praise, and left him believing that he had stood at the right hand of the Throne: "I was today crowned at Olympia. This is the greatest day of my life. I received a letter from Robt. G. Ingersoll the greatest living orator. . . . It is a letter which I shall prize forever. He says to study Shakespeare. Places Curran at the head of English orators, Danton of French and Cicero of all."[30]

The names of the forensic masters emphasized by Ingersoll—Curran, Danton, Cicero—were for Bowers golden names of golden men who spoke in golden tones. On 3 July 1895 the first Bowers diary opened with three telling words: "Studied Chatham tonight." On 6 July: "Finished Chatham and commenced Burke." Five days later: "Tonight, studied Grattan. I don't believe that either Chatham or Burke could excel Grattan's speech which accompanied his motion for a Declaration of Rights in any of the arts of oratory."[31]

What Bowers was doing here was scrutinizing speeches delivered by three eighteenth-century figures: Henry Grattan, advocate of Ireland's independence; William Pitt the elder, Earl of Chatham, architect of British victory in the Seven Years' War; and Edmund Burke, famous for many things. Significantly, no teacher told Claude he must evaluate those masterpieces. The youth pored over them, often after school at the Indianapolis Public Library, simply because he admired them, and because they fit so helpfully into his chosen course of self-instruction.

Other diary samples illustrate the sustained pattern of his reading program. On 4 August Claude studied John P. Curran, "that delightful Irish orator whose fervent eloquence meant so much to the Irish patriot." On 7 August he finished Curran. "How graceful and beautiful are his speeches!" Came September, and "at the Library I sent down for the lectures of John Quincy Adams on oratory." And so it went month after month—John C. Calhoun, more Adams, more Curran, Ingersoll, more Burke, still more Calhoun.[32]

While home study with an oratorical preoccupation was central, Claude concurrently familiarized himself with facets of life and death. He regularly read newspapers, kept up on national and world events, and saw a big-league baseball game. He went to the theater, took walks in the country, dabbled in class politics, "had a great time down town" with friends, and occasionally visited kinsmen in Boone, Clinton, and Hamilton Counties. In addition to such pursuits, the lad rose at half past three in the morning to carry the *Indianapolis Sentinel* and received eight dollars a month for his work. He attended trials in the state and federal courts, thought a Cass County girl's eyes "as beautiful as two lone stars," and found the smell disagreeable when he climbed the stairs to a medical college dissecting room, but after awhile he "realely enjoyed the carving of human flesh."[33]

With two friends Bowers tramped to Mozart Hall to hear James Keir Hardie, British labor leader and parliamentarian. Reactions? Hardie's "delivery is ordinary. . . . His sentiments were reasonable, and he impressed me with his sincerity." At the City Hall Claude watched John Philip Sousa conduct a band concert and found him

"a determined looking man of medium height" with forceful gestures. Jane Addams of Chicago, founder of Hull-House, spoke at
Bowers's high school and won his esteem: "She seems very earnest
in her work and she is a friend of the workingman through and
through." Claude did not have the money to hear "the sweet
inspiring voice of the peerless [Nellie] Melba." But nothing could
keep him away from English's Opera House the next night when
Ingersoll appeared. "If ever any mortal could play with the feelings
of man, he can," the youth noted. "His voice, though not powerful, is fine. In the higher keys it is shrill, penetrating, flexible. His
gestures excell any I have seen. None are useless. All are in harmony with the thought. They are smooth and easy."[34]

The open-mindedness Claude expressed in his diary was evident
in his daily life. One of his six best friends was a Jewish boy. He
admired another Jewish youth whom he knew less intimately and
found the local rabbi's daughter "very attractive" and "highly gift-
ed in the power of literary expression." Not infrequently he "would
single out a colored boy or girl," stopping to chat or bestow publicly "some extra courtesy." Bowers resented the "low base race
prejudice" exemplified when a "brilliant" black college student,
Ezra Roberts, was unfairly treated in a speech contest. "The judges
lose—not Roberts," Claude concluded.

In the opinion of a classmate, it was from his mother that
Bowers derived his concern for people of different creeds and colors. Though he did not steadily attend religious services of any one
denomination, Sundays often found him listening to Rev. Thomas
I. Coultas at the Roberts Park Methodist Church, or "with fresh
admiration" to Rev. Joseph A. Milburn at the Second Presbyterian,
or walking "3 miles through the rain" to hear the Very Reverend
Denis O'Donaghue at St. Patrick's.

A school friend said that as an adolescent and adult, Bowers
"only had faith in one Supreme Being and lived the ethics and the
service to his fellow-men entailed by the ten commandments." Yet,
the year of his graduation, Bowers acknowledged that "I am drawn"
to Roman Catholicism, praising its "ancient history, the deep sincere reverence of the devotion, the quite heavenly purity of

monastic life, the lives of priests adorned of learning and purified by repose."[35]

The attraction of Catholicism may have been related to Claude's concentration on Chauncey A. Goodrich's 947-page volume, *Select British Eloquence*. Five of the speakers discussed by Goodrich were Irish, including Grattan and Curran, who were advocates of Catholic emancipation.[36] From *Select British Eloquence*, Bowers moved on to biographies of Curran, Grattan, Burke, the Irish patriots Daniel O'Connell and Robert Emmet, the playwright Richard Brinsley Sheridan, and the poet Thomas Moore. Orations, plays, and verses of those Irishmen became the teenager's favorite reading, and Bowers's identification with his "specialty" made him a proponent of home rule. Loving political and religious liberty, he resented the treatment of the Catholic Irish by the English—so much so that his first book would be *The Irish Orators: A History of Ireland's Fight for Freedom*.

In his teens Bowers also read a wide variety of works. Among his favorites were biographies of Alexander Hamilton, John Randolph of Roanoke, William Wirt, John C. Calhoun, Daniel Webster, Henry Clay, Lewis Cass, Charles Sumner, Stephen A. Douglas, Jefferson Davis, William H. Seward, Samuel J. Tilden, and James G. Blaine. Systematically, he perused the lives of United States presidents. Other books high on Claude's list were accounts of Demosthenes, John Bright, and Richard Cobden and histories by David Hume, Alphonse de Lamartine, and Edward Gibbon. Victor Hugo's *Les Misérables* was Bowers's first choice among novels. He roamed widely through Shakespeare, Milton, Byron, Shelley, Tennyson, Anatole France, Charles Dickens, Alphonse Daudet, and Gabriele D'Annunzio. Thomas Babington Macaulay's essays made a lasting impression. *Plutarch's Lives*, Lord Brougham's *Autobiography*, and *The Federalist* appealed strongly to him, as did James G. Blaine's *Twenty Years in Congress* and Thomas Hart Benton's *Thirty Years' View*.[37]

Bowers's literary absorption brought advantages in some classes at Indianapolis High School Number 1, then known as I.H.S. and later renamed Shortridge. While he had no affinity for science or mathematics and never really mastered a foreign language, he excelled in English and civil government courses. Entering the school at the northeast corner of Michigan and Pennsylvania Streets as a freshman in early 1894, he was greatly benefited by a young teacher, Ora Edson, who "gave me my first word of encouragement." Two other instructors whom Bowers liked were Robert M. King ("full of wit and humor") and Esther May Allerdice ("beautiful personally"). Charity Dye, who taught English and was an author, showed particular interest in the promising youth.

But the faculty member with the most permanent influence was Laura Donnan. She held bachelor's and master's degrees from the University of Michigan and had written *Our Government*, a textbook. Erect and dignified, with searching gaze, Donnan was "vivid in her teaching." Her voice, "though ordinarily warm and pleasant, had at times a booming quality which made her somewhat formidable though not less feminine." Loathing toadies, the Republican partisan in petticoats respected Bowers for having the courage of his convictions. She liked him because "I blurted out precisely what I thought" when, as a junior and senior, he began to gravitate back to the Democrats. Exerting "a decisive effect on my life," Donnan contributed to his self-reliance by recognizing his articles of faith—democracy and freedom. "My prospects were dark," Bowers would write, and "her faith in me was a torch."[38]

One of Bowers's closest associates in high school, George Langsdale, was, like Claude, a leader. Tall and thin, "like a cornstalk in October," Langsdale had a "striking" imagination and a "penetrating" mind. Together the youths helped organize the school's Republican Club, wrote for the yearbook, debated, and shared an interest in oratory and literature. George's sister Kate was married to Beveridge, so Bowers had entrée to Beveridge's house, where Mrs. Beveridge warned the lads to walk on tiptoe while her husband composed speeches. George's father was president of the commission charged with constructing the Soldiers and Sailors Monument and permitted Claude to climb to the top of the unfinished obelisk in the center of the city, a thrill he never forgot.[39]

Fully three years younger than Bowers and Langsdale was Abraham Cronbach. A little fellow, with "small, black, bead-like eyes" and a "dark greasy complexion," Abie was considered by Claude "an extraordinary boy" and a "sort of genius" who did well in his studies. As Rabbi Cronbach, he was to become a widely known professor of theology. Claude's lifelong respect for Cronbach is foreshadowed in the diary: "He is wonderful—is Abie."[40]

The enfant terrible of I.H.S. was the equally bright but unpredictable Paxton P. Hibben. He was nicknamed Pax, which was a misnomer. Short, freckled, with sharp nose and sharper tongue, this son of well-to-do parents was "a reader such as I have seldom met." Aspiring to extracurricular leadership, he was repeatedly defeated when honors were at stake because he was "aristocratic," a "supreme egotist," and "extremely unpopular."

Privately Claude observed that Hibben could qualify as the darling of a Parisian mob, his speeches shallow—"words, words, words." Still the universality of his interests, his drive, and the intensity of his feelings caused Claude to enjoy his company. Hibben would have a colorful career. After Princeton and Harvard, he would enter the diplomatic service, newspaper work, and the army. He mixed with Russian revolutionary crowds at St. Petersburg in 1905, and ten years later in Greece, King Constantine I acted as godfather to Hibben's daughter. In the 1920s he admired Lenin, brought Bowers and John Dos Passos together, was secretary for the relief of Russian children, and directed that his ashes be interred in Moscow. When Paxton died in 1928, Claude noted with respect that his friend's "genius was for controversy and on the side of unpopular causes."[41]

Girls? At Whitestown in 1886, the seven-year-old Claude found Pearl Moody appealing. Ruby Cross attracted him when he was eleven, as did Marie Hall when he was fourteen. Three Marys—Vajen, Sayles, and Stubbs—were among the high school beauties to whom the boy paid tribute. Florence Dunning? "Her lips are red and inviting." Edna Kuhn? "A well rounded form that is the admiration of every boy." The diary, however, nowhere suggests a moonlight-and-roses love affair. Only when he was nearly nineteen and Hibben lured him into exploratory sessions sponsored by the "Spooners Club" did Bowers breathlessly exclaim: "Had a great time as usual, 50 kisses, 3 girls on lap, 25 embraces. Ye Gods! and still we live."[42]

Nor is there the slightest hint of anything more than admiration in Bowers's friendship with the young lady who meant most to him intellectually at I.H.S. Younger than Claude and behind him in school, Myla Jo Closser had a "wealth of dark hair brushed back" and "dark, queenly, mirthful eyes," which made her appear as "an oriental type" with an "independent air." Often, in the company of other boys, Claude was invited to Myla's Delaware Street house, where he was impressed by her den—full of books, papers, magazines—its walls lined with posters from Paris. The *Rubáiyát of Omar Khayyám* was a favorite of the hostess, and she also introduced Bowers to *A Tale of Two Cities* and other books. Myla Jo was petite and energetic, a spirited conversationalist, author in her teens of short stories published in an adult periodical, "poetic, witty, humorous—and she acts her words." There were linden trees near the entrance of the Closser house. Years later, when Bowers was on leave as ambassador and he and Myla were lunching together, he said: "There never was a place that smelled so sweet as Delaware Street of a summer evening." And Myla answered: "But, Claude, we were young then."[43]

Few prominent Americans of the twentieth century looked as frail as Claude G. Bowers. The mature man evolving from the I.H.S. years had a seemingly weak physique, contrasting with his oratorical wallop and his day-and-night labor on writing and research. It came as no surprise when a 1928 front-page story in the *New York Times* reported that Bowers's voice possessed "a strength and vigor belying the fragile stature of its owner."[44]

This frailty was equally noticeable before and during Bowers's high school days. One Whitestown contemporary would remember him as a "little, slim, peak-faced fellow" who "didn't look like he had much life or health at all." "C. G. B. as a youth was not dashing in appearance," Myla Closser observed, "but his brow was

Shakespearean, and he had beautiful and expressive eyes." Those big brown eyes, described as "soulful" and "mournful," certainly were among Claude's physical assets. Another was the high forehead about which nearly everyone commented. Still another was his wide mouth, turning up at the corners—now humorous in its implications, now pixyish in a questioning way.[45]

Most impressive of all was Bowers's voice, whose "depth and volume" in oratory or debate seemed so "strange" in comparison with his frame.[46] Large ears and a receding chin, the least attractive features of his head and face, were counterbalanced to a degree by Claude's thick, straight, and neat brown hair, carefully parted on the left side, and by a pensive and sincere expression, relieved by a rather large nose and an occasional twinkle in his eyes.

It was when young Bowers spoke—in private and, particularly, in public—that the power of his talent, character, and personality had a similar impact to his adult effectiveness. His phrases were unexpectedly graphic, sentences polished, and sentiments mature for a person well under voting age. Claude's platform presence appeared utterly natural, his unexaggerated gestures gracefully blending with the content of exposition or argument. His qualities of leadership were evinced by election as president of the High School Senate, president of the Readers' Club, president of the Oratorical Association, and president of his class. As an orator and a congenial spirit, he became an I.H.S. hero in an era before basketball supplanted speech as a route to Indiana high school applause. "Bowers! Bowers! He is ours!" girls and boys shrilly shouted in unison. And rafters rang with their acclaim.[47]

A special I.H.S. feature was the senate, which Donnan created and where Claude starred. This "legislative body" gave students practice in delivering speeches, sponsoring bills, and attempting to be parliamentarians. In his junior year Bowers criticized the senate for wasting "so much time in absolute foolishness—on useless points of order and things of that sort." But a few months later he could scarcely say enough in the senate's favor: "Here the heart expands, the mind soars, laughter sits enthroned, gaudy imagination comes down from ethereal heights, sits upon our shoulders and whispers in our ears. Here we fathom one another's natures, love, fight, and drown our quarrels in mirth's sweet pool. Long live the Senate."[48]

Perhaps Bowers's election as its presiding officer softened his attitude. More likely, he brought Donnanian qualities to the chair and reduced the foolishness. He shone, too, in a debate with the Industrial Training School on the south side of Indianapolis. Subject: "Are We Ready for the Dismemberment of Armies and for Submitting All International Questions to a Permanent Board of Arbitration?" Bowers, Langsdale, and two other boys represented the affirmative and won unanimously. Claude's humor entered his write-up of the event for the *Annual*: "Both sides were given the most courteous attention, and the *conclusion* of each speech was greeted . . . by the most generous applause." When one of the judges presented him with "a splendid little book" on argumentation, Bowers suspected that the donor "thought I needed something in that line very badly."[49]

Claude enjoyed the auditor's role as thoroughly as the participant's. He rarely passed up opportunities to hear orations and debates, listening to many at Tomlinson Hall, an imposing brick structure on the corner of Delaware and Market Streets. In addition to contests involving law school and college students, he attended Indianapolis meetings where the speakers included such eloquent oratorical and political celebrities as William Jennings Bryan and Beveridge.

The youth found Booker T. Washington "a magnificent orator." The famous president of Tuskegee Institute had a limitless store of anecdotes. "His style is mostly conversational," Bowers wrote. "Now and then as he becomes especially eloquent his voice rises and his form expands." Claude enjoyed several of his stories: "Its a mighty hard thing to make a good christian out of a hungry man." "The colored men down south are very fond of an old song entitled 'Give me Jesus and you take all the rest.' The white man has taken him at his word."[50]

Fellow townsman Beveridge, just then on the threshold of a national career, often spoke to Indianapolis audiences. Bowers heard him frequently, at first awestruck and later critical. Thus, in November 1897: "Of all orators of whom I know any-thing," Beveridge "can cram the most of severe thought into least space." "He is the orator complete." Ten months later, when Beveridge spoke on Labor Day: "That this orator whose brilliant sentences have been so accustomed to enliven and elevate the banquet hall of labors direct foe would have the audacity to appear as the counselor of labor could hardly be expected." "His speach was brilliant but it was the brilliancy of sophistry."[51]

Bowers's changing attitude toward Beveridge accompanied a gradual disenchantment with Republican policies and national leadership. In 1892 Claude's presidential choice had been James G. Blaine—rejected. Four years later he preferred Sen. William B. Allison of Iowa—defeated. William McKinley was nominated, and "I am disgusted"—this in mid-June 1896. Resenting the power of Marcus A. "Dollar Mark" Hanna, Bowers considered McKinley a moral coward for "whose abilities I have little respect." His opinion on the Republican platform? "It was written by the upper class. It was formulated in Wall street. Now has the interest of Wall St. ever been known to coincide with the interests of the masses?"

The youth warmed to Bryan from the moment the Nebraskan declaimed on the "Cross of Gold." On hearing the Great Commoner speak in Indianapolis during his first presidential campaign, Bowers would recall, "From that hour I thought in terms of politics." True, that same year Claude served on the executive committee of the High School Lincoln League that endorsed the McKinley-Hobart ticket.[52] But the break, long in coming, eventually was made.

A hobby rather than a vocational pursuit, the theater intrigued young Bowers as compellingly as the platform. And what actors and actresses he saw! Sir Henry Irving and Ellen Terry in *The Merchant of Venice*, Sarah Bernhardt in *Camille*, Helena Modjeska in *Macbeth*, and Julia Marlowe in *As You Like It*.[53]

There was excitement in being part of a pulsating Saturday night crowd, cramming its way into English's Opera House on the Circle. Well-to-do adults came in by the front door. But Claude,

George, and Pax went to the gallery for a quarter, "entering through an alley that was packed back to Meridian Street, and since gallery seats could not be reserved, the congestion in the alley was dense." On seeing the great English thespians Sir Henry Irving and Ellen Terry when he was seventeen, Bowers wrote: "This P.M. witnessed one of the genuine climaxes of my life. . . . My enthusiasm is so great that I am almost powerless to express my appreciation."

Bowers was enraptured by Bernhardt, marveled at "the genius of Modjeska," and became "a devotee of Marlowe." Though he wrote long and discerning diary reviews of plays, he seemed equally interested in the actress as female. Anna Held was but one beauty he adored. "The Idol of the French," said Claude, "was only on the stage about 30 minutes but she set every one crazy." Held "arouses all the animal passions in man." "Such a breast!" "Her eyes are languorous. Her legs are not fleshy but well formed. She has a very bad reputation. Then I envy her friends." It was Held's first American season, and she "took Indianapolis by storm" with "Oh, won't you come and play wiz me? / I've got such a nice little way wiz me!"

Held's appearance introduced Bowers to "the awesome mysteries of the stage door." Pax, aged seventeen, "had laboriously wrought a sonnet in French expressing his adoration and asking for an autographed photograph . . . of the actress." When she invited Bowers and his poet friend backstage, "We soon found ourselves standing beside the little charmer in the wings, not a little embarrassed by her state of undress," Bowers wrote. Pax addressed her in a "French no Frenchwoman could have understood, and the smiling lady replied in an English never before heard on land or sea. We had got nowhere when Miss Held's cue called her to the stage."[54]

Four decades later while ambassador to Spain, Bowers met another Frenchwoman whom he saw at English's Opera House, Lilie Boutier. Remembered as "one of a grand group of actresses" who played in Indianapolis, she was the Russian Countess Nostitz in 1936 when the diplomat and his family were entertained several times at her home in Biarritz. The adult Bowers then found Lilie "shapely and with a face still beautiful," but he also was able to appreciate her "keen intelligence."[55]

In addition to enjoying the theater, Bowers was involved in trying to realize an editorial ambition. As early as 1896, reading about Lord Brougham's accomplishments, the then high school junior had been impressed by the quality of the *Edinburgh Review*. Why, Claude thought, could he not model himself on the celebrated Scot and edit such a periodical in Indiana? Langsdale, to whom he confided the plan, proved enthusiastic, and together the boys compiled lists of prospective contributors—all more or less famous.

Invitations to submit prose or verse flowed from Bowers to ex-Secretary Carl Schurz, Booker T. Washington, Joaquin Miller, and others. Miller sent a poem, "Cuba Libre," Washington an article, and Benjamin Harrison—after careful interrogation of the Hoosier Brougham—showed restrained interest that was extraordinary for him. Bowers was encouraged. Bowers's editorial exuberance caused him to defer random ideas about advertising, and, reluctantly, he abandoned the project when harsh financial facts came to his attention.[56]

But waking from dreams of the *Review* did not involve total failure. The magazine plan not only put Claude in touch with public men but also led to the Bowers-Langsdale sponsorship of a lecture delivered by Joaquin Miller, with the understanding that the profits would go into a fund for the project. Miller's sole condition was that his friend, James Whitcomb Riley, would preside and introduce him.

When Miller arrived in Indianapolis, Riley and Bowers met the Indiana-born "Poet of the Sierras" at the railroad station. The tall, bearded writer was "wearing a slouch hat and waving a carpet bag vigorously, to the evident annoyance of his neighbors," and threw his arms around Riley's neck with the exclamation, " 'Jim Riley, I love you more than any man on earth!' " The youth was struck by the contrast between the two: "Riley short and slight, Miller tall and burly; Riley a veritable fashion plate, Miller almost a caricature of a rustic; Riley cool, quiet, dignified, Miller boisterous as a storm in the mountains."

Bowers and Langsdale had asked the speaker of the Indiana House of Representatives for permission to sell tickets on the floor of the legislature. The speaker "said he would do better than that— he would arrange a joint session with the Senate and do the poet the honor of asking him to address it." The youths plunked down their joint fortune of nine dollars to rent the fashionable Plymouth Congregational Church for Miller's appearance, which turned out to be a "brilliant success." The "church was packed, with the Governor and the Legislature in attendance. Riley's introduction was a beautiful prose poem. Miller's lecture was really blank verse, and charming. Later, when the complete works of Miller were pub-lished, Riley's speech was used as the introduction."[57]

When the Gold Democrats opposing Bryan held their national convention in Indianapolis in September 1896, Bowers seized that opportunity to become acquainted with its leaders in order to try to get contributions for the magazine—and in one case to establish a friendship. William Everett of Quincy, Massachusetts, was hard-ly a celebrity of the first rank. Described as "brilliant but erratic," he had taught in a private school near Boston and served in Congress.[58]

Calling on the former congressman, Claude later wrote asking him to contribute an article. The correspondence shows young Bowers at his worst and best. On the debit side, he led off by addressing the educator as "Edward" instead of "William," did some bragging about the high school's quality, and "hurled" in a "spirit of defiance" his and Langsdale's hope of having a "grander list of con-tributors than any Harvard paper ever had!"

The youth appreciated Everett's interest in his letters. When Bowers responded modestly that "I court your criticism," Everett composed a detailed reply. Blending criticism with humor, he noted that Bowers's letter had been "defective in spelling, in gram-mar, in construction." But above all "the stilted, inflated tone" was "wholly unworthy of what ought to be the simple spirit of young men, with a natural healthy sense of humor." "I have the well-deserved reputation of being a dreadfully poor speller," Bowers answered, "but this fault never before came home to me so forcibly and effectually as in your letter." Some of Bowers's points made a hit with Everett: "Your letter is a very delightful one, because you talk right out, and say what you think in words that really mean something to you." Yet the educator feared his young Hoosier friend was "studying Oratory too much as a specialty, as you might Geology." "Read more poetry, especially Shakespeare and Milton," Everett counseled. "The advantage also of studying history to an orator is infinite."[59]

In his many letters to his unofficial mentor, Bowers demonstrated the scope of his reading and revealed his inner self. Bowers discussed Joseph Addison's and Richard Steele's *Spectator,* Macaulay, academic freedom, concentrated wealth, high streetcar fares, "Pitchfork" Ben Tillman, Shakespeare, *Hamlet,* and Henry George. Now he is memorizing Sir Walter Scott's poetry. Now he explains why he prefers Hugo, Nathaniel Hawthorne, and George Eliot to Dickens. John Milton's diction is "simply wonderful," but Milton's classical allusions necessitate "frequent visits to the library for reference." Portions of François Guizot's *General History of Civilization in Europe* and a biography of Danton also were among his readings.[60]

In the final letter to Everett, after referring to the long-dead Lewis Bowers and to a deceased schoolmate, the young man wrote, "You must not think me morbid or gloomy. It is only when I am alone sometimes at night that I am hemmed in by all the demons of loneliness." "You alone know I am sometimes unhappy," Bowers continued. "When I feel blue, I shut myself up and fight it out. I go in smiling and come out smiling and my chums wonder how I always keep cheerful. . . .Your affectionate non-conformist Claude G. Bowers."[61]

Bowers's graduation from I.H.S. took place on the evening of 28 January 1898. Although three girls carried off the academic honors, Bowers was president of the class and also spoke on the commencement platform when ceremonies were held before a large audience at the Plymouth Church. Bowers sat in the front row next to his friend, Rabbi Meyer Messing's daughter Sara, calming her nervousness with cinnamon drops. His topic title, taken from

*Indianapolis High School graduating class of 1898. Claude Bowers is seated in the front row (fourth from the left).*
INDIANA HISTORICAL SOCIETY

Macaulay, was "Our Huns and Vandals." Of the nine speakers' efforts "all concede mine to have been the best, and all place Sara next." Boys carried Bowers on their shoulders after the exercises. The school's principal described "Our Huns and Vandals" as "better than many a college oration." The proud Bowers reflected, "My class is one of the very finest that ever graduated. The boys are big-souled fellows, and the girls are accomplished and . . . spirited."[62]

Even with diploma in hand, Bowers's connection with I.H.S. did not terminate on commencement night. The climax came two months later at Richmond, where the Indiana High School Oratorical Contest was held—Claude being eligible to compete, as he was a midyear graduate. Since early autumn he had been preparing for the preliminary intramural contest, which he won handily on 23 December, and then began rehearsing intensively for Richmond. His subject: "Hamilton, the Constructionist"—a highly creditable oration on the career and influence of Alexander Hamilton.

*Claude Bowers at the Indiana High School Oratorical Contest, Richmond, Indiana,*
*25 March 1898*

INDIANAPOLIS HIGH SCHOOL ALBUM (1898), INDIANA HISTORICAL SOCIETY

    Bowers chose twenty-three-year-old Maynard Lee Daggy, a
DePauw alumnus, to coach and prepare him for the Richmond event.
"He went over my speech with extreme care making several important suggestions," Bowers noted, describing Daggy as "a persistent
trainer" and "very particular about the pronunciation of words."

Once they went to Plymouth Church to test voice range and control, and the last practice was held at the high school.[63]

On Friday, 25 March 1898, Bowers walked to the Indianapolis Union Station "where I found the seven coach special packed and waiting for me." Entering the shed, "I was greeted with loud cries of encouragement but was not permitted to use my voice in reply." The nearly four hundred students were "very enthusiastic on the way over." All wore long blue and white streamers, and the boys carried decorated canes. Their arrival in Richmond was "inspiring."

Delegations came from throughout the state. Portland sent over a hundred students. The Richmond boys and girls outnumbered those from Indianapolis. "I was hurried off by a side street so as to escape the crowd and reached the great Wes[t]cott Hotel, decorated in Richmond colors," shortly before his boosters arrived and "made the hotel ring with awful yells." Bowers's principal competition came from a Richmond girl, Juliet Hollingsworth, who had finished second the year before. Other entrants represented schools in Madison, Plainfield, Portland, and South Bend. Daggy accompanied Bowers to the filled Bradley Opera House where he introduced himself to fellow contestants and "listened to the fearful din until the curtain went up."[64]

"History can not overestimate," Bowers insisted, "the real magnitude of Hamilton's services in forming and riveting the bonds of union." The contestant went on to declaim:

Alexander Hamilton possessed the imperial power of a Pitt, without his selfishness; the majestic eloquence of a Fox, without his vices; a Sheridan's brilliancy without his excesses; a Curran's forensic splendor, without his exaggerations, while within his wizard hand he held the organizing bond of a Richelieu, without abuse.

In the centuries to come, replete with rich prospects, the inquiring stranger, casting his eyes over happy and contented homes, may ask: "In whose majestic mind originated this splendid dream of liberty with law marching harmoniously

down the centuries? . . . And this sublime union of the sover-
eign States—who so broad-minded, so far-seeing, as to have
pierced the veil of futurity and bound them with a common
interest?"

And then the voice of history may proudly make reply:
"Alexander Hamilton was the nucleus of it all; his was the
dream that linked liberty and law; . . . and the Union—the
Union is but the crystallization of his logic and the everlast-
ing monument to the memory of his immortal mind."[65]

When the judges announced the results, Bowers was named the
winner with Hollingsworth runner-up. " 'Twas a mighty shout with
which we greeted" the decision, one of Claude's schoolmates
reported. The "pale, slight youth" from Indianapolis—"Our
Bowers! Bowers the Incomparable! Bowers the Mighty! Bowers the
Personification of Eloquence" had become the state champion.
"Indianapolis was yelling in earnest now. For ten minutes it was
kept up." As the audience of fifteen hundred filed out into the
night, the girls and boys from I.H.S. cheered "our victory" in the
street.[66]

When the Bowers rooters returned to their city by train the next
morning, "few are the persons along the road from Richmond to
Indianapolis who did not know that the I.H.S. was out on a holiday lark." The press carried accounts of the contest, and Bowers's
picture appeared in the *Indianapolis News*. On Sunday evening,
savoring his success, Bowers went to Delaware Street for a call on
Myla Closser. "Myla had a fan with my picture, a program, and,
upon demand, my autograph. She is a grand girl."[67] Thus the triumph at the Bradley Opera House trailed its garlands of juvenile
glory.

# CHAPTER TWO

# Journalist, Orator, and Politician

Bowers's next thirteen years, spent in Indianapolis and Terre Haute, witnessed the start of his career as a journalist and culminated in two exciting events—nomination for Congress at the age of twenty-five and a second House race at twenty-seven. In terms of intellectual conviction and partisan commitment, this 1898–1910 period proved decisive. His research on Alexander Hamilton led him to the conclusion that the conservative ideas of his subject were "obnoxious." The oratorical victor next perused and then steeped himself in the writings of Thomas Jefferson. Before the autumn of 1898, Bowers completed the long-developing shift from Hamiltonian to Jeffersonian allegiance and from the Republican to the Democratic party. Always thereafter he would define himself as a "Jeffersonian Democrat."[1] Those determinations proved permanent and of tremendous importance to the young Hoosier. In the press and on the platform, he quickly became an articulate spokesman for the Democratic cause. And he remained one of the most zealous of the breed.

With little delay, the twenty-year-old Bowers composed a ringing declaration of his new Democratic faith. In "What Is Republicanism?" he depicted the Jefferson-Hamilton ideological and political struggle as both basic and enduring. "Jefferson," he

said, "was as unlike Hamilton as democracy is unlike aristocracy."
Jefferson's "writings constitute the poetry of political expression.
They are as clear as the crystal of celestial truth, throb with the
pulsations of the human heart, and are as invincible with the
strength of the common people."

In a second article titled "Republicanism vs. the People," Bowers
related early American parties to later ones; he attacked trusts and
monopolies, called Sen. Albert J. Beveridge "the very reincarnation
of Hamiltonian commercialism," and charged Republicans with "hurrying us into the ancient pathway of national decay." Submitting the
two essays to *The Jeffersonian Democrat*, a Washington periodical, the
author saw them published in January and March 1900.[2]

By the turn of the century it was evident that college was not in
Bowers's future. "Quite early," he later recalled, "it was clear that
we could not afford a college education." No doubt because of his
prominence at Indianapolis High School, he was given an opportunity to attend college. The "very eccentric, very exclusive, very
rich and very eloquent" Addison C. Harris, a distinguished
Indianapolis lawyer, offered in December 1898 to defray Bowers's
expenses at Princeton University. But the prominent Republican
benefactor insisted that the Democratic youth promise not to enter
into politics until the age of forty if he accepted the proffered assistance. This was a pledge he was unwilling to make.[3]

Bowers's partisan politics led him into a career in journalism,
when editorial writer Jacob Piatt Dunn, Jr., of the *Indianapolis
Sentinel* was looking for a temporary replacement in the spring of
1900. Reading a statement of city attorney John W. Kern that
Bowers's *Jeffersonian Democrat* pieces were "crackerjacks," Dunn
sent for the magazine and decided to hire Bowers. Bowers claimed
that Dunn gave him the job to permit "his occasional meandering
in the woods beside a stream with hook and line." The young editor considered Dunn "an unusual man, a scholar, with a fine mind,
excellent in polemics." He also appreciated his "keen sense of
humor—indicated in my selection to write editorials at twenty-
two." Only two years earlier Bowers was delivering the *Sentinel* on
a dawn paper route, now he was writing the bulk of the editorials

*The young Claude Bowers*

for Indiana's principal Democratic daily during the second McKinley-Bryan campaign.[4]

Bowers's contributions to the *Sentinel* concentrated on national and international affairs. Inspired by the patriotic remarks of his teenage cohorts and the tide of aggressive nationalism, the youth was disappointed during the Spanish-American War that he could not enlist. But two years later the partisan Democrat was attacking the motives that had led his country to war. As ambassador to Spain in the 1930s, he would examine the embassy's correspondence and confirm his belief that the conflict was caused by "unreasonable" United States demands and "inspired by popular passion aroused by American newspapers." In 1900 he made anti-imperialism the main theme of his editorials, holding forth on such topics as "The Cuban Farce" and "The Puerto Rican Scandal." He also assailed the trusts, severely criticized Senator Beveridge, and appealed "To the Laboring Man."

The 1900 presidential campaign was the subject of many columns. When William Jennings Bryan came to Indianapolis in August for formal acceptance of his nomination, Bowers paid tribute to the Nebraskan's "keen sense of justice," "profound" moral convictions, and identification with "Jeffersonian principles." Bryan "has the eloquence of sincerity," the editor declared. "There is character in every word he utters. He says precisely what he means." Vice presidential candidate Adlai E. Stevenson, the editor asserted, "stands out in striking contrast to the buffoonery and egotism" of Theodore Roosevelt, William McKinley's running mate. Never a Bowers favorite, Roosevelt took a full share of lumps in the *Sentinel's* pages.[5]

Relinquishing the editorial chair when Dunn returned later in 1900, Bowers continued to contribute some pieces to the paper in 1901. In Bowers's eyes, Benjamin Harrison represented the "liberty-loving element" of Republicanism and "tried in vain to stem the imperialistic tide." Similarly, former Speaker of the House Thomas B. "Czar" Reed held Republican foreign policy in "contempt" because "he despises hypocrisy and injustice." Linking American and British imperialism, Bowers blamed the "mercenary and ignoble" Joseph Chamberlain for planning and consummating the "disgraceful assault upon the liberty and property of the Boers. No woman is weak enough, no child is young enough, and no person old enough to escape the malign hatred of those so-called Christian men who now dictate English policy."

Frequently Bowers commented on historical matters such as Emilio Castelar's role in championing Spanish republicanism, the French Revolution, the unification of Italy, and the fall of Charles Stewart Parnell. The Democratic party's "need of the hour"? A return to Samuel J. Tilden's democracy, which was "nothing more than Jeffersonian democracy applied to modern conditions." Bowers deplored plutocratic trends in America, arguing that the upper class "does not propose to yield an iota of its unjust privileges." He lambasted the Republican party and lamented that "no action will be taken against the trusts."[6]

Bowers's prominence as an orator at the turn of the century was in marked contrast with the anonymous nature of his role as a newspaperman. His partisan arguments and rapid-fire delivery so impressed audiences that he became known as the "Gatling-Gun Orator of the Wabash." At Lebanon in April 1900, his outspoken attacks on the Republicans enthralled the 534 diners at a Democratic love feast, and they roared approval when toastmaster Samuel M. Ralston lightheartedly "nominated" him for Congress though he was five and a half years under the constitutional age requirement.[7]

That autumn he spoke under Democratic State Committee auspices in Boone, Clinton, Hamilton, Marion, and Montgomery Counties, advocating the election of Bryan and also of Kern, who was running for governor. Appropriately, Bowers made his first stop on the campaign trail in Whitestown, where his former neighbors "packed the hall" to hear the hometown boy vehemently attack the Republicans for their imperialistic policies toward Spain's former colonies. But only polite applause greeted his speech. Afterward, a blacksmith advised the idealistic youth, "I think the boys would've liked it better if you'd gone into the price of corn and hogs." In December he spoke "earnestly and forcefully" on Jeffersonian Democracy before four hundred at Plymouth Church in Indianapolis. "Jeffersonian Democracy does not antagonize the lawful accumulation of wealth," Bowers informed his audience, but "the rights of capital must always remain subordinate to the higher and nobler rights of man." The press commented that Bowers had "an excellent voice" and "an easy stage presence."[8]

The next platform appearance came during a Jefferson celebration in the spring of 1901. Democrats, including Indianapolis mayor Thomas Taggart and future senator Kern, gathered in that city's Masonic Hall at a large meeting Bowers helped arrange. Already recognized by many as the dominant figure in state Democratic management, Taggart introduced Bowers, who presided. "We cannot hope for relief," he argued, "from the party that was founded by Hamiltonian plutocracy. . . . Jeffersonian democracy will yet blot from the statutes that class legislation which breeds monopoly." "Despotism has been wrinkled since the dawn of time. Liberty never grows old," the speaker went on. "Her smile is as radiant tonight as when she enticed our revolutionary sires to breast a British musket in her name."

Axt Hall at Franklin, Indiana, provided a November setting for another Bowers appearance. Addressing over five hundred fellow Democrats, he demonstrated his bitter disappointment at the GOP's virtual monopoly of the black vote—a complaint he would repeat for three decades. The partisan orator accused the Republicans of encouraging the migration into the state of black "criminals who prey upon the community with their crimes and immorality." The "industrious and intelligent negro is compelled to share in the general prejudice which the emigrant from the South has called down upon his race." This occurred, Bowers charged, because Republican politicians preferred subservient blacks who would vote the party ticket willy-nilly. Thus Indiana Democracy entered every campaign handicapped "by thousands of voters whose position is as unvarying as the north star." He asserted that both the 1901 Democratic candidate for mayor of Indianapolis and the 1900 Democratic congressional nominee there had been "elected" by the whites but "overwhelmingly defeated" by the blacks. Kern, also at Franklin, attributed his 1900 defeat for the governorship to the black vote. According to a newspaper account, Bowers's remarks "caught the crowd, for when he had finished he was given an ovation to which he had to respond with repeated bows."[9]

If the Republican black vote irritated Indiana Democrats, the presence in the state of two Kentuckians—William S. Taylor and Charles Finley—caused comparable aggravation. Bowers helped organize the Jackson Day Banquet of January 1902 in Tomlinson Hall, Indianapolis, where he spoke, denouncing what he called a "conspiracy." The high-ranking Kentucky Republicans were wanted at home in connection with the 1900 murder of William Goebel, the Democratic gubernatorial nominee wounded during a contested election who died shortly after he was sworn in. The Indiana Republican regime, however, refused to give them up. Taylor and Finley, Bowers asserted, crossed the Ohio River "like sneak thieves in the night" to avoid indictment. "And when they came," the Republican "rogues of Indiana celebrated their escape with a disgraceful carnival of debauchery." The Democrat's chastisement of the fugitives' Republican protectors was "interrupted by frequent bursts of applause."[10]

Bowers's last political canvass while still in Indianapolis came in the fall of 1902, when again the Democratic State Committee sponsored him as a stump speaker. At New Palestine in Hancock County, "the way he went after the leaders of the G.O.P. was a sin." He derided them and told the people that "the only way out of this political dilemma, and the clutches of Wall street and millionaires of this country, was to vote the Democratic ticket." He was applauded at every utterance. The tariff and trust issues were staples of other Bowers speeches delivered in Boone, Greene, and Putnam Counties and at Eden, Linton, and Shelbyville.[11]

The election of 1902, like 1900 and all election years of the period, climaxed in a Republican victory. Since the late 1890s the country had enjoyed what the Republicans labeled "McKinley prosperity." After McKinley's assassination the good times continued under Theodore Roosevelt. Bowers, however, gave no sign of being discouraged by voters' rebuffs of his candidates. Nor is there evidence that conceit inflated the ego of the orator who, barely twenty-four when 1902 closed, had advanced so rapidly into the limelight. Active and aggressive even though so frail that he could not obtain life insurance, he had developed the firmest of friendships with party leaders such as Kern and Ralston who regarded him as a Democratic asset. In sum, at least superficially, he seemed well advanced on the road to success.[12]

Yet Bowers found himself "in the depths of depression, ready to abandon all my boyhood ambitions." The basic trouble was financial. Living with his mother, who continued work as a dressmaker, he had earned small sums in 1898 and 1899 clerking for the Bowen-Merrill Company, subsequently Bobbs-Merrill. He worked in the company's law department, but on occasion he was drafted to perform manual labor he rather enjoyed—placing copies of best-sellers in packing cases. During the next two years Bowers made his living as a *Sentinel* employee. He was the paper's editor during Dunn's absence in the spring and summer of 1900, and Bowers continued to contribute editorials until August of the following year. He then tried his hand as a reporter for the *Sentinel*, a job he disliked and abandoned after one month.[13]

For the next fourteen months Bowers "turned to reading law in the offices of Burke and Warrum," two Democratic attorneys whose "exciting and eloquent debates" stimulated and entertained their young understudy. Since attending trials at the courthouse in Lebanon as a boy, Bowers would recall that "I had set my heart on law as a profession"—a goal his mother wholeheartedly encouraged. In Indianapolis the youth had haunted the criminal court after class and was fascinated by trial lawyers. But reading law contributed nothing to the family till, and reluctantly he abandoned his legal ambitions. He had offended Taggart by acting independently in planning the Tomlinson Hall banquet and thus was on the blacklist of "Oily Tom." So Bowers decided to go elsewhere and support himself as a newspaperman. In January 1903 he boarded a train for Terre Haute and a job on the *Gazette*.[14]

Early twentieth-century Terre Haute acquired an unenviable reputation on three counts of relative validity. Conservative citizens throughout the land knew it as the residence of Eugene V. Debs, recent Socialist presidential nominee and widely considered a dangerous radical. Moralists castigated the city as a reservoir of sin with a notorious red-light district, gambling dens, and numerous saloons, and critics also leveled the charge of political putridity. Despite such allegations, Bowers responded favorably to what novelist Theodore Dreiser would later term the "tang and go" of Terre Haute. The nearby coalfields, agricultural prosperity, flourishing industrial plants, and four railroad lines were bringing wealth and growth to this city of 36,000 on the Wabash River.[15]

Bowers, of course, was interested in Terre Haute's history and culture. Associated with William Henry Harrison and Zachary Taylor in pioneer times, it had been the home of Sen. Daniel W. Voorhees. In Terre Haute and later in New York, Bowers knew and admired Alice Fischer, the stage star, who "really loved the town." An early Terre Haute friend was the poet Max Ehrmann. Eventually the journalist would see a great deal of Theodore Dreiser, who was born there.[16]

In politics, the Democrats could usually count on Terre Haute urban majorities, and the Republicans on the vote in surrounding Vigo County. The Democratic leader, John E. Lamb, was fifty years old in early 1903—a curly-haired Irish American who had served a term in Congress. To one contemporary he seemed "pompous," to another "tough," and to a third a "dictator." But to his admirers the imposing, 250-pound lawyer was "strong, dauntless, assured." Shortly after moving from Indianapolis, Bowers called on the redoubtable Lamb, presenting a note of introduction from Kern. Bowers's "most valuable friendship in Terre Haute" seemed utterly improbable at this moment. For "after a glance at the scrawny, unpromising youth that I was," Lamb "received me with a cold, distant courtesy that discouraged me from seeing him again until a year later, when he sent for me."[17]

Throughout the intervening year, Bowers worked as a *Gazette* reporter. Although he always doubted his reportorial ability, he scored at least one "scoop"—the coverage of an outbreak of smallpox—which a rival Terre Haute newsman never forgot. Bowers also served as drama critic and occasionally as editorial writer. He lived in a plainly furnished bedroom at 206 South Fifth Street and took his meals in a boardinghouse.[18]

In spare moments he tried his hand at a novel—huddled near the stove in his room and scribbling by the light of a kerosene lamp. Titled "Tom Grady," the yarn featured a man and woman based upon the personalities of the Indianapolis political boss Tom Taggart and Bowers's classmate Myla Jo Closser. Instead of a "curt rejection slip," the aspiring author received a long letter from a prestigious publisher that included this rather disturbing statement: "to the effect that the man in the story was 'a distinct creation' but . . . the woman was not quite real." Bowers was puzzled, because Myla was as real as could be. Before he had time to rewrite the manuscript, he found himself involved in politics. And that ended his "career" as a novelist.[19]

Oratory, luck, and careful planning combined to launch Bowers as a congressional candidate. With times good and President Roosevelt popular, Republican prospects in 1904 seemed bright, including those of Elias S. Holliday, the unspectacular Fifth District incumbent. Yet gloom seldom appears on the surface when "outs" hold a love feast on the eve of a campaign. Certainly no pessimism infiltrated Bowers's January oration at the Terre Haute Jackson Club's annual banquet. After painstaking preparation, he captivated the Democratic diners with his polished speech. As had happened at Lebanon in 1900, but this time with utmost seriousness, county chairmen and others who rose after him urged that the newcomer run for the House.[20]

Lamb, absent that night, returned from a vacation to learn of Bowers's triumph. Having barely seen and never heard him, Lamb arranged for Bowers to appear on a program at the St. Patrick's Day Banquet sponsored by the Ancient Order of Hibernians. In his oration of 17 March Bowers declared:

> The time is coming when Ireland will be free. . . . But until that dream is realized, until the harps are heard again on the hills of Tara; until the savage laws are repealed and the

infamous tax masters are scourged forever from the land, . . .
until that time the Irishmen of America will continue to hold
up British brutality, hypocrisy and incapacity to the hatred
and contempt of every lover of liberty and fair play.[21]

Storms of applause followed storms of applause. He spoke so fast
that his staccato words sounded like "sheep terds [*sic*] falling on a
shingle." So eloquent was Bowers that, as he looked over at Lamb,
he saw tears rolling down the leader's cheeks. The "Gatling-Gun
Orator" thus surpassed his stunning Jackson Day performance.

The next morning, summoned to Lamb's law office, Bowers
heard the magic question: "How would you like the nomination for
Congress?" Quickly he answered he would like it. "Very well,"
Lamb replied. "There's hardly any possibility of a Democratic victory this fall. But you're a young man and can afford the sacrifice.
By making a speaking campaign in all seven counties you'll help
the local tickets and put the party under obligation to you in the
future. I suppose you have no money. We'll take care of that."[22]

Lamb had so much power in 1904 that he could make his decision stick. Thursday, 25 August, was the greatest day in Bowers's
life thus far. That day in Martinsville where the Fifth District
Democratic Convention assembled in the courthouse, Bowers was
"young in years but old in experience," said James Swango, who
presented his name. "He is a campaigner par excellence, and he
will take Brother Holliday down the pike at a killing pace." He was
nominated by acclamation. "Mr. Bowers was then called on," the
Republican *Terre Haute Star* reported, "and spoke enthusiastically
and vigorously on the issues. . . . He was repeatedly interrupted
with applause."

That night in Terre Haute a blaring band and a large delegation
from the Jackson Club accompanied Bowers in a partisan parade.
At the club rooms he expressed gratitude and promised to conduct
an active campaign. Attacking "inimical" Republican policies, he
said his criticisms would not be personal. "All my life the greater
portion of my warmest personal friends have been Republicans.
. . . A man can live without office—he can't live . . . happily with-

out friends." It was a gala occasion for the candidate who, only twenty-five years old, had resided in the district but twenty months.[23]

The 1904 presidential "contest" has been called "the dullest campaign in the memory of living men." Seeking a White House term in his own right, the incumbent Roosevelt found no stumbling block in his feeble opponent, Judge Alton B. Parker. The nominee refused to canvass the nation, barely budging from his Hudson River valley home. The Democrats' candidate for vice president, Henry Gassaway Davis, was an equally absurd albatross. This eighty-one-year-old West Virginian was unpopular with miners, of whom there were many in Bowers's district. In Indiana the Republicans' optimism increased when their senior senator Charles W. Fairbanks became Roosevelt's running mate, and his junior colleague in the Senate, Beveridge, canvassed for reelection.[24]

Bowers had a special problem of his own. Prior to his nomination the Democratic *Gazette* folded, and he accepted an offer as editorial writer for the Republican *Star*. Did this put him in an anomalous position? Less than one might suppose, as the *Star* tended to avoid partisan themes. Still, he had to submit a steady stream of copy to earn bread and butter, so in country hotels or wherever he might be, he gave parts of his nights to this responsibility.[25]

In the midst of such handicaps, Bowers had three assets and only three. First, Kern was running again for the Indiana governorship. Second, not only Kern and Lamb but also Bryan himself campaigned in the Fifth District. Third, Congressman Holliday, with all the advantages at his command, could never match Bowers on the stump.

By 1904 the Democratic congressional candidate had developed a well-defined set of political ideals. Most of these he shared with other adherents of the Progressive movement who were found in both major parties and who controlled American governmental institutions. Like his fellow reformers, Bowers sincerely believed that active participation by the people in the political system would make the government serve the interests of the majority instead of the special concerns of the wealthy. "The people are the great source of power," he confidently asserted. Thus Bowers favored primary elections to make politicians more responsive to public opinion and championed the expansion of democracy through women's suffrage and the direct election of senators. He joined other Progressives in demanding government control of monopolies and called upon elected officials to "regulate the great financial institutions of the nation."[26]

Firing his opening shot on 12 September at Staunton—population 696—Bowers defined as the most important issue the decision whether America would "be governed according to the Constitution" or "degenerate into a beneficent despotism." To the people of that Clay County community, he mentioned Parker only once and was greeted by a silence so "impressive" that he never repeated the error. In a region where coal miners lived, Bowers denounced recent events in Colorado mining areas, claiming that the miners there had been denied their constitutional rights and calling their incarceration in bull pens "the most despotic crime" in American annals. He likewise had much to say against corruption and extravagance in government and favored liberalizing pensions for Civil War veterans.[27]

What became Bowers's standard speech was paraphrased by the *Rockville Tribune*. Again emphasizing the Colorado miners' plight, he "recalled the warning of Mr. Bryan four years ago to the effect that a policy of imperialism would inevitably lead to the reign of the bayonet and the suspension of the Constitution." The tariff should be revised in order to "protect the people from extortion." Congressman Holliday had voted against investigating charges of corruption. Though a Civil War veteran, Holliday had "done nothing" for the old soldiers, while Bowers urged increases in pensions for Civil War veterans. Whenever he referred to his opponent, it was to criticize votes or policies. "The entire absence of personalities and abuse" was a constant in his presentation.[28]

In addition to Vigo, Clay, and Parke, the Fifth District comprised four other counties—Hendricks, Morgan, Putnam, and Vermillion. Bowers spoke in all seven, averaging two speeches a day—usually an hour and a half each—except for the customary Sunday respite. Holliday, old enough to be his grandfather and hailing from Brazil in Clay County, lauded Roosevelt as a great president whose administration was worthy of support. Though much less eloquent than Bowers, the whiskery lawyer had the advantages of being better known to the voters, of riding Roosevelt's coattails in a Republican year, and of addressing a nor-mally Republican constituency.[29]

Bowers's only recourse was to meet, persuade, and convince as many citizens as possible. He went to Clay City, Saline, and Paragon, to Russellville and Reelsville, to Byron and Tangier, and to Cory and other wide places in the road. At county seats, in country schools, barns, and village opera houses, the dedicated Democrat delivered his message. A Democratic paper in Putnam County described him as "brilliant" and "bustling with facts that cannot be successfully controverted." A Democratic county chair-man hailed him as "one of the best public speakers in Indiana." Danville's courtroom was "packed" when Bowers spoke. At Bowling Green, he "brought them in from all directions." "Large and enthusiastic audiences" greeted him at Caseyville and Mecca. "Not for years has Montezuma been treated to such a flow of ora-tory" as from this "master of the facts." Thus the Democratic and even sometimes the Republican press reported the challenger's efforts. Bowers "is a veritable 'little giant,'" the *Rockville Tribune* exuberantly exclaimed.[30]

It was hard going at times. Rock-ribbed Republican Monrovia—where Vice President Thomas Hendricks once had been stoned—denied Bowers the use of a hall, a vacant store, and the hotel porch. He had a packing box moved to a spot in front of the store's lighted window and spoke to a Republican crowd that "extended back into the blackness" and gave three cheers for his opponent.[31]

While the closing days found the Democratic candidate in and near industrial Terre Haute, he savored campaigning in rural areas where most of the voters lived. He particularly enjoyed horse-and-buggy drives "through the countryside when the forests were flam-ing with red and gold" and looked forward to dinner at the "farmhouse of one of the faithful, where we would be surfeited with fried chicken, cream gravy, spareribs, yeast biscuits, pie and cake." Meetings were enlivened by flaming torches and the fife and drum, and often the audience would be "farmers in their work clothes." The candidate's life on the road was not without difficulties. Some hotel accommodations were "primitive beyond compare," and he once awoke "to find my bedcover under three inches of snow that had drifted in through a broken windowpane."[32]

As expected, Bowers lost the election. Roosevelt's Fifth District plurality was 8,263 while Kern lost by 7,117, and Holliday had a margin of 5,091. Bowers carried Democratic Putnam County by 518 votes and wrested Clay County from Holliday by 72 votes—losing the other five. He led the ticket in many places and, as Lamb predicted in March, helped local candidates win. In the district it was more noteworthy that he ran 2,026 votes ahead of the well-regarded Kern than that he outscored Parker by a whopping 3,172. Nobody could conclude that the Terre Haute Democrat had waged "the dullest campaign in the memory of living men."[33]

Far from disheartened, Bowers received a cordial welcome the second week in November 1904 when he returned full time to the *Star*. From his desk he looked down on Terre Haute's main street, and when the weather was warm the open windows brought in the clang of the trolleys, the clomp of horseshoes on Wabash Avenue, and the occasional beep of an automobile horn. At the newspaper he was well liked. A "fast and prolific" writer, he customarily was waiting for galleys from the composing room when reporters and deskmen came to work. "So in the early afternoon," Bowers "had time for story-telling and speech-making" seated or standing near a friend's desk and waving an arm or a finger for emphasis. "On the slightest pretext," a fellow journalist later would recall, "he would take off into a flight of oratory as if making a political talk to eager Democrats."

The *Star*'s policy or lack of policy presented no special challenge to Bowers. Its absentee owner was Daniel G. Reid, a millionaire industrialist, who gave him wide latitude as to subjects—provided his partisanship did not obtrude. Because of the paper's soft attitude on many questions, the *Star* editorials proved less typical of their author than those he had composed in Indianapolis—or would later write in Fort Wayne and New York.[34]

On 30 August 1906 delegates to the Democrats' district convention at Rockville—under the trees of Beechwood Park—unanimously selected Bowers to run for Congress a second time. Roosevelt was still president and Holliday again the adversary. But runaway conditions no longer applied. Holliday, his standing damaged when he trailed the ticket in 1904, pitched his appeal on "just one more term." If reelected, he promised, it would be his final race.[35]

From the standpoint of national issues, prosperity still favored the Republican "ins." Although Roosevelt remained popular, there was much dissatisfaction with powerful trusts that thrust their tentacles into politics. This was the heyday of the muckrakers, and reform was in the air. Plutocracy and corruption were the enemies, said Bowers. These and his opponent's "inactivity" and refusal to run again for reelection if elected were assailed by the Democrat in his acceptance speech. "The coming fights in congress will be against the domination of certain colossal corporations that are defying the national government and in favor of that economic liberty and equality which form the basic foundation of American institutions," he insisted. "It will never be possible to control the corporations in the interest of the public as long as the manager of any political party can crawl like a sycophant and a sneak into the private offices of the plutocracy and to sell the fruits of a party victory to the highest contributor to a campaign fund." The candidate promised to "enter this campaign with my hands uncontaminated by the distribution of corruption money and with my wrists unmanacled by any pledge of any politicians. . . . If my election depends on my going out and buying American citizens like slaves upon the auction block," he insisted, "I would rather maintain my self-respect and walk into the shadows of defeat erect—and so I would ten thousand times."

After opening his campaign at Marshall, Bowers addressed meetings throughout the Fifth District. He delivered seventy-six speeches in eight weeks in cities, towns, and hamlets. The challenger paid tribute to Bryan and directed some of his fire at John D. Rockefeller, J. Pierpont Morgan, and Andrew Carnegie. Supporting the Grand Army of the Republic pension plan for old soldiers, Bowers also identified himself with "the miner, the farmer and the toiler in the shops." He lambasted the Republican bosses of Indianapolis and advocated the passage of legislation mandating an eight-hour workday for labor. While not assailing Holliday personally, he said the congressman "shamefully neglected" constituents' interests and "ought to be relegated to private life." From New Goshen he hustled to Seelyville, from Cope to Waverly, from Cloverdale to Stampton.[36]

Repeatedly, Bowers emphasized Holliday's promise never to run again, eliciting a reply of sorts. "I have never made a political speech in congress," Holliday admitted in an interview. "I have never claimed to be a great orator. . . . I have never claimed to be a brilliant man. . . . [But] if any man can point out a dishonest act committed by me, I will agree to withdraw." "I have delayed opening my campaign," the congressman added, "because of the extraordinarily little interest that the people are taking in politics."[37]

This interview underscored the differences between the two men's strategies. Young, dynamic, with "supreme vitality," Bowers sought to overcome the odds with eloquence and whirlwind coverage. In contrast, the elderly incumbent relied on a holding operation. So the challenger pressed on, with rare interludes of relaxation such as an October train ride with Bryan from Brazil to Terre Haute. On Bowers's lap lay the *Cincinnati Enquirer* with a report that Beveridge had dubbed Bryan a dreamer. "The dreamer lives forever," the smiling Bryan commented, "but the doer dies in a day." The Great Commoner then recounted the biblical story of Joseph, who was a "dreamer" but who "got the corn."[38]

The early returns of Tuesday night, 6 November, seemed to indicate an upset. Bowers increased his 1904 margins of victory in Clay and Putnam Counties, while substantially reducing Holliday's in Hendricks, Morgan, Parke, and Vermillion Counties.[39] Bowers needed a 1,118 plurality in his home bailiwick to shade Holliday in the stretch. Could he obtain it? Incomplete returns from most Vigo districts made this appear probable. The following morning men at Holliday's headquarters conceded the triumph of the Democrat. And as late as Wednesday at 2 P.M. Bowers was "confident of election."[40]

When tardy Terre Haute precincts reported Wednesday afternoon and night, Democratic optimism faded. The challenger won Vigo County by 164 votes—compared with a 2,139 deficit in 1904—but this was not enough. Bowers thus lost his second race for Congress. Quidnuncs speculated on the reason, particularly referring to unusual delays, and there was talk of "Republican skullduggery." Attention focused on a precinct in Terre Haute's Fourth Ward that delivered its 608 ballots to the canvassing board at 11:00 P.M.[41]

All agreed that Bowers's showing had been remarkable. His race, said the *Greencastle Star and Democrat*, "reflects credit and glory." He "made a fight in which he and his friends take pride," the *Rockville Tribune* agreed. The campaign had captured the voters' attention. Republican papers stressed the heavy vote in Terre Haute and "one of the fiercest local campaigns ever waged in Parke county." Meeting and greeting fellow citizens for eight weeks and delivering seventy-six speeches, Bowers lost the district by 953 votes, while the head of the Republican state ticket carried it by 2,887.[42]

Bowers proved a graceful loser. His unsigned editorial in the *Star* was entitled "The Election Over: Now Pull Together." No doubt deeply disappointed, he stated that "no bitterness" resulted from the outcome and "no sore places" needed to be healed. Despite such conciliatory remarks, he remained convinced for the rest of his life that "I was elected and counted out—no question about that."[43]

But Bowers's Terre Haute years were not given over to politics. It is doubtful if many Americans of his era saw more sides of life in a city the size of Terre Haute than Bowers encountered there. The theater, the Chautauqua, the pretty girls he knew, the warm friendships in and out of politics—all were meat and drink to him.

Bowers continued to read widely in various fields. He patronized the public library, and history and biography continued to be his favorites. For diversion he turned to poetry and fiction, including the *Rubáiyát*, Guy de Maupassant, and Honoré de Balzac. Local, Indianapolis, and other newspapers naturally were important to him. State, national, and international developments intrigued him. Editorially shackled in the political zone, he often depended on literature—and on the comparatively "safe" areas of history and European affairs—for the substance of his *Star* editorials.[44]

Many of Bowers's newspaper colleagues became his friends. Odd characters like Charles Timothy Jewett injected color into *Star* camaraderie. As city editor, the black-bearded, cane-carrying Tim guided younger men of promise—like W. Steele Gilmore, future editor of the *Detroit News*, and Philip S. Rush, subsequently a publisher in California—through reportorial apprenticeships. Rush responded favorably to Bowers, as did George H. James, the *Star* artist. James recalled Bowers's knocking out three or four editorials daily, using a two-finger technique on an L. C. Smith typewriter. To Rush, he seemed "rather of the intellectual type" who "may have been attracted" to Debs "for that reason." Gilmore remembered Bowers as brightening the routines of his fellow workers. "Ordinarily one member of the staff meeting another would say, 'Hi, Joe,' " Gilmore recollected. "But Claude more likely would say 'Joseph, my friend, it gives me great pleasure to greet you on this beautiful day.' But we all liked him."[45]

Bowers numbered among his other friends William F. "Billy" Cronin of the rival *Terre Haute Tribune*, Lamb, of course, and several Terre Haute physicians, principally Dr. W. R. Mattox, whom he frequently visited and who supported him politically. Through some of these men, Bowers made the acquaintance of attractive girls. One was Ann Cronin, Billy's sister. Another was Lamb's niece, Cecelia Parker. The journalist found opportunities to spend happy hours in the company of Ann and Cecelia as well as Grace Batchelder, whom he first met in Doctor Mattox's office. "The doctor introduced us, and we all had a pleasant period talking of my work at school," Batchelder later recalled. After discovering

she was majoring in English and history, Bowers was especially
interested, and two days later he asked her for a date. This was the
beginning of "a number of pleasant times." But her reminiscences
were of "too personal a nature to be published in a biography," she
later recalled.[46]

Of all Bowers's Terre Haute associations, one of particular
import was his friendship with Debs. The two first met in
Indianapolis in January 1899, when Maynard Lee Daggy introduced them, and Bowers found the older man "charming" with a
"caressing manner that is fascinating." In midsummer 1904,
shortly after the second Debs presidential nomination, the *Star*
editorialist scheduled an interview with the Socialist at his Terre
Haute residence. Scanning Debs's private library, he noticed,
among other conversation pieces, volumes by Jules Michelet,
Victor Hugo, and Thomas Dixon, the novelist and playwright.
Debs proved an admirer of Hugo ("A great soul. He was always
on the side of those who needed him") and a critic of Dixon.
("No man can write his name in immortal letters who takes the
ground that one race was created to be the bondsman of another
race.") For "three delightful hours" the presidential candidate
and the soon-to-be congressional nominee discussed books and
authors, as well as Debs's youthful hardships, self-education,
union activities, and jail sentence. Once again Bowers described
Debs as "charming" and "fascinating." "He is intense," Bowers
wrote, "enthusiastic, eloquent, fluent, and much given to gestures." "Whatever he may be politically, he is a . . . very lovable
man personally."[47]

Bowers's admiration for Debs never ceased. In Terre Haute
Bowers saw him frequently and never discovered "a flaw of any
consequence in his character." Debs criticized Bowers in their private correspondence because of their dissimilar views of the
Roman Catholic Church. Yet neither this nor Debs's speeches during World War I altered Bowers's long-held esteem. In his memoirs
he quoted James Whitcomb Riley: "God was feelin' mighty good
when he made Gene Debs, and he didn't have anything else to do
all day." Debs "was not a revolutionist" in Bowers's judgment.

"He was, rather, an evolutionist. He had no faith in force. He was an idealist, a poet and an honest man."[48]

Another celebrity whom Bowers observed close at hand was Bryan. The Bryan he first saw in the 1890s struck him as "remarkably handsome in a virile sense," with a "magnetic" glance and a "strong, mellow" voice "expressive of . . . sincerity" and "passionately earnest." Imagine the shock when in 1908 the Nebraskan seemed "on the verge of a collapse" and his hands "hung limply" over the side of the electric runabout in which he and Bowers were riding. But on approaching the Terre Haute baseball park where Bryan was to speak, a transformation occurred. "Then I realized that he had the rare capacity of relaxing utterly in the midst of a crowd. He had been resting!" Addressing a second throng that night, his voice became "as clear as a clarion." What interested Bowers was "the carrying power of that voice. I was standing beside him and it seemed to me that his tone was entirely conversational, and yet I noticed that every word reached those on the outskirts of the crowd a block away."[49]

Bowers's political mentor in Terre Haute was Lamb, whom he considered "one of the most amusing and consummate politicians I have ever known." Just as much as Ralston or Kern, and probably more than either of them, the big Irishman gave Bowers the essential recognition without which fledglings' wings are clipped. What a contrast they presented—the hefty lawyer and the fragile-appearing journalist, a quarter century separating the ages of the well-to-do lawyer and the young journalist whose wages at the newspaper never topped $1,000 a year. Yet they had so much in common—history, literature, oratory, politics, and devotion to the Democratic cause.[50]

Having won Lamb's total confidence, Bowers enjoyed the regular Sunday-morning gatherings in the law office where a few trusted souls were treated to Lamb's "acid wit" and "scorching sarcasm." Nor did any hours pass more merrily than those as John and Esther Lamb's guest at their home on South Third Street. Repartee sparkled in the dining room and also out on the front steps where the company might encompass almost anyone from Bryan to the policeman on the beat. "The real art of the time was conversation," Lamb's son has recalled. In the house and on the porch, "it was endless and informative."[51]

Though his relationships with other Terre Haute notables never approached his intimacy with Lamb, Bowers became close to two mayors of the city. He played a major part in the elections of both James Lyons and Louis Gerhardt. By December 1906 Bowers's connection with the *Star* had become less than satisfactory, because, in the last stages of the congressional campaign, the Republican newspaper had succumbed to pressure and plumped for Holliday. Furthermore, a position on the Board of Public Works paid $1,500—enough to enable Bowers to support his mother, who came to live with her son in 1906. So in December he gave up journalism for the post at city hall.[52]

As the second Democratic member of the bipartisan three-man board, Bowers developed abiding admiration for its chairman, Patrick B. Walsh. A former grocer with little formal education, Pat was the "most meticulously honest man I ever knew." One day Bowers wrote a personal letter and, wishing to get it in the mail at once, took a two-cent stamp from a city hall desk and stuck the stamp on the envelope. Walsh's "horrified" glance so impressed him that he never repeated the transgression.

Sewer contracts, the paving of streets, public transportation, and lighting were among the principal matters the Board of Works supervised. In Bowers's period the city constructed numerous streets, sidewalks, and sewers and built a garbage disposal plant— "all fine jobs," he later asserted, and never with the slightest suggestion that "they were not honest jobs." Weighing 110 pounds and disinclined to take himself too seriously, he could laugh with joshers who said he "jumped up and down" on a new brick street and "if it did not give . . . pronounced it sound."[53]

In addition to official duties, Bowers acted as "a liaison man between the Board and the Party." The two mayors were "not men of education and I wrote their speeches, messages, etc." When Lyons went out and Gerhardt came in, the newspapers ironically commented on the "marked similarity" of their styles. Bowers likewise composed and delivered many addresses on civic and other occasions. His memory was "prodigious." At one sitting he could type a speech long enough to last an hour and a half. This he reduced to half-hour length. Handing the copy to an associate, he more than once went through the whole thing orally without refer-ring to the manuscript.[54]

The associate in such instances was Frank Brubeck, clerk of the Board of Public Works and later superintendent of parks. A college graduate and erstwhile *Star* and *Tribune* employee, this prematurely gray six-footer was not a mover and shaker like Lamb but became Bowers's equally intimate friend. The personable Brubeck, nick-named "Blue Balls" by his friend, is linked with amusing stories of the lighter side of Bowers's life. The two men enjoyed cavorting with sexually available young women and had some high old times in the purlieus of Terre Haute. With a rare exception when he reached his fifties, there is no evidence that Bowers ever gambled. But he liked beer or an occasional highball and, when separated from Brubeck, fondly reminisced about their convivial times together. Still, if friends ordered too many rounds, Bowers, like Brubeck, "ditched his drink" into a convenient cuspidor. Thus he anticipated the evenings when, as an ambassador, he favored pot-ted palms as handy receptacles for cocktails.[55]

Concurrently, Bowers was more than passingly involved with Sybil McCaslin, an Indianapolis girl whom he saw often until 1911 and constantly thereafter. A graduate of Shortridge (formerly Indianapolis High School), Bowers's alma mater, she and Bowers met in 1901, when he was twenty-two and she was eighteen. He was the first man this beautiful brown-eyed brunette ever loved. Responding readily to his kisses the first time he embraced her, she remained devoted to him—with interludes of lovers' squabbles—throughout an astoundingly long courtship. During these years Sybil graduated from the Normal School in Indianapolis and then taught school.[56]

The first factor complicating the couple's amour developed when Bowers moved to Terre Haute. Seventy-five miles from the lady, and working extremely hard, he took advantage of Sunday respites to ride trains eastward for short Indianapolis visits. Distance, however, strained the affair. "I really do not know you at all," Sybil wrote to him in mid-1903. Later: "I don't know whether you have decided that you do not care for me . . . or really think that I no longer care." Yet, there were wonderful moments and hours. "My spirits are still way up," Sybil told him. "My dearest boy I am wild to kiss you now." "I need a little scolding and a little petting too. . . . A hundred kisses." "I like you in a tender, quiet, mood more than in a wildly passionate one except occasionally." "I want you to love me oh intensely, passionately and everlastingly."[57]

Such are samples of feelings reflected in some of the five hundred letters McCaslin sent to Bowers in the course of ten years. He wrote daily to her much of the time, and the number of his communications up to and including 1911 must have approximated two thousand. Meanwhile, Sybil taught school, which she detested, earning forty dollars a month and hoping that the day was not distant when she and her beloved would be married.[58]

Matrimony, however, was tucked back in a remote corner of Bowers's mind. Although able and ambitious, he made little money while on the staffs of the *Gazette* and the *Star*. When his mother stopped her dressmaking business in Indianapolis and came to live in Terre Haute, there were two mouths to feed. Although his annual pay at the Board of Works was $1,500, even this princely sum, in his judgment, was too small to support a wife.[59]

From at least one point of view, their situation was unfair. Sybil, in the main, was remarkably patient—exchanging expressions of endearment, reporting on her mundane routine, and looking forward to the Sunday or Saturday when her suitor might appear. The unfairness was due to the fact that her intended could follow his inclinations with available women, while she remained "true" to him. It all fitted the double standard of the era, there being a decided contrast between her Indianapolis abode on North New Jersey Street and the Terre Haute tenderloin where the light was low and the kicking high.

Her letters reveal no indication that Sybil knew about Claude's hanky-panky in the wide-open city on the Wabash. The tone of her missives demonstrates that, had she been aware of his dal-liances, the courtship would have ended abruptly. From the first, there were problems enough at the McCaslin residence. Back in the summer of 1903, the couple more than once had to do their "courting" in the presence of her mother and her younger sister. In February 1906 Sybil's mother heard that Claude was interested in a Terre Haute girl. Ironically, her source was in part correct, but she probably had the wrong girl in mind. He never did like his future mother-in-law; his distaste for her might have been less acute had she not been suspicious at this juncture.[60]

The romance reached its nadir in the middle of the decade. In both 1906 and the following year, there were long and, at least to Sybil, painful silences. When letter writing at last recommenced, it was not until November 1907 that "My dear Claude" was "Dearest Claude" again. In April 1908 Sybil rejoiced one day when "a gen-uine love letter" reached her. By June, Claude was "My Blessed Boy" and "The Dearest Boy in the World." Still he acted "bored" when she mentioned marriage that year.[61]

Nineteen nine proved pivotal. On 6 May they agreed to belong solely to each other. In June Sybil was "proudly wearing" an amethyst ring—a gift from Claude. That autumn she wrote: "I have enjoyed the last year and a half to the utmost. You have been delightful. . . . We have nothing to quarrel about." In March 1910: "We really understand as well as love each other."[62]

Bowers now called his fiancée "Bobbie" when she was happiest, most relaxed, and most responsive, reserving "Sybil" for the digni-fied side of her nature. Accordingly, she often signed love messages "Bobbie" or "Your own Bobby" or "Bob." During the spring and summer of 1911, when they were apart for longer than any other time in the rest of their lives, Bobbie-Sybil mailed Claude a sequence of particularly amorous messages.[63]

While love found its way, Bowers's political zeal was launching him as a junior participant in major Democratic developments. In 1908 Bryan made a third bid for the presidency. The partisans' meeting in Denver that July at the Democratic National Convention included Bowers, who attended as Indiana's youngest delegate. Although national chairman Taggart may have meant to be disparaging when he called Bowers "Babe," the twenty-nine year old from Terre Haute was closer to the convention's inner workings than Taggart, whom Bryan did not esteem.[64]

With Delegate-at-Large Lamb, a confidant of Bryan, Bowers left Terre Haute for Chicago, where they met Kern, already touted as a vice presidential prospect. Stopping off at Lincoln, on Bryan's invitation, the trio spent the night in the Nebraska capital, where the Bryans entertained them and nearly forty others at lunch. Afterward they continued the train trip to Denver where, to nobody's surprise, the Bryan forces held firm control.[65]

In the aftermath of ex-President Grover Cleveland's death on 24 June, a report spread that Parker, head of New York's uninstructed delegation, would present resolutions extolling Cleveland and inferentially criticizing Bryan. On Tuesday, 7 July, not long after the convention opened, Nebraska's Ignatius J. Dunn offered—and the delegates unanimously approved—different Cleveland resolutions acceptable to the Bryanites. To the press, Bowers identified Lamb as the substitute's main author: "I ran them off on the typewriter myself . . . and it was that copy that was read by Mr. Dunn." Many years later, Bowers, then ambassador to Chile, stated that he, not Lamb, composed them.[66]

Following "unpremeditated and spontaneous demonstrations" of support, the delegates nominated Bryan for the third time. The candidate's biographer asserts that forty men aspired to the vice presidential spot. But the likelihood of Democratic defeat in the autumn cooled the ardor of some prospective candidates. The anti-Bryan *New York Times* gleefully observed, "To state facts, the Vice Presidential nomination has gone begging for many days."[67]

Hoosier Democrats from the first had focused on Kern for the vice presidency. Kern, however, proved reluctant to consider seeking this office, citing as reasons his recent bout with tuberculosis and his rather modest financial means. Despite such objections, a Denver dispatch of Thursday, 9 July, to the *Indianapolis News* reported that "Indiana has started the boom for John W. Kern for the Democratic vice-presidential nomination." From their headquarters at the Albany Hotel, the Hoosier delegates went off in various directions to confer with Democrats from other states, "with the view to determining their possible reception of Kern's candidacy." Bowers's assignment consisted of Arkansas, Missouri, Nevada, North Dakota, and Washington. He found "Kern sentiment everywhere I went," and so did his fellow canvassers.[68]

Bowers wrote that on Friday morning the situation "shaped itself rapidly." Realizing that his selection would mean more to his three children "in the future than any amount of money I could leave them," Kern yielded to political pressure and allowed his name to be placed before the delegates. His long-standing political friendship with Bryan, dating back to the 1896 campaign, meant that the Great Commoner considered him an able and suitable running mate. In command of the convention with Bryan's blessing, Kentucky congressman Ollie M. James on Friday afternoon passed his chief's message along the floor: "Vote for Kern, boys." After gubernatorial nominee Thomas R. Marshall presented his fellow Hoosier's name, the delegates nominated Kern by acclamation.[69]

For Bowers, Denver spelled one of life's memorable experiences, and he relished his initial exposure to Democratic national leaders en masse. There for the first time he saw and heard congressmen, governors, and other party spokesmen whom he would know in later years. Oklahoma's blind senator, Thomas P. Gore, the Illinois fashion plate James Hamilton Lewis, future speaker Champ Clark of Missouri, young Francis Burton Harrison of New York, and big, bald, able James were but a few of the many on the scene.

As a champion of Bryan policies on the Resolutions Committee, Lamb was at the center of the convention. As Lamb's confidant throughout, Bowers seized the opportunity to study backstage developments. One highlight came when Bowers, Lamb, and Kern lunched for an hour and a half as Parker's guests, listening to his private disclaimers of any intention to embarrass Bryan in the proposed Cleveland eulogy. Renewing his acquaintance with Bryan at Lincoln, traveling west with Lamb and both ways with Kern, and rejoicing in the latter's recognition provided the young Democrat with fillips of a rare sort.[70]

To top it off, Terre Haute friends gave Bowers "a regular old-fashioned reception" on his return to city hall. Pulling off his coat at the Board of Works office and lighting a fresh cigar, he "was again ready to take up petitions, remonstrances, new streets, etc., when a great demonstration broke out in the reception room." Bowers looked in through the door to discover he was "in the midst of a crowd of city hall employees and officials, newspaper men and Terre Haute Democrats." Cries of " 'Speech, speech,' brought him out of his dream and he unfolded his tongue and was soon in the midst of an eloquent story of the Denver convention." Then followed a round of handshaking and three cheers in his honor.[71]

In 1908 Bowers was not a congressional candidate. He declined the nomination. However, changing factional alignments in the Fifth District undoubtedly led to that decision. Lamb's grip on the district was beginning to be loosened, and hindsight suggests that circumstances forced him to assent to a nominee other than Bowers. Though not on the ticket, Bowers campaigned with all his customary ardor. Starting in August with a foray into Uncle Joe Cannon's Illinois district, Bowers spoke frequently in Indiana and worked energetically for Bryan, Kern, Marshall, and his own replacement as candidate for Congress, Ralph W. Moss.[72]

The election results were mixed. Bryan lost to William Howard Taft in Indiana and the country at large, but Marshall defeated James E. Watson in the race for governor, and Moss also won, as did most of the Indiana Democratic congressional candidates. While the state senate remained Republican, the Democrats obtained a large majority in the Indiana House of Representatives that allowed them—on joint ballot—to elect a United States senator.[73]

From Bowers's point of view, two heartening developments occurred in the next year and a half. The first concerned the reputation gained by Marshall, who managed to establish a state board of accounts and to commence a moderate program of social and labor reform legislation. Bowers greatly respected the governor's success as an honest and efficient administrator. Ultimately this led to Marshall's selection as Woodrow Wilson's vice president.

Becoming friends in 1908, Marshall and Bowers remained on good terms until the former's death in 1925.[74] The second encouraging development was Kern's election to the Senate. In 1910 the Democratic State Convention selected him as its nominee, but his election depended on a Democratic legislative majority in the autumn polling. Kern's opponent was Republican incumbent Beveridge, through whose hushed house Bowers had tiptoed long before meeting Kern or Lamb. But 1910 was not a Beveridge year. Like their counterparts nationally, the Hoosier Republicans were deeply divided in their loyalties in the bitter feud between the followers of President Taft and those of his predecessor, Theodore Roosevelt. Beveridge was a Roosevelt confidant, and the more conservative Indiana Republicans sided with the Ohio incumbent. And Kern, conscientious in his homework, exposed Beveridge's votes against some of the legislation Progressives held dear, such as the Sixteenth Amendment "to lay and collect taxes on incomes."[75]

Meanwhile, Bowers, active as ever, campaigned in familiar and unfamiliar Hoosier settings, just as he had done periodically for a full decade. He spoke in Lebanon and Indianapolis—scenes of boyhood struggles and youthful dreams—at Gary and Hammond on the shore of Lake Michigan, and south of Terre Haute to the Ohio River. The November results gave the Democrats firm control of both legislative chambers for the first time since 1892. On 17 January 1911 the general assembly elected Kern to a six-year Senate term, and Bowers went with Kern to Washington as his trusted secretary and admiring friend.[76]

# CHAPTER THREE

# Washington

Claude Bowers's move to the capital placed him at the center of American politics—an ideal vantage point for a Progressive in the years before the Great War. He relished the chance to observe the ascendancy of the Democracy. By 1913 his party was in control of both the legislative and executive branches, which allowed Sen. John W. Kern to achieve an importance unusual for a freshman solon, to the delight of his hard-working secretary. In addition to political experiences, new friends and finally a bride made his Washington years memorable.

By 1911 the balance of American politics was shifting toward the Democrats. The William Howard Taft-Theodore Roosevelt feud deprived the Republicans of their majority in the House, and Kern joined twelve newcomers on his side of the Senate. The Hoosier fared well in his assignments. Kern was named to the prestigious Finance Committee and the Committee on Privileges and Elections and also became a member of the Democratic Steering Committee.[1]

Bowers's duties brought him into contact with Democratic senators. He soon was on cordial terms with Ohio's Atlee Pomerene, a "jolly" and "unaffected" senator "with whom I have a chat almost every day." He described Tennessee's Luke Lea, who admired Kern and called him Uncle John, as "something of a live wire . . . alive with a virility that thrills." Among other Democrats was Thomas P. Gore, "a marvelous man, this blind man." The Oklahoman's thrusts were "withering, his epigrams haunting in quality." Comparable was another Democrat, Isidor Rayner; no one could satirize Roosevelt more effectively. Rayner's contempt for Roosevelt, Bowers wrote, stemmed from the conviction that "Roosevelt is a hypocrite, dishonorable and dangerous to the perpetuation of our institutions and the liberty of our people." More than any other politician, Mississippi's John Sharp Williams delighted Bowers: "child-like simplicity, sincerity and mischievousness," also "the most dreaded tongue."[2]

Republicans fascinated Bowers at least as much. There was Robert La Follette, a short man with "hair standing straight on end," who "struts" about the Senate with "a smile of complacency upon his fighting face, an air of authority in his manner." The tall, broad-shouldered Albert B. Cummins of Iowa had "keen" eyes and a "graceful" bearing. The "lean-faced, nervous, youthful" William S. Kenyon of Iowa had appeal, as did the "profound" William E. Borah, whose face was "a little meaty" but redeemed by eyes revealing humor. The quintessential conservative, Elihu Root was "peaked and sharp," his face "a mask," his voice "cold, metallic, nasal—awful!" Henry Cabot Lodge was "a small man . . . with a jaunty and aggressive carriage." Of all the Republicans none titillated more than W. Murray Crane, Lodge's tiny colleague from Massachusetts, "and I often wonder if Taft takes Murray on his knee at these conferences."[3]

The novelty of the capital fascinated the Hoosier secretary. The city's leisurely tempo contrasted with the commercial bustle of even Terre Haute, and politics provided excitement. Although Washington's population of 330,000 hardly made it a world center, political celebrities and foreign diplomats gave it a cosmopolitan air. The district radiated charm, and tourists and residents alike beheld its shrines and enjoyed its tree-lined avenues and circles. Political rituals, cultural events, and social activities added to the city's appeal.

Washington attracted Bowers from the outset. Col. William R. Hollister, the right-hand man of Missouri's senator William J. Stone, took Bowers in tow on his first day in town, gave the newcomer a chicken supper at Hancock's, and introduced him to Shoemaker's, "the birthplace of the gin rickey." Bowers liked the Café République at Fifteenth and F, where one night he sat enthralled at a table with the Senate's raconteur, "Fiddlin' " Bob Taylor, who spun tall tales out of Tennessee.[4]

Art and beauty did not escape his notice. Bowers attended an opening at the Corcoran Gallery of Art, the guest of New York's senator James A. O'Gorman. "The scene was great," the young Hoosier exclaimed. "Statues lined the stairway. Women in low necks hovered close to the naked Apollos and blasé old roués leaned languidly against the legs of Venus." Likewise, he admired feminine charms in Peacock Alley at the New Willard Hotel. "Such beauty, such gowns, such strutting and spreading of peacock feathers. . . . See how these old grey beards around us grow dreamy as in some oriental harem."[5]

The cosmopolitan nature of the capital appealed to him. Jules Jusserand, the French ambassador, preceded Root to the rostrum at an Arlington ceremony: "The fine English oration of the day . . . came flowing . . . from the lips of a little Frenchman. . . . From fire to ice—that was the transition from Jusserand to Root!" One Sunday afternoon in May, Bowers went out to Benning Field "to see some aeroplanes fly—my first experience." "Alice Longworth was there," he reported. "She really has the blasé, hard, cold face of the fashionable demi-monde, and her reputation here is not the sweetest."[6]

The young man from Indiana found a place in a Massachusetts Avenue apartment across from the German embassy. His home away from home was room 240 of the Senate Office Building. He enjoyed his job "to the limit" and found his boss "a delightful fellow to work with." The secretary was a worker, dictating "about 100 letters a day and out of the 100 or so that come Kern does not hear of more than four or five." Bowers had the assignment of greeting visitors, taking them to lunch, and escorting them to House and Senate galleries. The secretary soon reflected, "Am enjoying the job to the limit," and as for the senator, "he is a delightful fellow to work with. . . . While I have always liked him I am growing decidedly fond of him."[7] Kern trusted Bowers and allowed him a great deal of freedom in carrying out his duties, a policy Bowers appreciated.

Secretarial duties did not take all his time. He made a point of listening to the more colorful speeches and debates in the House and especially the Senate. He sent a long column, "Washington Side-Lights," to the *Terre Haute Tribune* for publication every Sunday, and this continued until 1917. Elected to the National Press Club, he fraternized with correspondents. The "most interesting" was Gus J. Karger of the *Cincinnati Times-Star*, who saw Taft on confidential terms. Friendship with Arthur Krock of the *Louisville Times* lasted longest, increasing after the Kentuckian moved to the *New York World* and *New York Times*.[8]

Bowers corresponded with Frank Brubeck, Samuel M. Ralston, and John E. Lamb. He regaled Brubeck with candid reports, political and otherwise. "This morning I heard [Joseph] Cannon make the last stand" of the Old Guard in the tariff debate. The former Republican speaker "waved his arms, beat the table." "He has the courage of his convictions." Bowers wrote to Brubeck of flirtations in cafés and an episode one night when a congressional acquaintance took him to a house of assignation, the Republican paying for the fun, which did not develop as expected. After they undressed the girls, the congressman's partner became hysterical. "My girl shook her, slapped her, scolded her, threatened her, and stark naked she lay upon the bed and raised proverbial hell." At length they left for the Press Club and a drink. "I . . . ditched mine—our old trick."[9]

Convinced their party would capture the White House in 1912, several Democrats vied for the nomination. In Indiana Tom Taggart was busy touting Gov. Thomas R. Marshall for the presidency. Among the other Democratic aspirants were Gov. Woodrow Wilson of New Jersey and Speaker Champ Clark. Marshall was not Bowers's choice. His candidate for president? His own boss, Kern. "No one here takes Marshall seriously," the secretary reported, "and Kern is being talked up in the eastern papers and every day brings us Indiana papers booming him."[10]

The most eventful development for Bowers in 1911 was far removed from adventures in houses of ill repute. That year he married Sybil McCaslin. No hint of his intentions went to Brubeck or other friends because a second girl was pursuing Bowers and he did not want word to reach her. It is certain that the bride-to-be, who had written so devotedly to him during his Terre Haute years, understood. There were both serious and absurd overtones in all this, as he "had made the horrible blunder . . . not long ago" of placing letters to the other "Indianapolis damsel" and to Sybil in wrong envelopes. As he explained to Brubeck in December, "From that time on I had hell—more hell with the girl of whom I've often told you than with Sybil." The other girl expostulated both to Sybil and his mother. She threatened that if Claude and Sybil married "she would notify my wife's mother of the 'sort of person I am.' " Because of this, the wedding plans remained "a profound secret."[11]

At four o'clock on 29 November the Reverend Dr. Alfred Kummer of the Riverside Methodist Episcopal Church in Indianapolis united the couple. Bowers had passed his thirty-third birthday, and Sybil her twenty-ninth. The setting: the Morton Place home of her parents, George Hunter and Isabelle Jenkinson McCaslin. It was a small ceremony attended by Sybil's parents, her sister, Bowers's mother, the minister, and the bride and groom.[12]

The decision to marry Sybil was the best he ever made. A brunette with brown eyes, the Indianapolis native was attractive then and retained her beauty in their forty-six years together. Sybil got along with people, liked to read, enjoyed plays and concerts, was an acute observer, and politically knowledgeable. "She had great charm" and a "calm temperament in contrast to mine," Bowers wrote in his seventies. "I never heard her say a nasty word against any other girl." She came from a Democratic background; her father, an accountant, had run for office in Indianapolis.[13]

The couple spent the next six and one half years in Washington. They lived for three and one half years in the Cliffbourne Apartments on Calvert Street, near Connecticut Avenue—five rooms with a semicircular view of the District, close to Rock Creek Park. Sybil came to know the city almost as well as did her husband. Senator and Mrs. Kern gave a theater party at the National and another evening entertained them at the Arlington, a favorite of visiting royalty. Bowers planned something each day during the congressional recess. Fairfax was the object of an excursion, and Kern took Sybil and two women from Terre Haute to meet President Taft. When Bowers and his wife dined with the senator at the Willard, Sybil qualified as the "best looking girl in Peacock Alley."[14]

That winter Bowers's mother came to join them. Because he had the knack of snagging passes, his womenfolk witnessed drama as theatrical as anything on Broadway. Andrew Carnegie testified at Steel Trust hearings. "My wife and mother attended all three hearings. . . . He is to my mind the most colossal hypocrite of the age but as my wife says he is . . . lovable." Bowers looked in on a Senate Interstate Commerce Committee hearing. There the head of the American Federation of Labor, Samuel Gompers, pleaded "the point that men have rights that money should respect. . . . Carnegie was a condescending prince, Gompers a suppliant for crusts. It was nauseating!"[15]

Early in 1912 William Jennings Bryan, Governor Wilson, Speaker Clark, and Kern spoke at a Jackson Day Dinner. "I was very fortunate in having a seat within two yards of the speakers table," Bowers reported. Wilson's speech? A "masterpiece." He "is an exceptionally brilliant fellow. Magnetic, epigrammatic, forceful, earnest, and apparently sincere." Clark "made a colossal ass of himself by his conceit. He scatters. The more I hear him the less I think of his capacity." Bryan? "Marvelous." Senator Kern contrasted Andrew Jackson's and Roosevelt's attitudes toward powerful bankers. Though the Hoosier solon was not a candidate, Bowers told Brubeck, "It looks to me like Kern." "A dark horse is a probability and if a dark horse Bryan will name him and it will be Kern."[16]

That presidential year Bowers offered his partisan views on the GOP front-runners: Roosevelt, Taft, and La Follette. He sympathized with Taft and La Follette. The president "has made friends here by the . . . dignified manner in which he has met the curbstone bragging" of Roosevelt. Taft was "out of his element," but "no one can look into his jolly fat face and conceive it possible for him to sacrifice a friend on the altar of ambition." For Bowers, Roosevelt was "an enunciator of falsehoods," and his entry meant "the double crossing" of "poor" La Follette.[17]

Bowers followed the candidates of both parties. One afternoon he saw Clark "in an auto . . . on his way to Maryland to campaign." When he returned, "a handkerchief tucked about his collar" to protect it from perspiration and dust, the Indianan met him—"it reminded me of campaigning for county office." Bowers saw Taft come back after a sortie in New Jersey. "As his machine whizzed through the gates I noticed that . . . he had a care worn look and the customary smile was gone."

The candidates did not monopolize Bowers's time. Sybil and his mother went to hear him speak at an Irish-American meeting in the National Theater. He escorted them to Ladies' Day at the Press Club, where "we ate ice cream and cake and spiked lemonade and ogled the people." Divine Sarah Bernhardt and Detective William J. Burns were others whom he went to hear. The couple helped launch an opera singer, Helen Warrum, the daughter of an Indianapolis friend. They enjoyed picnicking at the Great Falls of the Potomac and attending Helen Herron Taft's garden party. "The setting was ideal. . . . The laughter of pretty women and the sing-song of the splashing fountain. It was just such a scene as Watteau loved to paint."[18]

The Hoosier secretary stood at the Press Club door as the president "waddled" in and sat five feet from him at Arlington on Decoration Day. When Bryan made himself at home in Kern's office, "I had to take the Colonel in charge. . . . I never saw such a whirl wind for work." In April "I was his secretary" and relished the problem of keeping Bryan from hearing anti-Bryan stories by two laughing senators in Kern's anteroom.[19]

Like Democrats throughout the land, Bowers was convinced that his party would win the White House. In mid-June the Republicans chose Taft as their standard-bearer, and the enraged Roosevelt formed a third party. When the Democrats opened their convention in Baltimore in late June, they were elated by the Republicans' split. Although not a delegate as in 1908, Bowers

looked forward to the drama at Baltimore. By May he believed that
the "wise ones" in his party "are expecting the unexpected—the
nomination of Kern." Members of the Indiana delegation, which
Thomas Taggart dominated, had a different idea—support of
Governor Marshall so that he might emerge as the running mate.
Considered a lightweight by some, Marshall never had a chance for
first place.[20]

The Democrats assembled in Baltimore saw one of the most
exciting, and protracted, nominating struggles in American history,
a contest between Clark and Wilson. After twenty-three ballots,
the exhausted delegates adjourned for the weekend. Rumor circu-
lated that Kern might emerge as the nominee. But how close the
senator came remains problematical. Bowers thought he "missed
the nomination by the breadth of a hair," but this is not in accord
with most historians' accounts. Yet Kern received one or more votes
on thirty-six of the first forty-three ballots. Bowers attributed
Kern's defeat to "stubborn insistence" of the leaders of the Hoosier
delegation, who cast every vote for Marshall through twenty-seven
ballots. Except for that, "it would have been easy."[21]

Indiana at last moved all but one of its thirty votes to Wilson,
and a series of less spectacular changes increased the governor's
count. On the forty-sixth tally, 2 July, he attained the requisite
two-thirds majority. That evening, on the second vice presidential
ballot, Marshall became Wilson's running mate.[22]

For Bowers, the convention must have involved frustration. The
loyal secretary would have dearly loved seeing his boss the nominee,
but Kern never officially became a candidate. In the *Tribune*, the secretary wrote that his time was spent on the convention floor, some
in Eva Taggart's box, and the rest with the committee on resolutions.
Yet he did not devote all his hours in Baltimore to political matters.
"I also had one unique adventure—the most remarkable I ever
expect to have. I flirted with a woman who is about forty-two years
old," he wrote to Brubeck. "Finally I concluded to return to the
hotel. The lady was faint with the heat. 'Would I mind escorting
her?' I would not. We had a mint julep—then another. Then she
went with me to my room. It was fine—Lord it was fine."[23]

As the Republicans had feared and the Democrats had hoped, Roosevelt's followers nominated their man to head the Progressive ticket. A fourth candidate was the Socialist Eugene V. Debs. "I count it as a privilege to be numbered among your friends," a pleased Bowers wrote his Terre Haute friend, "and I want to be among those to congratulate you—from the heart—on the honor you have received." "Your nomination will probably not get you the Presidency, but better than that I fancy, it will get you a very distinct place in American history." "Your words of congratulation are sweet and touching to me and I thank you for them with all my heart," Debs replied. "Just one expression from you is worth more to me than I would possibly get out of any office."[24]

Campaigning in Indiana, Bowers canvassed in a political climate different from any he had known. The Republicans were a party divided between the followers of Taft and Roosevelt. Bowers's old Lebanon friend, Ralston, was victorious and sent a photograph with the inscription, "Dear Claude—I appreciate all that you did personally to make me Governor of Indiana." Every Hoosier Democratic congressional nominee won election. Nationally Wilson triumphed and his party captured both houses.[25]

Returning to Washington, Bowers noted everything was changed. Such hardy Republican perennials as Cannon had gone down. "A once proud party is in sack cloth and ashes." The Democratic majority made Kern head of the Committee on Privileges and Elections, providing his secretary additional income as its clerk.[26]

Bowers, his wife, and mother continued to enjoy the sights and sounds. On Christmas Eve they rode a streetcar to the city's edge to witness the celebration of high mass at the Franciscan monastery. He and Sybil had a table in the Gold Room of the Ebbitt House on New Year's Eve and the next day "paid our respects to President Taft." Bowers went to the Press Club on Lame Duck Night when Cannon was the star attraction. Just prior to Wilson's inauguration, the couple viewed a parade of women demanding the vote, and Bowers attended what he described as the "first open air suffragette meeting ever held in Washington." He favored their cause and found the speakers attractive and their message compelling.[27]

On 4 March at the east front of the Capitol, the Princeton schoolmaster delivered his inaugural address. Twenty feet away, Bowers was "impressed" by the brevity, solemnity, and beauty. Sybil had begun keeping a diary and noted that just before he spoke "we were invited into the Press Section . . . and could hear him. His address was short, appropriate, scholarly, and politic. He was frequently applauded and he made a splendid impression." Bowers stopped to deliver a letter to Bryan and found the Nebraskan "radiant, glowing with health and in fine fettle." He had not admitted that he would be secretary of state, and Bowers decided to ask him. " 'It's Mr. Secretary now?' " " 'Well, it looks that way,' " Bryan said, "his eye twinkling. 'It all depends on whether the senate turns me down.' "[28]

Bowers reveled in Wilson's dramatic reforms. An enemy of the trusts and advocate of the government serving the majority, the Hoosier applauded the New Freedom's success in curbing the power of monopolies, protecting the pocketbooks of the middle class, and defending the interests of workers. As Kern's secretary, he took pride in the leading part his boss played in advancing the president's agenda in the Senate. While aware that these changes were creating a new role for government, Bowers's political partisanship blinded him to some of the defects of the Wilsonian administration. Attacks on the president's professorial egotism and self-righteousness were dismissed by the secretary as politically motivated, and, like so many other Progressives, he never realized that Wilson's agenda overlooked or reinforced nineteenth-century attitudes such as racism.

The young Hoosier continued to write a weekly column for the *Tribune* and noted a series of West Virginia outrages. A coalfield strike in 1912 had led to shootings, killings, martial law, and a military tribunal sentencing miners to the penitentiary without recourse to civil rights. Mary "Mother" Jones, an octogenarian agitator, also was locked up. Bowers would describe the miners as "brutally treated, shamelessly exploited, and denied the right to collective bargaining." This was "a story of tyranny and brutality as infamous and cruel as was ever born of the dynasty of the Romanoffs." At the start of the new Congress in April 1913, Kern, hearing of the problems in West Virginia, called for an investigation. Mine operators and their influential friends quickly reacted. An acquaintance urged the senator to call off the probe. Bowers was in Kern's office when the latter slammed down the receiver after telling the man, "I'll see you in hell first!"[29]

Although the governor of West Virginia claimed "Mrs. Jones is not now nor has she at any time . . . been in prison," Kern exposed this lie when he read the following telegram on the Senate floor.

From out the military bastille, where I have been forced to pass my eighty-first milestone of life, I plead with you for the honor of the nation. I send you the groans and tears of men, women, and children as I have heard them in this state, and beg you to force that investigation. Children yet unborn will rise and bless you.[30]

A resolution for a Senate investigation was debated. Pressure brought Mother Jones's release, and in mid-May she arrived in Washington, where Bowers hid her from the press and was her host in the Senate Office Building, while she pled the miners' cause to Kern's colleagues. "The day she walked into Kern's office I could scarcely believe that she could be the firebrand of whom I had heard, so grandmotherly did she look. Her eyes, however, were keen, penetrating and sparkling," the secretary later recalled. "Footsore but undaunted, she made the rounds of all the Senators, and the resolution was adopted after a bitter debate." Five years later, when Mother Jones called on Bowers in Fort Wayne, he found that her "spirit flamed as always" in her eighty-sixth year.[31]

In the short run, Kern focused on conditions in West Virginia. In the long run, the Senate resolution certainly was a factor in the gradual recognition of union and workers' rights. Senate approval was itself a victory for social justice. In 1918 Bowers would write: "For the first time in the history of the senate in a fight involving a contest between capital and labor the workers won." He retained the same opinion as an old man: "This, I think, was the first clear-cut victory ever won in the Senate by labor."[32]

Few occurrences pleased Bowers more than Kern's elevation to the post of majority leader. The Senate Democrats' unanimous decision was made even before Wilson took the oath. Kern played an important—and on occasion decisive—role in the New Freedom legislation. As his secretary, Bowers was increasingly busy. The senator allowed him to run the office without instruction. "I do everything connected with the senatorial job but serve on the committees [and give] speeches on the floor." Usually it was his secretary, not the senator, who had responsibility of "meeting the people," including constituents and job hunters who elbowed their way into Kern's anteroom. "A letter is opened," Bowers wrote. "A hand is shaken. The letter read. Then the telephone answered. Another hand shaken. A reply to the letter dictated. . . . And then all over again hour after hour." He found the turmoil trying "in a sense," but at the same time "mighty exhilarating." His journalistic and political background allowed him to take over when Kern "fairly shot from caucus to conference."[33]

Bowers was incapable of becoming enmeshed in mere routine and often found time to pursue various interests. Whenever something was occurring, he was apt to be on hand. Bowers listened to the maiden speech of Rep. Alben W. Barkley of Kentucky and with Sybil at his side heard Clark applauded when the Speaker backed Wilson on the tariff. The secretary informed *Tribune* readers on the personalities of congressmen. He rode streetcars between his apartment and the office—reporting Elihu Root sitting studiously aloof from other senators aboard the trolley. Bowers passed along "confidentially" the rumor that the president had heart trouble "of a rather delicate nature." Bowers broke away from Washington long enough to address an Irish-American gathering on St. Patrick's Day in Providence, Rhode Island.[34]

When Sybil's father fell ill, she returned to Indianapolis; the couple corresponded daily. "She's been away a week," he exclaimed to Brubeck, and "I have felt like one of the guests in Dante's

Inferno." "She will be away a week longer and the Lord knows how I will spend my time. . . . It's hell to be in love with your wife." As always, however, he found plenty to do. One of his preoccupations was a federal job for Brubeck, who eventually received an appointment in the Internal Revenue Service.[35]

Bowers provided *Tribune* readers with coverage of Democratic successes in 1913. The passage of the Underwood tariff, lowering duties for the first time since before the Civil War, and the Federal Reserve Act, a landmark of the New Freedom, won praise. As Senate Majority Leader, Kern used tact, parliamentary maneuvers, and appeals to party loyalty to persuade the narrow Democratic majority to pass the tariff revision, despite the strong opposition of several senators from his own party. Bowers's columns highlighted the president's close contact with the legislative branch, exemplified by repeated conferences with Kern at the White House and on Capitol Hill. Wilson's addresses to Congress were described as masterful, using "classic English." The future ambassador to Chile approved the president's foreign policy, praised his interest in Latin America, and insisted that "these southern republics . . . [are] vitally important to us."[36] That Bowers could meld regular newspaper contributions with his office duties was evidence of the industry that characterized his career.

Yet social life in the capital unquestionably meant just as much to Bowers as his serious occupations. A writer whom he knew well was Louis Ludlow of the *Indianapolis Star* and a future congressman from Indiana. Especially happy were the hours he spent with two congressional staffers, Frank Oliver of the Bronx and Shaemus O'Sheel, a New York poet. This trio shared rollicking humor and a love of Ireland. Bowers also relished discussing politics over cigars with Kern at the majority leader's quarters at the Congress Hall Hotel. The theater and weekend trips to Virginia entertained Bowers and his wife. They enjoyed dinners with Blanche and Charles T. Terry, a friend of Indianapolis pal Paxton Hibben. Formal events also met with their pleasure. At a reception on the White House lawn they mingled with other guests, afterward comparing Ellen Wilson with Helen Taft to the latter's disadvantage.

Sybil did not accompany her husband when, in June, he went to Boston to speak on "The Democracy of Woodrow Wilson."[37]

Bowers's 1914 *Tribune* contributions dealt with domestic issues, comments on the issues, and personalities. Passed to promote business competition, the Clayton Antitrust and Federal Trade Commission Acts were considered as "great remedial, constructive legislation." He made remarks about conservationist Gifford Pinchot ("a moneyed demagogue"), Kansas Republican Joseph L. Bristow (a "wordy warrior"), and Ohio Republican Theodore E. Burton ("magnetic as a brick"). A future friend, Navy Secretary Josephus Daniels, received the journalist's praise. Teddy Roosevelt with "outlandish hat" and "ruddy glow" came to Washington, and Bowers went to Union Station to see him—"a supremely selfish, self centered soldier of fortune, with his eye open for the main chance." Nothing was too minor to chronicle. Wilson's second daughter, Eleanor, liked to tango, and Borah was being stung by "the presidential bee." Bowers also mentioned John F. "Honey Fitz" Fitzgerald, the Boston politico and grandfather of Jack, Bobby, and Teddy Kennedy.[38]

The major event of 1914 was the European war, the "most horrible catastrophe," Bowers believed, "in the entire history of mankind." In the *Tribune* he interpreted it as the "greatest breaking down of civilization since the fall of the Roman empire." The contest between the Central Powers led by Germany and Austria-Hungary and the Allies including Great Britain, France, Italy, and Russia meant a host of problems for the United States. Bowers praised Senate legislation—opposed by the shipping lobby—that helped smooth the way for foreign vessels to register under the flag of the United States.[39]

How wonderfully the president met the emergency! Wilson "is a fighter—perhaps the most persistent and stubborn fighter" in the White House since Jackson. Bowers was equally outspoken in condemning the Republican senators—"the Black Horse Cavalry of Plutocracy." He sketched the scene, words of the diplomats, and remarks of Wilhelm von Schoen that Japan—on whose course of action many people speculated—hated America and Americans.

Later Bowers and von Schoen were acquainted, perhaps better than they would have preferred, when both served in Chile at the time of Pearl Harbor.[40]

Through 1915 the concern was German naval policy, U-boat attacks, and the torpedoing of the *Lusitania* in May, with 124 Americans among the 1,198 fatalities. There were loud demands for declaring war, but Wilson undertook to calm the clamor. In the *Tribune*, Bowers extolled the president's "character," "wisdom," and "conservative common sense." "Just think of what the sea tragedy of the other day would have meant with certain other people"— meaning Roosevelt—"in the white house!" The president "has met his duty . . . with a courage and consistency, that marks him as one of the greatest, safest and sanest leaders the American people have ever had." Because of this, he wrote, "There is no longer the feeling that we are close to war. It is probable that we have met the greatest crisis."[41]

Pro-Allied Americans, including Roosevelt, called Wilson wishy-washy. German and Irish Americans demanded that the United States condemn the Allied blockade of Germany. The Irish aspect of affairs placed Bowers in a curious situation. After years of interest in Irish history and engagements before Irish-American audiences, he sympathized with their attitudes. In his *Tribune* columns quasi-Anglophobic comments appeared, for, like Kern, he was unsympathetic to the preparedness campaign Wilson was mounting. In 1914–15 Bowers spent most of his spare time composing *The Irish Orators: A History of Ireland's Fight for Freedom.* Evening after evening, Sybil joined her husband in the Senate Office Building, reading while he wrote.[42]

The couple spent the summer of 1915 in Indianapolis, where he ran Kern's office and worked to finish *The Irish Orators.* It was a happy time, for Sybil was pregnant. Renting a house near Nineteenth Street, both did a great deal of reading and saw such friends as the Henry Warrums and Myla Closser Baker and her husband. Behind the Ruckle Street dwelling was a garden where the parents-to-be played at raising vegetables.[43] However, if the far-from-dexterous husband pulled up a single onion or radish, no evidence has been adduced.

Yet his dexterousness soon was tested when the baby arrived ahead of schedule on 2 September. "When we did go to the hospital," Sybil recorded, "it was in an ambulance with Claude holding the one hour old lady on his lap." Thus her father presided when Patricia joined the family circle. First Patty and afterward Pat, she accompanied her mother on an eastbound train in November 1915, a week after the new father went on in search of a new Washington apartment. He found it at the Prince Karl, corner of K and Nineteenth, where the family with Grandmother Juliet would remain until March 1917. Out in her carriage, Patty was a sidewalk hit with the wife of the British ambassador, and Claude was so delighted with Lady Spring-Rice's praise that Sybil accused him of degenerating into a British toady.[44]

While Wilson's harsh notes to Berlin tilted the United States toward the Allies, Bowers remained anti-British and pro-German in his *Tribune* columns in 1915 and 1916. Many of his contributions contained phrases like the "unexampled arrogance" and "criminal indifference of England to American rights" and "her shameful violation of all our rights upon the seas." He criticized Britain's seizure of American mails and attacked Anglophilic "snobs" in the United States.[45] By contrast, Bowers had good things to say about Germany. He assailed Congressman Augustus "Little Gussie" Gardner's "disgusting tirade against German-Americans" and declared: "There would be no U-boat crisis had there been no illegal determination" on Britain's part "to starve the civilian population of Germany." Did not England "lightly brush aside American protests" against violations of "international law and the law of humanity"?[46]

Still, only once did Bowers disagree with the president. Legislators introduced resolutions to warn citizens against travel on armed merchant vessels. Such measures, the secretary noted, were favored by the "overwhelming majority" of Democratic congressmen. Wilson opposed these proposals, arguing that Americans had the right to travel where they pleased, while Bowers opined in the *Tribune* that his countrymen "have no moral right to endanger the peace of their country to satisfy their whim for travel." What

Democrats regarded as a diplomatic triumph occurred in May 1916, when Germany yielded to Wilson's demands and gave up submarine warfare and tranquil relations ensued.[47]

In Indiana both Senate seats and the governorship were at stake, and Sen. Benjamin F. Shively's death made the situation more complex than usual. Taggart occupied Shively's seat by appointment, while Republicans picked Harry S. New and James E. Watson to run against him and Kern. Bowers lost no time telling readers the virtues of the Democratic candidates. He also praised his future friend Louis D. Brandeis, Wilson's nominee to the Supreme Court. Republicans on the Judiciary Committee opposed the Boston lawyer, the columnist claimed, because he "has served the people against the corporations" and because "he is a Jew." When the Senate confirmed Brandeis, Bowers was ecstatic.[48]

On 10 June 1916 Charles Evans Hughes became the GOP presidential nominee, and Indiana's Charles W. Fairbanks went on the ticket. The next week in St. Louis, Wilson and Marshall won renomination. Between the two gatherings, the president led a "monster preparedness parade" in Washington, and the Bowerses saw Woodrow Wilson marching "in white straw hat, blue coat, white trousers and shoes—looking the pink of physical condition. . . . No administration in history has accomplished so much in four years," the partisan onlooker exclaimed.[49]

In early May Bowers published *The Irish Orators*. Like his subsequent histories, the author chose heroes to praise and sought to shape opinion on a contemporary political issue. His subjects were nine Irish historical figures whom he had admired since high school. One message remained with the reader: Ireland deserved independence. Like his speeches, Bowers's writing betrayed the nineteenth-century origin of his literary and oratorical models. Hyperbole, repetition, verbal bouquets, and biblical allusions characterized his columns, books, and addresses. The modern reader is accustomed to a more prosaic style, but Bowers's contemporaries expected and applauded the Victorian excesses found in his writings and speeches. When introducing one of his orators, the author wrote, "Ireland found a voice for her unfortunate sons. It was the voice of genius—a voice so eloquent that its message . . . will instruct the world . . . as long as the language lives." And he continued, "It was the voice of that marvelous man, the most lovable, in many respects the most brilliant genius that Ireland has produced—the voice of John Philpot Curran."[50]

To promote the book, the author and the Bobbs-Merrill Company gathered encomia far and wide. The widely respected Archbishop of Baltimore, James Cardinal Gibbons, wrote the foreword and said, "The reader will find this valuable contribution to the story of Ireland's greatness impartial, instructive and interesting and of such appeal that he will not be satisfied until he reads to the end."[51]

The critical reception of the 548-page volume was favorable. Undiluted praise appeared in the anti-English *Review of Reviews*: "Impossible not to be inspired" by so "comprehensive and scholarly" a work—the "most complete book of its kind." The *Boston Transcript* was hardly less eulogistic, describing Bowers as "a master of his subject. . . . His heroes are truly heroic, daring in their opposition and admirable in their devotion to their cause." According to the *New York Times Book Review*, Bowers showed a "just appreciation" of his nine men, plus "a notable skill in psychological analysis." The *Catholic World* declared, "It is all well done." Adverse reactions concerned the author's one-sidedness. *The Dial*, while lauding the "glowing, vigorous, and eloquent style," faulted him for not presenting "all the truth." "If he had been a more discreet or experienced writer," the *Times* critic noted, "he would have blue-penciled a large number of his adjectives and thus have given more weight to his presentation."[52]

Later historians have assessed *The Irish Orators*. According to Robert E. Burns and Lawrence J. McCaffrey, some of Bowers's estimates were awry. Burns contended Henry Flood was "unprincipled" and Ireland "would have been better off without him," while McCaffrey found Bowers's depiction of Thomas Meagher "bad" and the Daniel O'Connell essay "fair but disappointing." On the positive side, McCaffrey confessed, "I never read a better short essay on [Charles Stewart] Parnell," and Burns called the volume "a respectable piece of work."[53]

The release of *The Irish Orators* was fortuitous. A week earlier, the Irish rose against the British on Easter Monday, capturing newspaper headlines. But sales were less than spectacular. The price was $1.50, within range of middle-income people. Yet only 961 copies sold between 1 May and the end of the year, with 360 sales in 1917. By 31 December 1917 royalties amounted to $201.81.[54]

Ex-senator Albert J. Beveridge's admiration of Bowers's book would be a factor in their friendship of future years. One day when Bowers was in the Senate chamber, Vice President Marshall sent a note from the dais: "You have certainly demonstrated that to teach history in connection with the actions and utterances of great men is more attractive and also more instructive than in the usual way." Mary J. O'Donovan Rossa, widow of one of Ireland's militants, could not lay down the "fascinating" volume and lauded the author's "charmingly eloquent style." Clark "went down into the dining room for breakfast sleepy headed and sleepy eyed. I had sat up all night reading your book. . . . It is one of the most interesting . . . written in this country in a quarter of a century."[55]

That summer Bowers witnessed a new birth of the New Freedom. Bills were enacted: the Rural Credits and Warehouse Acts brought applause from farmers; child labor and workman's compensation acts received labor support. The Shipping Act created a Federal Shipping Board and the beginning of a respectable merchant marine.

The political event of 1916 was the presidential contest. The GOP enjoyed the advantage of being the majority party, and this time united. Prognosticators predicted the election of Hughes. But Wilson's progressive record appealed, and his policy of neutrality— summed up in the slogan "He kept us out of war!"—proved popular. Nowhere was Republican organization in abler hands than in Indiana. Will H. Hays mobilized the GOP, courting the German, Irish, black, and Roman Catholic voters. Republicans sensed it was their year, but Democrats felt no comparable confidence. Taggart had been in Washington as a fill-in senator, leaving leadership in inexperienced hands. Nor did an unpopular Democratic mayor in Indianapolis and scandals in Terre Haute help.[56]

Kern's poor health prevented him from waging a vigorous cam-paign. Long tubercular, he was now in pitiful physical condition. The senator had worn himself out in behalf of Wilson and the New Freedom. Kern managed to return to Indiana and attempt a can-vass, but vocal problems made him "unable to speak," and when Wilson visited Indianapolis the senator remained "ill at home." His opponent, New, campaigned throughout the state.[57]

In 1916 Bowers was usually assigned to smaller towns. Starting on the trail 6 October, he spoke in seventeen counties, three in his own Fifth District. He proved popular. In Mecca, Parke County, every seat in the hall was occupied, with many standing in the rear. "One of the best ever heard," the *Daviess County Democrat* remarked of his speech in Washington, Indiana. When he spoke in Vigo County, even the headline in the Republican *Terre Haute Star* reported "Bowers Warmly Greeted at Political Gathering." His standard speech lauded the New Freedom. "Never in the history of the country," he asserted, "has business been as prosperous as it is today. . . . The skies of night are glowing from the furnace fires of factories running to their capacity. . . . Thanks to the constructive genius of Woodrow Wilson," Bowers insisted, the nation "had a financial system that was built upon the rock." Nor was foreign policy forgotten. How could the United States avoid war and enjoy peace? "The answer is the policy of Woodrow Wilson."[58]

Election night was dismal. New defeated Kern by 11,501 in a vote total of 662,677. Taggart lost the other seat, and the GOP won the governorship. In Indiana, Hughes beat Wilson by 6,842, but on the bright side, Wilson won nationally. When Bowers entered Kern's house after the election, he saw "a strikingly frail figure, a little sad but not too sad to smile and joke in his accustomed way, greatly disappointed but not so much so as to be embittered." The senator returned to duty in December, in a serious condition.[59] He died of tuberculosis the following August.

During Kern's last months foreign affairs dominated the nation. Despite Wilson's peace initiatives, in February 1917 Germany renewed submarine warfare. There was nothing for Washington to do but break relations with the Central Powers. Over the objec-

tions of a small minority, Congress in April—at Wilson's request—
voted for war.[60]

As Senate majority leader, Kern proved loyal to Wilson. A firm
proponent of reform, he skillfully steered controversial New
Freedom measures through the closely divided Senate. During his
four years in this post, his successful appeals to party loyalty and his
use of the caucus to make the will of the majority binding on all
members—as he had done in passing the Underwood tariff—
helped turn this office into an effective instrument of political
leadership. Bowers doubted that Wilson ever had "a proper appreciation" of Kern as "a self-sacrificing statesman and clever politician." But in 1914 the president did acknowledge his reliance on
his Senate leader. Referring to Kern's role as chair of the party's
Senate caucus, Wilson wrote him: "I am sure all Democrats are
indebted to you for the intelligence and conscience you have put
into that great task."[61]

Senator Kern seldom "gave any expression of his appreciation"
to his office staff. But on occasion he would write "a letter teeming
with affectionate appreciation." On his retirement Kern wrote to
his secretary:

> I have no words with which to express my earnest apprecia-
> tion of your faithful loyal service during the past six years. I
> have constantly leaned on you and you have never failed me.
> You have done more work and better work than any man in
> Washington that I know anything about and I want you to
> feel that I appreciate it all. My feeling towards you is that of a
> kinsman rather than a friend.[62]

In truth, Bowers was ready for another position. His enthusiasm
for his post had declined as the years passed. In addition to his distaste for office chores, he complained of lack of status. "A senator's
secretary was on a par with an elevator conductor," he lamented.
After his duties ended 4 March 1917, Bowers briefly continued as
clerk of the Committee on Privileges and Elections. On St.
Patrick's Day he spoke at a New York City dinner of the Ancient

Order of Hibernians. Meanwhile, he prepared to return to
Indiana, this time headed for Fort Wayne and its Democratic
paper, the *Journal-Gazette*.[63]

# CHAPTER FOUR

# Fort Wayne

Bowers's six years in Fort Wayne were crucial to his development as a journalist, historian, and orator. At the *Fort Wayne Journal-Gazette* he honed his editorial skills through hours of uninterrupted enterprise, and his pieces received recognition. In addition, he wrote *The Life of John Worth Kern* and *The Party Battles of the Jackson Period*, the first of his books to reach a national audience. And he continued as an orator to defend the Democracy, both within and without the Hoosier State.

His arrival in Fort Wayne coincided almost to the day with America's entrance into the First World War. Bowers's editorials sought to rally people in support of the army and navy. The German element of Fort Wayne was large, and many felt sympathy for the fatherland; nevertheless Fort Wayne responded to the challenge. As early as 19 April there were forty thousand marchers in a parade, termed "inspiring" by Bowers. The *Journal-Gazette* reported in mid-June that Fort Wayne, "which has set the pace for Indiana in every other line of patriotic activity," oversubscribed the first Liberty Loan.

A fervid and indeed eloquent tone sometimes characterized the new editor's offerings. Impressed by the war's "terrible solemnity," he wrote: "At first blush it is quite impossible to conceive of war in any other light than as a curse. . . . And yet men may, and at times must, war in sacred causes, else the man on horseback would ride rough-shod over the liberties and rights of the human race." In the spring of 1918 Bowers commended "Black Jack [John J.] Pershing, that beau ideal of a soldier." With him the sons of America "turned toward the thunder of the guns." Many editorials dealt with what civilians could do to help the war effort. The buying of Liberty Loan bonds, contributions of Fort Wayne women to the Red Cross, and victory gardens were three of the many home front causes he promoted with enthusiasm. He upheld the policies of Woodrow Wilson and attacked profiteers. Time and again he discussed the need for conservation of fuel and food. When the people of Fort Wayne and America did their part, the editor was quick with commendation.

Partisan as well as patriot, Bowers was disgusted by the acts of some Republicans. Gov. James P. Goodrich loaded the Indiana Council of Defense with members of his party, placing at its head the state chairman, Will H. Hays. Bowers was caustic when in mid-1917 Hays sent Republican agents across Indiana to raise a "$100,000 slush fund." "Call in your agents—let's 'get busy' for a greater cause," the journalist urged in "An Appeal to Mr. Hays." Even the *Lafayette Journal*, a Republican paper, said the money was to be used in the 1918 campaign.[1]

Bowers handled Hays more gently than he did Republicans—and Democrats, too—who in his judgment were misbehaving in Washington. Kern's successor, Sen. Harry S. New, opposed conscription although the army demanded it. "Can it be that you do not know," Bowers asked, "the miserable inefficiency of England until the near approach of disaster forced her to adopt the policy pursued by all their allies? Ah, senator, you are playing with fire and may get scorched." When Sen. Warren G. Harding discouraged Ohioans from subscribing to the Liberty Loan, this "notorious copperhead" committed an "act of infamy." Bowers scorned a Democrat, James Reed of Missouri, as "a disgrace to the republic." Influenced by "his food speculator friends," Bowers wrote, the senator dared to insinuate that "Wilson aims at a dictatorship and is a traitor." No one else in America "has so richly earned the Iron Cross from the kaiser."

The journalist praised Secretary of the Navy Josephus Daniels, who had been subjected to attacks. The editor lauded Secretary of War Newton D. Baker, "the little dynamo" from Cleveland "who owes his position to his nation-wide reputation for efficiency and cleanness." Secretary of the Treasury William G. McAdoo, a target for critics when he took over the regulation of railroads, had "a demonstrated genius for organization." When Republican senator William S. Kenyon of Iowa expressed confidence in a cabinet member, Bowers made effective use of the statement. Likewise, he put in a good word for the open-mindedness of Republican senators Knute Nelson of Minnesota and Porter J. McCumber of North Dakota. He praised Herbert Hoover's war work and was impressed by Franklin D. Roosevelt. The assistant secretary of the navy "wins people to him by his appearance of being earnest and of wanting to really do something." The editor predicted that Roosevelt was just beginning his career—"one that will be notable."

Bowers wrote knowledgeably on developments overseas. British and French politics, the floundering of post-czarist Russia, and even Spanish and Irish relationships to the war were examined. He introduced a host of European and American leaders to the *Journal-Gazette* readers: Georges Clemenceau, David Lloyd George, Alexander Kerensky, and Winston Churchill. Bowers's opinions of the British statesman proved prescient: "Winston Churchill stands out today as the one man in parliament who has at all times had the courage and the capacity to stand up in the face of jeers of enemies and tell England the truth to her face." The Hoosier predicted the time would come "when it will be conceded by the historians that his speeches were unique in that they went to the point and were wise in their suggestions."[2]

When discussing the Russian Revolution, Bowers demonstrated that he understood what was happening. In the spring of 1917, before Vladimir Lenin seized power, the editor observed, "In the resignation of Guchkoff, the provisional minister of war, we may read the story of the coming of 'the Reds.'" More significant for the editor was Kerensky's speech "in which he disclosed in pessimistic colors the utter hopelessness of the situation. . . . The nation is hopelessly drunk that dons the garb of democracy, and staggers with gleeful shouts of fraternity into the arms of autocracy. What will the morrow bring?" At the end of 1918, Bowers concluded, "This man Lenin is something new in the world. And while it may be said that the bolshevistic program is not new, . . . it is literally true that where other like movements lopped at the branches of our present civilization, this one aims at the roots." He argued that "the bourbonish reactionary is the advance agent of bolshevistic programs" and insisted that America's best hope for progressive social action rested with the Democratic party.

With the armistice of November 1918, attention shifted to the Paris Peace Conference where the overriding issue was the proposed League of Nations. Bowers wholeheartedly backed the League, asserting that America's participation in it was vital to world peace. Aware that membership in the body hinged on Republican support, he reminded readers of pro-League sentiments of such Republicans as William Howard Taft and Elihu Root. One of his strongest editorials drew attention to "more than 150" "powerful Republican newspapers nationwide" that wanted America in the League.

In the League fight, no enemy disgusted Bowers more than Henry Cabot Lodge, with Sen. Hiram Johnson of California a runner-up. Johnson at least was "open" in assailing Wilson's position; Lodge's opposition was "purely personal and partisan." Had not Lodge in 1915 favored an almost identical League of Nations? Yet now he was misleading "unwary" men by insisting on "meaningless and unnecessary reservations." Almost as reprehensible was Philander C. Knox, senator from Pennsylvania. The Knoxes and Lodges, Bowers said in 1919, were "endangering the future peace of the world" and would "threaten if not destroy the prosperity of this country" by undermining "the superstructure of European civilization." By setting forth on his transcontinental campaign for the League, Wilson "stands for the New Day. And the people will hear him gladly." But it was not to be. The president fell ill, and the Senate, guided by "reactionary statesmanship," rejected United States membership in the world body. "The League of Nations as it has been butchered by Lodge," Bowers asserted, "is only a grotesque cripple."[3]

Bowers chastised Republican and Democratic enemies of the League. Republican targets included Harding and Knox with their "venomous attitude." Indiana's James E. Watson was no better. Democrats Reed and Thomas P. Gore "would kill the hope of the world" to give the president "a kittenish scratch." After Wilson's stroke, Sen. Miles Poindexter of Washington heaped the "filthiest and the foulest abuse" upon the sick man. Bowers was outraged. The Republican senator was a "gutter Hooligan" with a "pompous pose" and a "jackass bray."

Was there no one beside Wilson whom the editor admired? Yes, he praised the Democratic leadership of Nebraska senator Gilbert Hitchcock. The editor likewise had good words for Republican senators George W. Wickersham and Herbert Parsons and other Republicans including Taft—quoting the ex-president's statement that senators "who are setting out to defeat this league of nations are those I would not trust over night." He lauded the Republican *Saturday Evening Post*, the *Philadelphia Public Ledger*, and the *Indianapolis Star* for their "courageous battle" for the League "against the army that is fighting with poison gas, and sprinkling the wells of information with the arsenic of falsehood."[4]

Because of his hostility toward the League, William C. Bullitt, later ambassador to France while Bowers served as ambassador to Spain, was anathema. After conferring with Lenin, Bullitt recommended recognition of the Bolshevik regime. When Wilson ignored this advice, Bullitt resigned from the State Department and urged the Foreign Relations Committee to oppose membership in the League. Bowers accused Bullitt of falsifying facts and defending "two monsters," Lenin and Leon Trotsky.

Bowers had no greater contempt for Bullitt than for Raymond Robins. This erstwhile social service worker also undertook to improve relations between the United States and Russia and testified before the Foreign Relations Committee. Bowers castigated Robins for pleading Lenin's cause "so persuasively" before the "sympathetic" senators and bristled at the announcement that this "special chum of Lenine and Trotzky" had been invited to help write the 1920 Republican platform: "All the socialists, all the communists, all the anarchists, all the bolshevists . . . have been extraordinarily faithful to Lodge's fight against the League." When Robins visited Harding following his nomination and was named to his executive committee, Bowers attacked the Republican candidate for so honoring this apologist for the "twin-devils of Moscow."[5]

The 1920 presidential contest was the subject of many editorials. Among Republicans, Harding attracted attention. Even in 1916 Bowers sensed the handsome Ohioan's potential, claiming he was the real "choice of the reactionary element." Senators Watson and New, Governor Goodrich, and all the others of their kind favored Harding, "the reliable standpatter of the traditional type." When Harding came to Fort Wayne in April 1920, the *Journal-Gazette* "welcomed" the candidate by assuring him that the paper had "no use for the things you stand for." The editor considered his address "a bromidic discourse" and the candidate a "reactionary."

When Harding became the GOP standard-bearer, Bowers gloated, "*We told you so!*" "And yet there was nothing remarkable in our prediction. . . . When Watson and New announced boldly for Harding months ago they knew what they were about." As for the nominee: "Many years ago the mind of the senator hardened . . . and he has not taken in any progressive ideas in two decades. He is the Ohio edition of James E. Watson."

For the Democrats at San Francisco, Bowers had no prophecy. In July James M. Cox won the Democratic nomination. A journalist and twice governor of Ohio, Cox was a staunch supporter of Wilson and the League. Bowers described the nominee as "a man of magnetic personality, with the victory habit," and "with a record of constructive achievement in the gubernatorial chair which has never been approached" in Ohio's history. His running mate, Franklin D. Roosevelt, was "a fine type of forward looking, fighting, progressive, standing for clean politics and efficient public service"—one of the "ablest and most intriguing men ever named for the vice-presidency."

The editor jeered at Harding's front porch pronouncements in Marion—"The Marionette of Marion Town" and the "Parrot of the Porch." "The plan evidently is for Taft to talk one way" to the pro-League people, "for Johnson to talk another way" to League adversaries, and "Harding to say nothing that means anything." While vacationing in Massachusetts that summer, Bowers questioned lawyers, businessmen, and laborers about their governor, Calvin Coolidge, Harding's running mate, and he heard "not one expression of real admiration." But Coolidge was secondary. What mattered were Cox's sponsorship of the League and the contrast between the stand for principle of Cox and the "shell game" of Harding. Including Fort Wayne on his tour, Cox was warmly greeted by a Bowers editorial: "WELCOME—TO A FIGHTING MAN."[6]

The 1920 cause was lost—the Cox cause, the League cause, the causes Bowers held dear. In Indiana, as nearly everywhere except in the less-than-solid South, Democrats and the League were defeated. Republican Warren T. McCray was elected governor, and Watson returned to the Senate. Yet the Democratic editor's faith persisted. On Wilson's birthday, 28 December, Bowers predicted that in the future the achievements of Wilson would rank with those of Washington and Lincoln, and they would be considered "the immortal trinity that justifies American Democracy to God."

In his editorials, whether defending or attacking, Bowers let few opportunities pass. He did not overlook the chance to scoff at Theodore Roosevelt, Jr. Young Teddy, he wrote, "admires the man [Harding] who called his father . . . a 'Benedict Arnold.' . . . That is a matter of taste. He knew his father better than most of us and if Harding's powers of description satisfy him no one should be excited about it." Taft came in for denunciation after an about-face on the League: "We have often commented upon the . . . spineless character of William Howard Taft, who usually begins right because his instincts are right but always ends by finding an excuse to indorse the thing he . . . condemned."

Editorials were low-keyed in 1921. Attacking what would develop into the Fordney-McCumber tariff, Bowers had good things to say for Charles G. Dawes when the banker became director of the budget. In a commencement talk at Tri-State College in Angola, Indiana, he praised Secretary of State Charles Evans Hughes. He commended a Harding address at Arlington on Armistice Day. Still, he expressed dismay at child labor, the American "industrial depression," and problems of American farmers, failures of Harding's so-called Normalcy. And the editor showed concern over trends in Europe, especially in Germany. Bowers did not ignore Count von Waldersee's statements that "hatred will stand guard in Germany" and "we must prepare for revenge." Bowers also informed his readers of the shocking desperation of "millions of half-starved" Russian peasants.[7]

In the 1922 Republican primary, Albert J. Beveridge opposed New. Few developments pleased Bowers more than when the onetime Progressive Beveridge delivered a blow to Harding—and conservatives of the Harding stripe—by vanquishing New. Samuel M. Ralston easily won the Democratic primary and went on to beat Beveridge. A friend of Beveridge, Bowers was restrained in his editorials, but he lambasted Harding for tax changes favoring the wealthy.[8]

The Ku Klux Klan was an issue in Hoosier politics, and Bowers was vehement in his opposition. Attacking the group for "proclaiming as its purpose the persecution of Jews, Catholics and negroes," as well as "people of foreign birth," he declared the Klan "a rejection of Americanism, a repudiation of the declaration of independence, a violation of the guarantees of the constitution. . . . If America is to be divided into racial and religious groups, warring upon one another, persecuting one another, boycotting one another," Bowers insisted, "the fair hopes of the republic's founders will never flower. For there is nothing so destructive, so hateful, so infamous, so ignorant, and so vicious as bigotry."

It took courage to write this in Indiana in 1922, for the Klan was powerful. But it took less courage to laud Democrats and roast Republicans, which Bowers did as frequently as ever. His editorials reflected more selectivity; such Democrats as New York's governor Alfred E. Smith received admiration. Bowers was hostile to James K. Vardaman, a conservative Mississippi Democrat, and called

Missouri's Reed "an alleged Democrat." He continued to find enco-
mia for such Republicans as William S. Kenyon of Iowa and Borah.
Nor was it a surprise when he assailed Lodge, Governor McCray, or
Secretary of the Interior Albert B. Fall.[9]

Bowers's editorials in 1923 were similar to those of earlier years.
In the White House Harding "kept faith with his party" by refus-
ing to be a leader. In 5-4 decisions the Supreme Court found the
Child Labor Act and the Minimum Wage Law unconstitutional.
The farmers' plight was terrible. Judge Elbert H. Gary, head of
United States Steel, loomed as a "new evangelist of the Lord" by
advocating more religion when his company insisted on at least a
twelve-hour day for the men in the mills. Abroad "Germany can-
not stagger on much longer under existing conditions." Britain's
Prime Minister Stanley Baldwin "is decidedly offensive to
Americans," and in Italy Benito Mussolini was "as impossibly reac-
tionary as Lenin is impossibly radical." Unrest in the Balkans,
killings in the Ruhr, Russians "eager" for another war—all, in
Bowers's judgment, proclaimed a collapse of world statesmanship.
There was one man in 1919 who "foresaw all this and tried to pro-
vide against it. . . . His name was Wilson. And they stoned him.
And now they are stoning one another."

One development gave Bowers a modicum of hope, for Harding
seemed to be supporting the World Court. The editor was skeptical; he paraphrased a remark of Will Rogers that Americans were
less interested in the World Court than in where to park their cars.
On the whole Bowers treated Harding less harshly than Lodge and
his cohorts. In Bowers's opinion their evident hypocrisy did not
apply equally to the Ohioan. In May 1923 Bowers referred pleas-
antly to Harding's "amiable" qualities. Comparing him and Lodge,
Bowers concluded that the "kindly gentleman from Marion" was
"no match for the cold-blooded old fellow from Nahant."

When Harding died in August the editorialist's tributes had
every mark of sincerity. Wrong and weak, Wilson's successor nevertheless was "kindly, considerate and personally lovable." Bowers's
policy toward Coolidge's administration was wait and see. While it
took time for the rascalities of Harding's cronies to come to light,

Indiana had enough scandal of its own to challenge honest men's credulity. That autumn a Marion County grand jury charged Governor McCray with larceny, forgery, embezzlement, and other crimes in 8 indictments and 192 counts. If the indictments were found true, Bowers pointed out, "this sitting governor of Indiana will go into history as a very prodigy of crime."[10]

In 1923 the editor was more outspoken on the Ku Klux Klan, whose reputed power was great. As the Klan issue waxed in warmth, he devoted more space to it, sometimes employing italics: *"When race is arrayed against race, and religion against religion, when neighbors become enemies because they worship in different churches, and when our people cease to be a people and become a miserable hotch-potch of quarreling factions,"* he maintained, *"we cease to be the America that was born of the Revolution."*[11]

Bowers's work was intense. Except for the final year, when he had the assistance of Harry M. Williams, he wrote six to fourteen editorials daily for a paper published seven days a week. He contributed a signed Sunday column titled "Kabbages and Kings," and in his last year in Fort Wayne he ran a book column. Although his writing assignments were many, Bowers received carte blanche to write what he saw fit from Lew G. Ellingham and Edward G. Hoffman, owners of the *Journal-Gazette*. He was friendly with Hoffman but believed Ellingham had little appreciation for his editorial work or oratory. Bowers gradually became dissatisfied with his job, and by 1921 he was looking for "an escape from the sort of grind to which I am subjected" at the newspaper.[12]

Bowers wrote two books while in Fort Wayne and began research for a third. Following Kern's death in 1917, his former secretary gathered data for his biography, and an Indianapolis press brought out *The Life of John Worth Kern*, with an introduction by Vice President Thomas R. Marshall. The work was a "personal tribute to an old chief." As in most of his histories, Bowers wrote about one of his heroes and wanted the book to influence current politics—to inspire Democrats to follow the path of reform. Kern was a great politician because he was "the consistent friend of social justice." The author's least creditable book from a stylistic

point of view, probably because it was written too fast, the biography was valuable for its discussion of Kern as a vice presidential
nominee and its emphasis on his senatorial accomplishments as
shepherd of New Freedom legislation. But the author was a politician as well as a historian. As a loyal Democrat, with political
ambitions of his own, he took pains to relate events "as fully as possible without unpleasantly affecting several prominent politicians
who are still upon the scene." Party factionalism, some of the intri-
cacies of the 1912 Democratic convention in Baltimore, and the
preoccupation of Kern's 1916 election campaign with German-
American voters were matters Bowers knew well but chose not to
cover. Favorable reviews appeared in such Indiana papers as the
*Kokomo Tribune*, the *Indianapolis Times*, and the *Indianapolis Star*,
among others. Former governor Ralston gave copies to all the
libraries in the state, and Hoosier novelist Meredith Nicholson
told Bowers that the book "grips the attention. It held me far into
the watches of the night."[13]

A much more important book was Bowers's *The Party Battles of
the Jackson Period*. The author originally thought "only of a small
tome on Jackson's Kitchen Cabinet," but his author-friend
Beveridge convinced him to broaden the scope to encompass the
Tennessean's presidency. For three years he worked on the book,
often "hammering away" four hours nightly, composing and
researching letters, diaries, and newspapers. Bowers insisted that he
was not writing the book to make money, but to gain "recognition
that might pave the way" to a better position. Beveridge encouraged him, advising him to "let the book have precedence over politics or everything else if you must make a choice." "After all that
is your bid for fame." When Bowers reported in early 1920 that his
manuscript had reached 226,000 words with seven chapters still
unfinished, his friend insisted he must "condense, condense, condense." Beveridge introduced the editor to his publisher at
Houghton Mifflin.[14]

Published in 1922, *Party Battles* was 480 pages and bore the
imprint of Houghton Mifflin. Again Bowers's subject was a hero,
and the book served to remind contemporary Democrats of their

party's democratic heritage. The author asserted that "the election of Jackson was due to the rising of the masses," and he vigorously defended his democratic policies. The seventh president organized his followers and thus inaugurated "party politics, in the modern sense." His enemy was Henry Clay, "the brilliant, resourceful, bitter, and unscrupulous leader of the Opposition." The new party system, according to Bowers, transferred "authority from the small coterie of politicians to the people in the corn rows," allowing the United States to become a "democracy in fact."

The book made fascinating reading. Bowers sought "to re-create the atmosphere of the period, so the reader feels he's there." The "miserable mud roads" of the capital, Washington gossip, political parades with "waving flags, branches and banners," political intrigue, stirring orations, and White House receptions filled the pages. No period in American history was "so susceptible to dramatization," Bowers believed, and his book offered proof. The insults hurled at Jackson by John C. Calhoun on the Senate floor, the political discord resulting from Sen. John H. Eaton's marriage to Margaret O'Neal, the "pretty daughter of a popular tavern-keeper," and the fight over the Bank of the United States, "the most bitter party battle ever waged," were vividly portrayed.[15]

Reviewers' appraisals were all the author could wish. Nicholas Roosevelt in the *New York Tribune* said Bowers had "produced one of the most interesting and readable historical studies . . . published in this country." The *New York Times Book Review* called *Party Battles* "brilliant," and in the *Indianapolis Star* Jacob Piatt Dunn, Jr., concluded that the book was "destined to a permanent place in the front ranks of American historical literature." Beveridge also reviewed the work favorably in the *Star,* to which the author responded, "I would rather have had that review than any of the others." Edgar E. Robinson wrote in the *American Historical Review* that Bowers's reliance on manuscripts was slight and noted that he had not consulted some standard monographs. But the Stanford professor was not hypercritical. While specialists, he said, might dig more deeply, it was not the author's intent to "add to our knowledge of the Jackson period by the presentation of new materials." Rather, he focused on "personal encounters" so as to depict "the struggle of leaders." Jackson was "the hero of the tale, although Mr. Bowers is not blind to the prejudices and short-comings of either the President or his subordinates." The reviewer concluded, "His book will interest and fascinate many readers." In the *Mississippi Valley Historical Review*, William E. Dodd of the University of Chicago could scarcely contain his enthusiasm. "He has used biographical material and fugitive reminiscences with a penetration . . . not . . . approached by [John Bach] McMaster, the first of American historians to magnify this kind of source." Some features of Bowers's account "need perhaps to be modified," but "few historians could have written so good and true a narrative of the Jackson epoch as has this layman." For Dodd, Bowers was a "better historian" than Beveridge.[16]

*Party Battles* proved popular. Houghton Mifflin sold the first printing of 7,000 and ordered another 8,500. Democrats were quick to praise the work. McAdoo found it "monumental and pro-foundly interesting," while Josephus Daniels declared it the "best book of the year." Although he "did not find myself in agreement with you at all times," Republican senator Watson considered the book a "remarkable production." *Party Battles* was Bowers's first volume to have a lasting impact and became a celebrated work among the many that emphasized the legacy of Jacksonian Democracy. Decades later he was elated when Jackson scholar Arthur M. Schlesinger, Jr., told him that it was " 'one of the books which first aroused my interest in Jackson.' " The success of *Party Battles* encouraged the author, and in 1923 he began research for a book on Thomas Jefferson and Alexander Hamilton that would be his most important work.[17]

Recent historians of Jackson have been outspoken critics of the views of Bowers and other champions of the seventh president. For these revisionists Jacksonian Democracy was a myth, and they deny that Jackson and his followers formed the backbone of the democratic movement. Despite the differences in the parties' rhet-oric, these historians maintain that "the same socioeconomic groups provided leadership for both parties." A number of modern works on local and state politics during the Jacksonian era support this conclusion.[18]

Fort Wayne was so impressed by the author of *Party Battles* that on 11 January 1923 it gave a banquet in his honor. Three hundred people heard Araminta Kern poignantly allude to the Kern-Bowers friendship. Charles M. Niezer, the toastmaster, voiced "pride and joy" in Bowers's recognition not only as a "forceful editorial writer" and "brilliant orator," but "an author of national fame and prestige whose work will be part of the literature of our nation."[19]

In addition to his editorial work and his historical writing, Bowers also devoted his efforts to politics and speech making in Fort Wayne. But Hoosier politics in Fort Wayne offered little comfort. He was involved in two election campaigns in 1917–18. The first resulted in supplanting Fort Wayne's Democratic mayor with a Republican, and in the second, Indiana voters sent an all-Republican delegation to the House of Representatives in Washington. The Twelfth District, which included Fort Wayne, reelected its incumbent, and every local race reflected the trend.

In 1918 Democratic leaders offered Bowers the nomination for secretary of state, the top spot on the ticket in a nongubernatorial year. Instead of accepting this, he chaired the resolutions committee that drew up the platform adopted in June at the party's state convention in Indianapolis. That spring he welcomed Champ Clark to Fort Wayne, where the Speaker opened the national canvass in the Majestic Theater, presiding at a meeting of Twelfth District Democrats. Bowers presented his Missouri friend as "the best loved man in public life." That summer, with members of the Democratic state committee, he presided at another Fort Wayne meeting. Vigo County Democrats invited him to Terre Haute, and he spoke elsewhere, doing his best to convince his audiences that Wilson was a great president who merited the support of a Democratic Congress. To no avail. The next year the editor was the unanimous choice for the chairmanship of the Indiana party, but he turned down the offer.

In 1920 Bowers was active in behalf of party candidates for state and national office. At the Democrats' state convention in

Indianapolis, Marshall was the temporary chairman. It was under-stood that the vice president's remarks concerning Wilson would be lukewarm, so the organizers announced that Bowers too would speak. He was to concentrate on state issues but also praise Wilson and defend the League. After flailing Governor Goodrich, Bowers turned his guns on the Republicans for "their campaign of misrep-resentation in their attempt to divide America" and for their oppo-sition to membership in the League. "Under the red flag of social chaos, under the black flag of anarchy, under the skull and cross bones of the flag of piracy, there you may look for the logical ene-mies of the League of Nations." The hero was Wilson, who fought for the League "before the American people, until under the pres-sure of his superhuman efforts he fell stricken in his armor upon the field of battle." When the speaker finished, "five thousand cheered for several minutes." After Bowers returned to his seat, the vice president leaned over to the orator and said, "Claude, I tried to help Wilson but he wouldn't let me." During the fall campaign Bowers took the stump in Cox's behalf in several Indiana towns and closed the Fort Wayne canvass, with Marshall at his side, the Saturday night before the election.

Bowers's banner year as a Hoosier orator came in 1922. On 16 February in Indianapolis he was one of four to address a banquet of the Indiana Democratic Editorial Association at the Claypool Hotel. There he first met Cordell Hull, the future secretary of state, who was national chairman and one of the speakers. As was his custom, Bowers evoked enthusiasm for the cause. With a vivid description of the world's plight, denunciation of the GOP record, and call for Democratic victory, he warmed his auditors' blood—transporting them from bitterness to laughter and on to zeal for righting wrongs. At the end, his speech was met with "a really remarkable unorganized and unscripted demonstration," accom-panied by cries of "Senator!" Robert G. Tucker, a political com-mentator, reported that Bowers "created a big hit" but "is not a candidate and it was said that he does not desire the nomination." This was stretching the truth. Ralston was expected to be the nominee for senator, and Bowers was not about to jeopardize his

*Claude Bowers's "Decoration Day" speech, 4 July 1917, Fort Wayne, Indiana*
COURTESY OF MANUSCRIPTS DEPARTMENT, LILLY LIBRARY, INDIANA UNIVERSITY, BLOOMINGTON

friendship with the former governor. More popular than ever, Bowers spoke in Vincennes, Huntington, and Marion, where he assailed the Harding administration for restricting immigration and changing federal taxation to benefit the wealthy.[20]

The demands of journalism, historical writing, and oratory precluded an active social life for Claude and Sybil Bowers. The couple rented an 1880-vintage, two-story, red brick house at 918 West Berry Street in an appealing residential section. Theirs was a simple life. Sybil did the marketing and cooking. Her only complaint was that Claude, though hardly a gourmet, would not tolerate leftovers and was an expert at detecting them. Patty, shy and engaging, was the center of attention. Her father looked after her education and read to her, and friends were impressed with her large vocabulary. He bought her so many presents that his generosity became legendary in the neighborhood. Terre Haute friend Frank Brubeck believed Claude was "so wrapped up" in his daughter that he warned him against spoiling her. The family enjoyed the companionship of Buster, Patty's dog, and in 1917 tended a "war garden" in the backyard. Bowers's salary was $3,000, but after necessary expenses he always had a few dollars left over to spend on occasional travel. Because he devoted so much time to writing, one might assume that life in Fort Wayne was dull for Sybil. Quite the contrary. There is no hint in the record that the dearth of teas or dinner parties bothered Sybil, who joined the College Club and the Fort Wayne Women's Club and was elected vice chairman of the District Federation of Women's Clubs. With her husband, she belonged to the Fortnightly Club, whose members read essays and participated in discussions.

After George Spayth's arrival as the *Journal-Gazette* cartoonist, the Spayth and Bowers families often picnicked in a park. Claude and Sybil took Patty with them on their summer vacations. The family visited the Ralstons at "Hoosier Home" on the edge of Indianapolis, went to the Dunes on Lake Michigan, and enjoyed New England. Sybil liked Fort Wayne so much that later she looked back to Berry Street with nostalgia bordering on wistfulness. But her husband was always more gregarious and resented the fact that except on two occasions "in six years there I was never invited to a home." "I was never a favorite in that town," he later concluded, "yet I remember it with affection."[21]

Trials and tragedies intruded now and then. Bowers's mother died in Washington in 1918. Patty was alarmingly ill in 1920 and 1923. In 1920 Billy Hoffman, her playmate, next-door neighbor, and best friend, fell in an accident at the Bowers house, fracturing his skull and dying within minutes. Someone poisoned Patty's dog, Buster, whereupon Bowers wrote an editorial flailing the poisoner in terms usually reserved for Senator Lodge.

Bowers's daily schedule was a full one. He ate breakfast and lunch at home, digesting the news along with the victuals. He rode a streetcar to the office, read papers and magazines, and hammered on his typewriter, mainly from two to five o'clock. During part of his Fort Wayne period, his cubbyhole office was on the first floor of the *Journal-Gazette* building; the rest of the time he shared space in an annex two blocks away. He dispatched copy steadily as each afternoon wore on, the last batch reaching the printer by six.

While type was being set, he and one or more of his colleagues ate at a little restaurant nearby or indulged in fried chicken at the YMCA cafeteria. After dinner Bowers returned to the *Journal* to read proof until eight. From eight until midnight, he worked on history in the newspaper office or at home. Smoking a cigar, coat off, vest unbuttoned, he went through the congeries of experiences familiar to authors of nonfiction. He devoted hours to private letters of public men, as well as relaxing with memoirs. He also dipped into general histories or batted out a paragraph or a page. It was hard work and always will be, but for Bowers less toilsome than for many, as he savored sorties into the past and the re-creation of personalities.

City Editor Lawrence (Levy) F. Levenberg was Bowers's closest Fort Wayne friend and companion. Another young man of whom he was fond was a reporter named Frank Roberts. Both were in their twenties, Hoosiers, knowledgeable, full of fun, and they knew how to listen, an important plus. For then as always Bowers was a raconteur, relishing candor with trustworthy friends. Charles Niezer, Guy Colerick, R. Earl Peters, and the youthful Samuel D. Jackson were attorneys he knew well. Margaret Colerick, the public librarian, recognized his literary potential and stocked the volumes he needed for research. Laura Goshorn Detzer, a former librarian, lived two blocks from Bowers's house. Detzer's hobby was eighteenth-century history and literature, and Bowers found her a congenial discussant of many themes.[22]

Celebrities came to Fort Wayne. Eugene V. Debs, Daniels, Mary "Mother" Jones, and Beveridge were among the wayfarers Bowers welcomed. The Debs reunion of 1918 occurred a few days before the Socialist's imprisonment, which the journalist considered a blot on Wilson's record. Daniels came on a Democratic mission, the Daniels-Bowers friendship blossoming there. Eamon De Valera's personality and attitude disappointed the editor when the Irish leader visited Fort Wayne. But Mother Jones was as delightful as ever. Bowers never forgot that when he took her to lunch the agitator asked for a stein of beer because it was "a restorative."

Of all the relationships, the most notable was with Beveridge. Since their political faiths differed, the Republican and the Democratic historians never could have been intimate without Clio as their muse. The Democrat in his early forties and the Republican in his early sixties developed a correspondence and saw each other on occasion each year. Beveridge not only encouraged Bowers's efforts but also gave him "fatherly" advice. In 1920 the Republican reported he had spoken with several Democrats and wanted to assure Bowers that his political reputation was " 'coming along' in fine shape." Beveridge was worried that Bowers's editorial and oratorical work was too taxing and continually warned him to "*take care of your health*," and he urged Sybil to see that he did so.

Bowers heard from, and wrote to, McAdoo and Cox, and exchanged letters with Dodd, but for the most part his correspondents were politicians rather than historians. Always aware of the value of favorable reviews for his works, he saw to it that Beveridge, Daniels, Dodd, and McAdoo reviewed *Party Battles*. One of the many volumes Bowers reviewed in the *Journal-Gazette* was Theodore Dreiser's *The "Genius."* Dreiser expressed gratitude, and before many months Bowers and the novelist were chatting amicably in New York.

The partisan journalist had his enemies. Republicans criticized Bowers through the local *Daily News* and then the *News-Sentinel*. Editor Jesse A. Greene often led the assault. Both were journalists, but the judgments and routines of Greene and Bowers were strikingly different. Greene was distastefully personal in referring to Bowers as "the chinless wonder," while the "wonder" preferred to operate at a higher level. Greene's tactics aside, he did not approach Bowers in his variety of talents, industry, or concentration.[23]

As disenchantment with his post at the *Journal-Gazette* grew, Bowers's ambition turned to politics. Although offered the chairmanship of the state party and nomination for secretary of state, he decided that he would be interested in serving only as governor, senator, or ambassador. In late 1919 he declined an editorial position in Wilmington, Delaware, deciding to remain in Indiana because of "the dangling of political prizes." Boss Tom Taggart did

not appear sympathetic to him, but Bowers believed that his service to the party would bring him its endorsement for governor or
senator. Following his triumph before the Indiana Democratic
Editorial Association in 1922, he was crushed when Ellingham, the
*Journal-Gazette* publisher and a force in the party, did not even
comment on his speech. This convinced Bowers that "the cards
were stacked against me." Despite his service to his party in
Indiana as an editor, orator, congressional candidate, United States
Senate secretary, and adviser to candidates and officeholders,
Bowers was acutely aware that he was not among the kingmakers
who controlled the state party. He concluded in 1923, "Well, life
is too short, the gamble too uncertain, and my obligation to my
family too real to grow old hoping."

Bowers's Fort Wayne achievements were substantial and transported him from Indiana to New York. His renown as a journalist
and reputation as the author of *Party Battles* brought him to the
national stage. The move to New York came about in a casual fashion. The editor of the *New York World*, Frank Cobb, mentioned to
Arthur Krock, "We need an editorial writer. A man who can think
and write and who believes the Republican party never did anything right and the Democratic party never did anything wrong."
Bowers's friend from Washington days replied, "I've got him. . . .
He's under a haystack in Indiana." Krock gave Cobb a copy of *Party
Battles*. He and Ralph Pulitzer, publisher of the *World*, were
impressed and began to read Bowers's contributions to the *Journal-
Gazette*. Pulitzer spoke to Senator Ralston and then sent Krock to
Indianapolis in early October to confer with Bowers at the
Claypool Hotel. Bowers insisted he must have editorial freedom
and wanted to be certain Patty would be able to attend a good
school. Krock assured him these concerns were not a problem. The
next week Pulitzer offered him a salary of $7,000—more than dou-
ble his current one—and promised him a lighter editorial load with
time to continue writing his books.

The editor was ready for a move. This would mean that he must
give up any idea of becoming a candidate for the Senate in 1926.
But this hope appeared remote, and Bowers reflected that most of

his friends in the Democratic leadership were on the national level. He reported Pulitzer's proposition to Beveridge, noting that "naturally there are some sentimental draw backs," and his GOP friend urged him "to take the New York offer." With little delay he did so because "I could not afford to turn down such an offer financially and partly to facilitate my work in writing books on history."[24] On a December night in 1923 City Editor Levy Levenberg drove Bowers to the train that would take him to Manhattan.

# CHAPTER FIVE

# New York

Bowers's decade in New York marked the high point of his career in journalism and, one must say, his importance as a historian. As editorial writer and columnist for both the Pulitzer and Hearst chains, he enjoyed a prominence from coast to coast. In the 1930s popular attention would turn to the radio, but in the 1920s newspapers reigned. For readers of America's dailies, his was a name to reckon with. And during his New York years Bowers published his two most important books about American history, making his name almost a household word.

The first two New York editorials appeared in the *Evening World* on Tuesday, 4 December 1923. To Wednesday's paper he contributed five, and Saturday he wrote all six. One of his most trenchant pieces was "President and World Court" on Friday. Theodore Roosevelt was the subject for castigation on his second Tuesday, and the following day he said complimentary things about Presidents Thomas Jefferson, Andrew Jackson, and Woodrow Wilson. He condemned the Ku Klux Klan and Henry Cabot Lodge three times within a week. He lampooned Sen. Hiram Johnson, lauded Sen. William Borah, contrasting him with Lodge, and discussed William G. McAdoo in connection with the Klan.[1]

For seven years Bowers contributed three editorials six days a week to the *Evening World*. In 1924 the Teapot Dome scandal, its perpetrator Albert B. Fall, and Fall's friend Edward B. McLean provided easy targets for the partisan editor. Bowers attacked them for entering the "invalids" camp at Palm Beach claiming illness and demanded that President Calvin Coolidge rescue the nation's "pillaged property." The editor aimed his sights at Secretary of the Navy Edwin Denby because he yielded control of the naval oil reserves to Fall. "DENBY SHOULD GO!" he insisted—followed at intervals by "YOUR HAT, MR. DENBY!" and "BUT THERE STANDS DENBY!" In February 1924 "Denby has at last done some thing he ought to have done weeks ago. He has sent in his resignation."

The editorials, like those in Fort Wayne, were not all critical. Bowers eulogized the Wilson cabinet vis-à-vis the Warren G. Harding crowd, this despite the employment of five Wilson cabinet members by the oilman Edward L. Doheny. Bowers took a lively interest in Jefferson Week when Gov. Alfred E. Smith proclaimed it, paid tribute to Miguel de Unamuno when Spain's dictator deported the savant, and extolled the stand of Columbia University's president Nicholas Murray Butler on Prohibition. Franklin D. Roosevelt, heading a Smith-for-president committee, was "an uncontaminated, out-and-out, Simon-pure Democrat." Painter John Singer Sargent, eighteenth-century pamphleteer Thomas Paine, nineteenth-century novelist Anatole France, and eighteenth-century philosopher Immanuel Kant came within the range of Bowers's topics.[2]

The Republican National Convention met in Cleveland in June 1924 to nominate Coolidge. The journalist's GOP friend Albert J. Beveridge considered Bowers's May editorial suggesting planks for the Republican platform "a masterpiece of sarcasm," demonstrating the party's "predicament in such startling fashion." Bowers asserted that the platform adopted in Cleveland was reactionary throughout. The tariff? Approval of enriching "the few" by exploiting "the many." Farm relief? "Utterly meaningless." On the "sinister threat" of the Klan? "Not one word." On Prohibition enforcement? Nothing. On scandals "that even shocked a Nation and shamed an

Administration?" Merely a protest against "publicity that has driven disreputables from high station." But the platform was less reprehensible than maneuvers of Indiana's senator James E. Watson, chairman of the resolutions committee and "liaison officer" between the national leadership and Klan Republicans in Indiana.[3] As Bowers saw it, Watson had persuaded Coolidge to remain silent on the Klan.

Bowers and the *Evening World* did their utmost for the Democracy when its representatives assembled in Madison Square Garden. Greeting delegates in his paper's columns on 24 June, he hailed them as representatives of a party "against special privileges and for equal rights." The next day he praised the keynote speech of Mississippi senator Pat Harrison for attacking "reeking" Republican corruption—without mentioning that he had helped the senator prepare his address. Fall, McLean, and Denby he paraded before the country. And so it went, issue by issue. Republican "chicanery" and "hypocrisy," the "crazy-patch tariff of all the interests," the 1,357 bank failures, the World Court, and the cabinet—Bowers emphasized them all.

But the Democrats' similar failure to take action on issues must have offended him. On the League of Nations, on states' rights, and dramatically on the Klan, delegates were in disagreement. They declined to denounce the Klan, instead condemning unnamed efforts "to arouse religious or racial dissension." In lieu of modifying the Volstead Act the delegates endorsed a strong states' rights plank with anti-Prohibition overtones. Still, Bowers found the platform "stronger than usual. . . . Struggle and compromise were inevitable. The platform is fortunate in not bearing more serious scars of the conflict."[4]

As to candidates, Bowers's position was unusual. Long on friendly terms with McAdoo, whom he saw in New York before and during the convention, he also esteemed Smith's record as governor. He worked for a pro-Smith paper. This meant fewer convention editorials. He praised Roosevelt's speech nominating the "happy warrior," but he considered "disgraceful" the rowdy conduct of spectators and marchers on the floor who "demonstrated on Smith's behalf long after Roosevelt sought to stop them."[5]

After many ballots the Democrats nominated the Wall Street lawyer John W. Davis, but Bowers had no illusions about his victory. "Fall in behind the leader who denounces bigotry, and intolerance and race prejudice," he exhorted. He ridiculed the "Coolidge of romance" and claimed the New Englander had been "fictionized" by hack biographers. The president was "the tacit tool of privilege." The choice of the blacks? The National Negro Press's executive committee, learning of strategy in Indiana, advised blacks to "vote against the party that makes common cause with their enemies." No other course, Bowers agreed, "was open to self-respecting men."

Davis denounced the Klan. The Democratic nominee asked Coolidge to take a similar stand, but the president sidestepped the issue. How revealing, Bowers exclaimed, was the "sinister silence" of the "cute and cunning" Coolidge compared with Davis's "forward-looking," "fighting," and "effective" speeches attacking the "corruption" and "crimes" of the regime "for which Calvin Coolidge stands." Meanwhile, Bowers's columns proclaimed "PILLOW CASES AND THE SMELL OF OIL" and "FORWARD THE BED-SHEET BRIGADE!"

Bowers considered Coolidge prosperity a myth. The president's policies had created "unrest and awakened the radical sentiment" that threatened to "hasten the day of reckoning." His campaign speeches seemed "characteristically bromidic, with the usual smattering of copybook platitudes." What a state the country was in. Labor deprived of constitutional rights, agriculture sunk in depression, "the Fiery Cross upon the hill, mobilizing bigots and fanatics."

If somewhere a Democrat hoped for a miracle, none was forthcoming. Coolidge won an overwhelming victory. Though Smith was elected to a third term, the Democrats had few other consolation prizes. Bowers concluded that progressives and liberals "must unite with the historic party which has won all the victories for progress and liberalism since Jefferson breathed into it the breath of life."[6]

The election over, Bowers turned to other matters. In concentrating on what was important to him editorially, Bowers was every bit as fortunate in New York as in Fort Wayne. Of New York's two Pulitzer newspapers, the morning *World* was far better than the evening. With Walter Lippmann as editor and Franklin P. Adams, Heywood Broun, and Alexander Woollcott as columnists, the morning paper may have qualified as the best editorial daily in the twentieth century. None of these luminaries had anything like Bowers's experience in politics. Aside from Herbert Bayard Swope in New York and Charles Michelson in Washington, no *World* employee rivaled Bowers in contacts with party leaders. That the *World* was politically oriented meant he was an addition to the staff. Pulitzer realized this and often was effusive in his praise.[7]

It probably was just as well that Bowers was not intimately associated with Lippmann. The morning *World* editor was more a philosopher than tactician or strategist. And for all the liberalism with which Lippmann's name was associated, Bowers thought more than once that his fellow journalist was essentially conservative and held him in low esteem. The transplanted Hoosier enjoyed working with Harold S. Pollard, who had reached his post through contact with Joseph Pulitzer. Pollard was interested in New York affairs. In the division of labor, Pollard concentrated on city and state and Bowers on national and international topics.[8]

Among Bowers's subjects in the mid-1920s were the Teapot Dome trials and the continuing national scandals. The *Evening World* hailed "A RIGHTEOUS VERDICT" when a court convicted the "crooked Director of the Veterans' Bureau" for conspiring to "rob the Government and steal from crippled soldiers." As Klan criminality in Indiana worsened, Bowers's editorials attacked D. C. Stephenson, Grand Dragon of the Indiana Realm, who went to prison for "the most loathsome murder in the Hoosier annals of crime."

Were there no good Republicans? President Butler of Columbia sided with Smith in supporting "a sane reorganization of the State Government." Bowers endorsed Beveridge's "vigorous defense of the primary as opposed to the convention system." Likewise commendable was a proposal by Nebraska's senator George W. Norris to abolish the Federal Trade Commission (FTC)—"worthless to the public" while packed by reactionaries. Here Bowers's judgment was off the mark, for the FTC was divided, with some members doing their best to get tariffs lowered under the presidential-discretion provisions of the Fordney-McCumber tariff. As to Elihu Root, his claim to fame was found not in his State Department or senatorial service but "in the part he played in the framing of the structure of the World Court."

Bowers found no one in the Coolidge administration worthy of his enthusiasm. Secretary of State Frank B. Kellogg might deliver a speech "admirable in tone." The editor also agreed with Kellogg's assertion at an Associated Press luncheon that the press had failed to cultivate better relations with Latin America. But the secretary could not avoid "a sly dig" at the World Court.[9] Again, Bowers's partisanship overrode judgment, for Kellogg, though a good Republican, was also a good secretary of state. He was a competent man who by and large made good decisions on policy.

A non-Democrat whom Bowers respected, Robert M. La Follette, died in 1925. Although Bowers opposed some of the Wisconsin senator's ideas, he found "much in his character as a public man to respect and admire." The journalist praised his ability and dedication to reform. Bowers chose to overlook the senator's run for the presidency in 1924—a candidacy that drew votes from Democratic malcontents who could not stomach Davis. Son Bob La Follette, who succeeded his father in the Senate, was the subject of a friendly editorial after his first months in office.

Looking overseas, Bowers commented on alarming developments in Europe. He was shocked that despite "treason in Bavaria," Adolf Hitler might be released after only five months in prison. But more "vicious" was the German "demand for anti-Semitic legislation." At Field Marshal Paul von Hindenburg's installation as president, "bands in the public squares" of Berlin played "imperial war songs." In Italy, Benito Mussolini "continues to give out interviews sneering at America." The Russian and Italian experiments were "identical" in seeking to control the people "by poking guns in their faces." In Spain, King Alfonso XIII, defending the dictator Gen. Miguel Primo de Rivera, predicted that "other nations will be obliged to abandon legality for a time." As in his judgments of domestic issues, good writing and bombast hid some of his omissions when treating foreign affairs. Bowers failed to emphasize the basic causes of these signs of nihilism. What Europe required was some years of economic stability, and France, Britain, and the United States might have contributed to this, but the former Allies proved unwilling to do so.

Of all international events of the 1920s, none encouraged Bowers more than the Locarno treaties. These agreements marked "the greatest move yet" for real peace in Europe, "the broadest, best-knit safeguard of boundary adjustments and arbitration pledges Europe has ever built against its arch-enemy, War." But Bowers reminded his readers that the results of the Locarno Conference might have been achieved "three years sooner" had America joined the League and been "as ready with help as with criticism." Still, like his optimistic contemporaries, he failed to recognize that the Locarno accord did not settle Germany's eastern boundaries—an omission that would bring a breakdown of peace in the next decade.

Coolidge's Latin American policy was another target of *Evening World* editorials. American selfishness led to an "ugly" involvement in Nicaragua where marines were sent on the pretext of protecting property. Nicaragua was part of a larger picture, for "we have failed miserably in understanding the South and Central American republics."

During 1925–28 a single ingredient of *World* and *Evening World* policy might have bothered Bowers. Ralph Pulitzer, Lippmann, and the others did not conceal their commitment to Smith for the presidency in 1928. After the 1924 defeat, Bowers argued that Jefferson, Jackson, and Wilson provided the Democrats with a platform, and he had no difficulty in adjusting to the *World's* policy. The editor was a friend of McAdoo, an unsuccessful candidate for the 1924 nomination, but he considered Smith a good governor and for four years contributed pro-Smith pieces. Bowers could not suspect—nor did his countrymen, then or for years thereafter—that McAdoo, a defender of oilman Doheny, was in his pay and that Smith was in the pay of a New York traction magnate.[10]

In 1927 the Jeffersonian Hoosier became an enthusiastic Smith backer. The *Atlantic Monthly* had carried a forthright Smith declaration on Roman Catholics' allegiance to their country and church. Designed to reduce prejudice and make Smith's candidacy more acceptable, it opined that "the Governor's is a great document that can be marked even now as historic." Noting that Smith had been elected governor four times "without the faintest suggestion that his religion stood in the way," the editor urged that "the old religious rancor that has returned to plague the Nation die forthwith and be buried."[11]

National politics became Bowers's focus for the next three years. In 1928 he wrote dozens of editorials praising the gubernatorial record and platform of Smith, while attacking his GOP opponent Herbert Hoover for playing a "game of political tag" in avoiding the issues. After the Republican landslide, Bowers saluted Smith for his campaign against religious bigotry and his defense of the interests of workers. But Hoover's popularity was short-lived. The stock market crash in October 1929 dramatically changed the political scene and provided Bowers with ammunition for many more anti-Republican editorials. "Never in the memory of living man has such ineptitude for government been displayed in this country as during the last year," he wrote in November 1929.[12]

The nation's economy turned down with a vengeance. The fortunes of apparently stable newspapers, such as Pulitzer's, changed. February 1931 forced a major decision on Bowers. That month the Pulitzer brothers sold the *World* to the Scripps-Howard chain. The morning paper was scrapped, and the *Evening World* was merged with the Scripps-Howard *New York Telegram*. Will Curley, managing editor of William Randolph Hearst's *New York Evening Journal*, made an offer. He "wants me to write a signed editorial daily for the Journal" at "almost twice what I get on the World. I am to be my own boss, select my own subject, write wherever I please, and not to be asked to write against my political convictions." There was also a possibility of his going on the *New York Times* but, if so,

"I cannot write politics" and "I imagine they would object to my making speeches." Bowers discussed matters with Arthur Krock and Bernard Baruch. The latter said that publisher Adolph S. Ochs might permit Bowers to do a signed column for the *Times*. "I do not think so, I cannot afford to assume an apologetic attitude toward my politics."[13]

The *Journal* was Bowers's choice—a fortunate decision. Neither Hearst nor Curley ever deviated from the letter or spirit of the stipulations, and Hearst "never made a suggestion" concerning editorials. Although Hearst made no secret of his dislike for Smith, Bowers continued to write in praise of the 1928 nominee. As head editorial writer for the *Journal*, he wrote five columns weekly that were carried coast to coast by the Hearst papers. His byline, often appearing with his picture, gave Bowers widespread visibility. Bowers later noted that his work there was "the most perfect in all my newspaper career." He encountered "no interference in the slightest" and considered Curley "more charming, juster, and fairer than any man on the old World." It was an interesting and, while it lasted, fortunate interlude. Bowers discovered that Hearst was not too difficult to work for—even while his attention at the time was shifting toward real estate, the source of his real wealth.

Bowers's partisan columns elicited the praise of Democratic leaders. In the months before the 1932 convention, he blamed the Great Depression on the Coolidge regime's "complete subservience to Wall Street" and argued that "Mr. Hoover has done little and has done the little that he did very late after irreparable damage had been done." After Roosevelt won the nomination, the journalist's support in the *Journal* was at least as strong as any other commentator in the country. The candidate should be compared to Jefferson and Jackson, Bowers maintained, for all three believed that "governments exist for the equal benefit of all the people, and for the protection of the public against the exploitation of the powerful monopolies." Following the Democratic victory, Bowers continued discussing the plight of the unemployed and the ideas of statesmen and economists to bring relief.[14]

In addition to his editorial work, Bowers had continued during the 1920s to write about history. The author of *The Party Battles of the Jackson Period* devoted most of his free hours to the preparation of *Jefferson and Hamilton: The Struggle for Democracy in America.* "Will power and the power of concentration," he believed, allowed him to finish his books. This volume, he claimed, was the result of "three years of grinding work." Since January 1923 he had been "cramming," and until publication in 1925 he spent weekends and evenings—"for three or five hours and sometimes longer"—at home reading and writing. Living in New York he had easy access to the New York Public Library and the Columbia University Library with their "many, many volumes of correspondence," "dozens" of pamphlets, and "all the leading newspapers," a favorite source. For months lunchtime was spent at the Astor Library.

*Jefferson and Hamilton* was Bowers's most important work. The first of his trilogy on the Virginian, it made the author the proponent of "Jeffersonian Democracy." Like his other books it focused on a hero and was meant to influence contemporary politics. An admirer of the third president, Bowers wanted to write his biography. On hearing Beveridge in 1923 declaim that the Federalist party disappeared "because the leaders lost contact with the people," Bowers decided to stress the continuing validity of Jefferson's democratic ideas. The result was "the stirring story of the Plutarchian struggle of Jefferson and Hamilton." Bowers insisted that the two personified "elemental differences that reach back into the ages, and will continue to divide mankind far into the future." He castigated the New Yorker for favoring "the rule of 'gentlemen'—the domination of aristocrats"—lauding Jefferson for taking "upon himself the organization of the forces of democracy." The Virginian was a leader "without a peer in the mastery of men," able to "mobilize, organize, and discipline." His inauguration meant that "the real American Revolution had triumphed."[15]

Bowers's biography, scholars admit, was "a potent, and most welcome, antidote to the one-sided productions of Hamilton worshipers." The author emphasized that he revised earlier volumes by

George Bancroft, John Bach McMaster, Henry Adams, and Lodge. "From the time of the Civil War on down practically every book written about Jefferson had attempted to damn him if only with faint praise," Bowers claimed. "That wasn't so strange, after all. It was political. The old Hamiltonian group was in power, and the writers of history didn't have the guts to combat it." Republicans such as Herbert D. Croly, Harding, Andrew W. Mellon, Butler, and Arthur H. Vandenberg extolled Hamilton.[16]

*Jefferson and Hamilton* was to offer lessons. The author warned his readers, "The spirits of Jefferson and Hamilton still stalk the ways of men—still fighting." Although he believed the work had "a far more permanent value" than politics, he insisted that it told his party what Jeffersonian Democracy was. Following the Democrats' factious convention and defeat in 1924, the author's message was clear: it was time to unite behind Jefferson's ideals.

Though Bowers's conclusions were at odds with those of earlier authors, his determination to make his biography relevant to contemporary politics was in step with such Progressive historians as James Harvey Robinson and Charles A. Beard. The latter was an admirer and epistolary friend of Bowers who maintained that history should enrich civic life.[17] This view contributed to the book's acceptance.

Bowers's dramatic literary style was a hallmark, and *Jefferson and Hamilton* was no exception. The author sought to make history readable and re-create "the reaction of the people to what was going on." He dramatized events and included such vignettes as the dinners and dances of Mrs. William Bingham, "the uncrowned queen of the Federalist group," and the "shouting, singing, laughing, drinking" at public houses. Many considered *Jefferson and Hamilton* Bowers's best-written book. "Your style is more finished and easier than in your other and earlier works," author Edgar Lee Masters assured him. Historian Samuel F. Bemis was as complimentary, confessing to the author that he was "a great admirer of your style and vigorous way of writing."

The first review came from Roosevelt. "I felt like saying 'At last' as I read Mr. Claude Bowers's thrilling *Jefferson and Hamilton*."

"It would be a supreme contribution to current thought if the simple historic facts of this book could be learned in the newspaper editorial rooms as well as in the homes and schools of America." Chastised for arguing months earlier that " 'the clear line of demarcation which differentiated the political thought of Jefferson on the one side, and of Hamilton on the other, must be restored,' " Roosevelt informed critics that they needed Bowers, as did "the romantic cult" that idolized Hamilton. History was interesting for portrayals of events and personalities but of special value because of application "of these facts to present problems." Roosevelt stressed "parallel or at least analogous situations existing in our own generation" and reported "a breathless feeling" when he considered what the nation might be like had Hamilton won. "I have a breathless feeling, too," he concluded, "as I wonder if, a century and a quarter later, the same contending forces are not again mobilizing. Hamiltons we have today. Is a Jefferson on the horizon?"[18] Roosevelt's review—the only one he ever published—appeared in Bowers's own paper.

Other reviewers also were enthusiastic. Davis praised Bowers's "rare dramatic power," while Senator Borah claimed the book was "more instructive than the most profound treatise on government." McAdoo complimented Bowers's knowledge of "practical politics down to the grass-roots," and Beveridge called attention to the author's "notable skill." In the New York Herald Tribune, Jefferson scholar William E. Dodd pronounced Jefferson and Hamilton "the most interesting book . . . ever written about the two greatest antagonists this country has produced." Commentators in the New York Times Book Review and the New York Evening Post offered similar opinions. The reception in scholarly journals was equally enthusiastic. The reviewer in the American Historical Review believed the work served "as a good antidote to the several recent studies extolling the marvels of Federalism and glorifying too exclusively the genius of Hamilton." While J. Fred Rippy of the University of Chicago considered events "over-dramatized," he praised the use of primary sources and concluded that "Mr. Bowers has written a great book."[19]

*Jefferson and Hamilton* was Bowers's most popular work, read by more Americans than any other single volume on Jefferson before or since. For months the book remained a best-seller. It went through thirty printings and was translated into French, German, and Italian. For a quarter century it was part of assignments to undergraduates and graduates. Columbia professor Allan Nevins claimed that his students "have honestly taken to it as to no other single book."[20]

The author was "swamped" with letters from readers. Col. Edward M. House received twelve copies for Christmas. Alice Roosevelt Longworth ordered ten and bought fifteen more. In Washington, Brentano's reported one thousand copies sold. "Everyone is reading it," said banker Otto H. Kahn. Gen. John J. Pershing presented a copy to Georges Clemenceau. At Charlottesville, Virginia, the audience cheered when Gov. Harry F. Byrd alluded to the work.[21]

*Jefferson and Hamilton* brought Bowers renown within his party. Pennsylvania's future senator Joseph F. Guffey claimed the book made Bowers "Democracy's Distinguished Author." James M. Cox considered him "the ablest of all our American political historians." McAdoo believed the writer had "rendered a great service to Democracy." Congressman Cordell Hull of Tennessee called the work a "godsend to democrats and to our country." Missouri's senator Harry B. Hawes claimed he owed his election to it. Roosevelt in 1926 urged Bowers to have "a cheaper edition" published to disseminate its message and thereafter sought to include him in party councils. Later, Roosevelt called upon the author for speeches and tried to identify himself and the New Deal with the Virginian and his ideals.

Bowers did not exaggerate when he asserted that "*Jefferson and Hamilton* unquestionably changed the drift of historical interpretation on Jefferson." According to one scholar, the book "signalized the movement of American historians to join the American people in admiration of Thomas Jefferson." Later works by academics such as Beard, John Dewey, and James Truslow Adams lauded the third president, and popular depictions tended to glorify him.[22]

Today *Jefferson and Hamilton* is a dated work. Subsequent scholarship has rejected the notion that the Virginian's deeds should be
used to justify present-day policies. While Bowers helped to renew
an appreciation of Jefferson, his biography approached hagiogra-
phy. The third president now appears complex, many-sided, defying political labels—even an "American sphinx." As a Progressive
suspicious of wealthy businessmen, Bowers's partisan convictions
caused him to dismiss the contributions of Hamilton and his allies
and blinded him to the positive aspects of the Federalists. As later
historians have emphasized, Hamilton as secretary of the treasury
helped create a stable currency and establish public credit on firm
foundations. His calls for government measures to promote manufacturing, such as protective tariffs, likewise have won the praise of
many contemporary scholars. Nevertheless, despite the biases of its
author, *Jefferson and Hamilton* continues to be considered "a landmark in Jefferson historiography."[23]

Bowers's success led the Thomas Jefferson Memorial Foundation
to enlist his support. Stuart G. Gibboney, a Virginian practicing
law in New York, headed a group intent on making Monticello a
national shrine. The foundation was in the position to be able to
acquire the title to the Jefferson mansion, but it lacked the funds
to make the initial payment. They were charmed by Bowers's book
and saw it as a torch lighting the way for America and the world to
restore the Sage of Monticello to his true stature. The leader of the
movement, Theodore Fred Kuper, a Moscow-born Jew, was full of
energy and ideas. Long a resident in New York City, Kuper with
steady selflessness transformed a dream into reality. He appreciated
the linkage of *Jefferson and Hamilton* to foundation hopes and
involved Bowers in everything connected with Monticello. The
Fourth of July, 1926, the centennial of Jefferson's death, was chosen as the dedication date. With the aid of President Edward A.
Alderman of the University of Virginia, Gibboney and Kuper
arranged an elaborate three-day ceremony. The first day Bowers
spoke. The climax came on the final afternoon when Alderman
awarded a Jefferson Medal to the author of *Jefferson and Hamilton*
for presenting "to the world the actual Thomas Jefferson." Bowers

remained a supporter of the Jefferson Memorial Foundation. In February 1933 the organization sponsored a testimonial dinner for him at the Astor Hotel in New York, where thirteen hundred guests, and a national broadcast audience, heard Democratic National Chairman James A. Farley assert that no one else in America had done more for the Democratic party.[24]

The 150th anniversary of the Declaration of Independence was also in 1926, and Congress created a national Sesquicentennial and Jefferson Centennial Commission. Gibboney and Kuper developed connections between the commission and the foundation. The honorary chairman was President Coolidge, who lauded Jefferson as an advocate of limited government. Gibboney became the commission's head, Bowers its secretary, and Kuper its factotum. The commission met in the East Room of the White House, where Vice President Charles G. Dawes, Speaker Nicholas Longworth, Gibboney, Bowers, and others were present. The president arrived, "walking rapidly but with mincing steps." Knowing that Felix Warburg, a Jew, had offered $100,000 to the Monticello fund provided a prominent Catholic and Protestant would do the same, Coolidge said soberly, " 'I will authorize Senator [Joseph T.] Robinson to notify Vice-President Dawes that it is the sense of this meeting that he donate a like amount.' " Bowers was amazed at the president's "mirthful mood and disposition to joke."

Leaving the White House with Majority Leader Finis J. Garrett, Bowers encountered Alice Roosevelt Longworth. Garrett introduced him as the author of *Jefferson and Hamilton*. With enthusiasm she said he had "almost converted me to Jefferson." Then, turning her head and looking out of the corner of her eye, she added, "Almost." Bowers was struck by her "wonderful charm and feminine fascination."[25]

Bowers's next book was *The Tragic Era: The Revolution after Lincoln*, published in September 1929. For three years he had been gathering material for this volume, consulting northern and southern sources. The journal of a Radical Republican leader from Indiana, George W. Julian, was lent by the congressman's daughter. The head of the United Daughters of the Confederacy asked members throughout the South to furnish letters and accounts covering the postwar years. Soon he was "overwhelmed with great material." "*THE WRITING IS THE EASY PART*," he observed. Again in 1927 lunch hours were spent poring over newspapers "page by page" at the New York Public Library. He gathered information on Thaddeus Stevens in Lancaster, Pennsylvania. "Continuously for four years," following an early dinner at home, he worked on the book.[26] He composed the first chapters in 1928 and delivered the manuscript to Houghton Mifflin in May 1929.

*The Tragic Era* glorified heroes and lambasted enemies. The latter were the Radical Republicans for whom "the Constitution was treated as a doormat" and who "put to the torture" southern whites, "pillaging the South." "The autocracy of military masters" and "intolerable" Reconstruction laws that "set aside the constitutional guarantees of the States" were blamed for depriving the majority of its rights. By "inflaming the freedmen with a false sense of their importance," the Radicals used the suffrage of freedmen to dominate the South for political ends. Stevens was singled out for his "extreme views," particularly his "obsession on negro rights." Heroes were white southerners "fighting for the preservation of their civilization"—particularly the women, for even disaster "could not rob them of their charm." Finally, in 1877 came "the South's redemption from military despotism." Other heroes were politicians opposed to Reconstruction, especially Andrew Johnson. The president fought "a memorable battle for constitutional rights and liberties" and suffered "for generations because of the slander of his enemies."

No aspect of Reconstruction received approval, and Bowers's treatment of African Americans was hostile, even racist. "Credulity," "childlike faith," "cupidity," "simple-minded" were used to describe African Americans. Their conduct was despicable, including "lustful assaults" on white women. The author noted they "were little above the intellectual level of the mules they drove." Even the ideals of racial equality that he attributed to some northern Radicals were "belligerent demands for social equality."[27]

The author's thesis was in line with his earlier notions of Reconstruction. He always expressed affinity for the South and equated the region with such virtues as hospitality and kindness. As he later admitted, since boyhood he had considered the North's treatment of the South "atrocious." In a 1901 address to Indiana Democrats, he argued that during Reconstruction "the most heartless fanaticism" deprived the South of its political identity and reduced it "to the last degree of degradation." And in numerous columns thereafter Bowers attacked Reconstruction. He maintained that "the masses of the people were victimized by the politicians" and argued that the Radicals were intent on a "systematic and persistent undermining of the Constitution."

Bowers's views toward race were established before 1929. Like white midwesterners of his era none of his friends or colleagues were black. In high school his contacts were limited to greeting "a colored boy or girl" and a sidewalk chat with Booker T. Washington, whom he admired. He lamented that racism had deprived a Butler College black from winning a debate contest, and as a journalist he penned dozens of editorials attacking the Klan and lynching. Despite his oft-stated advocacy of equality and liberty as a Jeffersonian Democrat, he was never an advocate of civil rights for African Americans.

In part Bowers's disinterest resulted from political considerations. By 1901 he concluded that so-called "Negro suffrage" was "the greatest curse" of Reconstruction, a GOP measure adopted "for the selfish purpose of perpetuating its power." Like many Indiana Democrats, he believed that "as the result of negro colonization by the republican party" the opposition received the votes of "20,000 political dummies." He described African-American voters as "unreasoning and unreasonable animals," "ignoramuses," and a "mass of ignorant brutality." Such views led him to defend the disfranchisement of African Americans in the South and call for the end of their migration to Indiana, so that Hoosier Democrats would be victorious and, ironically, "march on through the fields and factories carrying the blessings of universal liberty, economic opportunity and human rights."[28]

As many observers then and since have noted, one purpose in writing *The Tragic Era* was political. In 1928 Hoover was the Republican party's first strong presidential candidate in the South, so the work served to remind southern Democrats of Reconstruction measures. Bowers believed the book "will be the most powerful single factor in bringing the South back into line." Democrats were quick to realize the potential of *The Tragic Era*. Senator Hawes of Missouri believed "it would swing every state in the South." McAdoo thought the volume would have "a profound impression in the south."[29]

Readers found Bowers's prose compelling. He depicted "the reaction of the people to what was going on" and as always included entertaining vignettes and vivid descriptions. All aspects of Washington life were portrayed: streets "studded thick with barrooms," "the fashionable world, moving at a hectic pace," John Welcher's restaurant with its politicians, witty women, and "rich old wines." Stevens possessed "something between a sneer and a Voltairian smile upon his thin, hard lips," while the face of the "honest, inflexible, tender, able, forceful, and tactless" Johnson "denoted grim determination and even some bitterness."

As his books on Jackson and Jefferson, *The Tragic Era* proved a best-seller. It was a Literary Guild selection and quickly ran through printings. Libraries bought the work, and it was assigned reading. All in all, it sold 150,000 copies, more than any book ever written on Reconstruction.[30]

Contemporary reviews of *The Tragic Era* were generally favorable. It was "smashingly iconoclastic," Lloyd Lewis commented in the *New York Evening Post*. "The chapters on Reconstruction conditions in the South are masterpieces," said Krock in the *New York Times Book Review*. Hoosier author Meredith Nicholson discerned "constant evidence of painstaking research." Scholars lauded the book. For biographer Henry F. Pringle the story of the twelve years after Lincoln "is a shameful one, and Mr. Bowers tells it brutally, forcefully and without restraint." Professor William MacDonald noted that the author was not "wholly impartial," but concluded, "There is no history of the sordid epoch better worth reading."

Arthur M. Schlesinger, Sr., faulted Bowers for not noting that both good and bad events had occurred in the South during Reconstruction, but praised him as "the greatest living American practitioner of . . . personal history."[31]

The most critical evaluation came from the *Journal of Negro History*, where an unidentified reviewer, presumably editor Carter G. Woodson, did not write a favorable sentence about *The Tragic Era*. "The thinking element," he declared, "will take little notice" of the book, which was nothing but "downright propaganda." Bowers, Woodson claimed, was "an historically untrained politician with a cause to advance or an ax to grind," whose facts were "intentionally distorted." Unfortunately, the reviewer predicted, the volume "will probably have a large circulation among the gullible," and its "sinister influence" would make the teaching of history more difficult.

Bowers claimed that "*The Tragic Era* forced a complete reappraisal of men and measures of the reconstruction period." But he was wrong. Since the turn of the century academics and Progressives—in part tired of Republicans waving the "bloody shirt" and extolling the virtues of Reconstruction—had reinterpreted postwar history. Bowers's thesis was that of Professor William A. Dunning, whose *Reconstruction, Political and Economic, 1865–1877*, published in 1907, told of "the struggle through which the southern whites . . . thwarted the scheme which threatened permanent subjection to another race." This interpretation of Reconstruction held sway for decades.[32] Nevertheless, the popularity of Bowers's book identified him as the spokesman of the Dunning school for later generations of historians.

For more than a half century scholars condemned *The Tragic Era*. African Americans called for a counterbalance to Bowers's work. In 1934 W. E. B. Du Bois's *Black Reconstruction in America* considered *The Tragic Era* "propaganda" to prove "the North vengeful and the Negro stupid." But it was a profound change in racial attitudes, not historical scholarship, that overwhelmed Bowers's views. Following the 1954 Supreme Court decision outlawing segregation in public schools—where lawyers for the status quo cited *The Tragic Era* in their arguments—historians interpreted Reconstruction as an earnest attempt to incorporate the freedmen into American society. Kenneth M. Stampp, John Hope Franklin, C. Vann Woodward, and Eric Foner emphasized the efforts of Radical Republicans to educate the former slaves and guarantee suffrage. These authors found favor among reformers demanding civil rights for African Americans. But Bowers was hostile to this movement and believed that "the South never would acquiesce" to integration. He noted that civil rights tensions had "greatly increased" sales of his book in the region.[33]

Most contemporaries considered *The Tragic Era* another triumph, and Bowers was deluged with invitations to accept honorary degrees. As early as mid-January 1930 there had been eleven of them—and numerous others poured in. Many came from the South, but he went to the University of Notre Dame in June to give the commencement address and receive the LL.D. Then came more of the same at Holy Cross and the state universities in South Carolina, Alabama, and North Carolina.[34]

Despite their influence and popularity, neither *Jefferson and Hamilton* nor *The Tragic Era* received the Pulitzer Prize. In 1926 the jury unanimously chose *Jefferson and Hamilton*, only to be overruled by a committee at Columbia University supervising awards. Four years later the historians voted two to one for *The Tragic Era* and again were overruled. Bowers saw the whole thing as a matter of GOP shenanigans, claiming the publishers "resolved themselves into a Republican ward meeting to blackguard me." "The old traditional scheme of having little groups dominate the interpretation of history in the interest of the old Federalist and Abolitionist schools is dying hard," he concluded, and he focused his ire on "that blackguard Nicholas Murray Butler." The Republican president of Columbia had a history of interfering in Pulitzer decisions. Indirectly, Bowers faulted "the professors who feel they are ordained by God to have a monopoly on the writing of history." This assertion was too harsh, for Professors Nevins, Beard, and Dodd expressed their outrage to the author. There was a financial consideration. The committee members who refused him the

$2,000 prizes, he asserted, were "in the same class with porch climbers who would climb into my window and steal $4000 of my money."[35]

Bowers's third book during his New York years was *Beveridge and the Progressive Era*, published in 1932. Based on the senator's papers provided by Beveridge's second wife, it was a laudatory biography of a Republican. But the Hoosier hero was a Progressive reformer. The author sought "to paint a living portrait of a great orator, statesman, and biographer against the background of his stirring times." Bowers admired his subject for his denunciation of child labor, opposition to protective tariffs, and attacks "upon the greed and arrogance of the trusts." *Beveridge and the Progressive Era* sold 38,000 copies and was a Literary Guild selection.

Virtually all reviewers praised the volume, including Oswald Garrison Villard in the *New York Herald Tribune Book Review* and Arthur C. Cole in the *Mississippi Valley Historical Review*. John H. Finley called it an "enthralling book" in the *New York Times Book Review* and found the author's descriptions of the period "deftly and faithfully drawn." Because of Bowers's "balanced treatment," historians continue to praise this biography.[36]

The New York years were a remarkable time, when the energetic, talented, and lively erstwhile inhabitant of Indiana found himself at the center of journalism in the nation's metropolis. He did his best to move public opinion, not merely in New York but across the land, in the direction of the Democratic party. Bowers was an ardent Democrat from his youth. He wrote editorials to point out democratic virtues, which were not merely those of the people but of the party that descended from the country's first real Democrat, the Sage of Monticello. If some of Bowers's pieces displayed ignorance of domestic politics—his urging of McAdoo and failure to comment on the connections of prominent Democrats with oil interests—he hoped that the party of the common man and woman, even if it excluded African Americans in the South, would make American life more democratic. In foreign policy, too, he erred in some of his views—his overly partisan criticism of Secretary Kellogg and faith in the security achieved at Locarno—but he was an internationalist in an isolationist era. For Bowers the Republican party was the institution of wealth and conservatism, and its policies abroad must serve those interests. Whatever his shortcomings, he indeed did try to promote his democratic views, and the trying was always interesting as he set out his opinions during most of the 1920s in the Pulitzer papers and then in the early 1930s in those of the Hearst chain.

All the while he wrote books, and the trinity of volumes he produced—*Jefferson and Hamilton*, *The Tragic Era*, and *Beveridge and the Progressive Era*—were all widely read. His research was composed in fair part of original material—the letters of Jefferson and Hamilton, the diary of Julian, the papers of his late friend Beveridge, and always newspapers. The writing, quite properly, was vivid and therefore exciting; Bowers knew better than to make great topics, even small topics, dull. He reached audiences with his books, as he had done with his remarkable editorials. He left it to later writers, historians who preferred the lamp to the podium one might say, to revise his opinions—to announce that this and that lacked perspective, omitted sides to issues, and so forth. Meanwhile his countrymen could take their ideas, their hopes, and in the early 1930s, even their fears, and measure them against the experiences of figures of the American past. As Bowers knew well, it was the only measurement people could have.

# CHAPTER SIX

# Spokesman for the Democracy

In addition to his successes as a journalist and historian, Bowers's New York years were his most important as an orator and political adviser. His keynote address at the 1928 Democratic convention made him the public speaker for his party throughout the land. His political connections, in which he took great interest, brought him nearer power than ever before. His effect on the Democratic party was undeniable. He became a trusted adviser to Sen. Robert F. Wagner, and, more important, he became close to New York's two most influential political leaders. One was a national figure, Gov. Alfred E. Smith, and the other was his successor as governor and the man whose name became attached to the 1930s and 1940s, Franklin D. Roosevelt.

But more than politics fascinated Bowers during these years. Since childhood he had attended events and sought association and friendship with the famous. He continued to do so in Manhattan, the nation's intellectual and social capital. He saw friends from Indiana days: Theodore Dreiser, Albert J. Beveridge, William G. McAdoo, Arthur Krock, and Paxton P. Hibben. He made new friends whose names were known in the 1920s: Bernard Baruch, Adolph Ochs, Allan Nevins, Charles Evans Hughes, Max Reinhardt, Edgar Lee Masters, Norman Thomas, Henry L.

Stimson, Harry Elmer Barnes, John Dos Passos, and Henry Morgenthau, Jr. Bowers also encountered a host of foreign luminaries, including William Butler Yeats, Winston Churchill, and Ignace Paderewski.

Bowers's first foray into politics in New York came from his Indiana connections. At the invitation of Hoosier boss Thomas Taggart, he sat with the Indiana delegates at the 1924 convention in Madison Square Garden. The convention remained deadlocked between McAdoo and Smith. On 7 July all seemed in readiness for a compromise—Indiana's Samuel M. Ralston. In March the Bowerses had been guests of the Ralstons in Washington where the senator and Bowers had sat up until 1:30 A.M. discussing such a possibility. McAdoo agreed to release his delegates except those from California, and at Taggart's request Bowers drafted a statement on the Ralston candidacy. Suddenly it was off. On 8 July Ralston telephoned Taggart and insisted that for reasons of health he would not be a candidate.[1] The convention turned to John W. Davis.

The partisan journalist was "not delighted," believing the "intellectually brilliant" Davis had "given J. P. Morgan a monopoly on his intellect." Bowers maintained that the Democrats could have won with McAdoo, but he now had little faith in a Democratic victory. At Davis's invitation Bowers worked part-time at national headquarters in the Murray Hill Hotel in New York. While he came to admire the candidate as a person, he saw that Davis was unable to capitalize on Republican defects.[2]

Although Bowers never expected to participate in New York politics, by 1926 he found himself "into politics up to my eyebrows." His work in Wagner's first senatorial campaign won admiration. On meeting the candidate at the Manhattan Club in September, Bowers "fell in love with Bob Wagner." The feeling was mutual. The journalist liked his views and speculated that "his strength is in his lean, brown face lighted by deep, intelligent gray-blue eyes." They met again 6 October to plan Wagner's acceptance of the nomination. The candidate had prepared "a tentative speech," which was good but clearly not what was needed for the campaign. Wagner asked Bowers to draft the speech. "We talked over everything," deciding to concentrate on the record of Republican James W. Wadsworth, Jr., the incumbent. His vote for the Volstead Act and support of the Coolidge administration became the Democrats' targets.

The journalist did what was requested, to Wagner's satisfaction. Only once did the candidate veto an item in the speeches written by his Hoosier adviser. Bowers had included the admonition "Beware of Greeks bearing gifts." The ethnically conscious New Yorker struck this phrase from the text. Bowers recalled, "Then I knew I was in New York." A former state legislator, Wagner had been a judge for eight years and admitted his "utter ignorance of national politics." "It seems to be my business to put him in touch," Bowers remarked. The Wagner-Wadsworth contest turned out to be a warm one, with the Democratic candidate using Bowers's material.[3] Wagner had an advantage in running with Smith as his party's gubernatorial candidate. The *New York Evening World* carried pro-Wagner editorials, from Bowers's typewriter, on twenty-five occasions. Other newspapers backed Wadsworth or were silent.

Bowers's diary for 3 November proclaimed: "Smith and Wagner both elected. The only editorial page supporting Wagner was mine, but I used heavy artillery daily for three weeks." Wagner twice called Bowers to thank him, giving him credit for the victory, and the victor proved a good friend.[4] From the standpoint of affecting Congress, Bowers now had influence—the new solon would rank as one of the most influential senators. New York Democrats realized Bowers's value, and the erstwhile Hoosier became "one of us" on the sidewalks of New York.

Democrats recognized Bowers as the author of *The Party Battles of the Jackson Period* and *Jefferson and Hamilton*, but he was to make his mark on the party as an orator. Known as a forceful speaker in Indiana, he rose to national prominence in a series of addresses delivered in 1926 and 1927. One of his boosters was Congressman Harry B. Hawes of Missouri, who aspired to the Senate. He brought Bowers to St. Louis on 13 April 1926, the anniversary of Thomas Jefferson's birth. The theme was Jefferson as a party leader. The audience could not possibly miss the point that principles victorious in Jefferson's era were beacons to Democrats in the here and now. A thousand people crowded the Jefferson Hotel, where the speaker was embarrassed when greeted by "The Sidewalks of New York." When he sat down after forty minutes of eloquence, those present were "on their feet yelling like Indians." Hawes declared the speech "the best I have ever heard" and claimed Bowers's talk was responsible for his election.

Two nights later Bowers spoke in Pittsburgh for Joseph F. Guffey, national committeeman and an admirer. While the orator used much of his Missouri material, he tailored the speech to Pennsylvanians.[5] As in St. Louis his militancy, as well as his subtleties, inspired cheers.

The St. Louis and Pittsburgh speeches were typical of Bowers's presentations. His addresses constituted an oratorical art form that was his stock-in-trade. They were calls to arms, fighting speeches meant to move his listeners to action. Bowers avoided the claptrap of the sort to which political audiences often were subjected. He knew so much more about American history than the average politician, and he was so familiar with details of the past related to situations of the present, that officeholders and office seekers could readily relate the Jefferson-Hamilton struggle to conflicts in which they were embroiled. Moreover, his delivery was masterful. His sentences were constructed with care, and his timing was letter-perfect. Never boring, never long departing from the fundamentals as he saw them, and playing on the emotions of his listeners with skill that came from one who had been campaigning since 1900, he evoked enthusiastic applause early and repeatedly moved from climax to climax, usually concluding with a crescendo.

Even Bowers's nonpolitical speeches brought him into contact with Democratic leaders. In Fort Wayne the Fortnightly Club invited him to speak on Dreiser. In February 1927 the Detroit Athletic Club paid Bowers five hundred dollars for "Some Myths and Caricatures of History," and in Philadelphia he discoursed on Jefferson before the Democratic Women's Club. That year Bowers spoke twice in North Carolina. In May he addressed the bar association at Pinehurst. His host, Josephus Daniels, gave "a flattering introduction," and his talk on Jefferson as a lawyer "went off well." Speaking before the North Carolina Historical and Literary Association, Bowers was interrupted by constant applause when he protested the "historical 'framing'" of Andrew Johnson. But contemporary politics dominated his visits. Gov. Angus McLean told him that Sen. Furnifold M. Simmons was "gravely concerned" over Smith's nomination, fearing that many in North Carolina would not vote for a Roman Catholic. The senator wanted McLean to address the Jackson Day banquet in Washington and "to read Smith out." Bowers suggested that the governor instead "confine himself wholly to the fundamentals of Jeffersonian democracy."⁶

His popularity as an orator and writer prompted party leaders to ask Bowers to address the Jackson Day dinner in Washington. The presidential candidates were invited, and their followers also would be there. Party leaders feared that "conflicting speeches from presidential aspirants" might lead to bad feeling. Smith decided to absent himself. The major address fell to Bowers because "I was the only one all could agree upon." While preparing the Washington speech, the orator stole time for lunch with Roosevelt, Smith's campaign manager. Bowers found him seated at a huge desk, "his paralysis and its effect thus hidden," and noted his face was "finely chiseled—a patrician face." They conversed for three hours, but Roosevelt never mentioned the speech. Apparently Bowers had been invited for Roosevelt's perusal.⁷

On 12 January 1928 Mrs. Woodrow Wilson sat at Davis's right and Bowers on his left. Everyone "expected a cat-and-dog fight because of the candidacies and Prohibition, and the Washington correspondents had their pencils sharpened for the expected struggle." Bowers was disgusted at the Democrats' "quarreling about non-essentials" and reminded the faithful that their founders had stood "for democracy and against the oligarchy of a privileged class." His allusions to the battles of Andrew Jackson's period contained ever more telling relevance to the need for party unity. The speech was greeted with "one continuous series of demonstrations, the diners rising to their feet many times, with much shouting." Old-timers could not recall a recent address that elicited such a response, comparing it to William Jennings Bryan's "Cross of Gold" speech in 1896. Only Will Rogers's remarks that evening came close to Bowers's in appealing to the crowd. The humorist claimed that if the other speakers "had knowed what this little runt from New York was going to do you might just as well have washed up and gone home!" Daniels called Bowers "the man of the hour," and Davis considered the address "the best political speech I ever heard."[8] Unquestionably this was the oratorical masterpiece of Bowers's life, even greater than the keynote he would deliver later in the year.

The next evening at Hawes's, Bowers dined with twelve Democratic senators. Following his Jackson Day speech, a movement began to make him temporary chairman of the national convention to deliver the keynote. Hawes was "wild about the idea." The next afternoon Bowers reported that Democratic leader Daniel C. Roper is "dead set for me for the temporary chairmanship." Returning home Bowers discovered a basketful of letters and many articles about his speech. The *Chicago Tribune, Pittsburgh Dispatch, Baltimore Sun, Washington Star,* and *Christian Science Monitor* all were mentioning him for the chairmanship. Still, he did not believe that "it will work out that way." "If it comes, all right; if not, I shall not be disappointed."[9]

A woman of rare ability entered Bowers's life in 1928. Three times he was a guest of Elisabeth Marbury, author of the entertaining *My Crystal Ball,* "huge in bulk, and brilliant and agile in mind." She was an influential adviser to Smith and was "profoundly impressed" by Bowers's Washington address. She broached the temporary chairmanship to the Hoosier orator, saying she was "urging it on the Smith people." Guffey told Bowers that the governor's advisers were thinking of him for the nominating speech. The journalist, however, preferred to be the keynoter.

Invitations to address many groups poured in, but Bowers accepted few. One exception was Kansas City, where in March he spoke on Jeffersonian Democracy and met Judge Harry S. Truman.

The following month he gave the Founders Day Address on Jefferson at the University of Virginia and had a "long talk" with the young Jeffersonian scholar Dumas Malone.

On 15 April 1928 in Washington, Bowers extolled another of his heroes. The occasion: the unveiling in the Capitol of an Andrew Jackson statue. The principal speaker joined President Calvin Coolidge who "read a very good speech" and, concluding after no applause, left with his aides, "turning first to me and graciously shaking hands. My speech was well received, being frequently interrupted with applause, and at the close the audience stood." An amusing thing happened. Before the program, referring to President John Quincy Adams, Bowers remarked: "Mr. President, it was in this chamber that your most recent predecessor from Massachusetts strongly supported the foreign policy of Jackson." A pause. Then Coolidge ventured: "I well think he might."[10]

In April Bowers was named temporary chairman of the Houston convention. For months press reports had treated this "as a settled fact." Former ambassador James W. Gerard asked Bowers how his campaign for vice president was progressing ("I have heard that joke many times"). In June a former Oklahoma senator opposed to Smith told Bowers the party was "liable to nominate" him "if my speech at Houston makes an impression." Heady stuff? Hardly. Such suggestions, he noted, "had some circulation in the press," but Bowers gave "no importance to this at all."

Many Democrats in New York wished to give the keynoter advice about his Houston address. Much of it he found repugnant. From the remarks of some, "I gathered that a reactionary Republican speech would be just the thing." A New York committeeman advised him not to say anything that might please farmers, a counsel that had the "very opposite" effect. A friend of the oilman Harry F. Sinclair chastised him for editorially attacking the oil magnate. In Washington he saw Cordell Hull, the most "accomplished all-around statesman in either branch of Congress." His "idea of a keynote speech is precisely what I have in mind," making Bowers "feel more certain of my ground now." He met with Wagner and Congressman Frank Oliver of New York and went over "features of the oil scandal" with Montana's senator Thomas J. Walsh. Back in New York, he concluded that Washington advice "did not help me out much on the speech. It is plain that it is up to me to do what I think best, and that suits me just as well."[11]

Nor were Walter Lippmann's observations of help. On the first of May the Bowerses were guests of Eleanor Roosevelt at the annual luncheon of the Women's Democratic Union. Lippmann spoke and his words were "the most amazing to which I have ever listened." The *World* columnist made "a determined effort" to show that Democrats could seldom hope to win, and he blamed Smith's friends for not insisting that the governor come out against Prohibition. Bowers concluded, "Lippmann is not a Democrat. He does not care for Jefferson and is a great admirer of Hamilton, and that sort of Democrat is hard to grasp."

Smith in mid-June asked Bowers to come to the Biltmore Hotel, where he received his guest in underclothes and a bathrobe "with little smutches of dried lather on his face." Hearing the governor speak three years earlier, Bowers was surprised by "his crudeness and coarseness of manner," "his Bowery tone," and his "bar room presence and gesticulation." But this time Smith's "magnetism and dynamic force" won him over.

While Bowers was polishing his address, he attended a meeting of Smith's assistants. The candidate exploded over the foreign relations plank expressed in "high faluting language." " 'Now what does that mean?' " he demanded. " 'We want a platform that the man in the factory can understand.' " Bowers found "his husky voice" and manners unpleasant, but concluded that Smith was "a rough diamond."

Bowers arrived in Houston on Monday, 25 June, the day before his address and proceeded to Sam Houston Hall to get his bearings. For the first time the keynote was to be broadcast over a nationwide hookup, so the National Committee had scheduled the opening session for night to reach the radio audience. On Tuesday the Texas heat was awful. Throughout the daylight hours, the keynoter stayed under a fan and refused to see anybody. Late in the afternoon there was a terrific storm. His wife and daughter went to the convention

*Claude Bowers at the podium for his keynote speech to the Democratic National Convention at Houston, Texas, 26 June 1928*

COURTESY OF MANUSCRIPTS DEPARTMENT, LILLY LIBRARY, INDIANA UNIVERSITY, BLOOMINGTON

to watch the preliminaries. When the hour arrived for Bowers to depart, the rain still fell and no taxis were in sight. In the hotel lobby he mentioned his predicament to a man who darted out and hailed a passing car. "A moment later, a priest stepped out and motioned to me. I found that we had the Houston priest with two priests from Boston who knew me, and thus accompanied by three priests I reached the convention. What a story for the Republicans to get hold of for the benefit of the anti-Catholics."

The hall was packed with eighteen thousand people. Millions more, including Smith, listened on the radio. Calling on three decades of oratorical practice, the keynoter spoke for forty minutes without notes. He entertained his audience with an attack on the Harding-Coolidge years. "The American Democracy has mobilized today to wage a war of extermination against privilege and pillage," "the Gold Dust twins of normalcy." "We go forth to war for the cause of man," he insisted, arguing that "under the rule of this regime the average man has no more stake in the government for which he may be called upon to die than if he had never touched our soil." Cheering greeted his "demand that privilege take its hands out of the farmer's pockets and off the farmer's throat." The Republicans believed with Hamilton "in a government of the wealthy," while the Democrats believed with Jefferson that governments are "created for the service of the people." In closing, Bowers borrowed from Holy Writ and ordered the delegates "To your tents, O Israel," admonishing them to return home "to battle for the principles of Thomas Jefferson."[12]

Bowers was elated by the response. "Throughout there was constant cheering and two great demonstrations, one lasting fifteen minutes with a parade of all the standards." Ralph Pulitzer told him that never before had this happened for a keynote address. "There was more enthusiasm over the speech," Bowers asserted, "than during the whole of the Republican convention." The next day brought a flood of praise. "Deluged with telegrams. Seems the speech was a sensation. Papers are fulsome, declaring the speech the most notable in years. Telegrams call it the greatest political speech in twenty and forty years. One says in a century." The *Chicago Tribune* compared it to Bryan's "Cross of Gold" speech, while the pro-Republican *New York Times* considered it "about the most shrill 'keynote' ever sounded." That night Bowers sat in the press section with the *Evening World* crowd. Nine days earlier Roosevelt had told him that he had entirely rewritten his speech after reading the keynote. In placing Smith in nomination, Roosevelt "spoke exceedingly well," Bowers opined.[13] After the inevitable demonstration came the foregone conclusion: Alfred E. Smith for president.

Following the convention, Bowers represented the party in "notifying" Sen. Joseph T. Robinson that he had been chosen as Smith's running mate. The keynoter traveled to Arkansas for this formality. Twenty-five thousand people heard him deliver a ten-minute talk and Robinson's response at Hot Springs on 30 August.

The National Committee was eager for Bowers to take the stump. Around the country there were more demands for him to speak than for any other Democrat except Smith. Bowers was ready to go. His opinion of the Republican nominee, Herbert Hoover, was low; his disgust with the Republican record evident. But the *World*'s managers "hog-tied" their employee, "taking the position, strange to me, that if I was to do any speaking it would be better for me to take a leave of absence." Clearly influential was Lippmann, who published an editorial "to the effect that corruption must not be discussed in the campaign." This, in Bowers's judgment, constituted "a direct attack on my speech."[14]

Denied an oratorical role Bowers devoted his energies to pro-Smith editorials. He remained optimistic through September that the Democratic campaign would take on the GOP. Bowers noted that Smith was attacking corruption and following his keynote "absolutely," and Republican papers had launched a "terrific onslaught." In October he became disillusioned with the campaign, believing the national committee took "the lofty ground that all criticism of Hoover would be 'mud slinging.' " Bowers confided to his diary that "one of the most amazing things in this campaign is the fact that nothing is being done to dissipate the utterly false story of Hoover's wizardry in business during his sojourn of a quarter of a century in Europe." The journalist was distressed at the religious bigotry directed at Smith's Catholicism. But most disappointing was Smith's refusal to mention his keynote, leading Bowers to conclude that the candidate's advisers considered it "a dangerous speech."

John J. Raskob, head of the national committee, invited the Bowerses to Madison Square Garden for the campaign's close. There Roosevelt, nominee for governor, "got quite an ovation." When Smith entered, "there was a demonstration such as I have never seen before." Bowers was disappointed with his speech: "It might have been made in Des Moines or Topeka, and lacked the personal appeal I should have expected."[15]

On 6 November, when the Hoover landslide became apparent, Bowers unburdened himself in a postmortem. He concluded that bigotry accounted for the Republican vote. Just as disturbing was his conclusion that "the fool people have taken plutocracy to its heart."

For Bowers, contentment with radios, comic sheets, and automobiles purchased on the installment plan had made the many accept exploitation by the few. "I wonder," he ruminated, "if there isn't a good deal of the serf left in the average man and woman." Roosevelt won the governorship by twenty-five thousand votes while Smith was losing New York by a hundred thousand votes.

In 1929 Bowers became better acquainted with Smith. One March evening the Smiths and the Olivers joined the Bowerses as dinner guests of the Bronx politico Edward J. Flynn and his wife. The group of eight then went to the Ringling Circus. On an October afternoon Bowers called at the Biltmore to receive a copy of Smith's autobiography, *Up to Now*, and the former governor told him he had purchased *The Tragic Era*. The first night in November, Oliver drove Bowers and Pat to the Bronx to hear Smith and Mayor Jimmy Walker close the municipal campaign for that borough. The governor extended "a warm greeting" to Bowers, who considered his speech "a strong presentation of the issues."

Smith's cordiality contrasted with that of Eleanor and Franklin Roosevelt. On 19 November 1929, at a dinner of the Women's Fair Tariff League, Bowers was "seated beside Mrs. Franklin Roosevelt who is no friend of mine." Four days later, when he went to hear the governor speak, "Roosevelt greeted me as coldly and indifferently as humanly possible." Bowers thought the treatment was somehow connected with *The Tragic Era*. Then he remembered that Mrs. Roosevelt had been unfriendly even before its publication.

In October 1929 came the Wall Street panic, with stocks tumbling, fortunes lost, and much pessimism. Hoover came in for torrents of criticism. At Col. Edward M. House's on New Year's Day 1930, most seemed to agree that the president was "utterly stupid in politics," Bowers recorded. House told a story of Woodrow Wilson's opinion of Hoover. When someone referred to the Republican as "that damn skunk," the president objected, saying, " 'It isn't fair. A skunk, you know, has one white streak.' " Later that month young Bob La Follette told Bowers that Hoover was a failure—"without guts."[16]

In early 1930 Bowers accepted seven speaking engagements outside New York. In Washington Senator Hawes gave a stag dinner in January with sixteen senators present, and the honoree spoke about his works and about conspiracies in academic circles against Democratic interpretations of history. It was old home week in February when Bowers addressed the annual banquet of the Indiana Democratic Editorial Association in Indianapolis. He saw Laura Donnan, his high school teacher, and the widows of John W. Kern and Ralston. A delegation of farmers and friends from his boyhood village of Whitestown held a reunion. "At the conclusion of my speech I must have shaken hands with 800 people." His next stop was Terre Haute, where at the cemetery Bowers was touched to find his mother's grave decorated. "That sort of thing is peculiar to Terre Haute, reflecting the intense humanism of the place." At the Deming Hotel, he and others spoke. The next day he visited Mrs. John E. Lamb.

In March Bowers gave a lecture to the Young Men's and Women's Hebrew Association in Pittsburgh. Next he spoke at Holy Cross College in Worcester, Massachusetts, on "Thomas Jefferson and Religious Freedom" and also delivered an address to the Friends of St. Patrick at Albany. In Washington, the most remarkable episode at the Jefferson Day Dinner of the Women's National Democratic Club in April was the arrival of Alice Roosevelt Longworth. This congenital Republican had asked to come. She "has no use for Hoover," Bowers recorded, and "my flings at him were received with expansive smiles." That night Mrs. Wilson told Bowers her favorite for the presidential nomination was Newton D. Baker. Baker introduced Bowers that same month when he spoke in Cleveland. Bowers reported that Baker claimed "he had been too close to a President to ever crave the job, but that I cannot believe," Bowers observed.

In July Bowers was welcomed at Hyde Park and spent a pleasant day with the Roosevelts. The governor, lifted by two husky men into an automobile, drove his visitor around the estate. After lunch there was more talk of "politics and personalities" and no sign of earlier hostility.[17]

That summer and fall Bowers was delighted that the party was taking the offensive. The national committee distributed a hundred thousand copies of his article in the *Sunday World* advocating this course. In October, Bowers spoke over a nationwide hookup on "The Collapse of an Administration." Jouett Shouse, Raskob's aide, termed it the strongest speech of the campaign. The orator was elated when Smith in a Boston speech quoted from his address. Bowers predicted a landslide. "There ought to be one. Conditions are frightful. Bread lines, soup houses, everywhere." Five November 1930: "The Democrats have swept the country," capturing the Senate and almost gaining control of the House. Roosevelt was returned to Albany by more than seven hundred thousand votes. In December Bowers concluded that "present indications" pointed to Roosevelt's nomination for president.[18]

Bowers continued giving speeches in 1931. He delivered three in the South, one at the Washington Birthday Address at the University of Georgia, another at Emory University, and the third at the unveiling of John Tyler's bust in Richmond. The ceremony took place in the Hall of Delegates where Tyler had sat as a young legislator in the 1820s, and Bowers's remarks were carried over the air. The *New York Evening Journal* columnist, arrayed in the sash of a sachem, likewise was the speaker for the annual Fourth of July celebration at Tammany Hall.

In the fall of 1931 Bowers had his last experience with the offhandedness of Roosevelt. Calling by invitation, he was photographed with the governor and shunted aside for two hours. Bowers decided the affront was "a joke on me" and laughed it off "with the reservation that I would not see Roosevelt again until damn sure he wanted to see me." While his diary was full of favorable comments about Smith, the record included no praise of Roosevelt.[19]

There were so many prospects for the Democratic nomination that the national committee invited none of them to address the January 1932 Jackson Day Dinner in Washington. Instead, the headliners consisted of three of the party's previous standard-bearers, James M. Cox, Davis, and Smith, with Bowers as toastmaster. Raskob introduced Bowers, who spoke for fifteen minutes, "four being used up by interruptions, laughter and cheering." Afterwards he took his wife and daughter to Smith's room to be greeted by the inimitable Al.

The presidential nomination dominated Democratic politics. In February Smith announced he would accept the call. Bowers lunched with Charles A. Lindbergh and Harry F. Byrd, the ex-governor of Virginia, who was also in the race. In Washington for a St. Patrick's Day talk, Bowers visited House Speaker John N. Garner of Texas, who "clearly hopes for the presidential nomination but does not seem over-eager." The journalist went to see Senator Robinson who believed Roosevelt would be named "but is not enthusiastic about it." Pat Harrison also "seems to be for Roosevelt but with reservations like Robinson's." Back in New York, Bowers lunched with Montana sen-ator Burton K. Wheeler, who favored Roosevelt but believed he "lacks courage." Yet "we can elect him," Wheeler declared. Bowers wondered if the election of a weak man "would not put the party out of business for a quarter century." He left "a bit cynical."

In April Bowers went to Charlottesville to speak at the unveil-ing of Attilio Peccirilli's statue of James Monroe. Twenty-eight governors attended. The next day the orator for all occasions addressed the quadrennial mock political convention at Washington and Lee University. Then a blockbuster: the chairman of the Democratic National Executive Committee, Shouse, "amazed me by asking if I was to make the nominating speech for Roosevelt" at Chicago.[20]

Skeptical at the outset, Bowers learned in June that Roosevelt indeed had this in mind. Roosevelt, a reader of his editorials and admirer of his books and speeches, was ready to treat Bowers as a confidant. Since 1929 Roosevelt had asked Bowers during his speaking tours to report on Democrats who were his "good friends" and "carried political weight." At a "war conference" in Albany, Roosevelt's advisers urged Bowers to make the nominating speech. The columnist asked Will Curley of the *Journal* to get in touch with William Randolph Hearst, a Garner backer, because "without his gracious consent I cannot so conspicuously oppose him." The publisher answered he did not want to interfere with Bowers's views, but believed it would be less embarrassing "if he did not so conspicuously identify himself with any candidacy."

Invited to Albany, Bowers and the governor relaxed, quaffing beer. "Then we talked to the point. I explained the difficulties. 'Is there anything I can do?' he asked. 'Can I get in touch with Hearst?' I doubted the wisdom." Roosevelt wanted the speech to be " 'a fighting speech' " and enumerated points to emphasize. The candidate said that "an Andrew Jackson is needed now" and believed "he fills the bill." Two days later Bowers declined the assignment. The governor assured him "I know where your heart is."[21]

Prior to the convention, Bowers attended the GOP gathering, also in Chicago. He spent 12–16 June providing copy for the *Journal*. "Town . . . dull," he wrote in his diary. "No enthusiasm. Hotels not crowded. Delegates talk everything but politics." A monotonous keynote address "gave little heed to the realities" of the nation's plight. Eventually Hoover was renominated.

In Chicago again on 26 June, Bowers had a dual role—columnist and delegate. On the first ballot John F. Curry, the Tammany Hall chief, requested a poll of the delegation. "Everyone from Manhattan voted for Smith. I voted for him because he deserved at least a complimentary vote." While Sen. Alben W. Barkley of Kentucky was delivering his two-hour keynote speech, "everyone seemed to engage in general conversation." Rhode Island's senator Peter Gerry remarked to Bowers, "It seems to me that I remember a keynote about four years ago when there was no conversation." On the fourth ballot Roosevelt became the Democratic nominee. Flynn of the Bronx sent Bowers a message that Senator Wheeler "wished to see me on the platform. I know what that meant—a request to address the Convention." Believing that would be "undesirable," Bowers went to the hotel to hear Roosevelt's speech over the radio.[22] The explanation for his disappearance was that he wanted to be remembered for the Houston keynote and believed an unrehearsed 1932 oration would be anticlimactic.

During the summer Bowers conferred with National Chairman James A. Farley; Roosevelt's assistant, Louis M. Howe; and Eleanor

Roosevelt. Bowers had conducted himself in such a way as to make no enemies. On 3 July Roosevelt received him warmly and joked, "We've got to razz you for voting for Smith." Roosevelt's cordiality was evident when early in September Bowers went to Albany for dinner and to spend the night at the mansion. The governor "was in a happy, almost boyish mood." They discussed the campaign and the candidate's heartening experiences in Republican Vermont. "Good talk," the guest noted.

Bowers's campaign contributions were oratorical as well as journalistic. He made the renomination speech for Senator Wagner and on Columbus Day opened the Democratic Forum that Eleanor Roosevelt helped arrange at the Biltmore Hotel. There he castigated Hoover for a "brutal attitude" toward the unemployed. He counseled Texans Sam Rayburn and Garner, Roosevelt's running mate, on a Garner radio address. In late October and early November, Bowers hit the campaign trail—speeches at Terre Haute, Detroit, Buffalo, Syracuse—and found the audiences "wildly enthusiastic." The Indiana effort involved a hookup for three states.

In the midst of these travels Howe asked Bowers to substitute for Roosevelt in giving a forty-five-minute radio speech. Bowers read it at a New York City station. Broadcast nationally, it elicited congratulatory calls and telegrams "from everywhere"—some called it the "best of the campaign." Roosevelt's election, Bowers wrote 9 November, was "a landslide of almost unprecedented proportions." He also was elated that Wagner's reelection majority surpassed a million. "Now the Democrats have their opportunity," Bowers noted. "Will they rise to it?"[23]

Speaking engagements continued. In mid-November he spoke at the unveiling of a bust of an eminent conservationist, Richard Lieber, in Turkey Run State Park in Indiana. After being an honoree at a "successful authors" dinner, the next night Bowers joined economist Stuart Chase and novelists James Branch Cabell and Lion Feuchtwanger, as an invitee at a dinner for "authors of the year." Eleanor Roosevelt preceded Bowers at the podium. "Now that's over," she said to Bowers. "Now I can enjoy hearing you." He spoke on books and libraries, getting "quite a lot of laughter." The following month two thousand friends of Eleanor Roosevelt offered her a dinner at the Waldorf-Astoria. After Bowers's remarks, the honoree came to the microphone. He sat between her and her mother-in-law. When the orchestra struck up "Should Auld Acquaintance Be Forgot," Bowers noted that Eleanor Roosevelt "caught my hand."

In March came the electoral college dinner in Washington, the first ever, with Bowers as speaker. The dining room at the Willard was packed. Bowers met Henry A. Wallace, Harold L. Ickes, and Roper, all soon to be cabinet members.[24] Afterward he had a reunion with Hoosiers in town for the inaugural.

All the while the country was in awful shape. Just before Christmas someone robbed the cashier in a building next door to the Bowers apartment. The wretchedness of "millions out of work and hungry is increasing the danger. Never such a miserable Xmas season. None too much of good will toward men." Bowers was one of the fortunate Americans whose economic security remained intact during the depression. Never having invested in stocks, he did not suffer from the market crash. While the Beveridge book did not approach *The Tragic Era* or *Jefferson and Hamilton* in sales, royalty checks from Houghton Mifflin arrived with regularity. Salaries at the *World* and the *Journal* were substantial, and his savings drew interest. He could afford private schooling for his daughter, hired domestic help, and paid for a succession of European trips. It is an irony that one so poor from boyhood into his middle forties should now be comparatively affluent.

Life in Manhattan was pleasant. The apartment on Riverside Drive near Columbia University included a small room for writing, and the subway commute downtown lasted only a half hour. While at the *World*, Bowers occupied an office under the golden dome at the Pulitzer Building, lunched at a drugstore, and had supper before six o'clock with his family. While at the *Journal*, he wrote most of his columns at home.[25] His evenings were dedicated to historical writing, political events, or the couple's social schedule.

Sybil always preferred the tranquility of family life to political and social obligations. Because of this, she favored the less hectic days in Fort Wayne to those of New York and the capitals of Spain and Chile. One change she appreciated in her Manhattan life was a Virginian who cooked for the family. Although her participation was required at some dinners and reunions, her usual practice was not to attend her husband's speeches. Reading was her pastime.

Both parents continued to shower attention on Pat, who accompanied them on speaking trips. David Rockefeller was a classmate, but she was not impressed, considering him "a fat tub without too much brains." The proud father bragged of her "outstanding record in English and composition" and was pleased with her marks in French. In 1932 she entered Sarah Lawrence, then a two-year college, in nearby Bronxville. To her parents' delight, she was "enthusiastic about everything."[26]

Summer vacations afforded the family weeks together. Nearby places, such as the Delaware Water Gap, offered relaxation. Beginning in 1929 the Bowerses spent four summers in Europe. On the first of these they traveled for six weeks in England, Italy, and France, where Pat danced in the street on Bastille Day. In 1930 they visited France. In midsummer 1931 Bowers embarked on his European trip to meet his wife and daughter who were touring France and Spain. While on the *Ile de France* he shot craps and had beginner's luck; his tuxedo pockets bulged with money. "Funny experience, but no more dice for me," he vowed. The family went to Italy, and in Venice they floated in a gondola to the house of Charles T. Terry, a United States consul and friend from Washington days. When the intervention of the hotel doorman in Florence saved Bowers from paying an exorbitant fee demanded by his chauffeur, the exasperated visitor uncharacteristically wrote: "So does Mussolini make Italy safe for tourists. I came with a very deep-seated feeling against the dictator; I leave convinced that he is doing a great thing for Italy in probably the only way it can be done." In Paris Bowers saw the house of the famous orator of the Revolution, Pierre Vergniaud, whose life he would write. In 1932, for the fourth summer in a row, the family returned, this time to

England. They traveled to Paris, where he looked up Vergniaud references at the Bibliothèque Nationale.[27]

During these years Bowers found time for an amazing round of activities. Before *Jefferson and Hamilton* came out in late 1925, he did not lead a hermit's life. Aside from activities at the 1924 convention, his extra hours during his first two years in Manhattan had been consumed largely by the book—most social interludes were limited to just a few people of particular interest.

Bowers's friends from his Indiana days, Dreiser, McAdoo, and Beveridge, were the exceptions. For Bowers, Dreiser was "one of the most heroic and significant figures in our literary history." The "large, tall, and stout" novelist was "a delightful companion for a chat." Bowers and Dreiser began entertaining each other at dinner. Like her husband, Sybil was quick to observe their guest's "simplicity, his utter lack of pose." Sometimes his mistress Helen Richardson made a fourth.

Bowers usually saw McAdoo at the Vanderbilt Hotel and Beveridge at the Biltmore. In May 1924 the editor noticed McAdoo was "thin and worn and hoarse, but full of pep and fight." Meeting before the convention, they talked about the Klan and Pulitzer's opposition to McAdoo. After the Democrats selected Davis, Bowers extolled McAdoo for making one of "the gamest and most brilliant fights ever waged for progressive principles in this country." The defeated candidate inscribed a photograph "To Claude G. Bowers with my affection and admiration, William G. McAdoo," adding grimly, "You will get yourself fired yet."

That same summer he had the pleasure of presenting Beveridge to Sybil. The vigorous, athletic ex-senator "got her in a corner for ten minutes . . . exhorting her to look after my health." In November 1924 Beveridge told Bowers that "writing the *Lincoln* is the hardest job I ever undertook" and that Mrs. Beveridge predicted "my hero" would be Stephen A. Douglas. The following January Beveridge remarked: "I have not made up my mind what I think of Lincoln. I would not under any circumstances make a speech on him now." The last time Bowers and Beveridge saw each other was at the Biltmore in September 1926, when Wagner chanced to come by and Bowers introduced the former senator from Indiana to the future senator from New York. When Beveridge died in 1927, the journalist lamented that his death left "a void in the world of literature and politics."[28]

After publication of *Jefferson and Hamilton*, Bowers found time to participate in a wide range of social events and meet many of the famous or at least well known. Nineteen twenty-six was a year filled with invitations. At Colonel House's, he met the governor of New Jersey ("who has the appearance of a sublimated bartender") and the president of New York University. In Boston, Bowers spoke from the same platform with Theodore Roosevelt, Jr. In Washington the journalist dined with financier Perry Belmont, Sen. Walter F. George of Georgia, and ex-secretary of state Robert Lansing, "a fine-looking fellow" who "claims to be a Jeffersonian but I doubt it." In October he saw Baruch, ex-undersecretary of state Frank Polk, Krock, and Ochs's daughter Iphigene and son-in-law Arthur Hays Sulzberger. On occasion Masters joined Bowers for lunch to discuss Lincoln.

The journalist accompanied Congressman Oliver to Philadelphia in 1926 to see the first Dempsey-Tunney fight. Both boxers impressed him: Jack Dempsey's combativeness and Gene Tunney's calmness. The event took place in the rain, Bowers as impressed by the spectators as by the combatants. After Tunney's victory "there was no pushing, shoving, rushing. The vast bowl emptied as orderly as it had filled."[29]

Bowers's social whirl continued in 1927. Dreiser, wealthy after selling movie rights of *An American Tragedy*, held a series of "Thursday Evenings." In January the Bowerses attended the first of seven receptions at Dreiser and Richardson's apartment in Greenwich Village. Among the guests were novelist Ford Madox Ford, author W. E. Woodward, and Austrian theater director Reinhardt, who "looked more like a stockbroker than the great artist that he was."

In April "Sybil and I to dinner with Mrs. Franklin Roosevelt at her home tonight." Senator Wagner "sat on Mrs. Roosevelt's right, I on her left, Sybil beside the senator." The journalist was surprised to find her a Prohibitionist—no wine was served. That same month Nicholas Murray Butler and Bowers had a talk. He found that Columbia University's guiding spirit "looks the statesman rather than the school man" and suspected correctly that he had presidential ambitions. At Butler's he met Hughes, whom he found "very delightful and genial." It was unfortunate, the former secretary of state remarked, that "the papers of presidents are considered personal property." "Mrs. Harding took away all of Harding's and," with a chuckle, "destroyed some of them and sent the others to Marion."[30]

From May to November 1927 the Bowers couple saw more of Paxton and Sheila Hibben at suppers on Riverside Drive or in Greenwich Village. Hibben was having difficulties over his life of Henry Ward Beecher. The volume included a vivid account of the Beecher-Tilton scandal, and the preacher's family brought pressure on the publisher, who cut advertising and made life difficult for the author. Bowers gave Pax solace at lunches and favorably reviewed the biography when it was pubished in November.

Although Bowers and Hibben were enthusiastic playgoers in Indianapolis of the gay nineties, Bowers seldom attended the theater in New York. But there were two exceptions. During his first year on the *Evening World*, Maxwell Anderson and Lawrence Stallings, friends who worked for the morning paper, wrote *What Price Glory?*, dramatizing Stallings's war experience in France. The Bowerses attended its premiere. In October 1926 they went to the opening night of Dreiser's *An American Tragedy*.

From his window under the gold dome at the *World* building— usually with Sybil—Bowers observed parades honoring the famous. Lindbergh's reception in June 1927 was the most enthusiastic. With his wife and daughter, Bowers watched as the "almost childish boy" received the cheers of four million. Another parade feted Queen Marie of Romania, reputedly the "most beautiful, the cleverest, and the naughtiest queen in Europe." Another celebrated New York–born Gertrude Ederle, the first woman to swim the English Channel.[31]

Despite his writing and speaking schedule in 1928, there was no diminution in Bowers's social activities. At a January dinner party, he met George William Russell ("AE")—"the Dr. Samuel Johnson of the Irish"—who recited his poetry in a "strong, eerie monotone." At an April luncheon with Ochs, Bowers found the publisher the "same, comfortable conversationalist" and Ochs's son-in-law, Arthur Sulzberger, "a fine upstanding fellow." He also saw Oliver, Hibben, Masters, and Dreiser. The journalist lunched with Henry Seidel Canby, editor of the *Saturday Review of Literature*, established a friendship with Flynn, and with Sybil enjoyed a reunion with Mrs. Champ Clark.

In December Bowers devoted a large diary section to the "abuse" called down on Hibben by the Beecher family. His friend died of pneumonia that month. "What a tragedy. What a mockery too— the persecution of Americans who dare write the truth in history." Bowers was a pallbearer and reported that his friend's ashes were to be taken to Russia to be buried "beside those of John Reed outside the Kremlin walls in Moscow." That month the Bowerses attended Dreiser's "Thursday Evening" and joined Congressman Oliver and his wife "on an auto jaunt through a fine winter day into the beauty spots of Westchester," winding up at the house of Flynn, just appointed secretary of state by governor-elect Roosevelt.[32]

The climactic year 1929, which began quietly and closed with the crash, brought more of the same. The transplanted Hoosier encountered a different cast of characters when he attended a January housewarming of the poet Shaemas O'Sheel, a friend since Washington days. Most of those present were of the "flaming youth" variety, given to "making love pretty brazenly in the open." Among the guests was Dos Passos, a future Madrid friend. At a luncheon Bowers found the Socialist leader Thomas interesting but "in no sense comparable to Debs." On 27 March, Bowers attended the "most brilliant and spectacular party Dreiser has ever given," complete with dancers from the African Gold Coast. That autumn Bowers met historian Harry Elmer Barnes, a "robust young man" who "wears glasses and talks entertainingly." In October Churchill was a guest at Baruch's. Bowers was "rather disappointed" in his "almost pudgy" appearance, but was impressed by his talk on Anglo-American relations. At Butler's house in November, the journalist regaled the guests with campaign tales.[33]

For the next four years the Bowerses' social life continued as varied as in the past. At Baruch's party for South African general Jan C. Smuts in January 1930 were Bowers, Davis, Smith, three senators, one governor, Ochs, Morgenthau, and Robert W. Bingham, owner of the *Louisville Courier-Journal*. Two nights later he attended a *Times* dinner for Secretary of State Stimson. Unimpressed, the editor concluded that he was "a more clever lawyer than statesman." He continued to enjoy the company of Wagner, Oliver, and Masters. The couple became friendly with Alma Gluck Clayburgh, erstwhile opera star. Colonel House's 1931 New Year's guest turned out to be Paderewski—a "great mixer." Davis, Butler, Lippmann, and other regulars all came. The Bowerses dined with Yeats and heard him read his work. With Sybil and Pat and the Fred Kupers, Bowers spent hours in the studio of Peccirilli admiring his sculptures. At a dinner given by Morgenthau in January 1933, Bowers encountered Raymond Moley, a major Roosevelt adviser, the Farleys, and the mother of the president-elect.[34]

The years in New York were busy. The word kaleidoscopic best describes them. Almost incessant dining, if not wining, with people of importance or presumed importance consumed days and evenings. From their conversation came grist for editorials and perhaps even for writing books about figures of the Democratic past. For the onetime Hoosier it must have been a heady time. Although the Republicans were in control in Washington until March 1933, Bowers believed that sooner or later, in the ways of American politics, his party would obtain control—and then the editorial writer and historian could ascend to other duties, perhaps, or at the least to higher influence.

In retrospect one can ask whether the exposure to the crème de la crème was a good thing for Bowers. The answer, quite frankly, may well be that it was not. For here was a talented man, the erstwhile Hoosier, who had come to the nation's Babylon with a rich assortment of gifts, offering them to a political party that deserved the offering. But his talents were being mortgaged to an almost frothy outlook, obtained at lunches and dinners with luminaries from the worlds of not merely politics but of economics, the arts, and scholarship. Beveridge was a talented writer and worthy of cultivation. Some others, such as Butler—an administrator of quality but more politician than scholar—were not as worthy of cultivation. Bowers was drawn to what sparkled. But he had been attracted to the famous since his youth.

And yet, perhaps, fate had drawn him to the nation's metropolis, and there in many ways he flourished. The Great Depression and the troubled and indeed tragic 1930s lay beyond the prediction of even Bowers and friends who opposed the excesses of the Harding-Coolidge-Hoover years.

Bowers's career as a journalist, political obligations, and New York social schedule ended in 1933. Moley was the first to inform him that Roosevelt planned to name him ambassador to Spain, precisely the post he wanted. He preferred a foreign appointment to a position in Washington and believed service in Madrid would be within his means. The soon-to-be secretaries of commerce, state, and the post office—Roper, Hull, and Farley—as well as Senators Guffey and Wagner, had urged the president-elect to offer Bowers a diplomatic assignment. On 23 March Bowers heard Roosevelt on the telephone—the voice "clear, confident, buoyant"—convey the awaited message: "That Spanish matter is all right." After Senate confirmation, Bowers submitted his last newspaper column on 10 April.

The next morning the ex-journalist arrived in Washington. After calling on Hull, Bowers conferred with Undersecretary William Phillips and was helped by John C. Wiley, a former counselor at the embassy in Madrid. "Apparently we have but one matter of importance pending," the novice ambassador concluded—problems involving the monopoly granted by the Spanish government to the International Telephone and Telegraph Company (ITT). Bowers discussed with Commerce Secretary Roper "the evident wish" of some at State to postpone negotiations of a trade treaty with Spain in order to "use it as a club in the interest of the Tel. and Tel." Roper agreed this was "unthinkable." Hull explained his opposition to "the idea of making tariff readjustments in the interest of trade a mere club to be used in the interest of the telephone company." The new ambassador concurred.

At his second White House conference, Bowers mentioned the matter of using the tariff to protect ITT's Spanish interests, and Roosevelt "waved it aside with a vigorous shake of the head. 'Oh of course not. That is the old diplomatic method, outdated now.' " Reminding his guest that " 'I am a Jeffersonian Democrat,' " the president confessed his distress over the trend toward dictatorships: " 'Italy is gone, Japan is gone. Germany under Hitler is a menace.' " Roosevelt then stressed that the United States was eager to have Spain join the ranks of the democracies. As he was leaving, the new ambassador received a photograph inscribed "To Claude Bowers from his old friend, Franklin D. Roosevelt."[35]

During those spring days, Bowers interspersed his study of State Department documents with calls on Assistant Secretaries Wilbur Carr and Moley, Speaker of the House Henry T. Rainey, and Senators Royal Copeland of New York and McAdoo of California. He chatted with Senators Barkley, Byrd, and James Hamilton Lewis of Illinois and Attorney General Homer S. Cummins and saw Breckinridge Long, now ambassador to Italy, Ruth Bryan Owen, minister to Denmark, and Krock. He lunched with Senators Robinson, Harrison, and Frederick Van Nuys, Indiana's new solon, and Vice President Garner; dined with Wagner; and was entertained by the diplomat John Wiley and by Spain's ambassador. Bowers took notes for his next book, a volume on Jefferson's presidency. He visited his cousin Doll Bowers and saw Congressman Oliver throughout.[36]

Before they left for Spain, the Bowerses were the guests of Louis Wiley of the *Times* at a dinner in New York. There they met former ambassador and Mrs. Ogden H. Hammond, who had been in Madrid until 1929. The good-looking banker proved too conservative for the new envoy. More to Bowers's taste was a May party at Bridgeport, Connecticut, sponsored by friends who called themselves the "Irish Parliament." It turned out to be "a farewell to me," and the speeches continued far into the night. The real bon voyage occurred several days later. Pat Bowers, who stayed at Sarah Lawrence, Kuper, and others of the faithful went to the pier to wave good-bye when the ambassador and his lady sailed for Europe on the *George Washington*.[37]

# CHAPTER SEVEN

# A Hoosier's Spanish Adventures

Reporters, welcoming Americans, and representatives of the Spanish government greeted the couple as they stepped off the Sud-Express in Madrid. At fifty-four Bowers was embarking on a career he never expected, and he could not foresee that it would span two decades, under three presidents, in the Old World and the New. Bowers had been an observer of events, exercising influence through journalism, oratory, and historical writing. As a diplomat he became an actor and acquired a stage.

The most telling event that 22 May 1933 took place at half past four. With his tie askew and in shirt sleeves, the ambassador invited reporters to his Ritz Hotel suite, where he told them that the Spanish public as well as the government should be informed of American policies. His impromptu conference made a favorable impression. One newspaper claimed that Bowers's arrival began a new era in Spanish-American relations.

The ambassador took up residence in the palace of the Duke of Montellano, a three-story stone structure occupying an entire block near Madrid's center. It contained dozens of rooms and a chapel. The gate opened to a courtyard, and a dining room and ballroom were on the ground floor. Another room contained

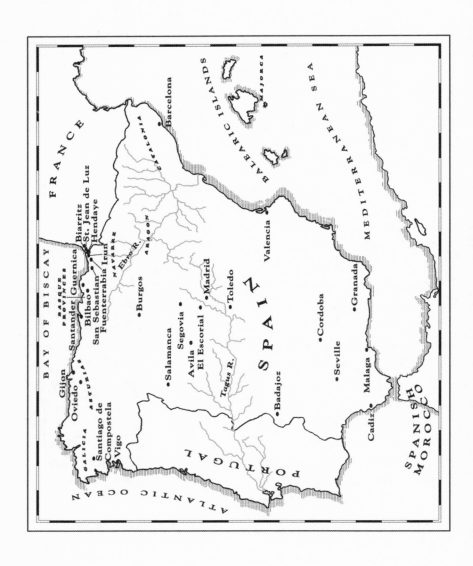

*The Palace of the Duke of Montellano, Madrid, Spain*
COURTESY OF MANUSCRIPTS DEPARTMENT, LILLY LIBRARY, INDIANA UNIVERSITY, BLOOMINGTON

paintings by Goya. Behind the embassy was a marble terrace that opened to grounds considered the finest in Madrid, with a large fountain, statuary, formal garden, tennis court, and buildings for staff, cars, and coaches, as well as polo ponies. Some seventy pine, horse chestnut, and plane trees provided shade, while high walls offered privacy. Previously Mexico's dictator Porfirio Díaz and Spain's Queen Victoria Eugenia were guests in the palace, and following World War II the present king of Spain, Juan Carlos de Borbón, would reside there while studying in Madrid.

Bowers was proud of the deal he struck to lease the palace. Knowing he must live within his salary of $17,500, he offered $1,000 a year in addition to the State Department's $9,000 subvention. Eager for protection in case of unrest, the duke agreed. The palace was attended by a butler, doorkeeper, footmen, cooks, maids, and gardeners.[1]

The capital's boulevards, parks, and monuments impressed the new *madrileño*. The Castellana boulevard ran along the Montellano gardens, allowing Bowers to stroll past the Gothic-gingerbread post office and the Cibeles fountain, through the Retiro Park, and on to the Prado Museum with its neoclassical entrance. The old section with narrow streets and the Plaza

Mayor, scene of bullfights and autos-da-fé, cast a spell on Bowers the historian.

Nor did events escape his observance. Although he did not understand Spanish, he enjoyed parliamentary debates at the Cortes. Prime Minister Manuel Azaña's "few gestures" and "fluent tone" impressed him, as did the "irony, sarcasm, humor, invective, mimicry," and wit of Indalecio Prieto, the moderate Socialist leader. Bowers was accompanied to bullfights by the reporter Rex Smith and admired the spectacle of the corrida, "the grace, beauty and daring of the matadors" and the "breathtaking charge of the bull," which Bowers believed "would quicken the pulse of a statue." When Smith reported that the ambassador was moved by the spec-tacle, animal lovers at home protested. But he had criticized bull-fighting in the *New York Evening World* and vowed to return only when escorting visitors.

Bowers's interest in Spain inspired him to travel. In the south Cordoba, the Moorish capital, Cadiz, "a sparkling white city by the sea," and Seville with its "superb cathedral" were early destinations. To the north the medieval pilgrimage center of Santiago de Compostela, the Basque lands, and the Catalonian capital Barcelona all fascinated the ambassador. Nearer Madrid Philip II's mausoleum-palace at the Escorial, the largest building in sixteenth-century Europe, and Toledo, perched high above the Tagus River just as painted by the city's adopted son, El Greco, became favorite sites. But more than geography attracted the ambassador's eye. Workers in the fields reminded him of "harvest day at my grandfa-ther's forty-five years ago," and he remarked on the "character and intelligence" of an old farmer bronzed by the sun, an illiterate wait-ress in an Andalusian café, and laboring peasant women.

José (Pepe) Torres Rueda took him on his rounds and drove the family in the ambassadorial Packard. Pepe knew no English, and his boss never was able to speak Spanish, but they became friends. After half a year Bowers confessed, "I have been to France, Italy and England annually now for seven years and none approach Spain." Travel gave him a feel for local conditions. After each trip he ridiculed stories of atrocities, police brutality, and strikes, and he took pleasure in noting that his predecessors seldom left Madrid.[2]

Bowers found the diplomatic corps charming. All the ambassadors were interesting, he wrote, and two or three he considered fascinating. He "got along swimmingly" with the papal nuncio, Monsignor Federico Tedeschini, "a gracious, handsome man" who had read *The Irish Orators*. The dean of the corps was Count Johannes von Welczeck, whose distaste for the Nazi regime impressed him. The transplanted Hoosier found French ambassador Jean Herbette "fascinating" on first encounter, but his opposition to the Republic led to disapproval. Bowers's best friend was Sir George Grahame, "the most charming of all my colleagues," whose "views on the Spanish situation" were in agreement with his. The Englishman was politically adroit and helpful to Bowers. In his will Grahame would leave the American some choice silver.

The United States ambassador detested protocol and told Roosevelt he did not wish to hold dinners for promotional purposes. Nevertheless he was forced to host dinners as well as cocktail parties and luncheons. And with Sybil he attended innumerable functions. Soon he was complaining that protocol was a "hard master." A raconteur, Bowers enjoyed relating his difficulties. Unaware that protocol forbade guests to sit until the ambassador was seated, he once wondered why the women remained standing, only to discover that they were waiting for him to take his place. Bowers was forced to learn how an ambassador should accompany a lady to another room: "The woman would stand back for me to pass first; I stood back for her; she stood back for me; at length in disgust I would bolt through."[3]

The envoy's taste was not changed by aristocratic entertainment. He became tired of French cooking and criticized diplomats' drinking habits. As in Terre Haute he sometimes poured out his drink—but in Madrid potted palms, not cuspidors, received his offerings. He considered social functions tiresome and complained to his wife, "The idle meaningless chatter of this society is most disorganizing to my mentality." Yet Bowers had to reciprocate. One Christmas two balls were offered at the embassy, with two hundred guests from twenty nations dancing and consuming vast quantities of food and drink, including lobster, ham, chicken, champagne, whiskey, and sherry. Bowers was disappointed that most Americans were businessmen and Republicans and was chagrined that they were against democracy. At the British embassy church he criticized "the extreme unction" with which Americans sang "God Save the King."[4]

Bowers enjoyed receiving visitors with his wife and watching her escort guests. Sybil found the round of diplomatic obligations tiring and stressful, so she was relieved that others handled entertainment arrangements. On the day of a function, "I had nothing to do but inspect," she noted. Sybil received the Order of the Republic, a decoration that pleased her husband. Often Pat served as hostess, and her father remarked that she conducted herself like a veteran.

Friends were made outside the diplomatic circle. John Dos Passos and Ernest Hemingway occupied a special place in the envoy's affections. A "tall, slightly bald, eager-eyed, young man of thirty-five," Dos Passos proved a conversationalist, and Hemingway was "a charming, unaffected fellow, boiling over with boyish exuberance." The ambassador was impressed by Hemingway's confession that he wrote The Sun Also Rises "in three weeks in hotels in Spain," adding modestly "as anyone can tell." Both authors joined Bowers for lunch and worked on his Spanish. Among his friends were several journalists—Jay Allen of the Chicago Tribune and Smith of the Associated Press. United Press reporter Lester Ziffren became a confidant and later an embassy employee under Bowers in Chile. Nobel Prize poet Juan Ramón Jiménez discussed Theodore Dreiser with the ambassador, and Luis Quintanilla painted Bowers's portrait.

An early guest at the Montellano Palace was Franklin D. Roosevelt, Jr., who arrived unannounced in a cheap summer suit. A visit to the Prado and a drive to the Escorial preceded a meal of cold soup containing baby octopus in an inklike broth. A matador dedicated the bull to Roosevelt, and President Niceto Alcalá Zamora received him. The ambassador escorted Alma Gluck

*Ambassador Claude Bowers, with his wife Sybil and daughter Patricia, receiving guests at the embassy, Madrid, Spain*
COURTESY OF MANUSCRIPTS DEPARTMENT, LILLY LIBRARY, INDIANA UNIVERSITY, BLOOMINGTON

Clayburgh, the diva, to Segovia to see its Roman aqueduct and imposing medieval castle, and he took Arthur Krock to Toledo to see Bowers's favorite painting, El Greco's *Burial of Count Orgaz*. A host of politicos arrived. The family accompanied Sen. and Mrs. William G. McAdoo to northern Spain and went with Jimmy Walker to Toledo, where following drinks the former mayor used a napkin to pretend to be a bullfighter.

The most amusing visitors were William Randolph Hearst and his companion Marion Davies. On hearing of the arrival of the motion picture goddess, Bowers acted like a puppy: "They say Marion Davies is along. Lord! Lord!" Seated next to the actress he observed her serve her dog under the table and felt the animal wagging its tail against his leg. He hoped it was the actress.[5]

All the while Bowers marveled at his circumstances. "At nine the butler comes in, draws the curtains, opens the shutters, and brings in my breakfast. At two, lunch. At six, tea. At nine thirty, dinner." Mornings were devoted to business, and he worked on his writing after lunch. His correspondents included J. Edith

Monahan, a Hoosier editor at Macmillan; his friends Frank Brubeck, Levy Levenberg, and Myla Jo Closser; Meredith Nicholson; and a "bright young fellow" at the *Fort Wayne Journal-Gazette*. Dreiser informed "Don Claudio Boweroso" that "a letter from you is like a half-dozen of the best pages of Tacitus." Evenings found him at home in the company of his wife and daughter, reading histories, plays, and novels by Salvador de Madariaga, Jacinto Benavente, Vicente Blasco Ibáñez, Anatole France, Maxim Gorky, and James Joyce. Before retiring he typed his diary on the Underwood typewriter he had used since his days in Indiana.

In Madrid Sybil adjusted better to changes in everyday life than her spouse, although both took advantage of the cultural offerings of the capital. She noticed the contrast between the careful, expensive grooming of the diplomats and the dress of her husband. "Claude is extremely stubborn about clothes." She studied Spanish and soon got along well, even conversing with the prime minister. Expecting to remain in Madrid only a few years, Bowers never studied the language. After two decades in Spain and Chile, he managed to communicate only in broken Spanish with his chauffeur and to scan newspapers. Both Bowerses attended plays at the Teatro Español by Golden Age dramatists such as Calderón de la Barca, contemporary theater pieces, *zarzuelas* (Spain's popular musicals), and dance programs, and they saw American films. Following dinners at restaurants around the Plaza Mayor, especially at Hemingway's hangout, the Casa Botín, they visited nightclubs.[6]

Pat relished her status as the ambassador's daughter, making friends and taking part in a swirl of activities. Able to speak French, she became fluent in Spanish. In the autumn of 1933 she returned to Sarah Lawrence, graduating the next spring. Back in Madrid she enjoyed various entertainments—tea dances and balls, tennis at the Montellano Palace, and golf at two country clubs. Her enchantment with life in Spain gave pleasure to her parents. "She is, I think, by odds, the most popular girl in the diplomatic circle," her father bragged.

Sybil's health became a concern for her husband, since during the years in Spain it deteriorated markedly. An initial problem was diagnosed in 1935 as a severe abscess of the liver. Attention by physicians and six months at a clinic in Santander brought her recovery, but she was never again in good health. Nervous tension caused by his wife's illness forced Bowers to consult a doctor for the first time in thirty years.

Summer stays on the Bay of Biscay were a highlight. The Madrid court fled the capital in July and August for the north, just as European society flocked to Biarritz and St. Jean de Luz in nearby France. In 1934 parents and daughter spent three weeks in San Sebastian, where their balcony overlooked the beach. The Prince of Wales was vacationing in Biarritz, and Bowers noted that foreign residents complained that the prince's casual attire "lowers the tone" of the resort. He was seen at a nightclub "with Mrs. Simpson, his latest mistress, looking much dissipated and unhappy."[7] The next summer the ambassador returned to San Sebastian.

The embassy chancery was in the Montellano Palace, and Bowers's upstairs office was close to his living quarters. In the morning he met with the staff and handled reports, dispatches, and diplomatic appointments. The chancery closed for lunch at two. Officials at the foreign ministry were not available in afternoons, so the staff pursued their own activities. For Bowers this meant writing. Around six o'clock came social obligations—dances, cocktails, receptions—and dinners began after nine.

Bowers's appearance and conduct belied his station. " 'A little man who looked as though he had been thrown into his clothes from a long way off,' " he sometimes wore his hat at work, forcing Sybil to intervene. Never exercising, save to walk their Scotch terrier Lucky Lass, Bowers had developed a noticeable potbelly. Limited to three cigars a day, he chewed them to make them last. He had a reputation as a storyteller and enjoyed regaling his fellow workers with anecdotes.[8]

Lacking administrative experience, Bowers was an inefficient boss. Correspondence disappeared, often reappearing in his coat pockets, and he was unable to delegate responsibilities. He tried to oversee all aspects of embassy work—public relations, commercial negotiations, consular affairs, and communications with Washington. He often bragged, "I have stayed on the job and personally determined on everything done at this embassy," and he observed, "If one does the work in this spirit, it is not a loafer's job."

Long before he became an ambassador, Bowers's liberal views had drawn his interest to Spain. As an editor he had praised republican leader Emilio Castelar in 1901 as "a child of American democracy" and noted that social tensions were increasing because the Spanish people "have never been given the slightest consideration by the Government." Alfonso XIII in the 1920s had supported the dictatorship of Gen. Miguel Primo de Rivera, whom Bowers attacked for his "suppression of freedom of speech and the liberty of the press." He predicted that "sooner or later Rivera will go." In 1930 the dictator did go, and Bowers observed the growing hostility toward the monarchy. The king left Spain following the victory of republicans in municipal elections.

The Second Spanish Republic was established in 1931, with Azaña the head of a coalition of his Republican Action party, the Socialists, and other groups. A writer and reformer, the prime minister championed "a profound transformation of society" to avoid social revolution. The coalition enacted an agrarian reform law, social welfare legislation, and separation of church and state. But cracks appeared in the alliance of moderates and leftists. The Socialists demanded more changes, while the Anarchists encouraged land takeovers. In January 1933 the National Workers' Confederation attempted an uprising.[9]

Voters in 1933 dismissed Azaña's government and brought in the center-right parties. Bowers maintained that the Azaña government was not given enough time to consolidate its position and attributed its defeat to Catholic women who were granted the vote. The Confederation of Autonomous Rights (CEDA)[10] was the big winner. This group of right-wing parties led by José María Gil Robles, together with their monarchist allies and the large landowners' Agrarian party, made up the largest block in the

Cortes. The Radical party and other centrists made up the next largest. Basque and Catalonian parties also elected deputies. The Socialist delegation was halved, and members from Azaña's Republican Action occupied eight seats. The lone Communist, Bowers believed, looked like a stockbroker.

Center-right governments headed by Radical prime ministers in 1934–35 reversed the Azaña reforms, causing opponents to label these years the Black Biennium. For Bowers this period was like "the struggle of the first twelve years of the United States when the Hamiltonians were fighting democracy and trying to establish a plutocratic republic." Conservatives' attacks on separation of church and state, he asserted, made a mockery of the Republic, and the government's opposition to social legislation convinced him that reactionaries were in charge.

The Socialists turned to revolution in 1934. In Madrid their call for a general strike caused problems. The ambassador reported there was no bread, but the chickens in the embassy basement guaranteed "enough eggs to last a siege." The next day in Barcelona, a Catalonian state within a federal republic was declared, but it was forced to surrender the following day. In Asturias a miners' strike backed by Socialists, Communists, and Anarchists was quashed by the army. Aware of the fighting and bloodshed, Bowers criticized the military excesses—rape and murder—used to suppress the workers.

Bowers believed that the 1934 revolution undermined the democratic process and handed the government to right-wing republicans "who are not likely to make any very drastic reforms in the educational, or social system of Spain. Thus the plan of the original republicans who established the republic is defeated." Thirty thousand political prisoners awaited trial, and many Socialist leaders were arrested. Azaña, although an opponent of the rising, was detained for months.[11]

Divisiveness led to dissolution of the Cortes. Noting the bitterness, Bowers feared the ensuing campaign: "All in all, it looks bad for Spain, and if she pulls out without much violence and possibly civil war, it will be a marvel." The election in February 1936 was

Spain's last for four decades. Monarchists and other rightists cooperated with CEDA. The Socialists, the Republican Esquerra in Catalonia, and Azaña's new group, the Republican Left, formed the Popular Front. The Communist International had called for such alliances to oppose fascism, so the small Spanish party was a partner.[12]

Bowers concluded that a rightist triumph would be tantamount to disaster. He surmised that the "shifty" Gil Robles sought "a restoration of 16th-Century ideas." But the Marxists also were targets of the ambassador's scorn: left-wing Socialist Francisco Largo Caballero was "an extremist" and the Communists "stupid and brutal." Bowers considered Azaña "the ablest man in Spain" and celebrated his victory. "My man Azaña is back with a great bang." For the next three years Azaña headed the Popular Front, and his government acted quickly, granting political prisoners amnesty. Bowers praised Azaña's promises of reforms, but he feared that the revolutionary demands of the leftist Socialists were only helping the fascists.

Following the election tensions rose to a crescendo. The rightists were determined to bring down the government, and the leftists were divided. Peasant invasions, a split between reformist and revolutionary Socialists, battles between Anarchists and Marxists, attacks on orators, assassination attempts against Socialist leaders, and the arrest of José Antonio Primo de Rivera, jefe of the Falangists, weakened the Popular Front. Bowers informed Washington of rumors that "the army is planning a coup d'etat in order to put an end to public disorder and to save Spain from what they appear to believe is a real danger of communism."[13] The assassination of monarchist leader José Calvo Sotelo in July 1936 would increase tensions and lead to civil war.

While observing Spanish political developments, Bowers was encountering problems with the careerists at the State Department, who hindered his effectiveness. Some Washington professionals assumed they should direct diplomacy without regard for political appointees, and they proved hostile to Bowers. Two of his chief adversaries were William Phillips and Jay Pierrepont

Moffat, who shared an aristocratic background and a conservative political outlook. Phillips was a Boston Back Bay Brahmin, while Moffat was named for his ancestor John Jay, the first chief justice. Phillips had opposed Bowers's appointment. Assistant Secretary of State Raymond Moley reported that the transplanted Hoosier's "charming lack of tonishness gave Phillips an attack of horrid misgivings." When as ambassador-designate he met Undersecretary Phillips, Bowers found him "a bit stiff, very polite, and very cold," noting that he "has the precious Harvard manner and seems supercilious. Not easy to take from a Republican." As head of the Division of Western European Affairs, Moffat was quick to criticize Bowers, accusing him in 1933 of "putting the cart before the horse" in negotiations with the Spanish government. The hostility of Phillips and Moffat continued through Bowers's years in Spain.

The Democratic appointee also had important friends. His association with Secretary of State Cordell Hull dated to 1922, and Bowers did not hesitate to write the Tennessean. Hull, however, was a political appointee, and Phillips became his trusted adviser. Another Democrat, Judge R. Walton Moore, became assistant secretary of state and proved a loyal defender, and Bowers enjoyed working with Wilbur Carr. A careerist concerned with personnel, Carr gave attention to Bowers's staff recommendations. The ambassador's most important ally was the president, whom he often wrote. Roosevelt's replies were prepared at the State Department, often by Assistant Secretary Sumner Welles, but the president always included personal observations. Roosevelt concerned himself with a number of specific Spanish-American issues—automobile and wine quotas, tobacco exports, loans, joint declarations in support of democracy, and treatment of American firms.

Bowers's prejudices against career diplomats seemed justified when he observed the political views and social behavior of American diplomats in Madrid. The New Deal Democrat was shocked that "practically all the career men are rabid Republicans of the big money variety." He had only disdain for the "procession of multi-millionaire predecessors here," especially his predecessor Irwin Laughlin, a wealthy conservative and supporter of Alfonso

XIII. A man of influence in GOP circles, Laughlin socialized with the Moffats. Tired of hearing employees attack the New Deal before foreigners, Bowers claimed to have stopped this by threatening to remove anyone indulging in such criticism. Moore supported him: "The service should be divested of such inexcusable features as you described." Bowers complained that the embassy was "saturated with monarchist sentiment" and staffed with millionaire secretaries. The Jeffersonian biographer remembered his Virginia hero had warned that no one should "stay in Europe without periods in the States lest they lose contact with the people in America and sympathy with American institutions."[14]

On one matter he enjoyed the support of career men. In 1933 cuts in department appropriations meant a decrease in salaries. "The money question is coming to be a most serious one," Bowers noted. His commercial attaché had to give up his home telephone. New Deal appointees in Berlin, Geneva, and Copenhagen complained, and some in the State Department urged Bowers to appeal to political friends. He wrote dozens of letters, including pleas to the president, Commerce Secretary Daniel C. Roper, Sen. Robert F. Wagner, and Rep. Frank Oliver. "Your letters are always exceedingly welcome," Roosevelt replied, predicting approval of increased funding. Legislation granting relief would have been enacted without Bowers's help, but nevertheless careerists joined in praising his efforts. "I know your letter alone," Carr wrote, "when brought to the attention of the people in Congress, made many conversions." The political envoy did not exaggerate when he lightheartedly referred to himself as "a hero of the service," a unique moment in his twenty years as a diplomat.[15]

Despite differences Bowers was able to work with his staff, although initially he encountered problems with Counselor Hallett Johnson. A friend of Phillips, Johnson had served in Madrid in the 1920s until conflicts brought his transfer. Bowers complained that Johnson was "prone to try to create the impression outside the chancellery that he really is the real ambassador." The envoy confronted his counselor and believed he had "him toned down quite a bit." A modus vivendi was reached in mid-

1934, and Johnson impressed his boss thereafter as loyal and cooperative.

Bowers's wealthy, conservative first secretary, Walter Schoellkopf, proved a dedicated friend. The ambassador considered this modest man a hard worker and appreciated his judgment. Carr found this gratifying, since Schoellkopf never stood high in the estimation of his colleagues. He and his wife Anna became favorites of the Bowerses. Pat was a guest in their London house for the coronation of Edward VIII, and their son Horton later served as Bowers's secretary.

Military attaché Col. Stephen Fuqua was another staff member the ambassador valued. Overlooking the colonel's conservative views, he appreciated Fuqua's rapport with Spanish officers. Fuqua accompanied the envoy on visits to military ceremonies, told him of the growing importance of the "brilliant" Gen. Francisco Franco, and carefully tracked the military actions during the Asturian miners' revolt in 1934.

Bowers's favorite was his secretary, Biddle Garrison. The red-headed six-footer was a Princeton alumnus who spoke Spanish and French and presented a letter of introduction from Senator Wagner. Garrison accepted a job without salary, until the ambassador was able to place him on the payroll.[16] He ran errands, worked as a translator, did office work, and served as a jack-of-all-trades.

Spanish politics was the subject of most of the ambassador's dispatches. He enjoyed debates at the Cortes, speaking with officials, and absorbing talk at gatherings. Representatives of American corporations, particularly the International Telephone and Telegraph Company (ITT), were familiar with government discussions and reported them. British Ambassador Grahame provided intelligence, and reporters shared their findings. During the Asturian revolt Bowers credited the reliability of his accounts to his relations with correspondents, and he was proud that his dispatches carefully covered political alignments. "During the last four years," he reported in December 1935, "there have been sixteen Cabinets. There have been twelve crises since June, 1933."

Bowers's dispatches disagreed with the views of most diplomats. Ambassador Laughlin had warned of Bolshevist influences, and his overestimation of Communist strength helped prejudice the State Department against the Republic. Bowers presented a different view, asserting that there was not the slightest possibility of either a communist or fascist dictatorship. Other embassy officers continued to exaggerate the party's strength. Johnson stressed the possibility of " 'great danger for the country from Communist agitation.' " From Moscow Ambassador William C. Bullitt reported that the Soviet Union "thinks that, in the course of three months, Spain may become communistic." ITT officials also sent alarmist reports. By 1936 many at the State Department were convinced that Azaña's government was susceptible to Communist domination and were suspicious of Bowers's denials.[17]

The ambassador's dispatches in 1936 proved misleading. Admiration for Azaña led him to underestimate the tensions that proved deleterious to the Republic. He was aware of "panic stricken Rightists"—the cousin of the Duke of Montellano brought more Goya paintings to the embassy for safekeeping—and Bowers closely followed the disturbing events. But he downplayed their importance. "Amazing rumors afloat," he reported in March, including one that he had been stopped by strikers, threatened with death, and forced to pay for his release. "The stories of revolutions, etc., in the American press are a disgrace to journalism—mostly lies," he asserted three months before the outbreak of civil war. "There are some communists, numerically unimportant, and some fascists, equally unimportant," he noted, "and they shoot at one another occasionally but no one minds."

Bowers ignored what one historian has called an "atmosphere of violence" that undermined the chances of a democratic government, and he refused to believe differently. Twenty years later he would continue to dismiss the disorders, asserting that there was more crime committed in two weeks in New York City than in the last two years of the parliamentary Republic in Spain.[18]

In the spring of 1936 Bowers reported rumors of an army revolt, but he gave them little credence. Shortly before the military rising, he informed Hull, "The objective of the 'Fascists' is evidently to weaken the Government's authority to the point where a military coup d'etat may be successfully engineered," admitting that "the purely political aspects of the situation appear to be becoming more serious." Two days before the coup, he reported the murder of Calvo Sotelo, noting this "may have far reaching results."[19]

The ambassador was in sympathy with the aims of the Spanish Republic, which in his assessment were made by Jeffersons and Washingtons. When Bowers presented his credentials in 1933, the government spared no efforts to make the ceremony a celebration of American support. He was escorted to the former Royal Palace by the presidential guard. Following his brief speech, Bowers spoke with President Alcalá Zamora, and the envoy found the executive "a decent and honest man" with an "exceptional executive ability."

A novice political appointee, Bowers was determined to be successful. His first assignment was a request from Roosevelt to determine if Spain would support an appeal from Washington calling on democratic nations to oppose dictatorship. Foreign Minister Fernando de los Ríos enthusiastically backed this initiative. Elated by his reception at the foreign ministry and in the press, Bowers bragged to Roosevelt that he had made "an unusual appeal to the Spanish." The president congratulated him for "the splendid relations you have established with Rios."[20]

Bowers believed in personal diplomacy. An opponent of the Spanish-American War, he searched embassy records concerning the 1898 conflict. His conclusion? The diplomatic correspondence "bears painful proof that we forced the war. The sinking of the *Maine* certainly was not the work of the Spaniards." Aware of criticism of an inscription at Annapolis blaming a Spanish mine for sinking the battleship, the envoy wrote Roosevelt asking that the wording be corrected. The president agreed and discovered that academy officials had changed the inscription. He urged Bowers to let this be known.

A crisis in the summer of 1933 allowed Bowers to throw himself into his duties. An intoxicated American on Majorca hit a Guardia Civil, sending the policeman to the hospital. All five in the American party went to jail, and the possibility of six years behind bars inflamed the American press. Their trial became a cause célèbre. On Majorca a mob protested the assault, cables criss-crossed the Atlantic, and Bowers visited the foreign ministry, where he saw Azaña. The five prisoners were released on bail, but for nine months the affair upset relations. In September Hull wrote the ambassador that pressure for prompt settlement was coming from senators and representatives. In February 1934 Spain's Supreme Court pardoned the Americans.

The envoy was pleased to see the Majorcan affair resolved. Azaña credited "the tact, judgment and understanding of the Spanish point of view by Ambassador Bowers" for the amicable ending, and Washington concurred. Roosevelt assured Bowers, "From all sides I hear the excellent work you are doing," and Hull added his appreciation for "the energetic manner in which you have pushed this case to a conclusion."[21]

On his arrival in Spain one controversial matter greeted Bowers, the monopoly enjoyed by the National Telephone Company of Spain (CTNE), a subsidiary of ITT. The company's association with the monarchy led to republican demands that the contract be canceled without indemnification. Roosevelt defended the agreement and told Bowers before his departure, "The matter of the Tel and Tel is simple. The company entered into the contract in good faith and put its money into the building of a great telephone system. We expect of course that the terms . . . will be observed." Hull insisted that the contract went to "the very heart of international confidence." Bowers realized that the telephone company's rights were dear to many at the State Department. Professionals such as Phillips and Moffat received reports from the firm's Madrid director, Capt. Logan Rock, and Col. Sosthenes Behn, ITT's founder.

As a Progressive Bowers had opposed the influence of large corporations, but like other New Dealers he recognized the positive role of private firms. While he lamented businessmen's conserva-tive views, he defended their investments. He hurried to the for-eign office in November 1933 to protest a proposal limiting CTNE's rights. A December parliamentary debate over the tele-phone concession turned into a shouting match between monar-chist and Socialist deputies, causing Moffat to surmise that "the sword of Damocles hangs over the telephone contract." The Popular Front victory in 1936 brought new problems for ITT, for the CTNE management had favored the right. "Of all corpora-tions," Bowers complained, the telephone company "has the least business mixing in Spanish politics." In May the government pub-lished a decree altering the ITT agreement, and Washington instructed Bowers to intervene. The Spanish foreign minister apol-ogized to Bowers and promised to rescind the measure. Bowers cabled Hull, "Anticipate no trouble on this score," and a relieved Behn thanked the ambassador. General Motors, Ford, National City Bank, Twentieth Century Fox, the Associated and United Presses, Firestone, and General Electric were other firms that did not hesitate to request his assistance.[22]

A chief concern of Bowers was improving Spanish-American trade. Hull and Roosevelt emphasized trade relations and sought lowered tariffs, and Spanish officials, too, were intent on fostering commerce. The stumbling block was the large trade deficit with the United States. Because of the depression, Spain's exports fell by 70 percent in the early 1930s. Washington's restrictions on the import of Spanish wines and taxes on cork brought reciprocal measures, particularly discriminatory quotas on American automobiles.

Bowers was convinced that trade would benefit both nations. He regarded strengthening the Republic a goal of United States policy, but the department was not sympathetic. The Madrid government's threats to expropriate ITT's subsidiary made Washington reluctant to consider major concessions. The ambassador counted on the president, the secretary of state, Commerce Secretary Roper, and Agriculture Secretary Henry A. Wallace to promote increased trade. Roper liked Bowers's suggestions on tariff concessions and showed them to the president.[23]

Some of Bowers's pleas met with success. He stressed that the United States imported only 365,000 gallons of wine from the Republic, while the quota granted more than a million to Mussolini's Italy. Moffat disagreed, arguing that the Spanish wine quota was a large one. Bowers appealed to the president, urging him to show "a generous disposition to consider the trade desires of Spain." Roosevelt consulted Phillips, who noted the department had offered Spain increased wine imports if Madrid would purchase an additional $150,000 of American tobacco. In his reply Roosevelt joked, "Can't you encourage the Spanish smokers and tobacco chewers!" Spain's refusal to buy additional tobacco incensed Moffat, who accused Bowers of downplaying the importance of concessions. Over the State Department's opposition, the president in 1934 instructed the Tariff Commission to increase the quota for Spanish wines. To encourage cooperation, Roosevelt persuaded the Export-Import Bank to grant a $675,000 loan to Spain.

Bowers helped resolve another irritant to Spanish-American relations, an embargo on Spanish grapes. Washington feared that Mediterranean fruit flies might be introduced with the grapes. The ambassador appealed to Wallace to rescind the restriction, and the Agriculture Department in 1934 approved the importation of Spanish grapes after observing import precautions. "Our generous treatment on wine and the removal of barriers against grapes," Bowers reported, "has completely changed the feeling in government circles here." The foreign minister noted the grape embargo had been an irritant for a decade.[24]

Passage of the Reciprocal Trade Agreement in 1934 led to Spanish-American trade negotiations that summer. Roosevelt and Hull wanted an accord. The secretary considered Spain a high-tariff country and welcomed Madrid's pledge to end discriminatory practices. In September both nations promised the other fair quotas, but Phillips observed that the announcement of trade discussions did not mean that they would be concluded. Events surrounding the start of negotiations presaged the difficulties that plagued the endeavor. On the day talks were announced, the Agriculture Department held up shipments of Spanish olives for sanitary reasons. As Bowers noted, this publicized blunder was "unbearably stupid."

The success of negotiations in Washington depended on mutual concessions. Spain's trade deficit with the United States grew from $17 million in 1933 to $19 million the following year, strengthening the Republic's resolve to demand favors. Washington agreed that Spain needed to reverse this imbalance, but the State Department found it difficult to agree to specific concessions. Political pressures required Spanish concessions to convince the American public that a sufficient quid pro quo had been reached. Washington called for increased imports and asked Spain to purchase additional United States tobacco for the government's cigarette monopoly. Madrid claimed this was impossible, but agreed in 1935 to buy tobacco from Algiers.[25]

The automobile industry was the most vocal advocate of increased Spanish imports. Detroit supplied half of Spain's vehicles in the late 1920s. The Spanish Republic was worried about its trade deficit in 1933 and limited United States automobile imports to 23 percent. To avoid "the fire of criticism from our opponents here," Hull suggested the United States furnish 40 percent of Spain's new cars, although Bowers argued this was impossible. Madrid in 1935 agreed to increase the automobile quota from 472 to 2,000, and in turn Washington permitted the import of more grapes and sardines.

Hull was hopeful in July 1935 that a trade agreement would be reached. Phillips urged the president to permit larger reductions in duties on a variety of imports, including cork stoppers, onions, capers, olive oil, and garlic. The secretary of state informed Bowers that these duties would be lowered. A draft treaty was completed in October, and Hull reported to the ambassador that an agreement was at hand, as did the Spanish prime minister.

But the bilateral accord was never signed for a new obstacle appeared. Spain's trade deficit had created a foreign currency shortage. By 1936 Spanish firms owed American exporters $15 million, and American companies were waiting almost a year for payment. Azaña suggested that Washington extend a loan to the Republic, but several months earlier Spain had agreed to pay all outstanding debts due British and French merchants. Hull viewed these agreements as discriminatory and refused a loan.[26]

By early 1936 the State Department was convinced that there would be no accord. The foreign ministry reached the same conclusion and raised tariffs on a number of American goods. The start of the civil war in Spain that summer and the presidential campaign in the United States in the autumn ended the talks.

The State Department viewed the failed negotiations as proof of the Republic's hostility. Although Roosevelt, Roper, and Hull expressed appreciation for Bowers's assistance, professionals at the State Department regarded his pleas to the president and the secretary as amateurish attempts to determine policy. "As is the case with so many new Ambassadors," complained Moffat, "he seems to regard his role as primarily that of Ambassador of rather than to Spain, and gives all of the Spanish arguments without assuring us that he presses our case in Spain with anything like the same vigor." For Bowers the department was to blame: "It looks as though the old regime still runs things in Washington. I cannot believe that Hull is not imposed on."[27]

As the Spanish situation was worsening, there were startling changes in American politics. Bowers was not merely enchanted by his surroundings in Spain, but by the news from the now faraway United States. The accession of President Roosevelt and the enormous changes under the New Deal signaled a new era of hope, even as the newspapers recounted the awful decline in America's standard of living. One-third of the workers were unemployed, and the incomes of those who possessed incomes had declined by one-third. Bowers lauded the New Deal, arguing that Roosevelt's "struggle resembles that of Jackson's time"—the victor will be "Democracy or Plutocracy." Following "the twelve year debauch of the Grand Old Party," he asserted the president was revamping the business system to meet economic needs. When Roosevelt wrote that "Congress is doing a splendid piece of work," the ambassador concurred. His comments on Roosevelt bordered on adulation: "Roosevelt seems to be doing a magnificent job and if he succeeds

he will be the greatest President since Jefferson, for he will have
made the nation in conformity to the needs of humanity."

Bowers, an outspoken Progressive for decades, had advocated
government control of big business since the 1890s. But the New
Deal went beyond regulation, for the government assumed responsibility for the economy. The Tennessee Valley Authority, Social
Security, the Agricultural Adjustment Administration, and the
"Blue Eagle" were novel departures. The ambassador supported this
new role and criticized Progressives and conservatives who
opposed Roosevelt. Bowers cast scorn on Al Smith for attacking
the New Deal, accusing him of "going over to the Wall Street
crowd bag and baggage" and labeling him a "he-prostitute kept by
the Du Pont millions."[28]

The envoy continued working for his party. James A. Farley,
head of the Democratic National Committee, furnished information that Bowers translated into speeches. A Bowers-authored
address by Farley at the Kentucky Democratic Convention in 1935
impressed Barry Bingham, editor of the Louisville Courier-Journal,
who called it "one of the strongest political statements I have ever
had the pleasure of hearing." But Farley's detractors complained
that he believed he was an orator, when in fact he was delivering
speeches composed by others.[29]

A trip to the United States in June 1935 was an ordeal. Bowers
lamented, "My experience in New York and Washington was
dreadful. A lunch and dinner every one of the thirty days with
conferences with politicians in between—a squirrel in a revolv-
ing cage." In the capital he saw Senators Alben W. Barkley of
Kentucky and Sherman Minton and Frederick Van Nuys of
Indiana. A long talk with Farley found Bowers promising weekly
contributions for use in campaign speeches and literature. His
meeting with Hull centered on politics, not foreign relations, as
did his "long chat" with Secretary of Commerce Roper. In New
York twenty friends gathered for dinner, and Smith spoke. The
1928 nominee, "looking like a prosperous man of big business,
now, very neatly dressed," praised Bowers's Houston keynote "in
the most extravagant terms."

Two appointments with the president were the highlight of the trip. "God I'm glad you are back," Roosevelt declared. Bowers commented on the president's "soaring spirits" and an "exceedingly fit" countenance, only to have his secretary remark, "Yes and he does it without benefit of clergy." This reference to his irregular church attendance caused the president to smile "a bit sheepishly." Roosevelt told his guest, "The people have not been in control in this country since the Civil War. First the railroad ran things, and then the industrialists, and then the bankers took over the country. . . . Today the bankers have got the people by the throat." The recent Supreme Court decision overturning the National Recovery Act (NRA), the chief executive insisted, reflected Chamber of Commerce opposition to the legislation. "It's amazing," he ruminated, "how little these big moneyed men know of the country and the spirit of the people." Roosevelt talked "freely of the coming election, predicting a bitter battle," and noted, "We shall have hardly a metropolitan newspaper with us." Whom did he see as his opponent? Herbert Hoover, a prediction that the ambassador relished: "Let us pray that he be. What a joy ride!" Bowers noticed the president's hand shook when lighting a cigarette and asked Roper if this were new. The commerce secretary replied, "Yes, since the NRA decision."

Bowers returned to Spain "worn to a rag," but elated that Roosevelt's reelection was assured. At the president's request he prepared a brochure, "New Deal Objectives and Results." Although pleased to fulfill such requests, the envoy complained, "I hear too much from America regarding politics." A proposed campaign trip to the United States in 1936 caused consternation. Joseph F. Guffey urged Bowers to return, and Hull wrote that Roosevelt would like him home for "some very special and highly important work to be done here in Washington," tasks "no other person is quite so well equipped to do as yourself." Dreiser agreed and wrote "Claudio" Bowers in February 1936 that Roosevelt was "a dunce" if he did not make the ambassador return for the campaign. The secretary of state wired Bowers in June that the president hopes "you will be able to get back by the first week in

*The Villa Lore Artean in Fuenterrabia, Spain, where the Bowers family was vacationing when the civil war began in July 1936*

COURTESY OF MANUSCRIPTS DEPARTMENT, LILLY LIBRARY, INDIANA UNIVERSITY, BLOOMINGTON

August at the latest. He thinks that this is of really great importance."[30]

In July 1936 Bowers was ready for a vacation near San
Sebastian before returning to the United States. Sybil's illness,
trade negotiations, and Spain's charged political atmosphere had
taken their toll. In a rare visit to a physician, he had been ordered
to rest. In Fuenterrabia he rented the Villa Lore Artean that
looked toward St. Jean and Biarritz across the bay in France. Some
hours were spent on speeches for Roosevelt's reelection, but political concerns were remote. The family visited the charming
medieval section of Fuenterrabia, inspected the castle of Charles V
that dominated the town, and took motor trips along the Basque
coast. On his second day the contented ambassador admired the
view and concluded, "I have never seen a more peaceful scene."[31]
Nine days later the outbreak of the most violent war in Spanish
history would shatter this peace.

# CHAPTER EIGHT

# The Spanish Civil War

The revolt against the Republic began on 17 July 1936 and turned into a war lasting three years. Aided by Adolf Hitler and Benito Mussolini, the insurgents defeated the government while the world democracies looked on. More than half a million people perished, and the conflict determined the future of the nation for four decades. Bowers did not exaggerate when he referred to these years as Spain's Tragic Era.

In Fuenterrabia news of trouble with the Foreign Legion in Spanish Morocco reached the ambassador the next day, together with a call from the embassy warning of a coup. Gen. Francisco Franco's role as "the instigator of the rebellion" soon was public knowledge, and Bowers noted that rumors of risings in Seville, Cadiz, and Barcelona and the resignation of the prime minister were bad omens. "It all looks like the long delayed showdown to determine whether the fascists and monarchists or the republicans and democrats are to run Spain." His support for the Republic was immediate. "My heart goes out to these fine but poor people who are defending themselves against fascist repression and tyranny." For him President Manuel Azaña was "one of the greatest men in Europe. He is the Spanish Jefferson."[1]

The unrest in Spain forced Bowers to cancel his return to the United States for Franklin D. Roosevelt's second presidential campaign. He had expected to speak from Boston to San Francisco, and columnists joked that the Democrats considered the civil war a Republican plot to keep Bowers out of the country. President Roosevelt assured reporters that his envoy would remain abroad "as long as the present disturbed conditions continued."

An astonished ambassador sighted the Coast Guard cutter *Cayuga* in front of his villa on 25 July. Its officers brought rumors of his whereabouts—one asserted he was in hiding from the "reds" in a castle. Bowers recommended that the battleship *Oklahoma* remain at Bilbao and the *Cayuga* near San Sebastian. "Our whole concentration," he insisted, "must be on protecting American lives."

Two days later the *Cayuga* brought "panic stricken men" from San Sebastian: Hallett Johnson, Walter Schoellkopf, and Biddle Garrison. With them was Edward J. Flynn, Bowers's vacationing friend from the Bronx. Johnson described the situation as "deadly peril" and implored Bowers to leave Spain, an idea Bowers considered cowardly. Schoellkopf reported that Secretary of State Cordell Hull had called him, emphasizing that the ambassador should not endanger himself and his family. Flynn joined the chorus. That evening the Bowerses crossed the border into France and stayed in Hendaye.[2]

The envoy's attention focused on evacuating Americans. Assistant Secretary Wilbur Carr asked him to board the *Cayuga* to visit ports along the north coast, and for the next nine days he lived aboard this "floating embassy." After stopping in Fuenterrabia the cutter sailed to Bilbao, where Bowers found that executives of the Firestone Rubber Company were worried that the government might take their factory. He met with the governor, who promised not to interfere with the plant or its secret formulas. The *Cayuga* stopped at six other ports, and seventeen American and Cuban refugees came aboard. Bowers was the only ambassador personally to participate in evacuating his citizens. Elsewhere his assistants helped hundreds of Americans leave Spain.

After the *Cayuga* rescue an article appeared in the *Army and Navy Journal* claiming that Bowers had attempted to assume command of the ship. Acting Secretary William Phillips denied these allegations. "A putrid piece of low politics inspired by the assumption that I am to enter the campaign for Roosevelt" was the envoy's explanation. Though his relations with naval officers were "most cordial," he later complained the navy did not keep ships nearby for emergencies as did the British and French.[3]

Bowers located his embassy in France, informing Hull that travel to Madrid was impossible. The region around Hendaye and nearby St. Jean de Luz and Biarritz became the diplomatic capital of Spain. Most observers predicted a short conflict and expected to return soon to Madrid, but by October a despairing Bowers remarked, "The Lord only knows how long I shall be here." When hotels in Hendaye closed for the season, Bowers rented a house in St. Jean and established the chancery in the Miramar Hotel. Southwestern France proved a logical site, as Hendaye became a doorway to the peninsula. "My going to Madrid," he noted, "would confine my picture of the situation to Madrid alone, since I would have not such means of communications there as here."

At this time the ambassador found himself in difficulties at home. "We all feel that Bowers himself ought to be in Madrid," opined Phillips, who reported that Hull concurred. But chaos in the capital forced Phillips to admit in late August, "We are indeed fortunate that Mr. and Mrs. Bowers were not in Madrid." Enemies of the New Deal attacked the Democratic envoy. Republican congresswoman Edith Rogers of Massachusetts asked Phillips why Bowers was not in Madrid; the undersecretary claimed she was trying to discredit the political ambassador. Bowers was lambasted for leaving Spain and "making no attempt to return to his post" by the *Chicago Tribune*, owned by Robert R. "Bert" McCormick, a Roosevelt rival since Groton. New Deal supporters came to the envoy's defense. The *Louisville Courier-Journal* asserted, "The reason he did not return to Madrid hardly needs an explanation." The ambassador insisted that the hostile editorials were motivated by "partisan spite." "I fully share your indignation," wrote Acting

Secretary of State R. Walton Moore, and Roosevelt's letter particularly delighted Bowers: "We are kindred spirits!" "Some day we will have a chance to sit down together and plan our own form of revenge on Bert McCormick and the like."[4]

Meanwhile the embassy in Madrid became a refuge for 170 United States nationals. Mattresses and food came from the Ritz Hotel, and cows were brought to the stables. The embassy did not admit Spaniards seeking—and willing to pay for—protection. Some legations granted asylum to wealthy Spaniards, providing in Bowers's opinion hiding places for enemies of the Republic. When the rebels attacked the capital in November, the government moved to Valencia, and Washington closed the mission in Madrid. The Goya paintings remained unharmed, but a shell destroyed furniture in the ambassador's bedroom.[5]

During the long conflict that followed, most of the Spanish army supported the coup, as did conservatives and the Roman Catholic Church. For the generals their cause was a "Crusade," and they called themselves Nationalists, while their opponents branded them rebels, insurgents, and fascists. Much of the navy and air force remained loyal, and the government received support in the cities. Backers of the Popular Front were labeled Republicans or loyalists—their opponents called them Communists or reds.[6]

At the start of the war, the insurgents won impressive victories. In the north they controlled Galicia, Navarre, and most of Aragon, as well as Avila, Segovia, Salamanca, and Burgos, where Bowers noted monarchist sentiment was strong. Majorca, Oviedo, and Seville also were taken. But two-thirds of the country remained under Republican control, including Madrid, the Mediterranean coast from Barcelona to Malaga, and the Basque Provinces. Transported from Spanish Morocco with German and Italian help, Franco's troops moved northward in August. "Badajoz is in the hands of the rebels," Bowers reported, then Toledo. The Basque cities near the French border were captured, and Bowers heard "a shivering reverberation and a whistling sound" as the insurgents bombed Irun opposite Hendaye. "An almost full moon shed its radiance on the grim scene though nothing was visible but the occasional flare or the firing of cannon."

The horror of war soon became apparent. Correspondents told Bowers that in Badajoz "the rebel army of Franco slaughtered two thousand people." When Irun fell he reported that insurgents fired on civilians. From the International Bridge the ambassador watched "ineffably pathetic" scenes: "Hundreds, thousands of women and children and old men poured across the border." Likewise, Bowers was shocked by the violence in the Republican zone—church burnings, confiscation of property, shootings without trial. But he insisted that he knew of "no instance of an atrocity where the commission was on orders of the government."

The civil war lasted three years and brought many political changes. The junta in Burgos named Franco head of government. The Republic depended on Socialists, Communists, and Anarchists, and Francisco Largo Caballero became prime minister. Bowers changed his opinion of the Marxist Socialist, calling him in 1936 "an honest man and able." Inclusion of Communists in his government troubled the ambassador, but he concluded that their participation in the Popular Front required this.[7]

Hitler and Mussolini furnished crucial aid to the Nationalists. Bowers reported that Italian arms, ammunition, planes, and pilots, as well as German planes manned by German aviators, were being contributed for Franco's forces. France and Britain refused the sale of war materials to the Republic, and at France's invitation twenty-seven nations—including Germany, Italy, Britain, and the Soviet Union—formed the Non-Intervention Committee to stop aid to either side. Despite the accord, Bowers noted that arms and ammunition from Italy and Germany poured in. He excoriated "the utter rottenness of the fake non-intervention pact" and condemned the League of Nations for not opposing intervention. When the Soviet Union sent planes and tanks to the Republic, he wrote that this occurred only after Germany and Italy had refused to stop helping Franco.[8] While relatively few Russians were sent to Spain, Moscow used the Comintern to recruit soldiers for the Republic. Forty thousand volunteers

*A building in Irun, Spain, after the city fell to the Nationalists in September 1936*
COURTESY OF MANUSCRIPTS DEPARTMENT, LILLY LIBRARY, INDIANA UNIVERSITY, BLOOMINGTON

enlisted, the majority of whom were Communists. From the United States came three thousand, mostly in the Abraham Lincoln Brigade. While admitting that some of these volunteers were Communists, Bowers emphasized that many were liberals and socialists.[9]

The battle for Madrid drew the world's attention in late 1936. Franco announced that he would capture the capital in November. "No one believes that the Government can stand up under the hopeless disadvantage of the German and Italian planes," Bowers wrote. The rebels advanced to the periphery of the city but no far-ther. When Hitler and Mussolini recognized Franco's government in November, Bowers feared this threatened a European war.

Elsewhere Nationalist victories continued. Malaga fell in February 1937, Bilbao in June. The Basques had no chance against the German guns and planes, Bowers lamented. "This fascist crush-ing of the Basques is one of the most atrocious crimes in modern times." Next Santander and Gijon to the west were captured.

Major political changes continued in 1937. The generalissimo united his followers into the Falange, and parties were outlawed, creating according to Bowers "a totalitarian state based on the fascist program." Military losses exacerbated the Republican divisions. Left-wing Socialists, Anarchists, and the members of the Workers' Party of Marxist Unification (POUM), an anti-Stalinist group, advocated a revolutionary regime. Moscow entered the dispute, and the Spanish party extended its power behind the scenes. Joseph Stalin wrote Largo Caballero telling the government to attract bourgeois support "to prevent the enemies of Spain from regarding her as a Communist Republic." Azaña's middle-class Republicans, moderate Socialists, and Communists insisted that winning the war was their first priority.[10] Bowers was not aware of the Communists' importance nor of their attempts to disguise it. For him the struggle was a war of fascism against democracy. He wondered how the Communists enjoyed such prominence, but believed that those who feared their strength had fallen "into the trap of Fascist propaganda." Bowers emphasized that Communists held insignificant portfolios and reiterated, "A victory by the Government will *not* mean a Communist state." President Roosevelt replied that conservative editors were "playing up all kinds of atrocities on the part of what they call the Communist government of Madrid."

In the beleaguered Republican government Communist power increased. A major supplier of military aid, the Soviet Union exerted a decisive influence. In the spring of 1937 Anarchists and POUM members turned against the Popular Front. In Barcelona "hell has broken loose with the Anarchists at war with the government," Bowers wrote. When the revolt was smashed, he reported to the State Department that this was more important than winning three battles. Anarchists and dissident Marxists were persecuted, and POUM leader Andrés Nin, earlier Leon Trotsky's secretary, was murdered by the Soviet secret police. Unaware of Moscow's role, Bowers defended suppression of the Anarchists and Trotskyists. At odds with the Communists over control of the army, Largo Caballero resigned and was replaced by a moderate Socialist, Juan Negrín, who cooperated with the Communists. Believing Negrín's choice was dictated by moderates as well as the Communists, Bowers cabled Hull that this change would make Azaña "the real directing force in the Foreign Office."[11]

For the Republican regime the remainder of the conflict was a series of military defeats and international disappointments. Government offensives west of Madrid and in Aragon in 1937–38 ended in retreat. By the spring of 1938 a dejected Azaña played a minor role. The defense minister, Indalecio Prieto, believed the war lost and was angry at the Communists for usurping his authority. Negrín demanded Prieto's resignation, citing his defeatism. Prieto's dismissal was a Communist goal, and he saw this as the cause of his ouster. Bowers initially accepted Negrín's explanation, but later the ambassador wrote Hull that he was not satisfied with the official version.

The Republic launched a diplomatic offensive on 1 May 1938, reiterating respect for private property and promising the removal of all foreign troops. Bowers wrote Washington, "The issue is clear as crystal now in Spain—fascism vs. democracy, legality vs. force." But London and Paris dismissed this initiative. British prime minister Neville Chamberlain sought to appease the fascist dictators, hoping to avoid a European war. In September came the "Great Betrayal of Munich," as Bowers labeled it, when Britain and France acquiesced to Germany's demands on Czechoslovakia. For Bowers, Chamberlain was the "cup bearer of the fascists." "When I think of Al Capone being in prison and Chamberlain being Prime Minister," Bowers wrote, "I almost question the justice of God."

The government fought on, its troops surprising the enemy at the Ebro River in July 1938, but the Nationalists regrouped. United States warships evacuated Americans from Barcelona on 25 January 1939. The next day, without artillery or planes to match those of Mussolini and Hitler, the city fell. At the French border Bowers witnessed "hundreds of women and children, many babies in arms, and young girls . . . herded together by the roadside in the rain awaiting transportation to a temporary refugee camp. It was pitiful." Nationalist troops entered the capital on 28 March.[12]

All the while Bowers followed political events back in the United States. Roosevelt's campaign to enlarge the Supreme Court found him with Roosevelt, claiming the court was "packed" against progressive government for fifty years. He, too, approved the president's subsequent campaign to defeat conservative Democratic opponents. Concern for the southern vote led to his disapproval of Sen. Robert Wagner's support of an antilynching bill—Bowers considered it "patronizing toward the South." He continued sending speeches to James A. Farley and Joseph F. Guffey and corresponding with Democratic officeholders.

But loyalty to the Democratic party had its limits. Twice he refused party requests. The war forced him to decline an appeal from Daniel C. Roper to contribute an introduction to a book on the New Deal, and diplomatic duties made him turn down Roosevelt's suggestion to return during the 1938 congressional campaign. When the Democratic Congress rejected an appropriation bill to establish a Jefferson memorial, Bowers swore: "To hell with such a party!" When Guffey urged him to delay publishing his Spanish memoirs because his views might offend some party faithful, Bowers declared, "Whenever a book in support of democracy becomes dangerous to the Democratic party, the party loses all interest to me."[13]

For three years the Bowerses lived in France. Life in St. Jean was dull, and the gloomy, rainy, winter weather went well with the gloomy news from Spain. The family in 1937 leased the Villa Eche Soua, "Our Home" in the Basque language. Situated atop a knoll east of town, the stone residence had two huge salons with lofty ceilings that looked out on a golf course and the "purple-clad Pyrenees" in the distance. Bowers ruminated, "In looking at sheep I can forget the savagery of men." His mornings were dedicated to work at the Miramar Hotel, while he spent the afternoons writing. At dusk, Bowers often walked along the country roads and ate dinner with his family around 8:30. On short wave he heard Roosevelt's speeches. However, "the most dramatic talk in my experience," Bowers confessed, was Edward VIII's abdication address. The family went to movies, but reading was their favorite entertainment. An eclectic reader, the ambassador devoured biographies, novels, histories, and memoirs, as well as detective stories. Throughout the war twenty Spanish servants resided at a nearby hotel at his expense.

*Ambassador Claude Bowers in his office at the Miramar Hotel, St. Jean de Luz, France*
COURTESY OF MANUSCRIPTS DEPARTMENT, LILLY LIBRARY, INDIANA UNIVERSITY, BLOOMINGTON

Few guests reached St. Jean, but Ernest Hemingway's visits were special. He regaled his host with war tales, and Bowers was impressed with his "living dangerously and joyously" in Madrid. One visitor, John W. Holcombe, transported Bowers back to his Hoosier childhood. Bowers recalled that "on the roof of a chicken coop at my grandmother's" he had read Holcombe's biography of Thomas Hendricks. "The old man's eyes beamed," and he wondered if this had something to do with turning the youth's attention to history and biography.[14]

Residence in France did not diminish Bowers's diplomatic responsibilities. As in Madrid, he continued to oversee all aspects of the embassy's operation. The war involved him in a prisoner exchange, the release of a captured American ship, and aid to Spanish civilians, as well as correspondence with Washington. By the second year he was worn out by constant work and his "suppressed rage over the Spanish war." He met with staff members to assess events, draft reports, and make assignments. As always his dress was unfashionable—his tie was usually askew, and he wore high-laced shoes. On his physician's advice, he cut back on smoking but chewed unlit cigars. Bowers remained an inefficient manager, continuing to stuff letters into his pockets and remaining unable to delegate duties. Opposed to the pro-Franco sentiments of his colleagues, he insisted on writing his own dispatches.

The war years brought staff changes. Johnson's "hysteria and blatant advocacy of the rebel cause" hardly made Bowers rue his transfer to Warsaw. The ambassador found his replacement, Walter Thurston, "a delightful fellow," who was assigned to Valencia and Barcelona. Bowers considered Col. Stephen Fuqua one of the ablest men he had known, and he found his military reports invaluable. Aware that censors were listening to their telephone conversations, he and the colonel referred to the Republicans as the home team, and the Nationalists as the visitors. Garrison continued as his secretary, translator, and friend.

The political views of the embassy staff remained a disappointment to the Democratic envoy. Bowers reflected in October 1938: "There was Johnson, counsellor of the embassy—with Franco and the fascists. There is Schoellkopf, first secretary—with Franco and the fascists." Likewise for Fuqua. The ambassador was irate with Charles A. Bay, the consul in rebel-held Seville. Bowers complained to Hull that "Bay describes the *Constitutional Government of Spain, which we recognize, as 'the Reds.'*" The department forced Bay to change his labels, if not his convictions.[15]

In France the ambassador continued to participate in the local diplomatic life. He found representatives of the totalitarian states aggressively fascist, but many from democratic nations were indifferent or opposed to democracy. French ambassador Jean Herbette shocked Bowers when he told him that the Spanish generals should come together and end the war. The British ambassador, Sir Henry Chilton, also opposed the Republic and said London should recognize Franco on the slightest pretext. The foreign colony was equally reactionary, and Bowers concluded, "When one contemplates these titled and aristocratic parasites about here, centuries old exploiters of the peasants and workers, the wonder grows how the people have waited so long to strike."

Bowers's many social obligations proved time-consuming: receptions for Washington's birthday and the Fourth of July, open house at Christmas, teas for the diplomatic corps, cocktails for visiting naval officers. "Recently we sat down to arrange dinners to repay obligations," he complained. "It required five dinners, each with twenty covers." Teas at the home of Russian countess Nostitz were a tie with his past. His hostess was the actress Lilie Boutier, whose performance he had enjoyed as a boy in Indianapolis. Betty Pack was another favorite. Married to a British diplomat, the Minneapolis native was young and pretty, and Bowers, aware of her travels to Madrid and Valencia, admired her sense of adventure. Unknown to her spouse, and to Bowers, Betty was a spy for British Security Coordination (BSC). After her husband's transfer to Warsaw in 1938, she employed her charms to befriend Polish engineers and Nazis in Berlin. Sir William Stephenson, BSC chief, lauded "this most exotic of lady spies" for helping unlock the puzzle of the Germans' Enigma cipher machine.[16]

All the while Bowers's dispatches to Washington furnished valuable information to the administration. Within days of the arrival of Mussolini's troops and Hitler's airmen, he was reporting it, and his prediction that a rebel victory would be impossible without help from the Axis powers proved accurate. Bowers emphasized that the Non-Intervention Committee served to permit the fascist powers to support their Nationalist allies, while preventing the British and French from selling arms to the Republic. Likewise his analysis of France's unwillingness to permit military shipments— British pressure and internal political problems—was correct. Thanks to journalists' reports, Bowers quickly informed Washington when the German Condor Legion bombed civilians in Guernica. He also reported crimes committed by Republicans, condemning "the reign of terror in Madrid," but his assertion that Nationalist acts were "ordered and carried out by the highest military authorities," while those in Republican Spain were "the work of revolutionary mobs taking advantage of the breakdown of the state," remains a point of contention.[17]

Some of Bowers's information was inaccurate. Although he reported that the generalissimo possessed "more than ordinary military brilliance," he incorrectly informed Roosevelt that Franco was "lacking in energy for the field." Ignorant of the caudillo's political acumen, Bowers time after time overestimated dissension in the Nationalist camp, and he exaggerated the strength of the Republican army. Even after the battle of the Ebro in 1938, he reported, "There is scarcely anyone today who believes the war will end in a military victory."

His dispatches were mistaken concerning Communist influence in the Republican government. He dismissed the party's growing power and defended its role, assuring Hull that the Communists were not "mischief makers" but supporters of the government. Bowers was unaware of their power in ousting Largo Caballero as prime minister and Prieto as minister of defense, as well as in persecuting Anarchists and members of POUM. Critics have emphasized Bowers's ignorance of Communist influence. Salvador de Madariaga, a historian and friend, praised the ambassador's stand "for the right of our people to freedom," but lamented "his refusal to see communist influence in quarters where it was unfortunately only too strong." Burnett Bolloten, a historian of the civil war, agreed: "There can be no doubt that Bowers's political ingenuousness and sympathy for the Republican cause obscured his judgement." Even a leftist Republican, Ramón Sender, considered him "an honest man so impressed by the strength of our arguments that he refused to see the shadows being cast over us by Moscow's sinister Machiavellianism."[18]

The envoy's wartime duties included support of American firms whose investments—primarily in banking, manufacturing, and communications—totaled $80 million in 1936. International Telephone and Telegraph's subsidiary, the most prominent foreign company, was a political target, but the Telefónica continued to provide service in each zone. As Bowers reminded Hull, "Both sides in Spain are very keen about maintaining reasonably friendly relations with us in the hope of post-war advantages."

United States relations with the Nationalists remained unofficial. They refused in 1937 to permit the reopening of the

American consulate in Bilbao and pressed Washington for recognition. The State Department rejected formal ties, but permitted a Franco agent in New York to validate shipping documents. In exchange the Nationalists allowed consulates in their territory, but their representative wrote Burgos that the department would be "obligated to deny" this understanding if it appeared in the press. Bowers was not informed.

The Nationalists' capture of the American tanker *Nantucket Chief* in January 1938 led to a diplomatic conflict. The ship was carrying oil to Barcelona when its cargo was confiscated and the crew incarcerated. Bowers considered the seizure an act of piracy. The department instructed him to resolve the matter informally, and he sent a letter demanding the crew's release. On hearing that the captain would be placed on trial, Bowers urged Washington to send a ship if the Nationalists did not back down. When the captain was given a seventeen-year sentence, Franco's New York representative telegraphed Burgos to free the captain and the ship. In February the insurgents informed Bowers of the release of both.[19]

More important than negotiations over the *Nantucket Chief* was the freeing of Americans in the Lincoln Brigade captured by the Nationalists. In May 1938 the Marquis de Rialp, a Franco emissary, asked Bowers to oversee an exchange of twenty-nine pilots held by the Republic in return for fifteen airmen in Nationalist hands. The *franquistas* did not have twenty-nine pilots as prisoners, so the marquis included fourteen captured Americans. Washington told Bowers to transmit the marquis's proposal to the Republicans, who agreed to negotiate. "For the first time since the war began I have brought the two parties together," Bowers informed the White House. When both sides refused to trade aviators, Bowers pressed for freeing fourteen Italian infantrymen for the fourteen United States veterans. The Americans crossed to Hendaye on 8 October. "It was an event," Bowers noted, "because these are the first military prisoners who have been exchanged since the war began." They told of Americans beaten and shot by their captors. The White House, State Department, and Friends of the Abraham Lincoln Brigade

*Ambassador Claude Bowers hosting Basque refugee children at the embassy residence
in St. Jean de Luz, France*

COURTESY OF MANUSCRIPTS DEPARTMENT, LILLY LIBRARY, INDIANA UNIVERSITY, BLOOMINGTON

lauded Bowers's help, Norman Thomas commended him, and
Mussolini's government expressed appreciation.[20]

Bowers's offices were not limited to official representations. He
spoke with the American Friends Service Committee in 1937 and
complained to Hull that the United States had done nothing to
help hundreds of thousands of children. The secretary answered
that American relief operations must be carried out by a neutral
organization. The Quaker committee established the Spanish
Child Welfare Association in 1938 to assist both sides. Encouraged
by Eleanor Roosevelt, Bowers served as honorary chairman, and
the National Broadcasting Company carried his appeal for funds.
He recorded a talk in Paris for Spanish relief, and Hemingway sped
him from a cocktail party to the studio. Fifteen thousand copies of
a Bowers appeal for funds were mailed from St. Jean.

The ambassador asked Washington in 1938 to appoint a commission to distribute food to civilians as the United States had
done for the Belgians and Armenians. Roosevelt replied that he

wanted to make a large contribution, but, as Bowers expected, the president refused to appoint a commission and encouraged the Red Cross and the Friends to increase their efforts and offered them flour and wheat. Roosevelt asked a dozen citizens to form the Committee for Impartial Civilian Relief in Spain to raise funds for the Red Cross, and Bowers obtained Nationalist and Republican cooperation.[21]

Washington was determined to avoid involvement in the civil war. Acting Secretary Phillips asserted at the start of the conflict, "This government will, of course, scrupulously refrain from any interference whatsoever in the Spanish situation," a decision Roosevelt reaffirmed. Although the United States did not sign the nonintervention agreement, Hull saw the accord as the best means to prevent the spread of the conflict. At Roosevelt's request, Congress amended the Neutrality Act in 1937 to outlaw the export of arms, ammunition, or war implements to Spain. Bowers endorsed these measures, and the president assured him the United States would follow "complete neutrality in regard to Spain's internal affairs." The ambassador urged Hull to remain aloof, and the secretary agreed.

Bowers changed his mind in 1937. Increased Axis aid, Guernica, the British-French appeasement policy, and the Non-Intervention Committee's interdiction of aid to the Republic convinced him that Washington's policy was wrong. The United States was "getting into a hypocritical position," Bowers wrote in June. While American law forbade arms sales to any nation at war, Italy and Germany were doing so, and the United States was selling them war materials. Washington was setting aside international law by refusing to sell arms to the government of Spain. Bowers kept his newfound opposition to himself. He believed that American neutrality stemmed from "a desire to stay out of quarrels at home"—to placate isolationists and Roman Catholics—so he viewed a change of policy as unlikely.

Still, he continued to warn Washington of the Axis threat. "The Civil War ceased to be a civil war many months ago," he assured Hull on the first anniversary of the conflict. Bowers predicted that "with every surrender, beginning long ago with China, followed by Abyssinia and then Spain, the fascist powers with vanity inflamed will turn without delay to another such country— such as Czechoslovakia—and that with every surrender the prospects of a European war grow darker." He assured Roosevelt that the Spanish contest was a struggle between fascism and democracy.[22]

The world situation worried Roosevelt. He assailed "the present reign of terror and international lawlessness" in an October speech and condemned the murder of women and children "with bombs from the air." Neither isolation nor neutrality, Roosevelt added, was a defense against international anarchy, and he urged a quarantine against nations violating the rights of others. But the address found little support, and Hull never endorsed it. For Bowers the president's speech reflected his warnings. While admitting that Roosevelt's remarks also applied to Japanese atrocities in China, the ambassador observed that "not one count in the indictment of fascist savagery does not apply to Spain."

The ambassador was encouraged when sixty congressmen in January 1938 called for repeal of the embargo against arms sales to Spain. "The time has come," he wrote Roosevelt, "when all democratic countries everywhere will have to stand up and be counted for fascism or against it." Bowers became more outspoken when following "the wholesale gangster murders" by German and Italian pilots at Barcelona he was told that some of the bombs were of American origin. "How sick our silly neutrality looks since Italy or Germany can get munitions from us." At a press conference Roosevelt admitted, "It probably is true that American-made bombs have been dropped on Barcelona by Franco airplanes."[23]

Supporters of the Republic in early 1938 believed the administration was preparing to lift the embargo. At Hull's request Arthur Krock wrote a *New York Times* editorial on 20 March "to prepare the way for a move to repeal the Neutrality Act." At a meeting at the State Department, Hull mentioned the president's concern and said Roosevelt would overrule any harsh policy toward the Republic. Bowers received a cable in April from Jay Allen, then a

Spanish Republican agent in Washington: "Great White Father
[Roosevelt] gave intimation of concrete execution our action Stop
This possible legally by proclamation that civil war no longer
exists." This proclamation would have permitted the president to
act without legislative approval. Roosevelt sought advice from the
department and attorney general, but conflicting interpretations,
Hull's hostility, and a divided public prevented action.[24]

Bowers urged the department on 10 June 1938 to lift the
embargo on military sales. To Roosevelt he insisted that the
Non-Intervention Committee was responsible for prolonging
the conflict. The way to end the war was "to restore to the legal,
constitutional, democratic Government of the Spanish people
its right under international law to buy arms for its defense." He
assured the Spanish foreign minister in late 1938 that the
prospects for lifting the embargo were bright. The Republic's
decision to dismiss its foreign soldiers, he believed, turned the
conflict into a war of fascist aggression. Hull in November
admitted "the possibility of an announcement by the President
that he would ask Congress to repeal the Spanish embargo
measures in January." Jay Pierrepont Moffat reported Roosevelt
anxious to do so, but Hull opposed this. Bowers informed the president and secretary in December, "The policy of prohibiting the
sale of planes to the legal Government of Spain is resulting in a
wholesale slaughter of women and children." With "some degree of
parity in the air forces the fascist forces in Spain would be
defeated." When Roosevelt asked Hull to help draft a reply, the
secretary answered, "It is hardly necessary for you to write further to Mr. Bowers in reference to neutrality legislation."

To a joint session of Congress on 4 January 1939 the president
encouraged the belief that the embargo was about to end. He
warned that neutrality laws might operate unfairly, aiding an
aggressor and harming victims. "The instinct of self-preservation
should warn us that we ought not to let that happen any more."
Bowers claimed Roosevelt almost quoted from his letters in the
statement on neutrality. To Hull the ambassador repeated, "We
should consider whether the Democracies of the world can con-

tinue to refuse to sell to the legal Government, which is the friend of the Democracies, the material necessary for its defense."[25]

Efforts to repeal the embargo came to naught. The Foreign Relations Committee refused to act. Chairman Key Pittman dismissed the Republic's chances and warned that ending the embargo would stir a religious controversy in every state. Hull opposed any change, maintaining that the United States should focus on the "broader policy of our role as neutral in the event of a European war."

The Nationalist victory ended Bowers's ambassadorship. Following British and French recognition of Franco, Secretary Hull on 2 March ordered him home for consultation to "free our hands for establishing relations with the Franco government." In Washington, Bowers met with diplomats, politicians, and friends. At the State Department Sumner Welles gave him the impression that Italian and German intrigues in South America had turned him against the Nationalists. That evening he went to Pittman's house, where his host confessed, "I am afraid I made a mistake about the embargo." At a White House luncheon Roosevelt greeted Bowers: "I have made a mistake. You have been right all along." He had admitted to the cabinet on 27 January that the embargo had been "a grave mistake," that the United States should have allowed the Republic "to come to us for what she needed to fight for her life against Franco—to fight for her life and for the lives of some of the rest of us as well, as events will very likely prove." Bowers ruminated in his diary, "I could not but wonder why my advice, so completely vindicated by events, was not taken in time." Roosevelt explained to him, "I have been imposed upon by false information sent me from across the Street," nodding his head toward the State Department. Until his dying day Bowers believed Roosevelt would have changed American policy in 1938–39 had he not received bad advice.[26]

The Washington visit was crowded with meetings. Senator Guffey reported Roosevelt's statement to him that Bowers had been "exactly right throughout the war" and the president's promise to offer him another ambassadorship. At a luncheon hosted by Guffey, Bowers noted his friends' sympathy toward the Republic.

The Spanish war dominated conversation at a dinner given by Harry B. Hawes, and a relieved guest, Moffat, admitted that Bowers was "a really unusual talker" and less partisan than anticipated. The envoy was surprised when Hull was reluctant to discuss Spain but found the Republicans friendly when he spoke before the House Foreign Relations Committee.

And what can one say in conclusion about Bowers's diplomacy during the civil war? In the aftermath of the war's end, he sought to defend himself by misleading the American public about his views on American policy. He implied that he always had favored United States intervention, but this was not true. In 1936–37 he endorsed neutrality and the embargo, a fact he never mentioned. With the passing of time Bowers perhaps came to regard advocacy of the Popular Front as tantamount to support for a changed policy. In letters to three historians he stressed his opposition to the embargo, and in his memoirs he attacked neutrality. Nowhere did he mention his initial defense of Washington's policy.

Like Bowers, many administration stalwarts opposed United States policy in Spain, and he influenced their opinions. Harold L. Ickes, Henry Morgenthau, Welles, Felix Frankfurter, Eleanor Roosevelt, Josephus Daniels, William E. Dodd, and Senators Claude D. Pepper and Guffey concluded by 1939 that United States policy had been wrong. Ickes had urged Roosevelt to end the embargo and wrote Bowers, "You and I see eye to eye in this whole matter." The president's wife told him she complained to her husband about neutrality, and Pepper insisted that not supporting the Republic was Roosevelt's greatest mistake. Guffey concurred. Frankfurter in 1939 told Guffey: "When I was entitled to have views on things—before I came to the Court—the services of the Ambassador in connection with the awful struggle in Spain evoked my admiration." Dodd asserted that he and Bowers agreed on Spain, and Daniels wrote, "You are eternally right in saying that for the Spanish crimes the three great democracies must take full responsibility in history." Welles later claimed that Washington's policy toward the civil war was a major error.[27]

In truth Hull was the only important New Deal official who defended United States policy. In his memoirs he argued that opponents of neutrality represented extreme groups unable to realize that Washington needed to take "the broad course of working along the same lines as Britain and France." "Bowers, himself a liberal, promptly took sides in the Civil War," Hull stated, and sought to make "policies conform with the vital interests of the liberal forces prosecuting one side of the war." The secretary's memoirs surprised Bowers. He believed Hull's policy set aside international law to appease the Axis and considered him "a very black reactionary and a damn poor democrat." Who else would condone appeasement in Spain and placing "the petty Franco on the throne"?

The ambassador told Welles in late March 1939 that recognition of the Nationalists was necessary to protect United States investments. But Bowers insisted that the victors must pledge not to carry out reprisals. "We have those guarantees," the undersecretary assured him, and Washington offered in April to establish relations. Franco's subsequent persecution of Republicans made Bowers doubt Madrid's pledges. Hull admitted in his memoirs that Franco had made no promises, and later on Bowers's questioning Welles was unable to name the Nationalist who had given him the guarantees.

Bowers returned to France and brought an end to his affairs. He went to a Basque hospital, which as ambassador, protocol had prevented him from visiting. There veterans, some without arms and others without legs, sang a welcoming song. He reflected that evening, "I would rather have their friendship and affection than the respect of any totalitarian tyrant in the world, and so I would a hundred thousand times."[28]

The civil war was over, and Bowers was unemployed. In 1939 he considered an offer from the *New York Post*, but understood that Roosevelt intended to appoint him to another embassy—Poland, Belgium, and Canada were mentioned. Fearing a European war, he did not want to go to Poland or Belgium, and the United States mission in Ottawa was a legation not an embassy, so he dismissed it.[29]

He accepted the embassy in Chile after the president assured him it was "a post of great importance to us in the fight against fascism."

Bowers noted that Chile was one of the two best assignments in South America. The Popular Front candidate, Pedro Aguirre Cerda, had won the 1938 presidential election, reminding him that Chile had "a functioning democracy, the one most deeply rooted in tradition in all South America." He wanted two employees to accompany him. Fearing Pepe Torres would be arrested if he returned to Spain, he arranged for his chauffeur and family to join him, and Garrison agreed to continue as his secretary.

When the Bowerses left St. Jean on 13 June 1939, two Basque girls presented them with flowers and a book. The former Basque minister of justice, Jesús María de Leizaola, and Hemingway saw them off at the Paris station.[30]

During his years as ambassador to Spain, Bowers continued writing, producing three books. Writing provided relief. Indeed he credited the hours composing *My Mission to Spain: Watching the Rehearsal for World War II* with keeping him sane. He prepared another Thomas Jefferson manuscript as a diversion, *Jefferson in Power: The Death Struggle of the Federalists*. He had researched materials at the Library of Congress in 1935 and corresponded with fellow Jefferson biographer Dodd. The manuscript was published by Houghton Mifflin in 1936. Bowers's most charming book, *The Spanish Adventures of Washington Irving*, was issued in 1940.

*Jefferson in Power* treated the president's two administrations, considered unexceptional by many. Bowers disagreed, finding them "brilliantly successful." For him the Republican victory in 1800 was a peaceful revolution supported by landowners who had defeated the monied interests in the East, represented by the Federalist party. The author accused Henry Adams, John Bach McMaster, and Edward Channing of denigrating Jefferson's accomplishments. "It is time to challenge these prosecuting attorneys," he insisted, calling them "sword-rattlers of the ivory tower." Jefferson's presidential terms saw democracy triumph. Among his accomplishments were internal improvements, doubling of the national domain, and successful financial arrangements.

The book was well written, and this, rather than historical revisionism, accounted for its popularity. Bowers sought to "re-create, as flesh and blood, the characters of this drama": the arch traitor Aaron Burr ("captivating to women and fascinating to men"), "blithesome" Dolley Madison, and even Alexander Hamilton "in the shining armor of his genius." Backstairs gossip, treason, crooked diplomats, bribery, flirtations, and tavern brawls filled the pages.

Bowers arranged favorable reviews. Robert La Follette, Jr., promised to critique it for *The Progressive.* "If you think the book good and will say so in thirty words for the use of the publisher I will appreciate it no end," the author wrote Dodd, who found it "exceedingly good." Daniels reviewed it for his *Raleigh News and Observer,* and Hull and George W. Norris offered publishable comments. Hawes agreed to review it for the *St. Louis Post-Dispatch,* as did Meredith Nicholson for the *Indianapolis Star.* Bowers insisted that his interest in promotion was not pecuniary: "I am *not in need of money* at all. I am interested in the circulation of the book."[31]

Gilbert Chinard in the *American Historical Review* considered it "a welcome corrective," a "vivid, brilliant, and penetrating piece of work." Enthusiastic reports appeared in the *Mississippi Valley Historical Review* and the *Journal of Southern History.* Henry Steele Commager claimed that Bowers "has rescued Jefferson from the barbed pens of the Federalist historians." Reviewers in *The Yale Review* and *The Nation* were more critical, faulting the author for "exaggeration and oversimplification" and for not stressing economic factors. *Jefferson in Power* reminded Democrats of Roosevelt's political struggles. Daniels asserted, "While you were careful not in a partisan way to compare the bitter fight against Roosevelt with that which was waged against Jefferson, it stood out clear from the very presentation of the facts of history." Roper wrote that Jefferson's problems were like those the president was facing, and Roosevelt himself praised the book.

*Jefferson in Power* was a commercial success. Full-page advertisements were placed in the *New York Times* and the *New York Herald Tribune.* Houghton Mifflin reported "orders of somewhere around twelve or thirteen thousand copies, which is very good for a book of this price in these times." On publication day the house sent Bowers $4,815.18 based on advance sales of 11,435 copies. In the autumn of 1936 it was on best-seller lists.

Bowers was pleased by election to the National Institute of Arts and Letters in 1937. Twice passed over for a Pulitzer, the author appreciated membership in the society—"the most distinguished organization of writers and artists in our country." He joked that selection had to have happened "during a sleeping sickness of Nicholas Murray Butler." Also chosen were John Dos Passos and Sherwood Anderson, causing Bowers to imagine that the electors "decided to hold their noses and have it all over with the non-comformists at one time."[32]

*The Spanish Adventures of Washington Irving* was an account of one of Bowers's predecessors in Spain. Houghton Mifflin assured the author, "Coming from you, one American envoy to Spain, writing about another, it will attract a great deal more attention than if it were merely the product of some research worker and ready writer." For his amusement the author re-created the Spain that Irving loved, "followed the trail of Irving on his romantic journeys, visiting his old haunts, the houses in which he lived or visited, the groves where he had spread his picnic lunches." Bowers viewed portraits admired by the New Yorker and discovered correspondence in the embassy, but the greatest treasures were found in a forgotten trunk. The book recounted Irving's three years as a writer in Spain in the 1820s and as American minister from 1842 to 1846. It focused on personalities: his "paternal partiality for the child Queen, Isabella," her reputation "as reactionary in her politics and a bit careless in her morals," and her plotting generals. Nor was local color omitted: the Prado, Bowers's favorite boulevard, was packed with leaders of fashion. He could not resist comparing Irving's endeavors to his own. Both were fascinated by Spanish politics and concerned with high tariffs against American products. Bowers appreciated Irving's complaints about State Department policy and protests that he was not kept informed.[33]

Only 3,373 copies of the book were sold, but it met with critical acclaim. Novelist Elliot Paul lauded the author's "excellent evocation of Spain of one hundred years ago." Others concurred: "A romantic and richly colored narrative" (*Indianapolis Star*); "Mr. Bowers has recaptured the flavor of the past and restored a Spain that has gone" (*Saturday Review of Literature*); "The Spain of Irving's day smolders on every page of his book" (*New York Times Book Review*). The *Christian Science Monitor*, the *Boston Evening Transcript*, *The New Yorker*, and *Time* magazine offered similar encomia.[34] Chilean publication of *Las aventuras españolas de Washington Irving* in 1946 also was greeted with enthusiasm. Santiago's *La Nación* thanked the author for providing "these savory pages." In Madrid the Falangist newspaper *Arriba* stated that his depiction of nineteenth-century Spain contained "no mistakes, no errors, no controversies, nor are there any when the author compares the countryside, places or buildings of yesterday with those of today." Bowers was pleased that the translation was selling "like hot cakes."[35]

Bowers's Spanish memoir did not appear for fourteen years. Its 437 pages included political observations but little on his personal life. His diary was the principal source. By November 1937 he was working on the twenty-third chapter and predicted the manuscript would be finished when the war ended. Treatment of the prewar years included politicians and intellectuals and underscored his love for Spain. Azaña, "the bulwark of the Republic," was his hero and the monarchist José Calvo Sotelo his villain. Bowers also sought to expose fascist aggression and show how diplomacy contributed to the destruction of Spanish democracy. He emphasized the Axis's military aid to Franco and condemned the democracies for refusing to sell war material. The Non-Intervention Committee was a target of his scorn—"a loathsome farce," "a stench."

His acceptance of the ambassadorship to Chile in 1939 postponed publication of his Spanish memoirs. World War II further delayed it because its treatment of Chamberlain might have been misinterpreted as anti-British. Bowers believed the Allied victory in 1945 was the appropriate moment, and President Harry S. Truman saw "no earthly reason why the Spanish book cannot be published now." When the State Department insisted on approving the manuscript, Bowers refused: "I cannot afford to have my impressions and story censored by anyone in or out of the State Department." Political considerations also contributed to postponing publication. He feared the book might embarrass friends in the Senate by stirring up Catholic hostility. *The Memoirs of Cordell Hull* in 1948 caused Bowers to add a concluding chapter, reviewing his reports to the department, sharpening his criticism of policy and the diplomatic establishment, and relating in detail his 1939 meetings with Hull, Roosevelt, Welles, and the Foreign Relations Committee. *My Mission to Spain* was published in 1954 following Bowers's retirement. The next year *Mi misión en España* came out in Mexico City, then *Ma mission en Espagne, 1933–1939* was issued in Paris and *Ma Missione in Spagna, 1933–1939* in Milan.[36]

As expected, liberals lauded Bowers's memoir. Historian Gordon A. Craig congratulated him for "bluntly and eloquently" demonstrating the danger of appeasement. In the *Manchester Guardian* J. B. Trend, another historian, praised the account for exposing "the inept dishonesty of the so-called 'non-intervention.'" *New York Times* journalist Herbert L. Matthews asserted that the memoir was the work of "a true American democrat," and Arthur M. Schlesinger, Jr., wrote, "*My Mission to Spain* breathes the robust and fearless spirit of our Jeffersonian tradition." *Le Figaro Littéraire* considered it "an important eyewitness account," while *Le Canard Enchaîné* called Bowers "one of the few lucid diplomats of the period." Spanish Republicans extolled the book, and the government-in-exile awarded him the Order of Liberation of Spain.[37]

The volume proved controversial as well. Thomas J. Hamilton faulted the author for overlooking "the internal weaknesses of the Spanish Republic," and Anthony West in *The New Yorker* chided him for not resigning because of Washington's policies. Two critics berated him for not mentioning the Communists' persecution of the Trotskyists. Conservatives and Catholics, too, offered criticism. Santiago's *El Mercurio* lambasted the book for displaying "every type of prejudice and bias" against Franco. The *Indianapolis News* accused the author of overlooking Soviet intervention, and

*Commonweal* charged him with underestimating "the destructive forces within the Left."

*My Mission to Spain* was a memoir, not a historical work. A zealous partisan, the author omitted material that did not support his views. Following the war Spanish Republicans informed him that Communist pressure had forced Negrín to dismiss Prieto as minister of defense, but Bowers chose not to include this. He confessed to Fernando de los Ríos that mention of this incident would "give comfort to the enemy." But he admitted that Largo Caballero's ouster was due to Communist pressure.[38]

Back in the United States in June 1939, Bowers visited friends in New York and Washington. His most important powwow was with the president. Bowers noted, "As he grows older he takes on the appearance of Andrew Jackson, his hero." When Roosevelt asked what he had observed since his return, Bowers answered that many were wondering if he had finished his speech accepting a third term. The startled president shrugged his shoulders and remarked, "It is not good for a party to revolve around one man." His guest replied that the issue was "not so much the man as the man's policies," adding that this might require his renomination. A State Department messenger interrupted the reunion to say that Hull would be over with a statement favoring repeal of the embargo. This made Bowers feel ill.[39]

After shopping, many dinners, and a night at the theater, the family boarded the *Santa María* on 11 August. The ship called at ports in Panama, Colombia, Ecuador, and Peru. Then came Chile, their home for the next fourteen years.

# CHAPTER NINE

# Chile

After fourteen years in Chile the Bowers family "agreed that we had never been so happy or so much among friends as in this lovely land between the mountains and the sea." But in August 1939 the ambassador could not have imagined what lay ahead in Santiago. Chilean relations during World War II required his attention for the next six years, and in the postwar period he worked on solidifying the economic, military, and cultural links that characterized Chilean–North American relations during the cold war. On retirement in 1953, Bowers could say that twenty years as ambassador to Spain and Chile made him the third-longest-serving head of foreign missions in the history of the foreign service.[1]

After eighteen days at sea, the *Santa María* on 29 August reached Valparaiso, where the envoy was impressed by the city's green hills and modern buildings. He was met by embassy officials and complained that there was "no escape" from posing for newspaper photographers. The family visited the adjoining resort of Viña del Mar, and the ambassador observed that its casino was "much larger than that of Monte Carlo."

The journey to the capital inaugurated his infatuation with Chile. Bowers described the coastal mountains and the central

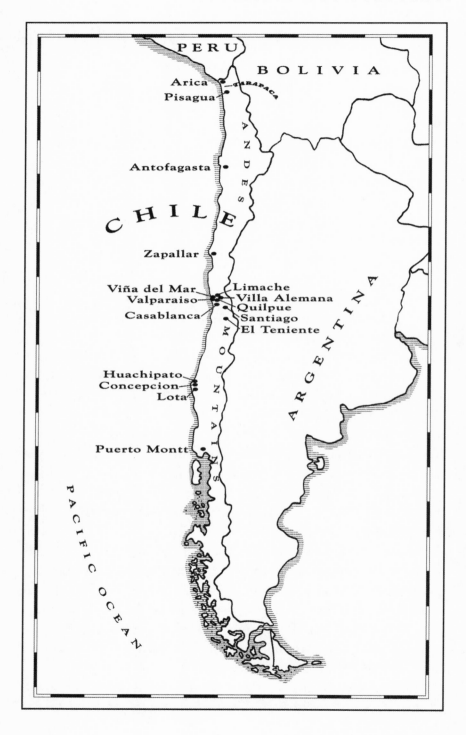

valley as "the most beautiful country I think I have ever seen."
Atop one ridge the party beheld "a picture spread before us so startling beautiful that we stopped the car for an unhurried view." En
route the threesome made the first of many offerings at a church
dedicated to travelers near Casablanca, where their car was halted
by a picturesque religious procession.[2]

That evening the family drove through the gate of their new
home, where reporters and members of the staff and the American
community greeted them as they alighted under the porte cochere.
Guests filed into rooms on the ground floor connected by a long
corridor lined with marble columns. In the middle was the main
salon with its beamed ceiling and huge fireplace. An adjacent
salon to the left was "furnished in the French style" with cherubs
adorning the walls, and refreshments were served in the dining
room at the right end of the corridor. The envoy noted that Lucky
Lass, the family's Scotch terrier, appreciated the gardens surrounding the residence and was "delighted to see grass again."

Bowers described his new home "as a palace or a large mansion"
and believed it was "the most beautiful owned by our
Government." Constructed for a Chilean nitrate magnate, the
three-story rectangular structure with its neoclassical facade, bal-
conies, and terraces still stands facing a park along the Mapocho
River several blocks east of downtown. The family's spacious quarters included a dining room and former chapel that became the
library. Adjacent was a sunroom. On the second floor the couple
occupied separate bedrooms, and a room on the third was reserved
for writing. Pat's room and two guest accommodations were also on
the second floor. The government paid for the butler, a footman,
and two groundsmen, while Bowers hired nine others, including
the chef of a former Chilean president.[3] The servants lived on the
third floor, and the chauffeur Pepe Torres and his family resided in
an apartment above the garage.

Although he never had been to South America, Bowers was far
from ignorant about Chile. His dozens of editorials on Latin
American subjects and diplomacy demonstrated his interest in the
region. After his appointment, he spent the next months reading

Chilean history and met with former president Carlos Dávila in New York and Chilean specialists at the State Department.

He was aware that Chile's political development differed from its South American neighbors. Following independence, the new nation had faced the same disorder as the other Hispanic states, and Bowers compared this strife between liberals and conservatives to the struggle between Hamiltonians and Jeffersonians. Unlike elsewhere in Spanish America, chaos gave way to stability in Chile. In the Constitution of 1833 the Chilean oligarchy established a strong government, and the discovery of silver and agricultural exports provided a base for social harmony. Between 1879 and 1884, Chile annexed rich guano, nitrate, and copper lands after a war with Bolivia and Peru, and the country's orderly life attracted immigration and investment. As Bowers emphasized in a 1939 address, United States diplomats and investors had played an important role in Chile throughout the nineteenth century.[4]

By the 1890s the legislature had increased its powers, creating a parliamentary regime, and in the 1920s the political system again was overhauled. The legislature had proved unable to produce coalitions, and the presidency was unable to lead. Urbanization, labor unrest, and a dissatisfied middle class demanded solutions. Liberal Arturo Alessandri, the paladin of the reformers, became president in 1920, but in 1924 army officers, led by Carlos Ibáñez del Campo, forced him to seek asylum in the United States embassy. There on the table in the study, Alessandri later told Bowers, "I signed my abdication." In his New York editorials Bowers had lauded the Chilean leader for favoring separation of church and state and promoting social legislation.

For Bowers, Alessandri's overthrow was "only another instance of the power of reaction and the sword—the sword in the hand of reaction." Popular support returned Alessandri to the presidency, and the Constitution of 1925 increased the executive's powers and the state's role in society. But the new system broke down in 1927 when Ibáñez orchestrated his own election. His regime ended with his resignation in 1931, and Alessandri became president in 1932, remaining in power for six years. In the 1938 presidential contest,

*Ambassador Claude Bowers leaving the United States embassy, Santiago, Chile, to present his credentials, 7 September 1939*

the Radical, Socialist, and Communist parties formed a Popular Front and nominated Pedro Aguirre Cerda, a Radical. Like Spain and France, Chile chose the Front. The Communists remained outside the cabinet, but the Socialists occupied several minor portfolios. In St. Jean de Luz Bowers had expressed his satisfaction with Aguirre Cerda's election and made fun of conservative diplomats who called him a "red."[5] But political stability could not be taken for granted. The month before the election Chile's National Socialist movement attempted a coup, and four days before Bowers's arrival Ibáñez tried to overthrow Aguirre Cerda.

The envoy's first month in Santiago proved taxing. "War in Europe is now on," the unsurprised ambassador wrote in his diary on 1 September, three days after arrival. "Hitler has sent troops against Poland." The war became the focus of his efforts for the next six years.

Against the backdrop of war, Bowers presented his credentials on 7 September. "A fine and handsome troop of soldiers" accom-

panied the ambassador, who rode in an open carriage along the
one-mile route to the Moneda where he presented his credentials.
Built as a colonial mint, this neoclassical building was the presidential residence and housed the Ministry of Foreign Relations.
National anthems in the plaza, brief speeches by Bowers and the
president, introductions, and a conversation between Aguirre
Cerda and the envoy proved an ordeal. Bowers was impressed by
the "rather short" executive, with his "dark and full" face. The
Chilean spoke English fairly well and stressed that the Radical
party was not really radical, making "it clear that the Government
does not include communists." Bowers admired his host for "trying
to do in Chile what Roosevelt was attempting in the States."

The ambassador set out on courtesy visits to other heads of
mission. He first called on Monsignor Aldo Laghi, the papal nuncio and dean of the corps, a liberal cleric whom Bowers liked.
Bowers's British counterpart, Sir Charles Bentinck, was "an
ardent friend and defender of Chamberlain," but both established
close ties between their embassies to oppose the Axis. Bowers
found Baron von Schoen, the German ambassador, "a charming
man of culture," but noted that he "carefully evades all matters of
any interest—especially the war." By 15 September Bowers had
visited the ambassadors of France, Italy, Japan, China, Mexico,
Colombia, Peru, Bolivia, Brazil, and Paraguay.

Bowers plunged into his duties. His staff of thirteen occupied the
top floor of a new building overlooking the Moneda, but World
War II brought changes. "We have greatly increased the personnel
here," the ambassador noted in August 1941, "until we have more
than forty—as big as the biggest in Europe before the war." By 1945
the embassy counted more than two hundred employees as coun-
selors, secretaries, attachés, members of military and aid missions,
FBI agents, and consuls. In 1950 the mission numbered three hundred, and the chancery moved a block away to a new eleven-story
building, occupying the top six floors. Bowers was proud of his people, once asserting, "I have a very fine staff from top to bottom,"
insisting that "each man knows his onions and all are keen about
their work."

The ambassador tried to follow a regular schedule. Never able to read Spanish well, he scanned three Santiago dailies each morning, and Pat translated interesting articles. Then Pepe drove him to the chancery around ten o'clock in a new black Buick sedan. The large staff forced Bowers to change his office habits: he held few staff meetings, delegated many assignments, and never entered the chancery coffee shop. To the distress of some in Washington and of several careerists who served under him in Santiago, Bowers was not interested in the day-to-day operations of the embassy. While he gained the respect of colleagues for not meddling in their work, the ambassador's relaxed attitude did not promote efficiency. On occasion the State Department complained that routine reports arrived after long delays. But Bowers was careful to oversee important government-to-government matters, noting with pride that "I pass on all dispatches sent to Washington."

His dispatches received a mixed reception. Secretary of State Cordell Hull and Undersecretary Sumner Welles praised him for "extremely helpful" reports, and Roosevelt found his views "interesting and thoughtful." Believing he had not written enough during the Spanish Civil War, Bowers wrote often from Chile. But Roosevelt and some at the State Department considered his correspondence too frequent. Roosevelt told Welles the envoy's letters were "beginning to be excessive." Still, the president dutifully answered—Bowers counted ninety-two letters from the president between 1933 to 1945; however, many were composed by Welles. The ambassador complained that Hull "replied to my letters with three and four lines until I ceased writing him except on very special occasions." Laurence Duggan, chief of the Latin American Division, believed the department should not bother to answer all of Bowers's mail.[6]

After lunch at home, the ambassador took a nap or read and then returned to the chancery until it closed at five. Most days his schedule was interrupted by visits to ministries or *actes de présence* at official or social functions. Whenever possible he spent time at his typewriter.

Bowers remained an unconventional head of mission. His kindness toward and repartee with his stenographers won their loyalty, but they despaired of his habit of filing dispatches in his coat pockets. He typed his letters to Roosevelt and Hull, as the misspellings attest. He continued to display a rumpled appearance while chewing unlighted cigars, and problems with his feet caused him to wear old shoes in the office with a space cut out to accommodate a splayed toe. On occasion colleagues had to remind the absentminded diplomat to change shoes before leaving the chancery.

The ambassador developed close relationships with several members of his staff. Cecil Lyon, who served as the secretary of the embassy from 1940 until 1943, was a special friend. Related to several Chilean aristocrats, he proved a helpful connection with conservatives and also became a translator for Bowers. "I have not in my more than ten years as ambassador had anyone under me for whom I have had such affection," he reflected in 1943, "and his work has been excellent." The secretary in turn appreciated his "countless kindnesses." Lyon would return to Chile as ambassador. Donald Heath, a political counselor who discussed Chilean events with his boss, wrote most of the weekly reports. On two occasions when Bowers did not take his advice, Heath so informed Washington without notifying him. Nevertheless he believed that Bowers was a "very good ambassador" and liked serving with him. Heath was another of the five officers under Bowers in Chile who became ambassadors. A secretary in Madrid, Hugh Millard came to Santiago in 1944 and remained for three years. "If you can take it," Millard wrote in 1947, "I should be most happy to serve you again for the third time."[7]

The ambassador's favorite was Biddle Garrison, whom he asked to look after "a million and one things." The aide wrote reports and served as a press liaison, translator, and social adviser. Attempts to have Garrison appointed an embassy secretary failed, but he received a salary as an "American clerk." He left Santiago in 1947 to return to the French Basque Coast where he worked at the Chilean consulate.

Two others were close aides. Lester Ziffren, a United Press correspondent and friend in Madrid, became press coordinator. On

*Ambassador Claude Bowers at his typewriter, Santiago, Chile*
COURTESY OF MANUSCRIPTS DEPARTMENT, LILLY LIBRARY, INDIANA UNIVERSITY, BLOOMINGTON

Sunday afternoons over a drink the stocky newsman met with the ambassador in the embassy sunroom to review the week's schedule and to orchestrate press releases. An Anglo-Argentine and *New York Times* stringer in Chile, Carlos Griffin served as cultural informant and translator. Ziffren returned to the United States following the war, but Griffin remained throughout Bowers's ambassadorship.

The envoy was unhappy with several people. Bowers left no doubt who was boss and expected United States diplomats to be partisans of democracy. His first counselor, Wesley Frost, was hostile to the Popular Front and insinuated that he advised Washington on

Chilean affairs. He wrote letters to Duggan, who sent them to Bowers. Bowers considered Frost a prima donna, and in 1940 he was sent to New Zealand. The ambassador found Col. Ralph H. Wooten, his military attaché, and wife "incomparable snobs" who "hate the present government and mingle with its enemies." On hearing that the colonel was being reassigned, Bowers remarked, "It is just as well." The staffer who caused the greatest difficulties was Allen Dawson, a counselor appointed at the request of the State Department. Dawson bragged that he would bring things into line, but he had emotional problems and shocked embassy employees with his fits of temper. After a family argument, he locked himself in his eighth-floor office and jumped out a window to his death.[8]

During his first two years Bowers dealt with the Popular Front. An outspoken opponent of dollar diplomacy, he welcomed Roosevelt's Good Neighbor policy. The ambassador urged Washington to grant his host government preferred treatment, believing this would strengthen Chilean democracy. The State Department criticized him for being too friendly, but claims that Chilean politicians manipulated Bowers were unfounded.

Washington sought to guarantee the import of copper, nitrate, and other materials, while Santiago wanted to replace its European markets. Aguirre Cerda established the Chilean Development Corporation (CORFO) to promote development, and Bowers showered Roosevelt with letters urging Export-Import Bank credits for CORFO and additional copper purchases. Always interested in South America, the president promised Bowers, "We want to do all we can." In 1940 exports to the United States were triple those before the war, and by 1942 the Export-Import Bank had extended $22 million in credit. Both nations agreed to a fixed price for copper, insuring a steady supply, and Washington promised to purchase copper and nitrates.[9]

Exposing German influence demanded Bowers's attention. "We are engaged here, more than elsewhere in South America," he insisted, "in hand to hand battle with the Nazi and Fifth Column." Pro-German sentiment was strong. The military traced its origins to Prussian instructors in the nineteenth century, thousands of

Germans had settled in the south, and German investment was important. Before the war Germany was Chile's principal supplier of pharmaceuticals and a major importer of agricultural products. Despite a failed coup in 1938, Chile's National Socialist movement continued its activities. With the benefit of hindsight many have viewed the Nazi menace as "spy-mania," but Hull, Roosevelt, and the FBI shared Bowers's concern.[10]

Defense was a primary consideration, and Roosevelt asked Bowers to suggest Chilean-American military conversations. United States military officers arrived in Santiago for secret meetings at the embassy in 1940, and the ambassador was elated that both sides agreed to "a detailed plan of cooperation of our two armies and navies in the event the Barbarian of Berlin attacks the Americas." Washington made supplies available, and Chilean officers were invited to the United States. In 1941 the two nations began negotiating a lend-lease agreement.[11]

Diplomacy exerted economic and political pressure to oppose Nazi influence. In 1940 the American and British embassies compiled black lists of firms believed to be supplying materials to the Axis. Some of these companies used their influence to have the Chilean government protest the lists, but this only convinced Bowers that the effort was successful.

Santiago was divided on the German threat. Off the record, two of Aguirre Cerda's foreign ministers expressed concern, but the president refused to believe in a fifth column. Bowers concluded that the administration lacked the courage to oppose Adolf Hitler. Under pressure Chile in 1941 ordered the German consul in Valparaiso to leave after he granted fraudulent passports to the crew of the *Graf Spee*, a German warship sunk off Montevideo. When the Santiago intendant prohibited the showing of the American anti-Hitler film *Parson Hall*—while permitting pro-Nazi films—Bowers persuaded the government to overturn the decision.

Chilean Communists opposed the Allies following the German-Soviet pact in August 1939. Early in the war the Communists were as vicious as the Nazis, Bowers complained, but the Socialists denounced the Communists' stance and withdrew from the center-

left alliance. By early 1941 rivalries among the Popular Front dis-
solved the coalition. After the German invasion of the Soviet
Union in June 1941, Bowers noted that overnight the Communists
became friends for the duration, later admitting that their anti-
Allied position had been a mistake.[12]

Aguirre Cerda became terminally ill in 1941. As a vineyard
owner he was known as "Don Tinto" (Mr. Red Wine), and in
November *Time* magazine implied he had a drinking problem.
The article caused a furor, and Bowers urged Roosevelt to
denounce it. At a press conference on 25 November, the day of
Aguirre Cerda's death, Roosevelt labeled the *Time* assertion "a
disgusting lie."

Following Pearl Harbor, all American republics broke relations
with the Axis except Chile and Argentina. Myriad factors account
for Santiago's delay: fear of attack along the coast, the German-
Chileans' influence, determination to demonstrate sovereignty by
resisting North American pressure, and Axis military successes.
But the pro-neutrality stance of government leaders proved decisive in postponing the rupture of relations. However, government
representatives for more than a year after Pearl Harbor suggested
that a break was imminent. On 8 December 1941, Foreign
Minister Juan Bautista Rossetti Colombino assured Bowers that
Chile was in absolute accord with Washington, and earlier the foreign minister had declared Chile's determination to support any
American nation attacked.[13] But the government refused to break
relations, claiming it wanted to give the victor in the 1942 presidential election freedom of action. Bowers expected the new executive to sever ties.

In 1940 at an inter-American conference in Havana, the
nations had agreed to consider any attack by a non-hemispheric
state an attack against all. At the Conference of American
Republics in Rio de Janeiro in January 1942, Undersecretary
Welles sought a united front. When Argentina and Chile
refused to back a resolution calling for a break with the Axis, the
undersecretary agreed to a declaration "recommending" that
American nations do so. This compromise came without con-

sulting Hull, who was "very angry" and claimed he spoke to Welles "more sharply than I had ever spoken to anyone in the Department."

The Radical Juan Antonio Ríos was elected president in February 1942 with Socialist and Communist support, defeating ex-dictator Ibáñez. Bowers praised the "tall, slender, handsome" Ríos, but distrusted his conservatism and "never felt he was friendly." Ríos professed admiration for the envoy but was critical when speaking off the record to Americans, who relayed this to Bowers.

After the Rio conference the ambassador told Rossetti the United States viewed severing ties as necessary to continental defense. Ríos's new foreign minister, Ernesto Barros Jarpa, "shocked" Bowers when he made it "very plain" he was opposed to breaking relations unless Chile were attacked, but Barros Jarpa promised to cooperate in supplying raw materials to the United States and pledged to act in the interests of continental solidarity. The foreign minister agreed to go to Washington to consult, but he kept postponing his trip, a decision that offended Welles. By May the ambassador concluded that the foreign minister was "the great obstacle." Bowers met with the president and Barros Jarpa on 18 May to explain why the United States believed Chile was not cooperating.[14]

Bowers's solution was to be patient, fearing attempts to press Santiago would destroy pro-American sentiment. Since Chile was a democracy, the ambassador believed any change would come through public pressure, and he worked with politicians who favored breaking with the Axis, supplying them with information. Former foreign minister Rossetti in his newspaper La Opinión was a proponent of the Allies, as were the Socialists and Communists. Gabriel González Videla, leader of the left wing of the Radicals, favored severing ties, as did some Conservatives, and several cabinet members urged Ríos to side with the Allies. Bowers also joined with the British, Brazilian, Mexican, and Chinese ambassadors to convince the administration. He encouraged rallies by pro-Allied groups, arranged letter-writing campaigns to newspapers, and cultivated the press. Always eager for recognition, Bowers was pleased when Roosevelt applauded his "vigorous campaign" to change Chilean policy.

The envoy tried to remove obstacles to breaking relations. Many feared German and Japanese submarine attacks should Chile sever ties, and Ríos told Bowers he would like to know he had Washington's backing. Roosevelt wrote that "President Ríos may of course count on the support of the United States."[15]

Barros Jarpa insisted that Chile's neutrality "prevents the inter-ference of the Axis with the movement of war material to the United States." He said that Washington appreciated Chile's coop-eration and was satisfied with its neutrality. The British ambassa-dor reported to Bowers that Ríos also claimed this. Welles and Hull wrote that Dávila was erroneously reporting to Santiago that the United States "fully understands" the Chilean position.

Bowers mistakenly considered Ríos pro-German. Ríos's opposi-tion to breaking relations came from domestic political considera-tions, and he later explained that rupture was a "difficult task" because his cabinet and public opinion were divided. For Ríos the foreign minister's assertions of United States satisfaction with Chile's position offered an excuse for doing nothing. Other con-siderations contributed to the government's reluctance to change its position. Barros Jarpa's cousin, Tobías Barros Ortiz, the pro-Nazi ambassador to Berlin, defended neutrality and "deliberately misin-formed" Santiago about German military successes.[16]

The ambassador took every opportunity to insist that the United States was "by no means satisfied with the Chilean position." He explained in February 1942 that Washington wanted Santiago to break relations and reported a "blunt conversation with the President and Barros Jarpa" in May. The next month Bowers had an "extraordinarily frank and I think forceful two hours" with both, emphasizing United States wishes. He assured the department that no misunderstanding was possible. Nor were his statements limit-ed to diplomatic circles. The cover of Santiago's weekly magazine of political satire, *Topaze*, depicted the ambassador and the foreign minister sparring.

The embassy increased pressure on the Moneda to take action against spying, for the FBI considered Chile a center for German espionage. Bowers told Ríos and Barros Jarpa that spies at the

German embassy had made Chile "a Nazi base for operations," and the ambassador complained that a German radio station near Valparaiso was sending reports of ship movements. Barros Jarpa claimed that charges of Nazi activity lacked "any foundation." Except for forbidding the German embassy to send cables in code, the government took no action. In June Bowers presented the foreign minister with a long report offering "absolute proof" of subversive activities.[17]

Throughout 1942 Washington received word that Chile was about to break relations with the Axis powers. Rossetti assured Welles in January that Santiago would sever ties. In June Barros Jarpa indicated he was seeking a pretext, and Ríos implied that his policy was leading to a break. The pro-Allied Chilean ambassador in Washington, Rodolfo Michels, without consulting Barros Jarpa, told Bowers and the department that Ríos had decided to abandon neutrality. The ambassador wrote Roosevelt in July that he was hopeful that the Chilean administration was about to change policy.[18]

Michels in August told Hull that Ríos was ready to act, and Roosevelt invited the president to Washington, expecting him to announce his changed policy. Welles told Michels that Ríos must do so before departing. During a September trip to Santiago the Coordinator of Inter-American Affairs, Nelson A. Rockefeller, also emphasized that it was imperative that the Chilean president break relations with the Axis powers before going to Washington. Barros Jarpa and Ríos were opposed to this, but the foreign minister assured Bowers that on the president's return Chile's problems with the United States would be solved. The minister in September told Bowers that Chile "will break relations," but the ambassador suspected Chile would not do so. When Barros Jarpa publicly denied charges of Nazi espionage, Bowers concluded that he "deliberately lies."[19]

Ríos's refusal chagrined Hull, Welles, and Bowers. The ambassador wondered if it were not time to issue an ultimatum, and in Washington Welles informed Michels that assistance to Chile depended on breaking relations. Before a Boston audience on 8 October, an exasperated Welles urged Chile and Argentina not to permit their hemispheric neighbors "to be stabbed in the back" by Axis emissaries. The undersecretary claimed German radio trans-missions from Chile were responsible for sinking Allied vessels. While this charge proved false, Welles and Bowers were convinced it was true.

Welles's speech brought a storm of complaints. Alessandri labeled his remarks "totally unjustified," claiming Chile had not "broken our relations with the Axis, to exercise our sovereignty and in defense of national dignity." Barros Jarpa said the undersecretary was casting blame that "we cannot accept." University students demonstrated in front of the embassy and Axis sympathizers threw stones. Ríos wrote Roosevelt that because of the disagreeable atmosphere created by the speech he was forced to postpone his visit.[20]

The ambassador considered Welles's address a shocking mistake. Bowers believed the undersecretary had made Barros Jarpa a national hero and given him a weapon to continue his fight against breaking relations. "Nothing could have been more unfortunate," Bowers concluded. Hull, too, thought the speech an error and was angry that the undersecretary had not consulted him.

Bowers and Hull were wrong. Welles's speech proved a turning point. It demonstrated Chile's isolation and increased pressure from pro-Allied Liberals, Conservatives, Radicals, Socialists, and Communists. A cabinet crisis on 19 October forced the president to appoint ministers favoring a break. Barros Jarpa later admitted he was dismissed because of his opposition. The document Bowers had delivered in June outlining German espionage was published in the Chilean press in early November, convincing many that neutrality was a mistake. The entreaties of other Latin American nations and German military defeats in Russia and North Africa in late 1942 also encouraged a new policy.[21]

The appointment of Joaquín Fernández Fernández as foreign minister meant rupture. The president instructed his interior min-ister to take energetic methods against espionage, and Germans working with the radio transmitter were arrested. Ríos told Bowers that Chile was doing everything possible and informed the press that Chile would break relations if its interests and those of the

American continent recommended it. Fernández warned the Senate of the nation's isolation, and the president told Bowers that "a break has been decided on." In January 1943 Ríos informed Roosevelt and Welles that Chile had decided to break relations immediately. The Senate approved this on 19 January, and the next day Ríos announced the suspension.[22]

"You deserve all of our congratulations for your part in the realignment of Chile's foreign policy," Roosevelt wrote Bowers. "The victory which has been gained is as real a one as though it had been won on the battle fields." This delighted the ambassador. But Welles had composed Roosevelt's letter, adding in a covering note, "This reply is couched in terms which are perhaps more enthusiastic than are in reality warranted." While professing to admire Bowers's ability, the undersecretary believed the envoy had not been forceful enough in presenting the administration's demands. Others have made the same argument, suggesting he was the "unwitting tool" of Chilean politicians.

That Barros Jarpa and Ríos misrepresented the United States position was not Bowers's fault. Time after time he stressed Washington's insistence. The president and foreign minister did not want to do so and for months used every effort to avoid rupture, including feigning ignorance. Barros Jarpa admitted that the ambassador was explicit when insisting on Chile's severing ties. To his cousin in Berlin he wrote, "I am being strongly pressured from Washington to break relations." Some at the State Department disagreed with Welles's criticism of Bowers. The head of the Division of American Republics, Philip W. Bonsal, lauded the ambassador's "great good sense" in working for rupture.[23]

After Santiago broke relations, North American support increased. In March a United States–Chilean lend-lease agreement was signed, offering Chile $50 million in arms and munitions. Over the next months more than 150 planes, 385 trucks, and supplies of tanks, cars, and guns reached Chile. By the war's end more than $20 million in lend-lease equipment had been shipped, and loans to CORFO helped finance six power plants, a tire factory, and a cement works.

Santiago curbed German activities, but the United States was not satisfied. Communications with Berlin were suspended, the German embassy's activities were exposed, and the German Club and a pro-Axis paper were closed. Although the operators of the German radio transmitter had been arrested, its head enjoyed diplomatic immunity and remained in Chile for several months. Despite repeated requests from the United States embassy, the government did not liquidate the assets of German banks until January 1944.[24]

As a reward for breaking relations, Washington arranged for three official visits. In March 1943, Roosevelt dispatched Vice President Henry A. Wallace to Santiago, and in September Bowers accompanied Foreign Minister Fernández to Washington. Ríos had to remain in Santiago because a military coup in Argentina required his attention. At the White House, Roosevelt spoke with the foreign minister for two hours in French. In November 1945, Ríos finally made his state visit to Washington, where President Truman received him as "the representative of a democratic people." In New York Bowers helped arrange a special reception. Mayor Fiorello La Guardia asked Ríos to speak at the ceremony renaming Sixth Avenue the Avenue of the Americas, and President Nicholas Murray Butler of Columbia University made him Doctor Honoris Causa.

Following Chile's rupture with the Axis, Bowers's diplomacy proved controversial at the State Department. Convinced Chile was "furnishing us more essential war material than any other South American country," he argued for favorable treatment for mineral exports and military requests. Fernández called him "Chile's best attorney before the State Department," but Washington careerists criticized him for being too pro-Chilean. Some complained he had not stressed the importance the United States gave to German espionage, a charge which overlooked his many protests to the Foreign Ministry over delays in pursuing anti-Axis measures.

Only nations at war were invited to the organizing conference of the United Nations in San Francisco. Chile had broken relations with Germany, Italy, and Japan, but had not declared war on the Axis. Fernández was shocked at this requirement, but Ríos assured

Bowers he would take the necessary step. In February the president declared a "state of belligerency" with Japan, and Congress approved the declaration, thereby permitting Chile to join the United Nations.[25]

The rivalry between the United States and the Soviet Union dominated world affairs after 1945 and determined Washington's policy toward Chile during Bowers's last eight years. The Chilean Communists "took up the anti-Yankee slogans their Nazi cousins had just abandoned," the ambassador lamented. In 1946 Communist-led strikes first in the nitrate region and later in the coal mines were viewed as political protests by the government. The president declared a state of siege, and there was bloodshed before workers returned to the nitrate mines. Fearing a coal shortage, Fernández told Bowers that Chile wished to purchase thirty thousand tons of coal from the United States, but the strikes ended.

Although the Communists became the most outspoken foes of the United States, conservative and moderate groups—as well as the non-Communist left—displayed their enmity. In the decade after the war, a love-hate relationship appeared. A tense domestic political situation and difficult economic problems forced Santiago to call on Washington, but the ensuing aid often was criticized as inadequate.

Following Ríos's death in 1946, three major candidates sought the presidency, including two rightists—nominees of the Conservative and Liberal parties. The Radicals chose González Videla, whom the Communists endorsed. Each combination jockeyed for advantage. González Videla courted Communist support, and his refusal to repudiate their "campaign of vilification and falsehood against us" annoyed Bowers. He observed that even one of the conservative candidates "made indirect digs at the United States."[26]

Although the candidates considered United States support deleterious, the embassy and North American firms were approached by their representatives. Bowers told American interests to make no contributions and insisted they refrain from interfering in Chile's internal affairs. A Conservative solicited funds from Joe Cuzzens, head of the Chilean Electric Company, a North

American enterprise, but Cuzzens refused, citing the ambassador's warning. An official from González Videla's staff visited the ambassador to ascertain United States policy. "We have been approached by representatives of all the candidates," Bowers noted, "but they were all satisfied with our explanations." After his victory on 4 September, González Videla admitted to Bowers that United States companies had not contributed to any party.

González Videla won a narrow plurality thanks to Communist support. He assumed the presidency in November 1946 and gained congressional backing by appointing three Liberals as well as three Radicals to his cabinet. The Communists had refused to join the ministries of Radical presidents in 1938 and 1942 and again were reluctant, but González Videla insisted they participate.[27] The Communists agreed, heading three ministries.

Bowers and the Truman administration were aware that in accepting these portfolios the Communists had achieved more power in Chile than anywhere else in the Western Hemisphere. Washington, however, was groping for a policy toward the Soviet Union, and United States reaction was conciliatory. The ambassador criticized the harsh anticommunist comments Herbert Hoover made during a 1946 visit to Santiago and agreed with Wallace's plea for a more understanding attitude toward the Soviet Union. Bowers feared "a drift toward war with Russia which would wreck civilization."

Several considerations lessened the impact of the pro-Moscow ministers. Communists held posts in the French and Italian governments, and Bowers understood that González Videla was obligated to the Communists. The portfolios were second level, and Bowers found their minister of agriculture an intelligent man, well trained for his job.[28] The presence in the cabinet of three Liberals and three Radicals also limited the Marxists' influence.

González Videla played down the Communists' importance. At his invitation, Bowers visited the victor, who assured him he would not "take dictation from the Communists—and that their attitudes will not influence his foreign policy in any degree." When Bowers showed his host his 1928 keynote address attacking dollar diplomacy and advocating social justice, the Chilean read it aloud twice and "slapped my knee" with approval. Two decades later González Videla insisted he never had any doubts that Washington knew his government would remain a friend.

Admiral William D. Leahy, Truman's chief of staff, attended the presidential inauguration. Leahy had served as ambassador to Vichy France and was a friend of González Videla, who was the Chilean representative to the Gallic regime. At two meetings the president-elect told the admiral the Communists would not control the government and asked him to inform Truman.[29]

González Videla's position toward the Communists remained an enigma. He admitted to a *New York Times* reporter that the Communist party "acts under the direction of Moscow," but argued that the Communists had supported him and were useful. He maintained that Washington "must furnish money for Chilean development" and blamed his nation's misery on North America's "failure to furnish money." This statement enraged the ambassador: "We have given millions for a steel plant, power plants, cement plants, etc. and no other country has given a penny. It was an amazing exhibition of hostility to the U.S., or complete adherence to Russia, or of incredible ignorance of what the U.S. has done." Upon reflection, he concluded, "The man is drunk with victory and I shall await his views when sober."

The Communist cabinet ministers proved controversial. The Liberals, laissez-faire "big business boys," to use Bowers's phrase, attacked them. The so-called alliance of Manchester and Moscow divided the government. Outside the administration, Conservatives, right-wing Radicals, and Socialists clamored for their dismissal, and the Chilean Anticommunist Action Front was formed to demand their removal. Nondomestic forces also opposed Communist representation in the government. North American private investment accounted for 70 percent of Chile's foreign total and controlled the mining corporations and telephone and electric companies. These firms employed thousands and paid taxes.[30] United States private investment and government aid would not continue if the Communists played a major role.

When González Videla assumed the presidency, Washington did not curtail financial and military aid. In September the United States approved a $15 million loan from the Export-Import Bank to CORFO and continued making arrangements to furnish "minor vessels and auxiliary vessels" to the Chilean Navy. The State Department also expressed interest in negotiating a commercial treaty. Two months after the election Spruille Braden, Assistant Secretary of State for Latin America, observed, " 'We had taken great pains to demonstrate good will toward President González Videla, this in spite of a feeling of uneasiness in certain quarters at the inclusion of Communists in the Chilean cabinet.' "

While the Communists served in the administration, the only dispute that threatened United States–Chilean relations was a Communist-led strike against the Kennecott Copper Corporation begun in September 1946. The government ordered the company to submit the matter to arbitration, but management insisted that the workers' demands be omitted. Bowers criticized both the labor ministry and Kennecott for refusing to compromise, complaining that the company was behind the times in dealing with labor disputes.[31]

A resolution of the strike was important. Bowers reported that the Kennecott president, E. T. Stannard, was told by González Videla that "he could not break with the Communists so soon" and that he considered "full arbitration politically essential." Kennecott's failure to agree, the Chilean executive claimed, would force a takeover of the mines. Bowers informed Washington that Kennecott's refusal could push the government farther to the left. Undersecretary of State Dean Acheson cabled that any settlement that jeopardized copper investments would place Washington in an embarrassing position. "With all the good will in the world for Chile this Govt. might be bitterly criticized by press," he warned, "if it were alleged that at time when interests of thousands of Kennecott stock holders were endangered American Govt. had made additional loans to Chile."

In response Washington placed an informal embargo on credits, including funds for five ships and a tanker already contracted for. The Chilean embassy in Washington informed González Videla of this before Bowers was notified. When the president confronted him, the envoy could only tell him that the State Department had failed to alert him, assuring him he had "strongly advised against this threat." González Videla lectured Bowers that Washington's action might force him "to change entirely his foreign policy and look elsewhere for friends."

González Videla softened his stand in November. He told Bowers that worker demands would be included in issues to be adjudicated, admitting this was necessary to placate the Communists, but the president promised to name an arbiter who would dismiss their claims. Pressed by Washington and aware of González Videla's pledge, the company agreed. On 29 December the decision was announced, pleasing Stannard, who thanked Bowers.[32]

East-West tensions hardened into the cold war. The Soviet Union rejected participation in the Marshall Plan, and the Truman Doctrine offered protection to Greece and Turkey. Chilean Communist leader Carlos Contreras Labarca was accused of softness toward the United States and replaced by his critic, Ricardo Fonseca. The party increased its pressure on the president, asking him to name twenty Communists as governors and intendants.[33] González Videla appointed six.

The president in March 1947 attempted to mollify the Telephone Company, a North American firm involved in a dispute over an approved rate increase. To appease the Communists, González Videla told the company he could not sanction the authorized increase, but he urged the firm to take the matter to the Supreme Court, which would rule in the company's favor.

Municipal elections in April 1947 brought an end to the Liberal-Radical-Communist ministry. The two non-Marxist partners suffered a stinging defeat, while the Communists, the Socialists, and the Conservatives increased their votes. The Liberals resigned and were followed by the Radicals. The president was forced to dismiss the Communists, but he tried to avert a break. González Videla told Bowers that in the event of a legislative crisis he might form a ministry of the left, possibly including

Communists. "I sometimes doubt if the President measures the meaning of his words," the surprised envoy concluded.[34]

Washington feared González Videla was catering to the Communists, and the department told Bowers there would be no United States loans to Santiago. It pressed the International Bank for Reconstruction and Development to reject Chile's request for $40 million, until the government raised the annual repayment on its foreign debt from $7 to $11 million.

Bowers favored the credit and opposed Washington's stance. When González Videla objected to this hostile treatment, the ambassador confided to his diary, "The whole thing looks like Dollar Diplomacy back again in a big way." He wrote the White House, complaining that United States business interests were frustrating Santiago's attempts to raise funds. "You can rest assured that as long as I am President," Truman replied, "the gentlemen in Wall Street are not to control the operations of the International Bank." But the department did not change its policy, and the head of the Chilean desk insisted that settlement of the debt payments "is a *must*." He believed Bowers refused to recognize this and observed, "I doubt whether anything less than a volume of instructions would clarify for him our feelings up here."[35]

González Videla's break with the Communists came in August 1947. The party saw that advancement within the administration was impossible, and the Communist-controlled union closed the coal mines at Lota. The president decided on confrontation. On 19 August he declared the Communists "enemies of Chile" and dismissed them from their five governorships and one intendancy. He was granted "extraordinary powers" for six months, enabling him to normalize economic activities. The government accused the Communists of plotting to attack the carabineros, the national police, and agents questioned party leaders. González Videla assured Bowers that "the communists are finished as far as the government is concerned."

Thereafter events moved rapidly. Fearing a strike at the Lota mines, González Videla had asked Bowers in April for twenty thousand tons of coal as a reserve, and by August fifty thousand tons had arrived. When the strike was declared, Washington agreed to an additional one hundred thousand tons. After armed intervention the mines were reopened. The president had positive proof, he assured Bowers, that the Communist party was following instructions from Moscow. The Soviet, Yugoslav, and Czechoslovak missions were charged with directing the Chilean Communists and ordered to leave.[36]

González Videla was intent on crushing the Communist party. Convinced that "the Communists and their whole system is based on the theory that the bourgeoisie are timid and will not fight," the president went on the attack. He proposed the Law for the Defense of Democracy. Enacted with support from the Radicals, Conservatives, Liberals, and some Socialists, this measure banned the Communist party, removed members from the voting rolls, and made them ineligible for union offices. Bowers, though a liberal opposed to the anti-Communist hysteria and Sen. Joseph R. McCarthy's intolerance in his own country, believed the Communists were determined to overthrow Chilean democracy, so he favored the legislation. But he warned Washington that the measure would not eliminate Communist influence.

For half a century González Videla's reasons for turning against the Communists have been debated. Contemporaries saw them in the light of their convictions. Bowers believed the president changed his mind when he recognized that his Communist allies were working to wreck Chile with strikes and sabotage. Communists decided that González Videla never had intended to retain the ministers for more than six months, asserting that Admiral Leahy brought instructions from Washington to dismiss them. Certainly the hostility of other political parties toward the Communists and an awareness of United States attitudes were factors in the president's decision.[37]

Washington demonstrated its support of González Videla's attack on the Communists. The Export-Import Bank granted credits of $4 million to pay for the coal, and the State Department made no protest when the Chilean Congress added a 20 percent surcharge to the copper tax. Washington approved Santiago's plans to amortize interest payments due foreign creditors, permitting Chile to regularize its debt and receive additional United States funds. Anaconda Copper decided to spend $130 million on improvements and join Kennecott in investing in the steel mill being built under CORFO. In 1948 the International Bank for Reconstruction and Development approved $16 million in credit, the first to a Latin American republic, and the Export-Import Bank granted another $23 million.

United States aid remained important to Chilean economic development after World War II. In 1949 when the price of copper fell, the Export-Import Bank extended $25 million in credits. North American assistance went to a variety of projects, but its major contribution was to the Huachipato steel mill, CORFO's most ambitious project. Of Huachipato's cost of $88 million, $48 million was financed by bank credits. Bowers lobbied for this funding in his dispatches and in an appeal to Truman. On Huachipato's completion the State Department declared it an outstanding example of the benefits derived from United States financial aid.[38]

Throughout his Santiago years the ambassador was concerned with "the miserable condition of the poor" and appalled by "the feudal ideas" of the wealthy landlords and their treatment of the rural workers. He warned the department that improving the standard of living was essential. He discussed the nation's sanitation problems, deaths caused by poverty, substandard housing, and unjust working conditions and spoke with Chilean presidents and their wives about social problems, accompanying them to the inauguration of housing projects and medical facilities.

During the war funds were limited for social projects, but Santiago in 1943 signed an agreement with the United States Institute of Inter-American Affairs (IIAA) to cosponsor public health programs. Washington gave $5 million in the next decade, and Chile contributed millions. Dr. Theodore I. Gandy directed the IIAA in Chile and praised Bowers's support. By June 1948, some 1,300 separate projects had been completed and 634 were under way, including 86 hospitals, 319 dispensaries, dozens of laboratories, 10 schools of nursing and hygiene, and 123 water-treatment systems. The most celebrated was the sewage system installed in the Quinta Normal, a poor section of Santiago, where one hundred kilometers of pipeline were laid, benefiting one hundred fifty thousand.[39]

In his 1949 inaugural address Truman called for technical assistance to underdeveloped countries, a program known as Point IV. Bowers urged Chile to participate, and Washington and Santiago signed a series of agreements for programs in technology, agriculture and livestock, and education. To Bowers's disgust Communists, many Roman Catholic educators, and some usually pro–United States moderates complained that the educational agreement would subject Chilean education to North American influence, so this accord remained inoperative. The other agreements were approved by the Chilean Congress, and Point IV help was extended to low-cost housing.

Chileans lauded Bowers in appreciation for their new sewage system. Quinta Normal residents held a celebration each 4 July with Bowers the guest of honor. The three Radical presidents thanked him for his efforts and the national police presented him with a medal. Socialist senator Salvador Allende, a physician and later Chile's first Marxist president, praised the ambassador's concern for the nation's public health system. Contemporary press reports, and even occasional editorials long after he left Santiago, applauded "his passion for social justice" and his belief that "people should live with equal dignity and parity."[40]

Washington stressed hemispheric defense agreements after 1945, and Bowers worked to improve them. He believed that United States army, air, and naval missions were important in cementing cooperation among the services in both countries and urged their expansion. To demonstrate his interest in military affairs, he regularly attended reviews and graduations at the army and naval academies. In 1946 he helped arrange the purchase of sixty-seven aircraft by Santiago "at a low figure," and in 1950 he called on Truman to assist in selling two warships. The Chilean defense minister and Bowers in 1952 negotiated a military accord. Communists and Socialists viewed the agreement as an example of United States imperialism, and others argued it compromised Chilean sovereignty. Despite vocal opposition, the Chilean Congress approved the pact establishing military cooperation for a quarter century.[41]

United States–Chilean relations were a topic of debate during the presidential election in 1952. Though outlawed, the Communists backed Allende in his first presidential campaign. The Socialist senator promised to end the military pact, and Ibáñez ran as a nationalist opposed to the treaty. The Liberals and Conservatives united, while the Radicals presented their own candidate. Bowers considered Ibáñez "our enemy," condemning his dictatorial past and indifference to the Allied cause.

Inflation and a stagnant economy, coupled with disgust at party bickering, led almost half of the voters to choose Ibáñez. Following his election, the new president moderated his anti–United States stand. He assured Bowers that Chile would not renounce the military pact or establish relations with Moscow, or attempt to nationalize the copper industry or repeal the Law for the Defense of Democracy. Washington followed the ambassador's recommendation that no loans be made until Ibáñez demonstrated a desire to cooperate. Bowers's relations with the new president remained only civil during the ambassador's last months, and the ambassador complained that several of his ministers were super-Nazis. Still, Bowers helped promote United States displays of goodwill. At his suggestion Truman sent Eleanor Roosevelt to Ibáñez's inauguration, and in 1953 President Dwight D. Eisenhower had his brother Milton meet with the new executive during a South American tour.[42]

After World War II Chileans believed that Washington was taking their cooperation for granted. While the Marshall Plan poured billions into Europe's reconstruction, Chile, like many of its neighbors, complained that the United States neglected Latin America. Bowers realized that Communist threats elsewhere and spending limits were responsible for postwar cuts, but he saw them as "unnecessarily drastic, too much out of proportion." Such sentiments were expressed by many others—including Rockefeller,

Peter J. Grace, and some United States diplomats.[43] The ambassador's outspoken views on foreign aid only increased the hostility of many careerists at the State Department who saw him as too pro-Chilean.

Bowers's relations with the Chilean government were the focus of his ambassadorial labors, but semiofficial duties and personal diplomacy also made demands on his time. As in Spain, his family life and writing also offered a welcome retreat from his public schedule.

# CHAPTER TEN

# Don Claudio of Santiago

Bowers once again discovered in Chile that an ambassador's responsibilities were many. Some he detested, particularly protocol and social obligations, and others he liked, involving new friendships, projects, and hosting visitors. In addition Bowers devoted time to writing and to following, and on occasion contributing to, politics back home. As always, he enjoyed the pleasures of family life.

Much of his diplomatic work focused on trade and military agreements, breaking relations with the Axis, and Santiago's policies during the cold war. But in large measure the success of such efforts depended on goodwill, so Bowers used protocol and personal diplomacy to promote sympathy for his country. Despite the advances of age, he devoted much of his energy to his job.

The demands of protocol were complicated. Celebrating Chilean independence each 18 September was required of the diplomatic corps: a Te Deum at the cathedral, standing during the military parade, the crowded presidential reception, and the obligatory appearance at the opera. The Fourth of July meant a flag raising and national anthems, greeting Chilean officers and veterans, and dinners and dances sponsored by the North American community. He also represented his government at the inaugurations of three presidents and the funerals of two. Despite foot pains, Bowers chose to walk in the procession from the cathedral to the cemetery when Pedro Aguirre Cerda died, since the venerable Archbishop José María Caro Rodríguez was walking. Prayers for the pope on his name day, visiting embassies on national holidays, and placing wreaths on monuments were other duties.

Bowers nearly wore himself out. During the war he promoted the Allied cause by attending reviews at the military academies, as well as talks and rallies sponsored by pro-Allied groups. Bowers's predecessor, Norman Armour, had not cooperated with Señora Aguirre Cerda in promoting her special charity, a Christmas bazaar with booths sponsored by the international community. Bowers urged the American colony's participation, and the president's wife thanked him for "the magnificent work accomplished by Your Excellency." For fourteen years he presented diplomas at an English-language school founded by North Americans, Santiago College, and gave commencement addresses at Villa María Academy, run by United States nuns. He handed out prizes at fairs and awards at orphanages, spoke at the inauguration of clinics supported by United States charities, attended Fourth of July parties at public schools, arranged for the donation of an American flag to the cathedral, and served as godfather to twins named Franklin and Eleanor.[1]

He was determined to promote United States culture. Bowers gave lectures on history, North Americans who had been influential in Chile, and Chilean–United States relations, and the Chilean–North American Cultural Institute, an embassy agency, received his support. The ambassador gave talks at the University of Chile, the Catholic University, and the Chile-American Association and encouraged visiting countrymen to do the same. When Douglas Fairbanks, Jr., was in Santiago, Bowers wrote an anti-Hitler speech for the actor, who delivered the translated address in Spanish, not without nervous pauses, at the University of Chile. Using his publishing contacts the ambassador arranged displays of works by United States authors at the annual International Book Fair. Aware that most of his predecessors seldom left the capital, he traveled throughout the country from Arica in the north to Puerto Montt in the south.

"The social life here is the most trying feature of the job," Bowers wrote. "It is a shame diplomats are subjected to such meaningless punishment." There was three times as much entertaining as in Spain: luncheons, cocktail parties, and dinners given by the president, ministers, and the diplomatic corps and the many invitations from staff and Chilean friends. Complaining he had not eaten lunch or dinner at home for two weeks, he asserted, "Too much. Perhaps a diplomat's brains are supposed to be in their belly." Throughout his Chilean years his personal correspondence, diary, and dispatches were replete with similar comments, but he enjoyed one aspect of the functions. He often noted that "the women were very attractive and . . . some beautiful."[2]

Entertaining was an obligation. President Franklin D. Roosevelt wrote that during the war social events should be held to a minimum, but they continued. The ambassador hosted hundreds of functions: receptions, luncheons, and dinners for officials, members of the embassy, visiting Americans, and friends. Bowers's secretary handled the invitations and matters of protocol.

Embassy dinners often included legislators. The dining table seated thirty-two and was usually full. Bowers was careful to invite representatives from a spectrum of political parties. The liberal envoy admired several conservative politicos, including Eduardo Cruz Coke, whom he considered the best friend of the United States, and Miguel Cruchaga Tocornal. Three Radicals held the presidency, so many of their number were guests, and Eduardo Frei Montalva, later a Christian Democratic president, was a centrist whose friendship he cultivated. Bowers believed Oscar Schnake Vergara, a Socialist, was the ablest member of Aguirre Cerda's cabinet. A Marxist and future president, Salvador Allende, was another Socialist guest. When the Chilean Communists backed the Allies during the war, Bowers was quick to welcome them.[3]

Receptions, cocktail parties, buffets, and dances brought hundreds to the residence to celebrate the Fourth of July, Thanksgiving, and the Christmas season. The ambassador, his wife, and daughter greeted guests in a receiving line in the front salon. A reception with refreshments and dancing, he observed on 4 July 1941, created a "crush," including the president, his cabinet, and military chieftains. In 1949 he complained on 4 July that "a thousand hungry and thirsty Americans jam into the Embassy to raise hell."

One function was special: the wedding reception for Lola Torres, daughter of his chauffeur Pepe Torres. She attended a private school where she later taught, and in 1952 Lola married the son of the Chilean ambassador to London. At the embassy the newlyweds were greeted by rooms filled with flowers, champagne, cocktails, and a proud Bowers.

Entertaining Americans was a mixed blessing. Often dinners and receptions for United States congressmen, senators, and mayors amounted to obligations. The ambassador did not look forward to visits from the chiefs of military missions and heads of the Red Cross, the Export-Import Bank, the American Legion, the YMCA, and the Chamber of Commerce. Bowers was forced to give a dinner in 1949 for a guest he loathed, Col. Robert R. McCormick, owner of the *Chicago Tribune*. On the other hand the ambassador found Gen. Fulgencio Batista charming when the Cuban strongman visited in 1944, and an appreciative Roosevelt thanked Bowers. Remembering the dictator's love for alcohol during a trip to Washington, Roosevelt wrote that he hoped he had arranged for plenty of martinis.

The visits of many countrymen proved enjoyable. Antarctic explorer Rear Adm. Richard E. Byrd was the couple's first guest, followed by film stars Tyrone Power and Bob Hope, Gen. Maxwell D. Taylor, Adm. William F. Halsey, Walt Disney, old friend James A. Farley, and Dennis Cardinal Dougherty of Philadelphia. Bowers was happy to greet Waldo Frank and John Gunther, as well as his friend from Madrid days, John Dos Passos. Frank and Gunther were collecting materials for their works *South American Journey* and *Inside Latin America*, respectively. He discussed Chilean politics with both and arranged interviews. On reading Gunther's manuscript, he suggested changes concerning Aguirre Cerda so that the published work would not embarrass the embassy. The author agreed, assuring the ambassador that he could not have written those chapters without his help. Midwestern guests were special. Indiana businessmen appreciated Bowers's Hoosier hospitality and stories about their state, and President Herman B Wells of Indiana University remembered with nostalgia his visit to the embassy during a trip to Chile.[4]

Political guests, even Republicans, found a warm welcome. Herbert Hoover "presented the possibilities of embarrassment" because of Bowers's 1928 keynote address, but the two enjoyed conversation and renewed memories. The former president had listened to the speech and had some fun out of it because of the closing sentence, "To Your Tents, Oh Israel." Hoover said that Democrats might live in tents, but Republicans had houses. During his fact-finding mission to Latin America, Milton Eisenhower thanked the ambassador for making his Chilean stay "informative, interesting, pleasant and rewarding." Among the visiting Democrats were Rose Kennedy and her children Eunice and John. Bowers had known Rose Kennedy's father and found the grandson a "bright young fellow." "I am not surprised to find that he is politically ambitious." The ambassador and the future president talked for three hours.[5]

When Vice President Henry A. Wallace visited, seventy thousand people heard him praise their nation as "a great country of democratic traditions." Determined to see farmers and workers as well as political figures and businessmen, Wallace addressed forty thousand coal miners in Concepcion, handled himself on horseback, and spoke with farmers along the roadside. The vice president grew in Bowers's esteem on confessing that the 1928 keynote speech had given him "the final shove" into the Democratic party and that he had approved of Bowers's views during the Spanish Civil War.[6]

The most appreciated guest was Eleanor Roosevelt, the United States representative to Carlos Ibáñez's inauguration in 1952. Given the president-elect's friendship with Argentine dictator Juan D. Perón, Bowers feared the ceremony might be turned into an anti-Yankee festival, and he believed Mrs. Roosevelt's presence

*Left to right: Mrs. Ibáñez del Campo, President Carlos Ibáñez del Campo, Mrs. Eleanor Roosevelt, Mrs. Sybil Bowers, and Ambassador Claude Bowers. United States Embassy, Santiago, Chile, November 1952.*

COURTESY OF MANUSCRIPTS DEPARTMENT, LILLY LIBRARY, INDIANA UNIVERSITY, BLOOMINGTON

might demonstrate the popularity of the United States. Her five days in Santiago were crammed with visits to educational institutions, talks to women's groups, an homage at the Municipal Theater, dinners given by both the outgoing and incoming presidents, receptions, and luncheons. At the embassy she hosted a press conference—a rarity for a woman in Chile—and submitted to questions, some a bit delicate. She also was taken to a housing project and a slum "where the very poor live in miserable shacks and Mrs. Roosevelt went into the houses and talked to the people." Bowers noted that even the anti-American newspapers printed glowing reports of her visit. Mrs. Roosevelt enjoyed her stay and praised the ambassador's "wise guidance"; she told him he had "lived the Good Neighbor Policy." When the State Department congratulated him, calling her trip "a stroke of genius on your part," he reflected, "Commendation from the Department comes so seldom."[7]

Bowers's personal diplomacy depended on contacts with the diplomatic corps, members of the American community, and important Chileans. One favorite was Betty Pack, whom he had known in Madrid and St. Jean de Luz before her espionage work in Warsaw and Berlin. Her husband Arthur had been transferred to Chile, where he oversaw the black list for the British. Unknown to him or Bowers, Arthur was sent to Santiago, where his American wife had lived as a youth, to permit her to keep tabs on German activities. Fearing she might be shot as a spy if she returned to Warsaw, Bowers was relieved when she remained in Chile, and he helped her write propaganda articles.[8]

The ambassador cultivated United States executives. Despite his distrust of big business, he was aware of the importance of North American investment; four Chilean presidents assured him that United States capital was needed. His staff followed legislative proposals dealing with mining, and he protested when leftist politicians proposed nationalizing foreign firms and interceded when companies faced legal problems. United States executives cooperated with Bowers and were happy with his warnings against businesses contributing to Chilean political parties. When he asked them to provide funds and leadership for the Chilean–North American Cultural Institute, they did so. When United States businessmen in Chile were convinced that Thomas E. Dewey would be elected president in 1948, a group proposed to petition Dewey to retain Bowers. The envoy respected the United States managers and hosted luncheons for the heads of North American corporations, representing copper, banking, shipping, utilities, and manufacturing.[9]

Two Roman Catholic clerics were among the Protestant ambassador's friends. A North American Jesuit, Father Gustave Weigel, was a proponent of social activism and ecumenism, and conservative Catholic churchmen viewed him with suspicion. Bowers praised the priest's defense of the poor, respected his intelligence, and enjoyed his sense of humor. "A loveable character, sweet and good, honest and liberal" is how Bowers described another friend and frequent embassy visitor, José María Cardinal Caro Rodríguez.

Bowers held several Chilean politicians in high esteem and was friendly with many, but he was closest to Arturo Alessandri, twice president. He considered him a consummate politician and constructive statesman who had established his place in Chilean history by his sponsorship of social legislation and his role as a pioneer in the struggle for women's rights. Bowers's friendship with Alessandri was slow to develop because of his suspicions of Alessandri's opposition to the Popular Front. The two met informally, and soon both became admirers. The envoy was impressed with Alessandri's intelligence and found him "the most amusing and caustic conversationalist I ever heard." Alessandri in turn praised Bowers's *Jefferson and Hamilton* and his concern for Chile.[10]

Other Chileans became close friends. Trained at Columbia University, Amanda Labarca was the nation's leading feminist and an active supporter of the Chilean–North American Cultural Institute. Bowers judged her the most brilliant woman intellectual in South America. Agustín and Chavela Edwards were other favorites. The owner of Chile's major newspaper, Edwards was a Renaissance man—a sportsman, composer, pilot, and raconteur. His beautiful and charming wife was the darling of Santiago society; "there is no brighter, lovelier woman in Chile," the ambassador wrote. The Edwardses often invited the Bowerses to their home. After Dwight D. Eisenhower's election Señora Edwards urged President Ibáñez to request that Bowers be retained.[11]

Bowers's reputation as an author brought acceptance in intellectual circles. He became the first diplomat admitted into the Chilean Academy of History, and his address to the group on Minister Joel Poinsett's role in Chile's history solidified Bowers's reputation. The envoy was inducted into the Chilean Society of History and Geography and became a friend of Ricardo Donoso, editor of the Society's review and head of the National Archive.

One campaign of the ambassador received great acclaim. When Father Weigel gave him a tour of San Francisco Church, the oldest building in the capital, Bowers learned that its convent was to be demolished because of unpaid taxes. He brought this to the attention of the foreign minister and mentioned United States efforts to preserve Monticello. The minister lauded his interest in "the preservation of our city's most characteristic colonial monument" and credited his timely suggestion with moving government authorities to save the structure.[12]

The ambassador used his contacts to promote another successful venture. When the State Department did not respond to his proposal to sponsor internships for Chilean newsmen, he wrote ten publishers urging each to employ a visiting reporter for two months. Eight agreed. The ambassador next persuaded the Grace Line to offer special fares and arranged for them to visit dailies in New York and Washington. The journalists' stay was covered fully in the Chilean press. Roosevelt greeted the reporters at a news conference and assured his envoy that "you have every reason to be pleased with the results of your initiative." At Bowers's urging, the Carnegie Endowment sponsored the visit of twelve American newsmen to Chile, and Columbia University agreed to host twenty-nine Chilean professors and students for two months. The department congratulated Bowers on the success of the exchanges. Wesley Frost admitted to being a usually cynical old hand, but he was fulsome in praising his former boss: "I hope your biography, when it shall come to be written, will do full justice to this exploit."[13]

The ambassador's efforts to promote United States–Chilean understanding won the respect of many Chileans. Admirers in the press dubbed him Don Claudio of Santiago. The Nobel Prize poet Gabriela Mistral offered him "special thanks" for an American flag given to an orphanage named for her, and Viña del Mar awarded him the Civic Order of the Municipality, praising him for the "improved state of public feeling in Chile toward the United States."

Washington was aware of Bowers's activities and popularity. Following his 1944 visit to Santiago, the chief of the Division of American Republics, Philip W. Bonsal, noted the improvement in the position both of the United States and the embassy, crediting this to the Chileans' perception of Bowers. Never too shy to inform others, Bowers sent hundreds of letters, often with copies of his speeches, to Washington relating his accomplishments. Roosevelt was impressed and complimented him on his "multitude of current activities."[14]

On the tenth anniversary of his ambassadorship, before congressmen, senators, diplomats, and friends assembled in the
Chamber of Deputies, the government awarded him the Grand
Cross of the Order of Merit Bernardo O'Higgins, Chile's highest
distinction. Among the speakers was the chairman of the foreign
relations committee, who lauded Bowers's decade of service to
friendship between Chile and North America, adding that in the
history of Chile no such honor had been shown any other diplomat. Bowers jocularly responded that he was not a diplomat sent
abroad to lie for his country. His idea of diplomacy, he insisted,
was that a diplomat "is expected to cultivate friendly relations,
that the most important function of a diplomat is honestly to
interpret one country to the other, to wipe out false impressions
with the truth."

Letters of congratulations poured in from Cardinal Caro to
Senator Allende. The Socialist praised his "steadfast democratic
convictions" and thanked him "for making more effective, real and
permanent, the good relations between North America and
Chile." Bowers's staff and the household servants presented him
with engraved silver mementos. He likewise was pleased at the
favorable press coverage, even by *Time*, and President Harry S.
Truman's congratulations. Until his retirement politicians, educators, and journalists continued to sing his praise. In 1951 the
Catholic University of Chile awarded him an honorary doctorate.

Critics stressed that Bowers never learned Spanish. Able to scan
Santiago newspapers, he attempted to communicate in broken
Spanish only with his chauffeur. Why he never learned the language remains a mystery, though contemporaries offered explanations. His reputation partially compensated for his linguistic
disadvantage, but his inability to speak Spanish after twenty years
as envoy to Spain and Chile was a glaring fault. Although one
scholar argues that it led to limited understanding of Chilean culture, Bowers's successes belie this charge.[15]

The ambassador's popularity lasted long after he left Chile, and
his high standing did not make the job of his successor, Willard L.
Beaulac, easy. In his first year the new ambassador attacked

Chilean Catholics for opposing the overthrow of President Jacobo Arbenz in Guatemala, linking them with the Communists. This made Beaulac a target for many Chileans. Senator Frei said that Bowers "never would have dared take such a false step to wound the pride of this worthy nation in such a heavy handed manner." A cartoon in *El Mercurio* showed Beaulac reading a note in broken Spanish from Bowers: "It's preferable not to be knowing how to speak Spanish like me, rather than to be speaking foolishness." Beaulac had little regard for political appointees and saw government-to-government relations as his primary task. Conceding that Bowers was the most popular ambassador in Chile, Beaulac criticized him for spending time fostering "good relations with the Chilean people," arguing that this was not his job.[16]

Throughout his years in Santiago, Bowers continued to follow the fortunes of the Democratic party. Correspondence with leaders and legislators and three trips to Washington kept him abreast of politics, and he contributed counsel and campaign materials to his friends. Farley informed him that he and Cordell Hull might head the Democratic ticket in 1940, and the ambassador urged Hull to run if the president declined to seek reelection. But Bowers was delighted when Roosevelt came out for a third term. In September Roosevelt thanked him for "your useful comments" that would be of help in the campaign, and the following month the embassy received a telegram to be decoded by the ambassador only. Bowers knew it was a summons home for the campaign. Indeed, in it Sumner Welles said that the president "is anxious to have you make one or perhaps two addresses." Using his wife's poor health as an excuse, Bowers declined. To atone for this, he sent a campaign speech to Frank Oliver, and as suggested it was published in the *New York Times*.[17]

Unimpressed with the Republican nominee, Wendell L. "Willkie the Obscure," Bowers considered Roosevelt's 1940 reelection a defeat for the fifth column in the United States. Four years later he remained an enthusiastic Roosevelt backer and celebrated Roosevelt's fourth presidential victory at an election night dinner party. But he found one return distressing: "It is humiliating to me as a Hoosier to note that as in 1940 Indiana went into the anti-Roosevelt column."

Bowers's visit to Washington in September–October 1943 with Foreign Minister Joaquín Fernández Fernández allowed him to see his political friends. He met twice with Roosevelt and was shocked by his appearance, deciding he looked many years older than in 1939. Roosevelt offered a litany of complaints against newspaper columnists, former National Committeeman Farley ("going about the country attacking me"), Dewey ("just a prosecuting attorney and a poor one at that"), and Gen. Douglas MacArthur ("He has not done so much"). Bowers was pleased when forty-two senators, two Supreme Court justices, and Vice President Henry A. Wallace attended a dinner in his honor. The host was Sen. Joseph F. Guffey, for whom the ambassador continued to write speeches. Bowers remarked to one guest, "I don't think I've had the pleasure of meeting you." "Oh, yes you have," Senator Truman replied, recalling his introduction of him at a rally in Kansas City in 1932.[18]

After Roosevelt's death, Bowers became an advocate of Truman. In 1944, however, he had favored Wallace's renomination for vice president and was disappointed when Roosevelt chose the Missourian. In April 1945 Truman wrote the ambassador, "I have always been a great admirer of yours" and promised "to carry thru the policies of the President [Roosevelt] in regard to the Good Neighbor Policy." Later, when some careerists suggested that Bowers might be relieved of his post after so many years, Truman let it be understood at the State Department that "Mr. Bowers will remain as ambassador to Chile as long as Mr. Bowers desires."

Bowers became a staunch defender of Truman's Fair Deal, and the president's opponents met with the envoy's scorn. "Our people seem to have gone absolutely insane," he asserted when the Republicans captured Congress in 1946. Bowers in 1948 attacked Wallace for his advocacy of the Soviet cause and dividing the party. He feared that Wallace's candidacy would bring Dewey's election. But if Truman would disregard the "many smallbore

politicians without vision and without much political intelligence," Bowers believed the president would be able to win. "I am
jubilant over your election," he wrote Truman in November. It
proved that "the American people are as Democratic now as in the
days of Jefferson and Jackson if the Democrats go out fighting for
our principles."

Two trips to Washington during the Truman years renewed his
involvement in United States politics. In October 1945 he accompanied President Juan Antonio Ríos, and at the formal dinner at
the White House Bowers noted that his host singled him out for
attention, twice insisting he wanted a long talk. The ambassador
enjoyed sessions with Secretary of State James F. Byrnes, Hull,
Wallace, Nelson A. Rockefeller, Fiorello La Guardia, and Arthur
Krock, but had to cancel a meeting with the president. Pat called
to say that her mother was ill, forcing him to leave for Santiago.[19]

Bowers made another trip to the United States in April–May
1950, this time with his family and President Gabriel González
Videla. In New York the Chilean was feted at a lunch by
Rockefeller, and heads of businesses with interests in Chile—
International Telephone and Telegraph, Grace and Company, and
National City Bank—hosted dinners for the president. One event
was memorable—the visit to Hyde Park, where Mrs. Roosevelt
exclaimed to Bowers, "How delightful to see you here again." In
Washington, González Videla was "startled and delighted with
Truman's informality" when the president played the piano and his
daughter sang. Bowers met with Vice President Alben W. Barkley,
congressional friends, and Secretary of State Dean Acheson, and
enjoyed a Hoosier chicken dinner given by the Indiana Society.
When he met with Truman, Bowers mentioned Chile and its
needs, but the conversation focused on politics. The guest stressed
the Republicans' inability to think and speak in terms of the average man and attacked Sen. Joseph R. McCarthy's smear campaign.
His host compared the GOP's use of McCarthyism to the Whigs'
embracing the Know-Nothing crusade. Bowers was impressed, concluding "that history will pronounce him one of the greatest presidents I have no doubt." When Truman decided not to run in 1952,

*Claude Bowers and Patricia Bowers in the embassy garden, Santiago, Chile*
COURTESY OF MANUSCRIPTS DEPARTMENT, LILLY LIBRARY, INDIANA UNIVERSITY, BLOOMINGTON

Bowers backed Adlai E. Stevenson, sending him suggestions and also writing speeches for Farley.

News that the Democrats' years in the White House were about to end came during Eleanor Roosevelt's visit to Santiago in 1952. Eisenhower's victory, Bowers believed, was a triumph for the general, "not a repudiation of the Democrats and a triumph for the

Republicans." The ambassador predicted that his party would retake Congress. He was impressed by the speeches of Stevenson and Truman, an opinion the Missourian appreciated, noting that "there are some papers in this part of the world that seem to think that my contribution was less than nothing."[20]

While in Santiago, Bowers also followed Spanish politics. He wrote Roosevelt about the plight of the Republican refugees in Vichy France and helped Manuel Azaña's widow and family obtain exit visas. Señora Azaña's brother, Cipriano de Rivas Cherif, was sentenced to death in 1941, but thanks to international pressure his sentence was commuted to thirty years' imprisonment. Bowers urged Washington to seek his release, and on the day Roosevelt died he instructed his ambassador in Madrid to continue expressing concern. Rivas Cherif was freed in 1946 and joined his family in Puerto Rico.

Francisco Franco's cooperation with Adolf Hitler and Washington's relations with Madrid of course attracted Bowers's attention. Irate on hearing in 1940 that the United States was considering lending the "totalitarian regime in Spain" $100 million, he expressed his opposition to Roosevelt. "If it is impertinent to write my views, I hope that I may be 'pardoned something to the spirit of liberty.'" Roosevelt answered that no such credit would be granted to Madrid.[21]

During the Chilean years Sybil Bowers took pleasure in her contacts with wives in the American community, but she avoided a role in diplomatic life. She sewed for war relief on Wednesdays with other women at the embassy, participated in a book club, and belonged to the Association of American Women. Her hearing difficulties increased, making it hard for her to converse at crowded affairs. "Sybil is worn out with her activities," her husband lamented in 1945, "and has aged noticeably in the last two years."

Very different from her mother, Pat reveled in the diplomatic spotlight. She enjoyed dinner dances, often returning home at 4:00 A.M. She liked to entertain, once hosting a party for four hundred guests with an orchestra and a buffet that the ambassador considered ostentatious. Her popularity remained a source of pride to her father, but her life was not all play. She attended a Red Cross nurs-ing course for three years, served as a Red Cross volunteer, was on the board of the American Clinic, and assisted with receptions.[22]

Whenever possible the ambassador lunched with his family, and weekend afternoons he spent in the garden. Following Chilean custom the threesome took tea around six, sometimes played cards, and dined after nine. In the evenings they read or saw a movie; *Casablanca* and Charlie Chaplin's *The Dictator* were among their favorites. Bowers devoured mysteries, especially by Agatha Christie, but he also read novels, histories, and biographies by Thomas Mann, Winston Churchill, Samuel Eliot Morison, Marcel Proust, Evelyn Waugh, Virginia Woolf, André Maurois, and Howard K. Smith.

When he arrived in Chile, Bowers was showing a few signs of age. His feet bothered him, so at home he wore slippers. His wife and daughter played golf and strolled in the park, but the pater familias limited his exercise to promenades in the garden. As the years passed he chose to sit down at receptions, and his shoulders became stooped.[23]

The ambassador was never interested in financial matters. During the war years his salary was $17,500 and his living allowance $420, while royalties from his books brought him another $500 annually. Although his expenses almost equaled his income, Bowers often forgot to cash checks from his publisher, later finding them in coat pockets. Theodore Fred Kuper in New York continued to handle the ambassador's tax returns, send books, and run errands.

Summers were a time of relaxation for the family. During January, February, and March the diplomatic corps and the politi-cal elite fled Santiago for the Pacific, and Viña del Mar became the capital. The threesome, accompanied by several house staff, joined this exodus for a month or two. From 1940 through 1943 the Bowerses spent their summers north of Viña at Zapallar, a mecca for vacationers. There in a rented stone villa amid grounds aglow with flowers, the ambassador with book in hand "sat in a steamer chair looking down on sea or beach most of the day." For a few years the family went to Viña, residing each summer in a different house. Twice Bowers rented an estate in Limache, twenty miles from the coast, and they also spent two summers at Quilpue, ten miles inland, in a house surrounded by large grounds. They passed their last summers in Villa Alemana, between Limache and Quilpue. Reading and walks in the morning and backgammon and croquet in the afternoon were favorite pastimes.

For the ambassador summers were not all vacation. Each week a staffer brought materials, and Bowers went one or two days a week to the consulate in Valparaiso. The naval mission was there, so he accompanied his attaché on visits to ships. Pepe drove him to Santiago for events and appointments, and on occasion he was invited to the president's summer palace in Viña.

*Time* attacked Bowers in March 1944 for being "off in the country, relaxing on a long leisurely weekend," just when "the State Department frantically tried to get in touch with its Chilean Embassy." The charge was groundless, and several United States journalists and the American Chamber of Commerce protested, noting that Bowers remained in close touch with his embassy. The enraged ambassador believed this "silly attack" by "the scurrilous weekly" was repayment for his denunciation of the magazine's "monstrous attack on Aguirre Cerda." He was pleased when Roosevelt and Hull informed him that the State Department had come to his defense.[24]

Amid diplomatic duties and summer vacations, Bowers's writing continued. Because of his position, he declined to do an introduction to William E. Dodd's posthumous *Ambassador Dodd's Diary, 1933–1938*, instead contributing a review in the *New York Times Book Review* praising Dodd's opposition to Hitler. For the *Virginia Historical Quarterly*, Bowers wrote an article, "In Defense of Politicians," attacking cynicism toward parties and politicians. He believed this attitude was similar to the fascists' "in undermining popular confidence of popular government." The piece was reprinted by the Democratic National Committee. In 1944 he completed *The Young Jefferson, 1743–1789*, the final volume in his trilogy. The Library of Congress had sent him books, and Kuper's daughter in New York had done newspaper research. Like its two predecessors, the book praised the Virginian. "Had Jefferson died before Washington's inauguration," the author contended, "he would still be one of America's few immortals."[25]

Again Bowers sent page proofs to friends, requesting promotional comments and reviews. Supreme Court Justice Felix Frankfurter, Senator Barkley, and historian Charles A. Beard gave him quotable encomia, and an enthusiastic review by Wallace appeared in *The Nation*. The author went to great pains "to present the Jefferson of flesh and blood, the human being," and in a long review *Newsweek* asserted, "It is a very human, lovable Jefferson who emerges from these pages." Friend Dos Passos concurred, writing, " 'Young Jefferson': It's a first rate piece of work. It's simple. It's alive." President Nicholas Murray Butler of Columbia praised the book, and the author was also pleased with Maurois's glowing review.

*Young Jefferson* became a best-seller, running through three printings in the first ten days. The Literary Guild took fifty thousand copies, and Houghton Mifflin issued a three-volume set of the Jefferson trilogy. In 1948 Bowers discovered that, without asking, the War Department had translated *Jefferson and Hamilton* and *The Young Jefferson* into German. He was proud that these books were being used in "an attempt to make democrats of Germans."[26]

Historians gave the biography mixed reviews. Academicians chastised the author for misspellings, but their most serious criticism was his ignorance of recent scholarly articles on Jefferson. Bowers was prepared for this, believing that "professors who feel they are ordained of God to have monopoly on the writing of history usually resent others breaking in." Reviewers in the major historical journals praised Bowers's "flair for vitalizing the record of the past" and presenting the "achievements of Thomas Jefferson entertainingly and dramatically," "all in the best tradition of popularized history."[27]

Bowers finished another book, but it proved to be his most discouraging effort. In 1938 he had agreed to write a biography of the owner of the *New York Times*, Adolph S. Ochs, whose daughter and son-in-law offered ten thousand dollars and supplied materials. He finished it in 1942, but the daughter was disappointed. "Some people have queer ideas of biography and history," he complained. For them "all warts must be wiped out; and a really great man not be permitted to appear human." Bowers refused to make changes, and the family held the manuscript.

He continued to work on what became *Pierre Vergniaud: Voice of the French Revolution*. Published in 1950, it was the first biography in English on this defender of liberty whom the author had admired since childhood. The French translation received a prize from a French historical society. For Bowers Vergniaud was the interpreter of democracy among leaders of the revolution, and his principles were "precisely those of Jefferson." By contrast the author considered Robespierre the model for Hitler, Benito Mussolini, and Joseph Stalin. Bowers had begun collecting material on Vergniaud in New York and continued consulting sources in France. He knew no French, so his daughter in Santiago translated microfilm while her father typed notes.[28]

Most critics praised the work. Maurois in the *New York Times Book Review* congratulated Bowers for combining "exhaustive research and complete mastery of his subjects with the art of making a period, or a man, come alive again." The *London Times* admired "the easy sweep of the narrative, the skillful management of complexities of a dramatic story." "He makes another hitherto neglected democratic hero's life and times come intensively alive," claimed an Indianapolis reviewer. In comparing the political struggles of Vergniaud's time with the present, Truman wrote, "I don't think there is much difference." In Santiago *El Mercurio* judged the work an "extraordinary success," and the head of the National Archive considered it "a true profession of democratic faith."

As Bowers expected, historians received *Vergniaud* rather unenthusiastically. They took the author to task for not being aware of recent research on the French Revolution, while lauding his vivid style. Robert R. Palmer, whose review the author considered smug, noted that the work would revise no judgments on the French Revolution, but he praised Bowers's "commendable stand for humanity." Crane Brinton admired Bowers's narrative, while attacking him for abandoning "the detachment, the coldness, of the professional scholar."[29]

During his last years in Santiago the ambassador wrote *Chile through Embassy Windows, 1939–1953*, finishing it in 1956 in New York. The Spanish translation, *Mi misión en Chile*, was published the next year, and the English original came out after his death. Based on his diary, correspondence, and observations, he offered an introduction to Chile that he knew would please the Chileans. He sketched the nation's historical development, discussed United States–Chilean relations, introduced its leading citizens, and stressed its democratic institutions. The work was filled with admiration and praise for the country's cooperation with the United States. In a chapter on Chilean presidents he wrote glowingly of the three Radical party executives and stressed their friendship. The ambassador had respected Aguirre Cerda and González Videla, but in his diary he often criticized Ríos. Since he had detested Ibáñez, he only mentioned him in passing.

The author was seldom able to admit he made a mistake. Perhaps as a political appointee he feared such an admission might play into the hands of his enemies at the State Department. Like *My Mission to Spain*, *Chile through Embassy Windows* served as an apologia for his actions. Bowers's chapter on Chile "moving toward rupture with the Axis" depicted an ambassador much more confident than did his pessimistic diary entries. In attempting to demonstrate his popularity with Chilean officials, he even praised Ernesto Barros Jarpa's help as foreign minister in 1942. In his diary Bowers claimed the opposite, calling him "the best and most valuable ally the Axis has had in Chile."

Santiago reviewers were unanimous in their praise. "You are the most popular and most beloved North American citizen among the Chileans," author and journalist Joaquín Edwards Bello wrote. The nation's newspapers urged their countrymen to read *Mi misión en Chile*, and the Institute of Historical Research made him an Honorary Member.[30]

In the United States *Chile through Embassy Windows* was widely reviewed. Most commentators found the memoir a useful introduction to Chile. "An important contribution," the *Christian Science Monitor* concluded. "A record of a keen mind and vigorous personality," the *San Francisco Chronicle* averred, while the *Saturday Review* lauded the author for expressing "the genuine affection he felt for Chile and the Chilean people." Journalists familiar with Latin America were less enthusiastic, noting Bowers's uncritical treatment, but they considered the book "valuable for its considerable if slanted information." Academics found fault with the "amateur historian" for being "unsparing in his praise, but reserved in his criticisms." Nevertheless, contemporary historians agreed that "the volume can be read with profit," and one labeled it "an excellent book."[31]

Some years after publication, the book received a different sort of criticism. Following the rise of Fidel Castro and the growth of Communist parties in Latin America, scholars attacked United States policy for overlooking the region's problems. Without consulting his diary or dispatches, one historian accused Bowers of ignoring Chile's appalling social conditions and heaping "uncritical praise upon all the superficial aspects of Chilean life." Another found the ambassador's uncritical treatment unworthy of an "objective professional diplomat."[32]

*Chile through Embassy Windows* deserved criticism for overlooking the nation's defects, but it was incorrect to assert that Bowers was unaware of Chile's serious social inequities. His diary was replete with condemnations of the upper class's mistreatment of the poor. "All hail Chilean feudalism!" he wrote, on hearing that an aristocratic lady was excused for ordering the murder of a peasant. In letters to Roosevelt and in dispatches, Bowers castigated "the rich laymen, the 16th-Century land owners," warning that "communism will come" unless social injustices were rectified. His support of United States–funded sanitation, public health, and educational projects and his continuing appeals to Washington for increased aid for such programs demonstrated his concern for the miserable living conditions of so many Chileans.

At long last, after more years than the ambassador and his family ever anticipated, the end came to his service in Chile. It had been in many ways a wonderful time in which the erstwhile youth of Indiana, now a bowed and tired envoy, had done his best to maintain relations between one of the leading countries of South America and what once had been labeled the Colossus of the North. The world had changed dramatically from the time of his arrival on the eve of World War II. One American president had passed on, and another had followed. Upon the imminent inauguration of the third, the ambassador tendered his resignation. A political appointee, he knew that the formality of resigning, expected of all envoys upon the appearance of a new administration, this time would carry reality. President Eisenhower accepted his resignation on 3 August, congratulating him on his record in two important countries.

A succession of farewells proved a test of endurance. Honored by Chileans, the diplomatic corps, and the American colony, Bowers was also the subject of newspaper editorials. The Communists were the only group to welcome his recall—a hostility that pleased him. Laudatory editorials in the *New York Times* and the *Washington Post* were also sources of satisfaction.

On 2 September 1953 the Bowers family boarded the *Santa Isabel* for the four-week sea voyage home. Although he still considered himself "a Hoosier of the Middle West," Bowers believed that the East had been good to him, and he returned to New York.[33]

# CHAPTER ELEVEN

# Retirement

Returning home in his seventy-fifth year, Claude Bowers devoted the remainder of his life to politics and history. His political influence and importance as a writer never approached earlier levels, but his partisan fervor did not flag. He befriended a new generation of Democratic leaders—presidential nominee Adlai E. Stevenson, New York mayor Robert F. Wagner, Jr., and Illinois senator Paul H. Douglas—while remaining in touch with such contemporaries as Eleanor Roosevelt, Harry S. Truman, and James A. Farley. And Bowers again served his party as an orator and author. The three books he published in retirement were autobiographical, two dealing with his Spanish and Chilean experiences, the third his memoirs.

Age had not tempered his liberalism. He was outspoken in his disdain for President Dwight D. Eisenhower, whose administration, he believed, favored corporate interests at the expense of the people. His labor policies, the Dixon-Yates proposal to give away the Tennessee Valley Authority, tax relief only for the rich, and weak support of Israel—all were targets. Bowers considered Eisenhower the most incompetent president since Ulysses S. Grant, describing the White House as "the tomb of the well-known soldier." His high school classmate Myla Jo Closser cautioned him that his view of

Eisenhower seemed "pretty extreme," but his contempt for Richard M. Nixon, Eisenhower's vice president, knew no bounds. Nixon was "downright crooked," a "gutter scavenger." Eisenhower "ought to resign," he concluded, "but my God, it would then be Nixon."[1]

Bowers also was alarmed by Sen. Joseph R. McCarthy. The Wisconsin Republican was "our little Hitler," "a professional killer of the reputations of decent men." Bowers praised Secretary of State John Foster Dulles's defense of the foreign service against McCarthy's accusations—Democratic support the secretary of state appreciated. The former ambassador deplored the senator's attacks on Gen. George C. Marshall and Truman. He saw the former president in New York during McCarthy's assault, and both excoriated the "McCarthy gangsters."[2]

But McCarthyism was more than the senator. J. Edgar Hoover's cooperation with McCarthy had dragged the FBI into politics, moving the nation "that much closer to a police state." Bowers believed such perverters of patriotism considered all liberals communists. Writing to Eleanor Roosevelt, he remembered her forecast in Santiago the night of Eisenhower's victory "that it would be dangerous to express a liberal thought." "We are back in the days of the Alien and Sedition Laws," he asserted. When the Senate condemned McCarthy in 1954, he was proud that every Democrat had voted for censure.[3]

Bowers's role in Democratic politics was limited. In April 1954 he gave his "first open political speech in twenty years," to the National Women's Democratic Club. It attacked McCarthy's demagoguery, arguing that his anticommunist hysteria was serving the enemy by trampling freedoms. He belittled the detractors of Roosevelt and Truman, insisting that their administrations had done "a million times more" to combat communism than all "the noisy, self-advertising witch-hunters posing before the television as the star enemies of Moscow." Enjoying the address were Sen. J. William Fulbright of Arkansas, "a brilliant fellow," and Edith Wilson, the president's widow, whom the speaker had not seen since 1935.[4]

The retired ambassador discussed politics with friends. He often saw Eleanor Roosevelt, and the two exchanged letters. When a plaque to her was dedicated in 1956 at the Roosevelt School in Stamford, Connecticut, he composed the inscription. Through correspondence and occasional reunions Bowers and Truman remained in touch. "You and I agree," the Missourian wrote, "that the Democrats ought to take a definite stand on issues and fight for that stand." The former ambassador corresponded with Dean Acheson, who concurred that constructive criticism was the Democrats' duty. Friendship with Jim Farley continued, and Bowers's last diary entry concerned Farley's possible senate candidacy in 1958. He did not see his best Democratic friend from pre–New Deal days, Frank Oliver.[5] A devout Roman Catholic, the former congressman never forgave his opposition to Francisco Franco.

In retirement Bowers established contacts with several younger leaders. He spoke with Bob Wagner, the senator's son, at party functions. Senator Douglas consulted him, and he corresponded with Speaker Sam Rayburn, who assured him it was "the Jefferson theory, as you know better than I," that made the country prosperous. Sen. Thomas T. Connally of Texas appreciated Bowers's praise, and Sen. Herbert H. Lehman of New York went out of his way to show respect. Bowers met Albert B. "Happy" Chandler of Kentucky over lunch, finding him "a big hearted fellow" who speaks "the language understood on the street and around the cracker barrel in country stores," and he was delighted the governor had read his books. Bowers also respected Stevenson's liberalism and speeches. The Illinois governor urged him to send material and confessed, "I find it so difficult to write freshly and so often these damnable speeches, with so little assistance." Stevenson noted that in preparing an address he had consulted *Jefferson and Hamilton*.[6]

Bowers's participation in the 1956 presidential race was marginal. He urged Stevenson to wage a campaign "hitting hard and hitting high," but the cerebral nominee answered, "The former tempts me, but I think the latter is a more natural posture for me." Bowers's only role was as chairman of the West Side Stevenson for President Committee. He presided over meetings and gave talks, but he privately remarked, "None of it interests me much." He heard Stevenson at dinners at the Waldorf-Astoria and was impressed by his campaign, predicting a Democratic victory. Bowers was disgusted at Eisenhower's reelection and claimed the American people were "like children with a childish faith in the Great White Father."[7]

The partisan was not unquestioning in his Democratic loyalty. He detested Sen. Lyndon B. Johnson for acting like a Republican, working with wealthy Texans to give away oil rights. When Franklin D. Roosevelt, Jr., ran for New York attorney general in 1954, the candidate's host two decades earlier in Madrid declared that "he was running on his name and on no achievements of consequence." Bowers believed Republican victor Jacob K. Javits was "more liberal on principle than Roosevelt." Truman's support for New York governor Averell W. Harriman against Stevenson in 1956 met with Bowers's censure. He believed the Missourian was moved by spite, since Stevenson advisers in 1952 had urged the nominee not to involve Truman.[8]

Bowers was out of step with his party on civil rights. He never abandoned the racism he had displayed in *The Tragic Era* a quarter century earlier. Though he praised Eleanor Roosevelt for resigning from the Daughters of the American Revolution when they forbade Marian Anderson to sing in their auditorium, and the ambassador had gone out of his way in Santiago to invite the Haitian minister to dinner, he opposed expanded rights for African Americans. Upon hearing of the Supreme Court's decision in 1954 outlawing segregation in public schools, he lamented that a majority of students in some southern states would be black, causing trouble. For him the civil rights movement was motivated by politicians' desire to win the African American vote. He compared supporters of integration to "fanatics like the old abolitionists" and complained, "The fool Democrats are fighting among themselves on segregation and may split the party." He was pleased that Senators Richard B. Russell of Georgia and Samuel J. Ervin, Jr., of North Carolina had cited *The Tragic Era* in speeches to defeat "the abolitionists of our day."[9]

Chairmanship of the Woodrow Wilson Birthplace Foundation, a post he accepted at the request of the president's widow, gave him great satisfaction. In 1956, the centennial of Wilson's birth, he was to gather endorsements and financial support to maintain the president's house in Staunton, Virginia. But he complained that the post was "a headache because it takes so much time." President Truman, Rear Adm. Richard E. Byrd, and James M. Cox, among others, agreed to serve on the foundation committee. Bowers solicited funds, inviting "twenty millionaires to luncheon at the Lawyers Club." Arthur Hays Sulzberger of the *New York Times* contributed five thousand dollars, and Nelson A. Rockefeller gave a donation.[10]

Retirement did not end Bowers's interest in Spanish and Chilean affairs. He assailed the Eisenhower administration for "pouring hundreds of millions into Spain to bolster up a regime that does not tolerate freedom of the press or of speech or academic freedom, or the right of assembly." At the request of Arthur M. Schlesinger, Jr., he became a sponsor of Spanish Refugee Aid. The Veterans of the Abraham Lincoln Brigade invited Bowers to their twentieth-anniversary dinner in 1957, and he spoke on the Spanish Civil War at City College and Columbia University. He retained connections with the Chilean government, corresponding with the ambassador in Washington and attending events at the New York consulate. In Manhattan he saw Gabriela Mistral, Chile's Nobel Prize laureate in poetry.[11]

Bowers continued his oratory. He spoke in ten states and Washington, D. C., giving more than two dozen presentations. Some were informal—an after-dinner talk celebrating Theodore Fred Kuper's seventieth birthday, a homily at a service for a Spanish Republican, seminars on Thomas Jefferson and Reconstruction. Most were addresses. At Memphis State College he lectured on Jefferson, Andrew Jackson, and James K. Polk; at the University of Mississippi he spoke on Theodore Dreiser. To the New York Jewish Conference and at the Universities of Virginia and Kentucky he discoursed on Jefferson and civil liberties, while Reconstruction was his subject before the Kentucky Civil War

Round Table in Lexington. Civil liberties and inter-American relations were his topics at the Indiana Historical Society in Indianapolis and in Fort Wayne, before the Pan American Women's Association, and at Brooklyn College, Princeton, and Ohio Wesleyan. In 1955 he made his only television appearance on "The Man of the Year," a program devoted to Alexander Hamilton. His last engagement was in April 1957 at Yale, where he talked on United States foreign policy.[12]

Friendship with historian Allan Nevins led to seminars at Columbia. Nevins was president of the Society of American Historians and arranged for a radio lecture on "The Fight for Freedom: The Alien and Sedition Laws." Bowers was the luncheon speaker at the Society of American Historians' 1955 meeting and a representative to a conference on Responsible Freedom in the Americas at Columbia. As the United States representative he joined former Latin American presidents in presenting papers.

His lectures focused on contemporary issues, using Jefferson's and Jackson's concerns for individual freedom to warn of McCarthyism's threat to civil liberties. In "History's Warning Finger" before the Indiana Historical Society, the orator asserted that "hysteria is the natural ally of fascism, and we cannot forget that it was hysteria that swept the hysterical Hitler into power." When lecturing on inter-American topics, Bowers used the subject as a springboard to attack the Eisenhower administration for its disinterest in Latin America.[13]

In retirement Bowers visited familiar Hoosier places. In Indianapolis he saw an 1892 photograph of himself holding a campaign poster endorsing James G. Blaine for the Republican presidential nomination. He toured the north side of the city "now built up with the pretentious houses of the rich" and "old Fairview Park now the huge campus of Butler University." He dined in Terre Haute with Frank Crawford, a friend from the turn of the century, and in Fort Wayne he went by the house on Berry Street and the park where he had taken Pat on walks. Indiana University awarded him an honorary doctorate of laws, with President Herman B Wells, a Santiago visitor in 1941, presenting the degree.[14]

Speaking engagements brought Bowers new friends and experiences. At a talk to labor leaders he met Louis Hollander, the New York head of the Congress of Industrial Organizations (CIO). At his urging, Bowers wrote *Twenty Years of New Deal and Fair Deal Achievement—And This They Call Treason!*, a tract that enlisted Truman's praise. Bowers's trip to the University of Kentucky offered him his first view of the bluegrass country, Lexington's fine Georgian mansions, the college lodgings of Jefferson Davis, and Mary Todd Lincoln's school. His host was Holman Hamilton, a friend since Fort Wayne days; the guest was impressed with Thomas D. Clark, head of the history department.[15]

But the most enjoyable retirement hours were devoted to writing. "I sit at my typewriter writing books, articles and speeches as forty years ago," he noted in 1956, "and get as much thrill out of my work." The books on Spain and Chile saw print, and his memoirs were issued posthumously. His Memphis State lectures were published as *Making Democracy a Reality: Jefferson, Jackson, and Polk*, and ten pieces appeared as book chapters, articles, and a pamphlet, in addition to book reviews. Manuscript deadlines left him "over my head with work," but he bragged that he was good at keeping "my nose to the grindstone."[16]

After many revisions, *My Mission to Spain* finally appeared in 1954, and the next year the Spanish edition came out. The account of his Chilean years proved difficult. "I am slowly working on a book of my fourteen years in Chile" was his refrain. The problem was too much information, but "hard work, constant writing," allowed him to finish the book in 1956. The Spanish translation was published the next year, but *Chile through Embassy Windows* did not appear until a month after his death.

The author was elated by both books' reception. Spanish Republicans were enthusiastic over *My Mission to Spain*, and United States liberals expressed praise. The Basque government-in-exile sent formal thanks, and Truman asserted, "The book is something that has needed to be said for a long time." Likewise, Chileans greeted the Spanish translation of his complimentary Chilean memoirs with enthusiasm. Former president Gabriel

González Videla assured the author, "Your book is worthy of a monument," and an abortive movement began to create a Bowers foundation in Chile and name a plaza for him. The book remained on best-seller lists in Santiago for more than a year, going through four printings in ten months.[17]

Based on his diaries, *My Life: The Memoirs of Claude Bowers* was not published until 1962. The manuscript was almost completed before his death, and his daughter added a final chapter based on excerpts from his diary. Truman furnished a quote for the dust jacket. Filled with vignettes, *My Life* offered a personal view of seventy-five years of American history and portrayed Bowers's association with the leading personalities in politics, journalism, literature, and diplomacy. The most interesting sections for United States historians dealt with political events from the Wilson era through Roosevelt's election in 1932.[18]

The memoirs met with greater acclaim than they merited. While fascinating reading, the autobiography was uncritical and unfocused. Entertaining stories filled its pages, but the author offered few insights into the development of his political thought. These limitations did not bother reviewers, several of whom were friends—and others perhaps were moved by sympathy for the deceased author. Nevins enjoyed "this amusing book of anecdotal memoirs" displaying Bowers's "gusto for life: for friends, for liberal causes." An Indianapolis reviewer emphasized that the author remained very much a Hoosier. Critics in *The New Yorker* and the *Virginia Quarterly Review* offered no criticism, stressing the book's value for American history. A commentator in the *Christian Science Monitor* admitted that the autobiography "sometimes bogs down with trivial personal anecdotes with little point," but he praised its "warm-hearted sections."[19]

Bowers wrote in the family's third-floor apartment a block west of Central Park, with a "superb view of one-way traffic" on West Eighty-fourth Street, on the edge of the slums. His neighbors were Puerto Ricans, and from the windows he watched "pandemonium in the street"—children beating tin cans, loud preachers, men shooting craps. He did not like the New York of the 1950s and had a litany of complaints. "Not at all like the city I lived in for 12 years thirty years ago," he wrote during his first month back. "It is dirty!" "One is gouged at every turn." "I made a mistake settling here instead of in Washington," he later lamented. But Sybil liked New York. There she was not faced with social duties, and a maid took care of the household. Pat enjoyed accompanying her father to lunch and the theater and continued her travels abroad.[20]

Social life centered around friends. Ruth and Fred Kuper visited, as did Myla Jo Closser, but most guests were from the years abroad. A stream of Chileans arrived. Chavela Edwards, a Santiago favorite, often was in New York, and historian Eugenio Pereira Salas brought news. Former foreign minister Eduardo Irarrázaval Concha and ex-president González Videla also called. Cecil Lyon, by 1956 United States ambassador to Chile, paid visits, as did Bowers's Jesuit friend Gustave Weigel, and Santiago secretaries joined him for lunch or dinner.

On his return to New York, Bowers bragged that his health was "exceedingly good for my age." He remained a rapid talker and continued to display vigor, but by the 1950s he was "slender to the point of frailty, slightly stooped, pallid of complexion, and thin-voiced." There were intimations of mortality. Each day he read the obituaries, and he drew up his first will. He noted that his friends were "now old men in their seventies." Reminiscing with Bernard Baruch, he reported, "Much talk about long dead days." He retained his positive outlook, but his ruminations reflected a sense of closure. "Seventy-eight years ago in the little Quaker town of Westfield in Hamilton County, Indiana, I was born," he wrote on 20 November 1956. "The seventy-eight years since have had many lights and shadows. Happily I enjoyed the lights and never mourned over the shadows."[21]

In August 1957, with little warning, his good health ended. He found himself "weak as a kitten and very short of breath." Bowers had leukemia. During his hospital stays in the fall he had "great fun" kidding the student nurses, but was concerned that Sybil was so worried. Back in his apartment he followed a strict regimen of medication, diet, and naps.[22]

Bowers's illness was interrupted by happy events. Get-well wishes and greetings on his seventy-ninth birthday in November 1957 were welcomed, but he admitted that "I find it darn dull in my cell." Unaware of his illness, the Faculty of Philosophy and Letters at the University of Chile asked him in October to become an Honorary Member and offered the family a trip to Santiago in December. His acceptance was greeted with invitations and articles in the Santiago press. He did not make the trip.

Early in his eightieth year, on 21 January 1958, Bowers died. Four days later the Reverend Leopold Bernhard, pastor of St. Peter's Lutheran Church, presided over services held at the Frank E. Campbell Funeral Home in Manhattan. Among the one hundred attending were friends, including Ambassador Lyon, representatives of the City of New York and the Spanish Republican government-in-exile, the Basque delegate to the United Nations, and Chilean diplomats. Eleanor Roosevelt, Secretary of State Dulles, and President Carlos Ibáñez del Campo sent flowers. In Santiago a memorial program was held at the Chilean-North American Cultural Institute, where two Chilean politicians, one a Conservative and the other a Socialist, offered eulogies. Laudatory pieces appeared in the Chilean press, the *New York Times*, the *Washington Post*, and Indiana newspapers.

Bowers regarded Terre Haute as home, according to his daughter, " 'because that city gave him his first break,' " and he had informed Kuper that he wished to be buried in his home state. In Terre Haute services were held at the P. J. Ryan and Sons Funeral Home on 27 January. Among the pallbearers were John K. Lamb, son of John E. Lamb, the Terre Haute Democratic leader who had backed Bowers for Congress; William Cronin, a Bowers friend since their newspaper days in Terre Haute; and former governor Henry P. Schricker. Bowers was buried next to his mother in Highland Lawn Cemetery on a wooded hillside overlooking the city on the banks of the Wabash River.[23]

His wife and daughter continued living in their west side apartment, but Sybil Bowers later had to reside in a retirement home. She died in 1964. Pat returned to Sarah Lawrence, by then a four-year college, and thereafter worked for the Foundation Library Center, a philanthropic agency in New York. She saw that her father's papers were preserved. Nevins had urged Bowers to offer them to Columbia University, Truman had requested them for his presidential library, and the Library of Congress and the Roosevelt Library had sought them. In 1968 Pat Bowers sold the fifteen boxes of papers to the Lilly Library at Indiana University in Bloomington. She died in 1975 and like her mother was interred in the family plot.[24]

The theme in Bowers's life was advocacy of democracy. In journalism, politics, oratory, historical writing, and diplomacy he was a spokesman for democracy. He sided with the Democratic party in the days of William Jennings Bryan, was outspoken in progressive beliefs—supporting Republican Progressives, as well as Democrats—and became an unquestioning supporter of the New Deal and the Fair Deal. He never ceased to expound his liberal creed and to promote the Democratic party. His editorials, speeches, political counsel, and books urged his party to take a stand for the interests of the majority. He helped give Democrats a cause to espouse.

As a journalist and political adviser he lambasted big business, excoriated the "Gold Dust twins of normalcy," and supported nominees from Bryan to Stevenson. For three decades he championed Progressive reform, and when the New Deal expanded the state's role to oversee economic and social well-being, he defended this change, arguing that Roosevelt's accomplishments were equal to those of Jefferson and Jackson. Bowers stressed party differences, insisting that the Democracy was waging "a war of extermination against privilege and pillage," while the opposition was committed to a government of the wealthy. In advice to Hoosier politicos and to national leaders, he urged the party to stand for "democracy and against the oligarchy of a privileged class."[25]

Friends and acquaintances spanned these busy decades. In Indiana he had become a friend of Samuel M. Ralston; half a century later he discussed politics with Sen. Frederick Van Nuys and Governor Schricker. Presidential candidates from Bryan to

Stevenson were friends, as well as legions of party leaders from across the country. Nor were all Republicans enemies. He admired such Progressives as Robert M. La Follette and George W. Norris, and Albert J. Beveridge was his closest friend among Hoosier politicians. Bowers also respected the well-to-do who gave their talents to the common good. He held Baruch, Henry Morgenthau, and Rockefeller in high esteem.

Bowers wrote to support the democratic ideal and to influence his party. "My sole reason in writing historical books is to give a liberal interpretation," he declared, and "to reach the liberal and progressive element." *The Party Battles of the Jackson Period* and his Jefferson trilogy were read by the Democratic faithful. The 1920s was not inspiring for Democrats, but *Jefferson and Hamilton* served as a "shot in the arm," and Democratic chiefs from Cox to Stevenson credited Bowers with shaping their views. The most important leader influenced by Bowers's histories was Roosevelt, a self-proclaimed Jeffersonian Democrat and enthusiastic reviewer of *Jefferson and Hamilton*. His identification with the Virginian and his use of him for partisan purposes continues to be a subject of historians.[26]

But the author intended his histories to serve more than political ends. Convinced of the veracity of his beliefs, Bowers maintained his books would be definitive. Contemporary historians—presidents of the American Historical Association, Jefferson scholars, authorities on the South, and dozens of academic reviewers—lauded his works, and later Jefferson biographers who differed with Bowers recognized his importance. Dumas Malone confessed that *Jefferson and Hamilton* had " 'meant a great deal in my own life,' " and Merrill Peterson wrote to Bowers that "no one has contributed more to the awakened sense of Jeffersonian heritage in America than you have—on so many sides: scholarship, politics, journalism, patriotism."[27]

Scholarship has overturned Bowers's historical conclusions. There is much to criticize in his histories: his inherent racism, his disinterest in economics and intellectual trends, and his belief that history should offer contemporary lessons. Bowers's descriptions of individuals and events impress modern readers as overly dramatic, yet this style led contemporaries to purchase his books. The most severe criticism was of his partisan treatment. Bowers not only acknowledged this partisanship, but he also proclaimed it. As he noted, many writers had not treated Jefferson fairly, and his biography helped move the pendulum in the other direction. Likewise, *The Tragic Era*, to his view, was a counterpoint to historians who supported Radical Republicans and Reconstruction in the South.

One of Bowers's goals was to make his books appeal to the public. Sales demonstrated his success, and reviewers were unanimous in praising his style. His eight books—from *Party Battles* through *Young Jefferson*, published from 1922 to 1945—averaged about thirty-two thousand sales each. Scholars agree that *Jefferson and Hamilton* and *The Tragic Era* reached larger audiences on these subjects than any works before or since. As commentators have noted, Bowers should be classed with such popular, nonacademic historians as Barbara W. Tuchman and Bruce Catton. In defense of his books, Nevins made fun of academic critics, citing "Professor Dryasdust," an unpublished pedant of "morose jealousy," who reveled in making "mincemeat" out of Bowers.[28]

His popularity as an author and orator is difficult to imagine today. His speeches before the Great War and later during the radio age electrified audiences large and small, but their appeal is lost on later generations. The length and partisanship of his addresses, as well as his oratorical flourishes and carefully rehearsed and almost staccato delivery, are no longer expected fare in the television era. Likewise, his histories of Jefferson, Jackson, and Reconstruction, so laden with advocacy, have little attraction for the modern reader. But Bowers's audiences had different expectations. Their attitudes and tastes were formed in the nineteenth century when political partisanship was sharp, long addresses customary, and verbal adornment demanded. His clear-cut arguments were appealing.

As a diplomat in Spain and Chile, Bowers wanted the United States to bolster democracy. Roosevelt agreed, telling him in 1933 that he hoped to have the Madrid regime "'on our side of the table.' "[29] To strengthen Spain's democracy, Bowers urged the State Department to compromise in trade matters, and during the civil war he was one of the few ambassadors who favored the government. In Santiago he respected the nation's constitution, patiently working for Chile's break with the Axis. During the cold war he opposed the inclusion of Communists in González Videla's government.

Bowers's most important diplomatic legacy was his attempt to promote better understanding of the United States. At innumerable functions he spoke on history, culture, and politics and befriended Spaniards and Chileans representing a wide section of national life. In Madrid and Santiago he was the first ambassador to cultivate journalists, inviting them to informal press conferences, a novelty. Career diplomats like his successor in Chile belittled this; however, the cold war and the Alliance for Progress made embassy attempts to influence public opinion a staple of United States diplomacy.

His successes as an ambassador were limited. Perhaps he trusted too much in personal diplomacy, but he hoped thereby to ensure democracy, surely a worthy goal. His appeals to the White House won some tariff concessions with Spain and facilitated military exchanges with Chile, but Bowers discovered the limits of personal suasion. His difficulties with careerists in the State Department contributed to the failure of trade negotiations between Washington and Madrid, as well as the department's frustrations with Bowers's diplomacy in Chile's break with the Axis. His attempts to end the United States embargo against arms sales to the Spanish government came to naught. One ambassador's advocacy proved no match for the proneutrality sentiment at home and the State Department's determination to avoid involvement.

Bowers the biographer complained that some authors mistakenly painted over all defects in their portraits, not permitting a great man to appear human. Bowers had his defects. Like many partisans, self-righteousness colored his endeavors and caused him to overlook his mistakes. His inability to mention his early support of United States nonintervention in Spain and his later refusal to admit Communist influence in the Republican government were cases in point.

Racism was another of Bowers's shortcomings. As a schoolboy and an ambassador, he expressed sympathy and respect toward individual African Americans. Nevertheless, his attitudes on race reflected the prejudices of his generation. Although Chile had a large mestizo population, he claimed in 1939 that its people were "the finest in South America because there is no mixed Indian or negro blood." Like most Progressives he took no interest in civil rights; instead he defended the disfranchisement of blacks in the South and lamented their electoral strength in Indiana. His Jefferson biography did not analyze the Virginian's views on slavery, and *The Tragic Era* was filled with pejorative statements about African Americans. During the New Deal important liberals such as Harold L. Ickes and Eleanor Roosevelt supported the civil rights of blacks, but Bowers never altered his views. In 1950 he sympathized with South Carolinians who were determined to exclude African Americans from the Democratic primary, believing that these segregationists were "ready to fight again for their principles and civilization." Until his death, Bowers saw civil rights as "only the right of the darkies to sit in the classroom with the whites in the South."[30]

Bowers certainly possessed qualities that outweighed his defects. Friends invariably remarked that he was warmhearted. His care for his domestic help at his own expense during the civil war, his concern for the safety of his chauffeur Pepe Torres and family, donations during World War II to Margaret Palmer, a friend in need who had raised funds in France for the Spanish Republic, and efforts to save Manuel Azaña's brother-in-law Cipriano de Rivas Cherif from Franco's prisons offer examples of his generous nature. People who knew Bowers also emphasized his unassuming manner. "Absolutely devoid of affectation" was a typical assessment of his demeanor, a trait that reflected the habits and beliefs he had developed since childhood. "He has never taken on airs," one commentator reported when visiting him in Spain, and an old friend remarked that "a certain sort of humility" characterized Bowers's conduct in his last years, as it had a half century earlier. To a historian interviewing him in 1954, Bowers gave "the impression of thinking of himself as a small town Indiana boy who is proud and a little incredulous of the honors that have come to him."[31]

All in all Bowers stood among the illustrious Hoosiers who proved so important in national literature and politics during the first half of the twentieth century. Many were his friends or acquaintances: Dreiser, Booth Tarkington, Meredith Nicholson, Charles A. Beard, and the politicians Thomas R. Marshall, Charles W. Fairbanks, John W. Kern, Thomas Taggart, and Beveridge. While they were significant in national life, their fame diminished as the century came to an end. But in looking to the greatness that comes to only a few figures in the country as a whole, Indiana and the Middle West often have defined the hopes and progress of the nation. In this respect Bowers's greatness is indisputable.

# Notes

Unless otherwise cited, correspondence addressed to and copies of letters written by Bowers are found in the Bowers Manuscripts at the Lilly Library, Indiana University, Bloomington, as are all his diaries and his correspondence with Frank Brubeck. Holman Hamilton's correspondence and transcripts of his interviews are found in the Holman Hamilton Papers in the Division of Special Collections and Archives of the Margaret I. King Library, University of Kentucky, Lexington, as are the transcripts of Peter J. Sehlinger's interviews. All letters from Claude and Sybil Bowers to Jessie Moore are in the William Henry Smith Memorial Library of the Indiana Historical Society in Indianapolis.

## Introduction

1. Harry S. Truman, dust jacket for *My Life: The Memoirs of Claude Bowers*, by Claude G. Bowers (New York: Simon and Schuster, 1962).

2. James A. Ramage, *Holman Hamilton: A Biographical Sketch* (Pamphlet published on the occasion of his retirement) (Lexington, Ky., 1975), 6.

3. Claude G. Bowers, introduction to *Zachary Taylor: Soldier of the Republic*, by Holman Hamilton (Indianapolis and New York: Bobbs-Merrill, 1941), xi–xiv; Thomas D. Clark, introduction to *Kentucky Profiles: Biographical Essays in Honor of Holman Hamilton*, eds. James C. Klotter and Peter J. Sehlinger (Frankfort, Ky.: The Kentucky Historical Society, 1982), 3–7; Holman Hamilton, "Clio with Style," *Journal of Southern History* 46 (Feb. 1980): 5; Bowers to Hamilton, 12 Feb. [1952].

4. Hamilton to Bowers, 26 Jan. 1952; Bowers to Hamilton, [15 Feb.], 29 Mar., 20 Apr. 1952.

5. Holman Hamilton and Gayle Thornbrough, eds., *Indianapolis in the "Gay Nineties": High School Diaries of Claude G. Bowers* (Indianapolis: Indiana Historical Society, 1964).

## 1. "Bowers! Bowers! He Is Ours!"

1. As a youth Claude Bowers admitted he was a poor speller, a trait he retained throughout his life. In this book Bowers's misspellings have been corrected.

2. Holman Hamilton and Gayle Thornbrough, eds., *Indianapolis in the "Gay Nineties": High School Diaries of Claude G. Bowers* (Indianapolis: Indiana Historical Society, 1964), 32; U.S. Census for 1880, Jolietville, Washington Township, Hamilton Co., Ind., 13:20, bracket page 372D. Indiana Asbury University is now DePauw University, Greencastle, Ind.

3. Bowers, letter to Holman Hamilton, 15 Feb. 1952.

4. Bowers, *My Life: The Memoirs of Claude Bowers* (New York: Simon and Schuster, 1962), 1–2; Bowers to Hamilton, 15 Feb. 1952.

5. In *My Life*, 2, 5. Bowers erred in calling his grandfather Christopher instead of Christian. Lewis Bowers, fifth child and second son of Christian and Jemima, was the first of his parents' progeny to be born in Indiana.

6. Bowers to Hamilton, 15 Feb. 1952.

7. Ibid.; Bowers, *My Life*, 1, 334; Bowers to Hamilton, 13 Mar. 1952. Julia Etta's name first appears as Juliet (U.S. Census for 1860, Washington Township, Hamilton Co., Ind., 12:130, bracket page 354), but it was usual for official documents and city directories to record it as Julia Etta, Juliaetta, Juliaette, and Julia E.

8. U.S. Census for 1850, [Union Township], Boone Co., Ind., 2:362, bracket page 181½; Census for 1860, Washington Township, Hamilton Co., Ind., 12:30, bracket page 354; Bowers to Hamilton, 15 Feb. 1952; State of Indiana, certificate of Adjutant General Robinson Hitchcock, 19 Aug. 1952, Holman Hamilton Papers, Division of Special Collections and Archives of the Margaret I. King Library, University of Kentucky, Lexington.

9. Bowers, *My Life*, 1, 7; John F. Haines, *History of Hamilton County, Indiana: Her People, Industries and Institutions* (Indianapolis: B. F. Bowen and Co., 1915), 263; Lela Thomas, interview with Holman Hamilton, 11 June 1963.

10. See Sabine Jessner and Peter J. Sehlinger, "Claude G. Bowers: A Partisan Hoosier," *Indiana Magazine of History* 83 (Sept. 1987): 217–19.

11. Bowers to Hamilton, 15 Feb. 1952.

12. Bowers, *My Life*, 3–5; Larkin L. Beeman, interview with Hamilton, 11 June 1963; Claude Sortor, interview with Hamilton, 8 June 1963; Larkin L. Beeman, letter to Hamilton, 19 July 1963; Ralph W. Stark, letter to Hamilton, 21 July 1963.

13. Mildred Tipton Stubbs to Hamilton, 20 June 1963; Ben Tomlinson, interview with Hamilton, 11 June 1963; Stark to Hamilton, 15 Nov. 1962; M. E. Thalheimer, *The Eclectic History of the United States* (Cincinnati: Van Antwerp, Bragg and Co., 1881), 33, 197–98, 209–10, 236, 344–45; Bowers, *My Life*, 11–12; *Indianapolis Star*, 24 June 1928.

14. Claude G. Bowers, "The Reminiscences of Claude Bowers," interview with Louis Starr, 24, 30 Aug. 1954 (Oral History Research Office, Columbia University, New York), 2.

15. Bowers to Hamilton, 15 Feb. 1952; Bowers, *My Life*, 7, 11; Beeman and Sortor interviews; *Lebanon Patriot*, 25 July 1895; Boone Circuit Court, Civil Order Book 31 (4 June 1888–21 Feb. 1889), 249; *Lebanon Pioneer*, 26 July, 18 Oct. 1888.

16. *Lebanon Patriot*, 14 Mar., 4 Apr. 1889, 5, 19 Mar., 30 Apr. 1891.

17. Stark to Hamilton, 22 July 1963, 28 Nov. 1962; *Compendium of the Eleventh Census: 1890* (Washington, D.C.: Government Printing Office, 1892), pt. 1, 131; Hamilton and Thornbrough, eds., *Indianapolis in the "Gay Nineties,"* 95, 108; Bowers, *My Life*, 11–12.

18. *Lebanon Patriot*, 13 Aug. 1891; J. M. Rice, "The Public Schools of St. Louis and Indianapolis," *The Forum* 14 (Dec. 1892): 438, 442; Hamilton and Thornbrough, eds., *Indianapolis in the "Gay Nineties,"* 63; Abraham Cronbach, "Concerning Claude G. Bowers," attached to letter to Hamilton, 27 Feb. 1959. The number of the cottage was later changed from 317 to 607.

19. *Lebanon Patriot*, 15 Oct. 1891; Stark to Hamilton, 29 May 1963; Boone Circuit Court, Civil Order Book 31, p. 249.

20. Bowers, *My Life*, 7; Bowers, letter to William Everett, 15 Nov. 1897, William Everett Papers, Massachusetts Historical Society, Boston (hereafter cited as EP).

21. *Terre Haute Star*, 20 Nov. 1906.

22. Boone Circuit Court, Probate Order Book 13, p. 5; Sortor interview; Marion County, Ind., Marriage Record Book 24 (1892), 369; *Indianapolis Directory* (Indianapolis), 1892: 199; 1893: 494; 1894: 464; 1898: 208.

23. Bowers, *My Life*, 9; Bowers to Hamilton, 15 Feb., 13 Mar. 1952; Hamilton and Thornbrough, eds., *Indianapolis in the "Gay Nineties,"* 63–65.

24. [Max R. Hyman, ed.], *Hyman's Hand Book of Indianapolis* (Indianapolis: M. R. Hyman, 1897), 133, 258–66, and passim.

25. Ernestine Bradford Rose, *The Circle: "The Center of Our Universe," Indiana Historical Society Publications*, vol. 18, no. 4 (Indianapolis: Indiana Historical Society, 1957), 404; Bowers, *My Life*, 13–14; Rebecca Shepherd Shoemaker, "James D. Williams: Indiana's Farmer Governor," in *Their Infinite Variety: Essays on Indiana Politicians*, ed. Robert G. Barrows, *Indiana Historical Collections*, vol. 53 (Indianapolis: Indiana Historical Bureau, 1981), 195–221.

26. Harry J. Sievers, *Benjamin Harrison*, 3 vols. (Newton, Conn.: American Political Biography Press, 1996), 2:362, 3:256–57; Bowers, *My Life*, 27.

27. Gayle Thornbrough, letter to Hamilton, 21 Aug. 1969, verifies all the addresses mentioned in this paragraph.

28. Bowers, *My Life*, 17–18, 8, 22; Hamilton and Thornbrough, eds., *Indianapolis in the "Gay Nineties,"* 160.

29. Bowers, *My Life*, 27–29, 37; Hamilton and Thornbrough, eds., Indianapolis in the "Gay Nineties," 37, 88–89; Bowers, letter to Carl Schurz, 20 Sept. 1897, Carl Schurz Papers, Manuscripts Division, Library of Congress, Washington, D.C.; Bowers, letter to Ignatius Donnelly, 2 June 1896, Ignatius Donnelly Papers, Minnesota Historical Society, St. Paul.

30. Hamilton and Thornbrough, eds., *Indianapolis in the "Gay Nineties,"* 30.

31. Ibid., 15–16.

32. Ibid., 17–18, 26–27.

33. Ibid., 16–23, 26–28, 34–37, 39–44, 46–49, 64, 93–94.

34. Ibid., 29, 40, 33–34.

35. Ibid., 119, 143, 15, 24–25, 183–84; Sara Messing Harding, "Random Notes about Claude Bowers," Indiana Historical Society, Indianapolis.

36. Chauncey A. Goodrich, *Select British Eloquence* . . . (New York: Harper and Brothers, 1852), 382–98, 785–820; Bowers, *My Life*, 36.

37. Bowers to Hamilton, 29 Mar. 1952.

38. Bowers to Everett, 15 Nov. 1897, EP; Hamilton and Thornbrough, eds., *Indianapolis in the "Gay Nineties,"* 23, 42, 45, 51, 54; Fletcher Hodges, letter to Hamilton, 31 Jan. 1963; Bowers, *My Life*, 34–36; *Indianapolis News*, 9 Jan. 1963.

39. *The Annual: Indianapolis High School* (Indianapolis, 1898), 54; Hamilton and Thornbrough, eds., *Indianapolis in the "Gay Nineties,"* 30–31, 46, 51–52, 80–81, 84, 86, 88–90, 139n; Claude G. Bowers, *Beveridge and the Progressive Era* (Boston: Houghton Mifflin, 1932), 24, 57; Bowers, *My Life*, 13, 19.

40. Hamilton and Thornbrough, eds., *Indianapolis in the "Gay Nineties,"* 119, 149, 173, 190.

41. Ibid., 96–97, 109, 110, 115, 121, 152, 157, 181, 184, 205; Myla Jo Closser, letter to Hamilton, 29 Jan. 1959; John Dos Passos, interview with Hamilton, 23 Feb. 1965; *New York Evening World*, 8 Dec. 1928.

42. Hamilton and Thornbrough, eds., *Indianapolis in the "Gay Nineties,"* 107–10, 135, 149, 150.

43. *Annual* (1898), 55; Hamilton and Thornbrough, eds., *Indianapolis in the "Gay Nineties,"* 92–93, 153, 159, 195–96, 203, 220–21; Closser to Hamilton, 29 Jan. 1959.

44. *New York Times*, 27 June 1928.

45. C. Walter Schooler, interview with Hamilton, 8 June 1963; Martha Hawkins Norman, interview with Hamilton, 6 Aug. 1970; Beeman to Hamilton, 19 July 1963; Closser to Hamilton, 29 Jan. 1959.

46. Closser to Hamilton, 29 Jan. 1959.

47. *Richmond* (Ind.) *Evening Item,* 26 Mar. 1898; Hamilton and Thornbrough, eds., *Indianapolis in the "Gay Nineties,"* 94, 97, 105, 109, 110; Closser to Hamilton, 29 Jan. 1959.

48. Bowers to Everett, Christmas, 1896, EP; *Annual* (1898), 55.

49. *Annual* (1897), 39; Bowers to Everett, 13 Mar. 1897, EP.

50. Hamilton and Thornbrough, eds. *Indianapolis in the "Gay Nineties,"* 98–100, 103–4, 117–18, 142–44, 162–64, 168–70, 203–4, 217.

51. Ibid., 107, 198.

52. Ibid., 57, 59, 60, 69–70, 80–82; Bowers, *My Life,* 43–44.

53. Bowers, *My Life,* 17.

54. Ibid., 15–17; Hamilton and Thornbrough, eds., *Indianapolis in the "Gay Nineties,"* 42–43, 114, 129, 135–36, 179, 220.

55. Bowers, "My Spanish Diary," 16 Oct. 1936.

56. Bowers, *My Life,* 27–28, 30–32; Hamilton and Thornbrough, eds., *Indianapolis in the "Gay Nineties,"* 87–90, 98.

57. Bowers, *My Life,* 30–32.

58. Ibid., 37; Hamilton and Thornbrough, eds., *Indianapolis in the "Gay Nineties,"* 89–90; Samuel Eliot Morison, *Three Centuries of Harvard, 1636–1936* (Cambridge, Mass.: Belknap Press, 1965), 354.

59. Bowers to Everett, 30 Sept., 30 Oct., 21 Nov. 1896, EP; Everett to Bowers, 3 Nov., 3 Dec. 1896.

60. Bowers to Everett, Christmas, 1896, 30 Jan., 13 Mar., 15 Aug., 15 Nov. 1897, EP.

61. Bowers to Everett, 15 Nov. 1897, ibid.

62. Hamilton and Thornbrough, eds., *Indianapolis in the "Gay Nineties,"* 145–50; Harding, "Random Notes."

63. Hamilton and Thornbrough, eds., *Indianapolis in the "Gay Nineties,"* 103–4, 124–27, 145–48, 151–66; Maynard Lee Daggy, interview with Hamilton, 25 Apr. 1963.

64. Hamilton and Thornbrough, eds., *Indianapolis in the "Gay Nineties,"* 166–67; *Richmond Evening Item,* 25, 26 Mar. 1898.

65. *Annual* (1898), 5–6.

66. Ibid., 59–61.

67. Hamilton and Thornbrough, eds., *Indianapolis in the "Gay Nineties,"* 166–68; *Annual* (1898), 61; *Richmond Evening Item,* 26 Mar. 1898; *Indianapolis News,* 26 Mar. 1898.

### 2. Journalist, Orator, and Politician

1. Claude G. Bowers, *My Life: The Memoirs of Claude Bowers* (New York: Simon and Schuster, 1962), 39; Bowers, "Reminiscences of Claude Bowers," interview with Louis Starr, 24, 30 Aug. 1954 (Oral History Research Office, Columbia University, New York), 7; Sabine Jessner and Peter J. Sehlinger, "Claude Bowers: A Partisan Hoosier," *Indiana Magazine of History* 83 (Sept. 1987): 220.

2. Claude Bowers, "What Is Republicanism?" *The Jeffersonian Democrat* 2 (Jan. 1900): 549–62, and "Republicanism vs. the People," ibid. (Mar. 1900): 710–20.

3. Claude Bowers, letters to Holman Hamilton, 29 Mar., 15 Feb. 1952; Bowers, *My Life,* 159; Holman Hamilton and Gayle Thornbrough, eds., *Indianapolis in the "Gay Nineties": High School Diaries of Claude G. Bowers* (Indianapolis: Indiana Historical Society, 1964), 26n, 219.

4. *Indianapolis Press*, 5 Apr. 1900; Bowers, *My Life*, 40; Ray E. Boomhower, *Jacob Piatt Dunn, Jr.: A Life in History and Politics, 1855–1924* (Indianapolis: Indiana Historical Society, 1997), 45; Bowers to Hamilton, 3 Oct. 1952.

5. Hamilton and Thornbrough, eds., *Indianapolis in the "Gay Nineties,"* 176; Bowers, "My Spanish Diary," 3 Nov. 1935; *Indianapolis Sentinel*, 8, 9, 10, 11 Aug., 1 Sept. 1900.

6. *Indianapolis Sentinel*, 9 Aug. 1900, 10 July, 19 Aug., 2 July, 14 Apr., 27 Aug. 1901.

7. Bowers, *My Life*, 48; Hamilton and Thornbrough, eds., *Indianapolis in the "Gay Nineties,"* 9; *Indianapolis Sentinel*, 4 Apr. 1900; *Indianapolis Press*, 4, 5 Apr. 1900; *Indianapolis News*, 4 Apr. 1900; *Indianapolis Sun*, 4 Apr. 1900; *Indianapolis Journal*, 5 Apr. 1900.

8. *Indianapolis Sentinel*, 15, 18, 20, 27, 29, 31 Oct. 1900; *Indianapolis Press*, 17, 27 Oct. 1900; Bowers, *My Life*, 45; Bowers, *Jeffersonian Democracy* (Indianapolis: Bradford Press, [1901]), 4, 5; *Indianapolis Sentinel, Indianapolis News, Indianapolis Press, Indianapolis Journal*, 8 Dec. 1900.

9. *Indianapolis Sentinel*, 3 Apr., 6 Nov. 1901. See also *Indianapolis Press, Indianapolis News, Indianapolis Sun*, 3 Apr. 1901.

10. Ibid., 6, 9 Jan. 1902; *Indianapolis News*, 8 Jan. 1902; *Indianapolis Sun*, 8, 9 Jan. 1902; *Lebanon Pioneer*, 6 Feb. 1902. Concerning the death of Kentucky governor Goebel, see James C. Klotter, *William Goebel: The Politics of Wrath* (Lexington: University Press of Kentucky, 1977), 100–109.

11. *Indianapolis Sentinel*, 22 Sept., 2, 12, 18, 31 Oct. 1902.

12. Bowers, "Diary," 20 Nov. 1956; Bowers, *My Life*, 335; Samuel M. Ralston, letter to Bowers, 17 Dec. 1901.

13. Bowers, *My Life*, 48; Lois Stewart, letter to Claude McCaleb, 14 Feb. 1964, Holman Hamilton Papers, Division of Special Collections and Archives of the Margaret I. King Library, University of Kentucky, Lexington (hereafter cited as HP); Hamilton and Thornbrough, eds., *Indianapolis in the "Gay Nineties,"* 8, 187, 217, 222.

14. Bowers, letters to Hamilton, 13, 29 Mar. 1952; Bowers, *My Life*, 20, 38, 47, 48; *Indianapolis News*, 14, 16 Dec. 1901; *Indianapolis Sentinel*, 9 Jan. 1902.

15. *Literary Digest* 50 (16 Jan. 1915): 87–88; *The Outlook* 109 (31 Mar. 1915): 748; *The Independent* 82 (26 Apr. 1915): 138–39; Theodore Dreiser, *A Hoosier Holiday* (New York: John Lane Co., 1916), 396; *Indianapolis Sentinel*, 17 Oct. 1902; *Twelfth Census of the United States . . . 1900, Population* (Washington, D.C.: Government Printing Office, 1901), pt. 1, 143.

16. Bowers, *My Life*, 49–50; Bowers, letter to Max Ehrmann, 15 Jan. 1926, Max Ehrmann Papers, DePauw University, Greencastle, Ind.; W. A. Swanberg, *Dreiser* (New York: Charles Scribner's Sons, 1965), 74–75.

17. Philip S. Rush, letter to Hamilton, 20 June 1963; George H. James, letter to Hamilton, 18 June 1963; Frank Brubeck, interview with Hamilton, 29 Dec. 1961; John K. Lamb, letter to Hamilton, 9 Nov. 1962; *Who Was Who in America* (Chicago, 1942), 1:699; Bowers, *My Life*, 55, 56.

18. Bowers to Hamilton, 29 Nov. 1952; Rush to Hamilton, 10 June 1963.

19. Bowers, *My Life*, 51–52.

20. *Terre Haute Gazette*, 9 Jan. 1904; Bowers, *My Life*, 56. Bowers's Jackson Day subject was "Liberty and License."

21. *Terre Haute Gazette*, 18 Mar. 1904; Bowers, *My Life*, 56. Bowers's topic: "Ireland's Struggle toward Home Rule."

22. James, letter to Hamilton, 18 June 1963, quoting John E. Lamb; Bowers to Hamilton, 25 Mar. 1952; Bowers, *My Life*, 57.

23. *Terre Haute Star*, 26 Aug. 1904.

24. Paolo E. Coletta, *William Jennings Bryan*, 3 vols. (Lincoln: University of Nebraska Press, 1964–69), 1:350; Clifton J. Phillips, *Indiana in Transition, 1880–1920: The Emergence of an Industrial Commonwealth, The History of Indiana*, vol. 4 (Indianapolis: Indiana Historical Society and Indiana Historical Bureau, 1968), 89–92; John Braeman, *Albert J. Beveridge: American Nationalist* (Chicago: University of Chicago Press, 1971), 81; Claude G. Bowers, *Beveridge and the Progressive Era* (Boston: Houghton Mifflin, 1932), 208–14; Herbert J. Rissler, "Charles Warren Fairbanks: Conservative Hoosier" (Ph.D. diss., Indiana University, Bloomington, 1961), 158–63.

25. Bowers, *My Life*, 50, 57.

26. *Terre Haute Star*, 9 Nov. 1905, 4 Nov. 1906.

27. Ibid., 12, 27, 29 Sept. 1904; *Rockville Tribune*, 5 Oct. 1904; Bowers, *My Life*, 57.

28. *Rockville Tribune*, 5 Oct. 1904.

29. *Terre Haute Star*, 24 Sept. 1904.

30. *Rockville Tribune*, 21 Sept., 5, 12 Oct., 2 Nov. 1904; *Terre Haute Star*, 17, 29 Apr., 18, 22, 27 Sept., 2 Nov. 1904; *Greencastle Star and Democrat*, 2 Sept., 14 Oct. 1904.

31. Bowers, *My Life*, 58–59; *Terre Haute Star, Indianapolis Sentinel*, 29 Sept. 1904.

32. Bowers, *My Life*, 58.

33. *Biennial Report of . . . Secretary of State of the State of Indiana for the Two Years Ending October 31, 1904* (Indianapolis: Wm. B. Burford, 1904), 332–35, 361.

34. Benjamin F. Lawrence, letter to James A. Stuart, 7 Nov. 1962, HP; W. Steele Gilmore, letter to Hamilton, 5 Oct. 1965; Brubeck interview; *Who Was Who in America*, 1:1019.

35. *Terre Haute Star*, 15, 31 Aug. 1906; *Rockville Tribune*, 5 Sept. 1906; *Indianapolis News*, 30 Aug. 1906.

36. *Rockville Tribune*, 5 Sept. 1906; *Terre Haute Star*, 10–13, 15, 24, 26, 28, 30 Sept., 6, 7 Oct. 1906; *Terre Haute Tribune*, 20, 23 Sept., 6, 21 Oct. 1906.

37. *Terre Haute Star*, 24 Sept. 1906.

38. *Greencastle Star and Democrat*, 2 Nov. 1906; Bowers, *My Life*, 59–60.

39. *Biennial Report of . . . Secretary of State of the State of Indiana for the Two Years Ending October 31, 1906* (Indianapolis: Wm. B. Burford, 1906), 287; *Rockville Tribune*, 17 Oct. 1906.

40. *Indianapolis News*, 7, 8 Nov. 1906.

41. *Biennial Report . . . 1906*, p. 287; *Terre Haute Star*, 8 Nov. 1906; *Rockville Tribune*, 21 Nov. 1906; Bowers, *My Life*, 59. In his memoirs, Bowers understates the case.

42. *Greencastle Star and Democrat*, 9 Nov. 1906; *Rockville Tribune*, 21 Nov. 1906; *Rockville Republican*, 7 Nov. 1906; *Terre Haute Star*, 29 Oct., 4, 7 Nov. 1906; *Biennial Report . . . 1906*, pp. 264–65, 287.

43. *Terre Haute Star*, 9 Nov. 1906; Bowers, "Reminiscences," 20.

44. Brubeck interview; *Terre Haute Star*, 12, 15, 30 Sept. 1904, 1 June, 14, 19 Sept. 1906.

45. James to Hamilton, 18 June 1963; Rush to Hamilton, 20 June 1963; Gilmore to Hamilton, 4 Mar. 1966; Gilmore, letter to Hubert H. Hawkins, 24 Aug. 1965, Indiana Historical Society, Indianapolis.

46. John F. O'Brien, interview with Hamilton, 24 Oct. 1962; Jean Crawford, interview with Hamilton, 23 Oct. 1962; Brubeck interview; Grace Batchelder Drake, letter to Hamilton, 12 Jan. 1966.

47. Hamilton and Thornbrough, eds., *Indianapolis in the "Gay Nineties,"* 222; *Terre Haute Star*, 8 Aug. 1904.

48. Bowers, *My Life*, 52–55, 101; Eugene V. Debs, letter to Bowers, 22 Apr. 1914. The Debs letter included such phrases as "Priestcraft is the curse of Ireland," "that smooth and smug cardinal at Boston," "hypocritical ilk," and "blood-sucking leeches."

49. Bowers, *My Life*, 43–44, 60–61.

50. Ibid., 61–62, 55; James to Hamilton, 18 June 1963; Brubeck interview; Robert D. Heinl, Jr., letter to Hamilton, 11 Mar. 1968, quoting notation in his father's hand. The sole coworker believing that Bowers received over $1,000 was W. Steele Gilmore, who estimated the weekly wage at $20 (Gilmore, interview with Hamilton, 31 Dec. 1965).

51. Bowers, *My Life*, 55–56; Lamb to Hamilton, 9 Nov. 1962.

52. *The General Ordinances of the City of Terre Haute . . . Revision of 1906* (Terre Haute, 1906), 142; *City of Terre Haute . . . : An Index to the Common Council from January 1, 1908 to January 1, 1909* (Terre Haute, 1909), and *. . . from January 1, 1910 to January 1, 1911* (Terre Haute, 1911); *Terre Haute Saturday Spectator*, 10 Nov. 1906; Bowers to Hamilton, 13, 25 Mar. 1952; Brubeck interview.

53. Bowers to Hamilton, 13 Mar. 1952; *Terre Haute Tribune*, 21 June 1922; Bowers, "Reminiscences," 21.

54. *General Ordinances of the City of Terre Haute* (1906), 142–44; Bowers to Hamilton, 13 Mar. 1952.

55. Brubeck interview; Bowers, letters to Frank Brubeck, 27 Feb., 4 Apr. 1912, copy, HP.

56. *Fort Wayne Journal-Gazette*, 6 Dec. 1964; Sybil McCaslin, letters to Bowers, 10 Feb. 1903, 23 June 1904. Bowers saved her letters to him, but she did not keep his.

57. Ibid., 3 July, 1 Oct. 1903, 11 Apr., 5 July 1904, 10 May, 10, 16 Aug. 1905.

58. Ibid., 25 May, 13 Nov. 1903, 12 May 1904, 5 Apr. 1905, 23 Nov., 27 Dec. 1908, 5 Mar. 1909.

59. *Terre Haute City Directory* (Terre Haute, 1906), 108; Brubeck interview; Bowers to Hamilton, 13 Mar. 1952.

60. McCaslin to Bowers, 1 May, 15 Nov. 1903, 29 June 1904, 24 Feb. 1906.

61. Ibid., 10 Aug., 9 Nov. 1907, 17 Apr., 12, 14 June, 21 July, 10 Aug., 23 Nov. 1908.

62. Ibid., 12 May, 9 June, 4 July, 5 Nov. 1909, 16 Mar., 4 May, 29 July, 24 Sept. 1910.

63. Ibid., 29 Aug., 24 Sept., 26 Nov. 1910, 9 Mar., 2, 6, 16 Apr. 1911.

64. *Terre Haute Tribune*, 9 July 1908; *Terre Haute Saturday Spectator*, 18 July 1908.

65. *Terre Haute Tribune*, 9 July 1908; Bowers, *My Life*, 60; Bowers to Hamilton, 25 Mar. 1952.

66. Coletta, *William Jennings Bryan*, 1:401, 406; *Official Report of the Proceedings of the Democratic National Convention . . . 1908* (Chicago: Press of Western Newspaper Union, 1908), 31–35; *Indianapolis Star*, 9 July 1908; Bowers to Hamilton, 25 Mar. 1952.

67. Coletta, *William Jennings Bryan*, 1:407, 404, 409–10; H. J. H., "The Democratic Convention," *The Outlook* 89 (25 July 1908): 645, 654; *New York Times*, 11 July 1908.

68. Claude G. Bowers, *The Life of John Worth Kern* (Indianapolis: Hollenbeck Press, 1918), 156–57, 163; *Indianapolis News*, 9 July 1908; *Terre Haute Tribune*, 16 July 1908.

69. *Terre Haute Tribune*, 16 July 1908; John W. Kern, "Autobiographical Statement," 1910, James H. Stuart Collection, Indiana Historical Society; Peter J. Sehlinger, "John W. Kern: A Hoosier Progressive," in *Gentlemen from Indiana: National Party Candidates, 1836–1940*, ed. Ralph D. Gray, *Indiana Historical Collections*, vol. 50 (Indianapolis: Indiana Historical Bureau, 1977), 196; Coletta, *William Jennings Bryan*, 1:410; W. J. Bryan, letter to Bowers, 12 Jan. 1918; Bowers, *Life of John Worth Kern*, 164–66; H. J. H., "The Democratic Convention," 654.

70. *Indianapolis Star*, 11 July 1908; *Terre Haute Tribune*, 11, 9 July 1908.

71. *Terre Haute Tribune*, 16 July 1908.

72. Bowers to Hamilton, 25 Mar. 1952; Bowers, *My Life*, 60–62; *Terre Haute Tribune*, 6, 11 Oct. 1908.

73. Keith S. Montgomery, "Thomas R. Marshall's Victory in the Election of 1908," *Indiana Magazine of History* 53 (June 1957): 147–66; Phillips, *Indiana in Transition*, 105–6.

74. *Journal of the House of Representatives of the State of Indiana during the Sixty-Seventh Session of the General Assembly* (Indianapolis: Wm. B. Burford, 1911), 24; Rollo E. Mosher, "Tom Marshall's Term as Governor" (M.A. thesis, Indiana University, Bloomington, 1932), 70–90, 109–24; Charles M. Thomas, *Thomas R. Marshall: Hoosier Statesman* (Oxford, Ohio: Mississippi Valley Press, 1939), 56–111; Bowers to Brubeck, 15 Apr. 1913, copy, HP; Bowers, *My Life*, 62–64, 93–94.

75. Bowers, *My Life*, 64; Bowers, *Life of John Worth Kern*, 202–8; Sehlinger, "John W. Kern," 210–11; *U.S. Constitution*, Amendment XVI; Bowers, *Beveridge and the Progressive Era*, 394–401; Virginia F. Haughton, "John Worth Kern and Wilson's New Freedom: A Study of a Senate Majority Leader" (Ph.D. diss., University of Kentucky, 1973), 13–24.

76. Bowers to Hamilton, 25 Mar. 1952; *Indianapolis News*, 25 Oct., 5 Nov. 1910, 18 Jan. 1911.

### 3. Washington

1. Claude Bowers, *The Life of John Worth Kern* (Indianapolis: Hollenbeck Press, 1918), 216.

2. Bowers, letter to Frank Brubeck, [23 Apr.(?)], [June], 11 May 1911. (Copies of Bowers's letters to Frank Brubeck are in the Holman Hamilton Papers, Division of Special Collections and Archives of the Margaret I. King Library, University of Kentucky, Lexington.) *Terre Haute Tribune*, 25 June, 6 Aug., 9, 16 July 1911.

3. *Terre Haute Tribune*, 28 May, 16 June, 2 July, 6, 20 Aug. 1911.

4. Claude Bowers, *My Life: The Memoirs of Claude Bowers* (New York: Simon and Schuster, 1962), 66–67; Bowers to Brubeck, [23 Apr.(?)], 30 Apr. 1911; *Terre Haute Tribune*, 13 Aug. 1911, 23 July 1916.

5. *Terre Haute Tribune*, 28 May 1911; Bowers to Brubeck, 19 Apr., 6 June 1911.

6. *Terre Haute Tribune*, 16 July, 28 May 1911; Bowers to Brubeck, 11 May 1911.

7. Bowers, letter to Holman Hamilton, 13 Mar. 1952; Bowers to Brubeck, [23 Apr.(?)] 1911.

8. Bowers, *My Life*, 67–68; Bowers to Brubeck, [23 Apr.(?)] 1911; Arthur Krock, interview with Holman Hamilton, 16 Nov. 1965.

9. Bowers to Brubeck, 19, 30 Apr., 6 June 1911; *Congressional Record*, 62 Cong., 1st sess., 1911, 47, pt. 1:395–406.

10. John E. Lamb, letter to Bowers, 3 July 1911; Bowers to Brubeck, [23 Apr.(?)] 1911; *Terre Haute Tribune*, 28 May 1911.

11. Bowers to Brubeck, 19 Apr., 6 June, 21 Dec. 1911.

12. *Terre Haute Tribune*, 30 Nov. 1911; *Terre Haute Star*, 1 Dec. 1911.

13. Bowers to Hamilton, 13 Mar. 1952; Bowers to Brubeck, 21 Dec. 1911.

14. Bowers, *My Life*, 68; Bowers to Brubeck, 21 Dec. 1911, 12 Jan. 1912.

15. Bowers to Brubeck, 12 Jan. 1912; *Terre Haute Tribune*, 11 Feb. 1912.

16. Bowers to Brubeck, 12 Jan. 1912.

17. *Terre Haute Tribune*, 3, 10 Mar., 5 May 1912.

18. Bowers to Brubeck, 31 Jan., 25 Feb., 6 Mar., 4, 25 Apr., 14 May, 8 July 1912; *Terre Haute Tribune*, 9 June 1912.

19. *Terre Haute Tribune*, 28 May 1911, 10 Mar. 1912; Bowers to Brubeck, 12 Jan., 10 Mar. 1913.

20. Bowers to Brubeck, 12 Jan., 25 Apr. 1912; Bowers, *Life of John Worth Kern*, 274–80.

21. Bowers, *Life of John Worth Kern*, 277; *Terre Haute Tribune*, 7 July 1912; Araminta A. Kern, letter to Bowers, 12 Nov. [1912]; Bowers to Brubeck, 3, 8 July 1912.

22. Bowers, *Life of John Worth Kern*, 281; James P. Fadely, *Thomas Taggart: Public Servant, Political Boss, 1856–1929* (Indianapolis: Indiana Historical Society, 1997), 122–23.

23. *Terre Haute Tribune*, 30 June, 7 July 1912; Bowers to Brubeck, 8 July 1912.

24. Bowers, letter to Eugene V. Debs, 20 May 1912, copy, Holman Hamilton Papers (hereafter cited as HP); Debs to Bowers, 31 May 1912.

25. Bowers to Brubeck, 4 Jan. 1913.

26. *Terre Haute Tribune*, 15, 22 Dec. 1912; Bowers to Brubeck, 4 Jan. 1913.

27. Bowers to Brubeck, 4 Jan., 23 Feb. 1913; *Terre Haute Tribune*, 2 Feb., 9 Mar. 1913.

28. *Terre Haute Tribune*, 9, 16 Mar. 1913; Sybil Bowers, "Diary," 5 Mar. 1913, Claude G. Bowers Manuscripts, Lilly Library, Indiana University, Bloomington (hereafter cited as BM); Bowers to Brubeck, [Mar. 1913].

29. Bowers, *Life of John Worth Kern*, 297, 318; Bowers, *My Life*, 76.

30. *Congressional Record*, 63 Cong., 1st sess., 1913, 50, pt. 2:1402–3; Jones quoted in Bowers, *Life of John Worth Kern*, 318.

31. Bowers, *My Life*, 78.

32. Bowers, *Life of John Worth Kern*, 324, and *My Life*, 78.

33. Bowers to Brubeck, [1913]; *Terre Haute Tribune*, 16 Mar. 1913; Bowers, *Life of John Worth Kern*, 324; Peter J. Sehlinger, "John W. Kern: A Hoosier Progressive," in *Gentlemen from Indiana: National Party Candidates, 1836–1940*, ed. Ralph D. Gray, *Indiana Historical Collections*, vol. 50 (Indianapolis: Indiana Historical Bureau, 1977), 213–16; Walter J. Oleszek, "John Worth Kern: Portrait of a Floor Leader," in *First among Equals: Outstanding Senate Leaders in the Twentieth Century*, eds. Richard A. Baker and Roger H. Davidson (Washington, D.C.: Congressional Quarterly, 1991), 23–25.

34. *Terre Haute Tribune*, 5 July 1914; Bowers to Brubeck, [Feb. 1913], 15 Apr. 1913.

35. Bowers to Brubeck, 20 June 1913, 30 Jan. 1914.

36. Bowers, *Life of John Worth Kern*, 365; Sehlinger, "John W. Kern," 214–15; *Terre Haute Tribune*, 13, 20 Apr., 31 Aug., 29 June, 19 Oct., 16 Mar., 28 Dec. 1913.

37. Bowers to Brubeck, 14 Jan. [1913], 16 Sept. [1913]; Frank Oliver, interview with Hamilton, 26 Apr. 1963; Bowers, *Life of John Worth Kern*, 414; Sybil Bowers, "Diary," 14 Oct. 1913, BM; *Terre Haute Tribune*, 25 May 1913; Bowers, *The Democracy of Woodrow Wilson* (Washington: Benedict Printing, [1913]).

38. *Terre Haute Tribune*, 21 June, 29 Mar., 16, 23 Aug., 31, 10 May, 11, 18 Jan. 1914.

39. Ibid., 16, 23 Aug. 1914.

40. Ibid., 6 Sept., 4 Oct. 1914, 21 Feb., 27 June 1915.

41. Arthur S. Link, *Wilson*, 5 vols. (Princeton, N.J.: Princeton University Press, 1947–65), 3:312–79; A. A. Hoehling and Mary Hoehling, *The Last Voyage of the Lusitania* (New York: Holt, 1956), 227; William H. Harbaugh, *Power and Responsibility: The Life and Times of Theodore Roosevelt* (New York: Farrar, Straus, and Cudahy, 1961), 476; *Terre Haute Tribune*, 16, 23 May 1915. See also *New York Times*, 18 May 1915.

42. Link, *Wilson*, 3:401–55; Harbaugh, *Power and Responsibility*, 476–79; Carl Wittke, *German-Americans and the World War*, *Ohio Historical Collections*, vol. 5 (Columbus: The Ohio Archaeological and Historical Society, 1936), 24–25, 45–52, 59–65; Virginia F.

Haughton, "John Worth Kern and Wilson's New Freedom: A Study of a Senate Majority Leader" (Ph.D. diss., University of Kentucky, 1973), 263–71; Bowers to Hamilton, 13 Mar. 1952.

43. Sybil Bowers, "Diary," 1 Nov. 1915, BM.

44. Birth certificate 113-15-038077, Indiana State Board of Health, Indianapolis; Sybil Bowers, "Diary," 1, 7 Nov., 2 Dec. 1915, BM; Bowers to Brubeck, 28 Nov. 1915.

45. Terre Haute Tribune, 30 Jan., 6 Feb., 5 Mar., 9 Apr. 1916.

46. Ibid., 16 Jan., 16, 30 Apr. 1916.

47. Congressional Record, 64 Cong., 1st sess., 1916, 53, pt. 3 and 4, pp. 2756, 2958, 3120; Terre Haute Tribune, 12 Mar., 27 Dec. 1916.

48. Biographical Directory of the American Congress, 1774–1971 (Washington, D.C.: Government Printing Office, 1971), 1692, 1786; Cedric S. Cummins, Indiana Public Opinion and the World War, 1914–1917, Indiana Historical Collections, vol. 28 (Indianapolis: Indiana Historical Bureau, 1945), 213–15; Terre Haute Tribune, 2 Apr., 14, 28 May 1916.

49. Terre Haute Tribune, 18 June 1916.

50. Claude G. Bowers, The Irish Orators: A History of Ireland's Fight for Freedom (Indianapolis: Bobbs-Merrill, 1916), 127–28.

51. Bobbs-Merrill circulars for The Irish Orators, BM; Thomas L. Reilly, letter to Bowers, 22 May 1916; Bowers, foreword to Irish Orators.

52. American Review of Reviews 54 (July 1916): 119; Boston Evening Transcript, 24 May 1916; New York Times Book Review, 11 June 1916, p. 242; The Dial 60 (June 1916): 554–55; Catholic World 103 (Sept. 1916): 833.

53. Robert E. Burns, letter to Hamilton, 20 Feb. 1963; Lawrence J. McCaffrey, letter to Hamilton, 17 Apr. 1963.

54. Max Caulfield, The Easter Rebellion (New York: Holt, Rinehart and Winston, 1963); New York Times and Chicago Tribune, 25 Apr.–5 May 1916; Lois Stewart, letter to Claude B. McCaleb, 14 Feb. 1964, HP.

55. Champ Clark, letter to Bowers, 11 May 1916; Albert J. Beveridge, letter to Bowers, 20 Dec. 1916; Mary J. O'Donovan Rossa, letter to Bowers, 22 June [1916]; Bowers, My Life, 89–90.

56. Cummins, Indiana Public Opinion and the World War, 209–15, 220–32; Harold L. Ickes, The Autobiography of a Curmudgeon (New York: Reynal and Hitchcock, 1943), 189; Bowers, Life of John Worth Kern, 377–79; Wittke, German-Americans and the World War, 95.

57. Indianapolis Indiana Daily Times, 11 Sept. 1916; George C. Roberts, "Woodrow Wilson, John W. Kern and the 1916 Indiana Election: Defeat of the Senate Majority Leader," Presidential Studies Quarterly 10 (winter 1980): 67.

58. Rockville Tribune, 17 Oct. 1916; Washington Daviess County Democrat, 20 Oct. 1916; Terre Haute Star, 26 Oct. 1916.

59. Bowers, Life of John Worth Kern, 387–88.

60. Link, Wilson, 5:187–303.

61. Sehlinger, "John W. Kern," 217; Bowers, My Life, 89; Woodrow Wilson, letter to John W. Kern, 16 Mar. 1914, BM; Haughton, "John Worth Kern and Wilson's New Freedom," 185–241.

62. Bowers, Life of John Worth Kern, 413; Kern to Bowers, 17 Mar. [1917].

63. Bowers to Hamilton, [1953]; Bowers, "Reminiscences of Claude Bowers," interview by Louis Starr, 24, 30 Aug. 1954 (Oral History Research Office, Columbia University, New York), 23; Terre Haute Tribune, 18 Mar. 1917.

## 4. Fort Wayne

1. *Fort Wayne Journal-Gazette*, 15, 20 Apr., 2, 15 June, 12, 13 Aug. 1917, 2 Apr. 1918 (hereafter cited as J-G).

2. Ibid., 21 Apr., 16 June, 7, 23 Aug., 28 Dec., 13 May 1917, 1 Mar., 22 Feb., 25 Nov., 28 Jan., 4 Aug. 1918.

3. Ibid., 16 May 1917, 30 Dec., 6 Nov. 1918, 7 Oct., 1 July, 14 June, 5 Sept., 18, 20 Nov. 1919.

4. Ibid., 19, 21 Feb., 3 Apr., 20 Mar., 3 Aug., 29 Sept., 10, 19 Dec., 20, 22 June 1919.

5. Louis Fischer, *The Life of Lenin* (New York: Harper and Row, 1964), 353, 349–55; William C. Bullitt, *The Bullitt Mission to Russia* (New York: B. W. Huebsch, 1919), 18–31; J-G, 17, 30 Sept. 1919, 4, 9 Apr., 19 July 1920.

6. J-G, 10 Feb., 14, 16 Apr., 14, 15 June, 7, 8, 9, 20 July, 3, 13, 18, 27 Oct., 7, 25 Sept., 9 Aug. 1920.

7. Ibid., 28 Dec., 28, 19 June 1920, 22 July, 4, 23 June, 14 Oct., 11, 15 Nov., 8, 26, 28, 29 Aug., 12 Sept., 11 Mar. 1921.

8. Ibid., 5, 8 May, 9, 28 Sept., 4, 28 Oct., 2–4 Nov. 1922; Claude G. Bowers, *My Life: The Memoirs of Claude Bowers* (New York: Simon and Schuster, 1962), 97, and *Beveridge and the Progressive Era* (Boston: Houghton Mifflin, 1932), 531–35; John Braeman, *Albert J. Beveridge: American Nationalist* (Chicago: University of Chicago Press, 1971), 280–88.

9. J-G, 13 Aug. 1922; see Leonard Joseph Moore, "White Protestant Nationalism in the 1920's: The Ku Klux Klan in Indiana" (Ph.D. diss., University of California, Los Angeles, 1985); J-G, 28 Jan., 2, 16 Feb., 8, 9 Aug., 14 June, 20 Apr., 29 Nov., 27 Dec. 1922.

10. J-G, 21 Mar., 10, 14 Apr., 7, 28 June, 16, 24 July, 10, 15, 22, 31 May, 23 Feb., 3, 11, 23 Aug., 1 Dec. 1923.

11. Ibid., 29 Oct., 3, 15, 18, 21, 20 Nov. 1923; Bradford W. Scharlotti, "The Hoosier Journalist and the Hooded Order: Indiana Press Reaction to the Ku Klux Klan in the 1920s," *Journalism History* 15 (winter 1988): 122–31.

12. Bowers, interview with Holman Hamilton, 22 May 1956; Bowers, letter to Albert J. Beveridge, 4 Nov. [1923], 4 Oct. 1921, Albert J. Beveridge Papers, Library of Congress, Washington, D.C. (hereafter cited as AJB); Bowers, letter to Lawrence F. Levenberg, 26 Aug. 1947, copy.

13. Bowers, *The Life of John Worth Kern* (Indianapolis: Hollenbeck Press, 1918), 473, 252–53; Bowers, "Fort Wayne Days," Holman Hamilton Papers, Division of Special Collections and Archives of the Margaret I. King Library, University of Kentucky, Lexington (hereafter cited as HP); George C. Roberts, "Claude G. Bowers: Hoosier Historian and the Politics of Yesterday, Today, and Tomorrow," *Proceedings of the Indiana Academy of the Social Sciences*, 3d ser., 17 (1982): 64–65; J-G, 22 Dec. 1918; Meredith Nicholson, letter to Bowers, 20 Dec. 1918.

14. Bowers to Beveridge, 21 Dec. 1922, 21 Dec. 1921, 8 Apr., 11 Sept. 1920, AJB; Beveridge to Bowers, 24 Dec. 1921, 11 Apr. 1920.

15. Bowers, *The Party Battles of the Jackson Period* (Boston: Houghton Mifflin, 1922), 65, 67, 172, vi, v, 2, 245, ix, 446, 116–25, 322; Bowers, "Reminiscences of Claude Bowers," interview by Louis Starr, 24, 30 Aug. 1954 (Oral History Research Office, Columbia University, New York), 49.

16. *New York Tribune*, 3 Dec. 1922; *New York Times Book Review*, 10 Dec. 1922; *Chicago Evening Post*, 15 May 1923; *Indianapolis Star*, 23 Jan. 1923; Bowers to Beveridge, 14 June [1923], AJB; *American Historical Review* 28 (Apr. 1923): 558–59; *Mississippi Valley Historical Review* 10 (June 1923): 80–82.

17. Craig Wylie, letter to Hamilton, 30 Dec. 1960; William G. McAdoo, letter to Bowers, 22 Dec. 1922; *Raleigh* (N.C.) *News and Observer*, 21 Jan. 1923; James E. Watson, letter to Bowers, 27 Feb. 1923; Arthur M. Schlesinger quoted in Bowers, letter to Holman Hamilton, 15 Apr. 1951.

18. Edward Pessen, *Jacksonian America: Society, Personality, and Politics* (Homewood, Ill.: Dorsey Press, 1969), 154, 387, 67, 25, 388; Lee Benson, *The Concept of Jacksonian Democracy: New York as a Test Case* (Princeton, N.J.: Princeton University Press, 1961), 331; Gene Wise, "Political 'Reality' in Recent American Scholarship: Progressives versus Symbolists," *American Quarterly* 19 (summer 1967): 303–28.

19. *J-G*, 12 Jan. 1923.

20. Ibid., 6, 7 Nov., 19, 20 June, 11 May, 13, 15, 22 Aug. 1918, 21 May, 31 Oct. 1920, 10 Jan., 11 Feb., 11 Mar. 1922; Bowers, "Fort Wayne Days"; Bowers, *My Life: The Memoirs of Claude Bowers* (New York: Simon and Schuster, 1962), 92; Bowers, letter to Mary E. Tipton Corbin, 23 Dec. 1919, copy, HP; *Indianapolis Star*, 17 Feb. 1922; Bowers to Beveridge, 4 Nov. [1923], AJB.

21. Bowers interview; Frank Brubeck, interview with Hamilton, 29 Dec. 1961; Arthur Krock, interview with Hamilton, 16 Nov. 1956; Bowers, "Diary," 14 Oct. 1955; George Spayth, letter to Hamilton, 23 Apr. 1965; Bowers to Levenberg, 31 July 1935, 15 Aug. 1950, 15 June 1937.

22. Bowers interview; Bowers to Levenberg, 23 Nov. 1933, 26 Aug. 1947.

23. Bowers, *My Life*, 101, 78, 96–99, 153–54; Bowers, *Beveridge and the Progressive Era*, v; Beveridge to Bowers, 5 Jan. 1920; Brubeck interview.

24. Bowers to Corbin, 23 Dec. 1919; Bowers to Beveridge, 4 Nov., 16 Oct. [1923], AJB; Bowers to Levenberg, 15 June 1937; Krock interview; George Bittler, interview with Hamilton, 3 Dec. 1960; Bowers, *My Life*, 106; Ralph Pulitzer, letter to Bowers, 10 Oct. 1923; Beveridge to Bowers, 1 Nov. [1923]; Bowers, letter to Nellie [Sights], 22 Jan. 1928, copy, HP.

## 5. New York

1. *New York Evening World*, 4–19 Dec. 1923, 7, 5, 8, 24 Jan. 1924 (hereafter cited as *EW*).

2. Claude G. Bowers, letter to Albert J. Beveridge, 4 Nov. [1923], Albert J. Beveridge Papers, Library of Congress, Washington, D.C. (hereafter cited as AJB); *EW*, 18, 22, 30 Jan., 12, 15, 18, 23 Feb., 1, 19, 22, 30 Apr., 1, 24 Mar., 10 May 1924.

3. Beveridge to Bowers, 28 May [1924], AJB; *EW*, 5 May, 12 June 1924.

4. Claude Bowers, "Reminiscences of Claude Bowers," interview by Louis Starr, 24, 30 Aug. 1954 (Oral History Research Office, Columbia University, New York), 57; *EW*, 24, 25, 30 June 1924; James P. Fadely, *Thomas Taggart: Public Servant, Political Boss, 1856–1929* (Indianapolis: Indiana Historical Society, 1997), 189–90.

5. Bowers, letter to Holman Hamilton, 3 Aug. 1952; Bowers, "New York Journal," 18 May, 25 Sept. 1924 (hereafter cited as "New York Journal"); *EW*, 27 June 1924; Claude Bowers, *My Life: The Memoirs of Claude Bowers* (New York: Simon and Schuster, 1962), 119.

6. *EW*, 2, 7, 12, 27, 29 Aug., 3, 21, 29 Oct., 10, 12, 15, 17, 18, 26 Sept., 6 Nov. 1924.

7. Edwin E. Emery and Henry L. Smith, *The Press and America* (Englewood Cliffs, N.J.: Prentice-Hall, 1954), 504–6; Ronald Steel, *Walter Lippmann and the American Century* (Boston: Little, Brown, 1980), 197–99; Jonathan Daniels, *They Will Be Heard: America's Crusading Newspaper Editors* (New York: McGraw-Hill, 1965), 284–85; "New

York Journal," 10 Dec. 1923; Bowers, *My Life*, 101–10; Bowers, letter to Ferris Greenslet, 2 Feb. 1923, Houghton Mifflin Company Papers, Houghton Library, Harvard University, Cambridge, Mass. (hereafter cited as HMP).

8. Bowers to Beveridge, 20 Apr. 1926, AJB; Bowers, *My Life*, 108, 111; Edward L. Schapsmeier and Frederick H. Schapsmeier, *Walter Lippmann: Philosopher-Journalist* (Washington, D.C.: Public Affairs Press, 1969), 1–3, 66–68, 163–73; Bowers, "Reminiscences," 72.

9. *EW*, 2 Feb., 16 Nov., 31 Oct., 28 July 1925, 28, 31 Dec., 22 Apr. 1926.

10. Ibid., 2 Apr., 28 May 1924, 6 Jan., 24, 29 Apr., 19, 29 June, 19 Oct., 16 Dec. 1925, 12 Jan., 17 Aug., 28 Sept., 18 Oct. 1926, 5, 6, 11 Jan. 1927; James W. Barrett, *Joseph Pulitzer and His World* (New York: The Vanguard Press, 1941), 400; Schapsmeier, *Walter Lippmann*, 50–54; Paula Eldot, *Governor Alfred E. Smith: The Politician as Reformer* (New York: Garland, 1983), 379; Elisabeth I. Perry, *Belle Moskowitz: Feminine Politics and the Exercise of Power in the Age of Alfred E. Smith* (New York: Oxford University Press, 1987), 185.

11. Alfred E. Smith, "Catholic and Patriot: Governor Replies," *Atlantic Monthly* 139 (May 1927): 721–28; *EW*, 31 Dec., 18 Apr. 1927.

12. *EW*, 2 June 1928, 12 Nov. 1929.

13. Daniels, *They Will Be Heard*, 290–95; "New York Journal," 23, 14, 27 Feb., 3, 4 Mar. 1931; Emery and Smith, *Press and America*, 505–6; Frank L. Mott, *American Journalism: A History, 1690–1960* (New York: Macmillan, 1962), 642–44; *Indianapolis Star*, 16 Mar. 1931; Theodore Fred Kuper, interview with Holman Hamilton, 30 Aug. 1962.

14. Bowers, "Reminiscences," 70–71; "New York Journal," 10 Apr. 1933; R. Wagner, letter to Bowers, 5 May 1932; *New York Evening Journal*, 1, 15, 5 Oct., 8, 10, 21 Nov., 5, 30, 31 Dec. 1932.

15. Bowers to Beveridge, 4 Nov., 16 Oct. [1923], 2 Apr., 3 Dec. 1925, AJB; Arthur Krock, interview with Hamilton, 16 Nov. 1965; Bowers to Greenslet, 25 Mar. 1925, HMP; Bowers, "Reminiscences," 61; Bowers, *Jefferson and Hamilton: The Struggle for Democracy in America* (Boston: Houghton Mifflin, 1925), v, 29, 115, 107, vi, 510.

16. Merrill D. Peterson, "Bowers, Roosevelt, and the 'New Jefferson,'" *Virginia Quarterly Review* 34 (autumn 1958): 530; Harry L. Coles, "Some Recent Interpretations of Jeffersonian America," *Lectures, 1969–1970* (Indianapolis: Indiana Historical Society, 1970), 74–76; see George Bancroft, *History of the Formation of the Constitution of the United States of America*, 2 vols. (New York: Appleton and Co., 1882); John Bach McMaster, *History of the People of the United States: From the Revolution to the Civil War*, 8 vols. (New York: D. Appleton, 1883–1913); Henry Adams, *History of the United States during the Administrations of Jefferson and Madison*, 9 vols. (New York: C. Scribner's, 1889–91); Henry Cabot Lodge, *Alexander Hamilton* (Boston: Houghton Mifflin and Co., 1882); Bowers, "Reminiscences," 61; Merrill D. Peterson, *The Jefferson Image in the American Mind* (New York: Oxford University Press, 1960), 346; see Herbert D. Croly, *The Promise of American Life* (Indianapolis: Bobbs-Merrill, 1965); Nicholas Murray Butler, *Why Should We Change Our Form of Government?: Studies in Practical Politics* (New York: Charles Scribner's Sons, 1912); Arthur H. Vandenberg, *The Greatest American: Alexander Hamilton* (New York: G. P. Putnam's Sons, 1921).

17. Bowers, *Jefferson and Hamilton*, 511; Bowers to Greenslet, 24 Mar. 1925, HMP; Howard K. Beale, "Charles Beard: Historian," in *Charles A. Beard: An Appraisal*, ed. Howard K. Beale (Lexington: University of Kentucky Press, 1954), 146–47; Thomas Bender, "Making History Whole Again," *New York Times Book Review*, 6 Oct. 1985,

p. 42; Richard Hofstadter, *The Progressive Historians: Turner, Beard, Parrington* (New York: Alfred A. Knopf, 1968), 181–89, 292.

18. Bowers, "Reminiscences," 65, and *Jefferson and Hamilton*, 127, 510; Edgar Lee Masters, letter to Bowers, 6 Aug. 1927; Samuel F. Bemis, letter to Bowers, 25 May 1926; Arthur M. Schlesinger, Jr., *The Age of Roosevelt: The Crisis of the Old Order, 1919–1933* (Boston: Houghton Mifflin, 1957), 104; Geoffrey C. Ward, *A First-Class Temperament: The Emergence of Franklin Roosevelt* (New York: Harper and Row, 1989), 681; Roosevelt quoted in Graham J. White, *FDR and the Press* (Chicago: University of Chicago Press, 1979), 144; *EW*, 3 Dec. 1925.

19. *New York World*, 6 Dec. 1925; W. E. Borah review, *The New Republic* 45 (23 Dec. 1925): 140; William McAdoo review, *Literary Digest International Book Review* 4 (Jan. 1926): 83–86; *New York Herald Tribune*, 20 Dec. 1925; Florence Finch Kelly, "Jefferson and Hamilton Fought to Shape People's Destiny," *New York Times Book Review*, 20 Dec. 1925, p. 7; *New York Evening Post*, 5 Dec. 1925; Samuel Flagg Bemis review, *American Historical Review* 31 (Apr. 1926): 543–45; J. Fred Rippy review, *Mississippi Valley Historical Review* 13 (Dec. 1926): 426–27; see Beveridge's reviews, *Boston Evening Transcript*, 12 Dec., *Indianapolis Star*, 13 Dec. 1925.

20. Peterson, *Jefferson Image in the American Mind*, 347; Jack Temple Kirby, *Media-Made Dixie: The South in the American Imagination* (Athens: University of Georgia Press, 1986), 33; Allan Nevins, letter to Bowers, 16 Jan. 1928; Oliver Knight, "Claude G. Bowers, Historian," *Indiana Magazine of History* 52 (Sept. 1956): 253.

21. Bowers, letter to Robert N. Linscott, 4 Jan. 1926, HMP; "New York Journal," 17 Mar., 4 Sept. 1926, 4 Sept., 16 Feb. 1927; *New York Times*, 24 Sept. 1926.

22. Joseph F. Guffey, letter to Bowers, 31 Mar. 1926; James M. Cox, *Journey through My Years* (New York: Simon and Schuster, 1946), 245; William G. McAdoo, letter to Bowers, 17 Dec. 1925; Cordell Hull, letter to Bowers, 29 Dec. 1925, Cordell Hull Papers, Library of Congress; "New York Journal," 9 Feb. 1926; Franklin Roosevelt, letter to Bowers, 22 Jan. 1926; Bowers to Hamilton, [1952?]; Peterson, "Bowers, Roosevelt, and the 'New Jefferson,'" 530; Coles, "Some Recent Interpretations of Jeffersonian America," 83–84.

23. For the views of recent historians on Jefferson, see Peterson, *Jefferson Image in the American Mind*; Keith B. Berwick, *The Federal Age, 1789–1829: America in the Process of Becoming* (Washington, D.C.: Service Center for Teachers of History, 1961); Coles, "Some Recent Interpretations of Jeffersonian America," 68–85; Joseph J. Ellis, *American Sphinx: The Character of Thomas Jefferson* (New York: Alfred A. Knopf, 1997). For the conclusions of recent scholars on Hamilton, see Forrest McDonald, *Alexander Hamilton: A Biography* (New York: W. W. Norton, 1979); John C. Miller, *The Federalist Era, 1789–1801* (New York: Harper and Row, 1960); Stanley Elkins and Eric McKitrick, *The Age of Federalism* (New York: Oxford University Press, 1993); McDonald, *Alexander Hamilton*, 117, 163, 233–36, 361; Miller, *Federalist Era*, 64–68; Elkins and McKitrick, *Age of Federalism*, 115–17, 260; Peterson, "Bowers, Roosevelt, and the 'New Jefferson,'" 530.

24. Charles B. Hosmer, Jr., *Presence of the Past: A History of the Preservation Movement in the United States before Williamsburg* (New York: G. P. Putnam's Sons, 1965), 180–83; Kuper interview; James A. Bear, Jr., interview with Hamilton, 9 Nov. 1972; "President Alderman's Tribute," typed MSS, Holman Hamilton Papers, Division of Special Collections and Archives of the Margaret I. King Library, University of Kentucky, Lexington (hereafter cited as HP); *Indianapolis Star*, 4 July 1926; Bowers to Linscott, 5 July 1926, HMP; Kuper to Hamilton, 12 Apr. 1961; "New York Journal," 1 Mar. 1933.

25. "New York Journal," 24 Sept. 1926; Bowers, *My Life*, 133–35; Theodore Fred Kuper, "Collecting Monticello," *Manuscripts* 7 (summer 1955): 215–26; Peterson, *Jefferson Image in the American Mind*, 350, 386; Bowers to Beveridge, 17 May 1926, AJB.

26. Bowers to Linscott, 4 Feb. 1926, 18 Feb., [June?], 14 Jan., 23 May 1927, HMP; see Mary Elisabeth Seldon, "George W. Julian: A Political Independent," in Ralph D. Gray, ed., *Gentlemen from Indiana: National Party Candidates, 1836–1940, Indiana Historical Collections*, vol. 50 (Indianapolis: Indiana Historical Bureau, 1977), 29–54; Bowers to Greenslet, 8 Nov. 1927, HMP; Bowers "Reminiscences," 64.

27. Bowers, *The Tragic Era: The Revolution after Lincoln* (Boston: Houghton Mifflin, 1929), v, vi, 155, 215, 140, 342, 51, 198–99, 83, 80, 60, 54, 538, 44, 349, 454, 199, 198, 308, 358, 360.

28. Holman Hamilton, "Before 'The Tragic Era': Claude Bowers's Earlier Attitudes toward Reconstruction," *Mid-America* 55 (Oct. 1973): 235–44; Bowers, "Reminiscences," 63; Bowers, *A Truce to Negro Colonization* (Indianapolis: Bradford Press, [1901]), 1–6; *EW*, 28 May 1924, 7, 30 Oct. 1925, 22 Mar., 4, 18 June 1927, 4 Jan. 1929; Sara Messing Harding, "Random Notes about Claude Bowers," Indiana Historical Society, Indianapolis; Holman Hamilton and Gayle Thornbrough, eds., *Indianapolis in the "Gay Nineties": High School Diaries of Claude G. Bowers* (Indianapolis: Indiana Historical Society, 1964), 98–100, 117–18.

29. David E. Kyvig, "History as Present Politics: Claude Bowers' *The Tragic Era*," *Indiana Magazine of History* 73 (Mar. 1977): 17; Bowers, letter to Jouett Shouse, 26 Aug. 1929, copy, HP; Harry B. Hawes, letter to Bowers, 6 Sept. 1929; McAdoo to Bowers, 28 Sept. 1929.

30. Bowers, "Reminiscences," 65, and *Tragic Era*, 243, 251, 244, 84, 44, 25; Craig Wylie, memorandum to Hamilton, 6 Jan. 1961; Kenneth M. Stampp, *The Era of Reconstruction, 1865–1877* (New York: Alfred A. Knopf, 1965), 4.

31. *New York Evening Post*, 7 Sept. 1929; *New York Times*, 8 Sept. 1929; Henry F. Pringle review, *Outlook and Independent* 153 (11 Sept. 1929): 66; Meredith Nicholson review, *Indianapolis Star*, 7 Sept. 1929; William MacDonald review, *The Nation* 129 (18 Sept. 1929): 307; Arthur M. Schlesinger, Sr., review, *The New Republic* 60 (9 Oct. 1929): 210; Charles R. Lingley review, *American Historical Review* 35 (Jan. 1930): 382–83; *New York Herald Tribune*, 8 Sept. 1929; Nathan G. Goodman review, *The Historical Outlook* 20 (Nov. 1929): 351–52; James C. Malin review, *Mississippi Valley Historical Review* 16 (Mar. 1930): 561–64; Nathaniel W. Stephenson review, *Saturday Review of Literature* 6 (28 Dec. 1929): 600; David S. Muzzey review, *Current History* 311 (Nov. 1929): 212, 216–17.

32. *Journal of Negro History* 15 (Jan. 1930): 117–19; see Sherwin L. Cook review, *Boston Evening Transcript*, 7 Sept. 1929; Bowers to Hamilton, 1 Aug. 1946; William A. Dunning, *Reconstruction, Political and Economic, 1865–1877* (New York: Harper and Bros., 1907), 1; Eric Foner, *Reconstruction: America's Unfinished Revolution, 1863–1877* (New York: Harper and Row, 1988), 609–10; John Hope Franklin, *Reconstruction: After the Civil War* (Chicago: University of Chicago Press, 1961), 235–36.

33. See Anna J. Cooper to [W. E. B.] Du Bois, 31 Dec. 1929, in Louise Daniel Hutchinson, *Anna J. Cooper: A Voice from the South* (Washington, D.C.: Published for the Anacostia Neighborhood Museum of the Smithsonian Institution by the Smithsonian Institution Press, 1981), 180; W. E. B. Du Bois, *Black Reconstruction in America: An Essay toward a History of the Part Which Black Folk Played in the Attempt to Reconstruct Democracy in America, 1860–1880* (New York: Russell and Russell, 1934), 732; Foner, *Reconstruction*, xx; William H. Harbaugh, *Lawyer's Lawyer: The Life of John W. Davis* (New York: Oxford University Press, 1973), 514; C. Vann Woodward, *The

*Strange Career of Jim Crow*, 3d rev. ed. (New York: Oxford University Press, 1974), 8–10; Bowers, letter to Lester Ziffren, 14 July 1957, copy, HP.

34. "New York Journal," 16 Jan., 11, 17 June 1930, 12 May, 10 June 1931; *South Bend Tribune*, 2 June 1930.

35. "New York Journal," 12 May 1930; Bowers, letter to William E. Dodd, 2 Oct. 1933, copy; W. J. Stuckey, *The Pulitzer Prize Novels: A Critical Backward Look* (Norman: University of Oklahoma Press, 1966), 7–8; Bowers to Hamilton, 1 Aug. 1946; Nevins to Bowers, 26 May 1930.

36. Bowers, *Beveridge and the Progressive Era* (Boston: Houghton Mifflin, 1932), vi, 387; "New York Journal," 14 Sept. 1932; Greenslet to Bowers, 19 Sept. 1927, copy, and Bowers to Greenslet, 23 Dec. 1927, HMP; Wylie memorandum; *New York Herald Tribune Book Review*, 4 Sept. 1932; Arthur C. Cole review, *Mississippi Valley Historical Review* 20 (Dec. 1933): 437–39; *New York Times Book Review*, 4 Sept. 1932; Kirby, *Media-Made Dixie*, 37; Knight, "Claude G. Bowers, Historian," 255.

### 6. Spokesman for the Democracy

1. Claude Bowers, "Reminiscences of Claude Bowers," interview by Louis Starr, 24, 30 Aug. 1954 (Oral History Research Office, Columbia University, New York), 54, and *My Life: The Memoirs of Claude Bowers* (New York: Simon and Schuster, 1962), 116–17; Bowers, "New York Journal," 7 July 1924 (hereafter cited as "New York Journal"); James P. Fadely, *Thomas Taggart: Public Servant, Political Boss, 1856–1929* (Indianapolis: Indiana Historical Society, 1997), 192–93; *Boston Herald*, 24 July 1927.

2. Bowers, letter to Robert N. Linscott, 14 July 1924, copy; Bowers, "Reminiscences," 57; William H. Harbaugh, *Lawyer's Lawyer: The Life of John W. Davis* (New York: Oxford University Press, 1973), 225–28; Bowers, *My Life*, 120–24.

3. Bowers, "Reminiscences," 57–60; "New York Journal," 16 Sept., 6 Oct. 1926; Frank Oliver, interview with Holman Hamilton, 26 Apr. 1963.

4. *New York Evening World*, 4 Sept.–30 Oct. 1926; "New York Journal," 3 Nov. 1926; Bowers, letter to Albert J. Beveridge, 26 Nov. 1926, Albert J. Beveridge Papers, Library of Congress, Washington, D.C. (hereafter cited as AJB).

5. Bowers, "Reminiscences," 59; *St. Louis Post Dispatch*, 14 Apr. 1926; "New York Journal," 4 Sept. 1926; Bowers to Linscott, 20 Apr. 1926, Houghton Mifflin Company Papers, Houghton Library, Harvard University, Cambridge, Mass. (hereafter cited as HMP); Harry B. Hawes, letter to Bowers, 20 Apr. 1926; Bowers to Beveridge, 20 Apr. 1926, AJB.

6. *Fort Wayne Journal-Gazette*, 14 Dec. 1926; Bowers to Linscott, 14 Jan., 18 Feb., 23 May 1927, HMP; "New York Journal," 7 May, 3 Dec. 1927.

7. *New York Times*, 11–13 Jan. 1928; "New York Journal," 14 Dec. 1927, 4 Jan. 1928; Bowers, letter to Ferris Greenslet, 23 Dec. 1927, HMP; Bowers, letter to Holman Hamilton, 14 Feb. 1952.

8. "New York Journal," 15 Jan. 1928; Bowers, "Reminiscences," 74; *Washington Post*, 13 Jan. 1928; Bowers, *My Life*, 180; *Raleigh* (N.C.) *News and Observer*, 15 Jan. 1928; Meredith Nicholson, letter to Bowers, 11 Feb. 1935; Bowers to Hamilton, 14 Feb. 1952.

9. Hawes to Bowers, 9 Jan. 1928; "New York Journal," 15 Jan. 1928; Bowers, "Reminiscences," 74–75.

10. "New York Journal," 22, 26 Feb., 5 Mar., 15 Apr. 1928; Elisabeth Marbury, letter to Bowers, 6 Feb. 1928; Bowers, "Reminiscences," 75–76; Bowers to Roberts, 9 Feb. 1928, Holman Hamilton Papers, Division of Special Collections and Archives of the Margaret I.

King Library, University of Kentucky, Lexington (hereafter cited as HP); Bowers, *My Life*, 181–85, 192, 137.

11. *New York Times*, 7, 24 Mar. 1928; "New York Journal," 15, 27 Mar., 7, 15, 16 May, 8 June 1928; Bowers, "Reminiscences," 76; Bowers, *My Life*, 185.

12. "New York Journal," 1 May, 13, 15, 25–26, 28 June 1928; Bowers, *My Life*, 194–97, 189–90; Bowers to Beveridge, 1 Sept. 1925, AJB; Bowers, "Reminiscences," 79–82; Fred L. Israel, *Nevada's Key Pittman* (Lincoln: University of Nebraska Press, 1963), 63; Edwin A. Miles, "The Keynote Speech at National Conventions," *Quarterly Journal of Speech* 46 (Feb. 1960): 31; Richard O'Connor, *The First Hurrah: A Biography of Alfred E. Smith* (New York: G. P. Putnam's Sons, 1970), 196–97; Bowers, "Keynote," *The Political News* 10 (July 1928), copy, Claude G. Bowers Manuscripts, Lilly Library, Indiana University, Bloomington.

13. "New York Journal," 18, 26, 27 June 1928; *Chicago Tribune*, 28 June 1928; *New York Times*, 27 June 1928; Edward J. Flynn, *You're the Boss* (New York: Viking Press, 1947), 66–67.

14. "New York Journal," 30 Aug., 19 Sept. 1928.

15. Ibid., 19 Sept., 2, 18 Oct., 3 Nov. 1928; see Allan J. Lichtman, *Prejudice and the Old Politics: The Presidential Election of 1928* (Chapel Hill: University of North Carolina Press, 1979), 79–90; Harris G. Warren, *Herbert Hoover and the Great Depression* (New York: Oxford University Press, 1967), 41–50; Bowers, "My Spanish Diary," 29 Jan. 1935.

16. "New York Journal," 6 Nov. 1928, 21 Mar., 1, 19, 23 Nov. 1929, 1 Jan. 1930; Alfred E. Smith, letter to Bowers, 17 Sept. 1929.

17. "New York Journal," 24 Jan., 5, 6, 10, 18 Feb. 1929, 14 Feb., 5, 30 Mar., 12, 27 Apr., 12 July 1930.

18. Ibid., 4 Aug., 24 Oct., 5 Nov. 1930; Bowers, letter to Roger L. Scaife, 16 Dec. 1930, HMP.

19. "New York Journal," 21 Feb., 16–18 June, 4 July, 2, 28 Oct. 1931; Bowers, letter to [J. G. de R.] Hamilton, 6 June 1931, J. G. de R. Hamilton Papers, Southern Historical Collection, University of North Carolina, Chapel Hill; Bowers, *John Tyler: Address by Hon. Claude G. Bowers* (Richmond, Va.: Richmond Press, 1932); Franklin D. Roosevelt, letter to Bowers, 23 Sept. 1931.

20. "New York Journal," 9 Jan., 10 Feb., 19, 20, 24 Mar., 26, 28 Apr. 1932.

21. Roosevelt to Bowers, 23 Apr., 24 June, 19 July 1931, 18 June 1932; W. A. Swanberg, *Citizen Hearst: A Biography of William Randolph Hearst* (New York: Charles Scribner's Sons, 1961), 435–38; "New York Journal," 5, 7, 9 June 1932; Bowers, "Reminiscences," 89, 88.

22. "New York Journal," 12, 30 June, 2, 27 July 1932.

23. Roosevelt to Bowers, 1 Aug. 1932; Bowers, "Reminiscences," 89–91; "New York Journal," 8 Sept., 6, 12–13 Oct., 3, 9 Nov. 1932; Frederick Van Nuys, letter to Bowers, 28 Nov. 1932; Bowers, letter to Mary D. Carter, 20 Nov. 1932.

24. "New York Journal," 15 Nov. 1932, 24–25 Jan., 8 Feb., 3 Mar. 1933; "Authors of the Year Dinner Committee," typed transcript, copy, HP.

25. "New York Journal," 24 Dec. 1932; Bowers, "Reminiscences," 64; Theodore Fred Kuper, interview with Holman Hamilton, 30 Aug. 1962.

26. Sybil [Bowers], letter to Jessie [Moore], n.d.; Eleanor Roosevelt, letter to Sybil Bowers, 21 Apr. 1923; Bowers, letter to Nellie and Pete Sights, 6 June 1929, copy, HP.

27. Bowers to Nellie and Pete Sights, 6 June 1929; "New York Journal," 21 Sept. 1930, 6, 9, 15, 14, 18 Aug. 1931, 4–5, 16 Aug. 1932.

28. Bowers, "Reminiscences," 60; "New York Journal," 18, 21 May, 16, 20, 28 June, 28 Nov. 1924, 21 Jan., 8 Dec. 1925, 3 Sept. 1926; Bowers, *My Life*, 158, 160, 163; Bowers to

Beveridge, 19 May 1926, AJB; James M. Cox, *Journey through My Years* (New York: Simon and Schuster, 1946), 245; *New York Evening World*, 28 Apr. 1927.

29. "New York Journal," 4, 23 Sept., 25 Oct. 1926; Edgar Lee Masters, letter to Bowers, 17 May 1926.

30. Bowers to Beveridge, 7 Jan. 1927, AJB; Bowers, *My Life*, 165–66; "New York Journal," 25, 14 Apr., 4 Nov. 1927; Richard Lingeman, *Theodore Dreiser: An American Journey, 1908–1945* (New York: G. P. Putnam's Sons, 1990), 240–41, 283–84, 314; Thomas Bender, *New York Intellect: A History of Intellectual Life in New York City, from 1750 to the Beginning of Our Own Time* (New York: Knopf, 1987), 285.

31. Bowers to Beveridge, 26 Nov. 1926, AJB; "New York Journal," 5 Sept. 1924, 18 Oct. 1926, 6 Jan., 13 June, 15 Sept. 1927; Ann Douglas, *Terrible Honesty: Mongrel Manhattan in the 1920s* (New York: Farrar, Straus, and Giroux, 1995), 519, 454–55.

32. "New York Journal," 27 Jan., 6 Apr., 19, 21 July, 14 Oct., 14, 16 Nov., 5, 8, 13, 29 Dec. 1928.

33. Oliver interview; "New York Journal," 26, 30 Jan., 27 Mar., 15, 29 Oct. 1929; Nicholas Murray Butler, *Across the Busy Years: Recollections and Reflections*, 2 vols. (New York: C. Scribner's Sons, 1939), 1:359–61.

34. "New York Journal," 5, 7 Jan., 11, 18 Nov. 1930, 1 Jan., 6 Feb. 1931, 15, 29 Dec. 1932, 9 Jan. 1933.

35. Ibid., 23 Feb., 23 Mar., 11, 27, 28 Apr., 2 May 1933; Robert F. Wagner, letter to Bowers, 22 Dec. 1932; James A. Farley, interview with Hamilton, 25 Sept. 1967.

36. "New York Journal," 11–14 Apr. 1933.

37. Ibid., 24 Apr., 3 May 1933; Bowers, *My Life*, 265.

## 7. Spain

1. Claude Bowers, "My Spanish Diary," 22 May, 16 June 1933 (hereafter cited as "Spanish Diary"); *El Sol* (Madrid), 23 May 1936; Bowers, letter to Lawrence Levenberg, 23 Nov. 1933. (Copies of Bowers's letters to Levenberg are in the Holman Hamilton Papers, Division of Special Collections and Archives of the Margaret I. King Library, University of Kentucky, Lexington.) Fred L. Kelly, "Ambassador as Democrat," *Esquire* (Apr. 1937): 220; Bowers, *My Mission to Spain: Watching the Rehearsal for World War II* (New York: Simon and Schuster, 1954), 16–17 (hereafter cited as *My Mission*); Bowers, letter to J. Edith Monahan, 17 June 1933, J. Edith Monahan Collection, Holman Hamilton Papers (hereafter cited as MC); Sybil [Bowers] to Jessie [Moore], 18 June 1933; Bowers, letter to Josephus Daniels, 3 July 1933; Cordell Hull, letter to Bowers, 11 Apr. 1933, 123 Bowers/10, U.S. Department of State, RG59, National Archives, Washington, D.C. (hereafter cited as NA).

2. *My Mission*, 9, 39, 27, 20–23, 30–33; "Spanish Diary," 14, 24 June, 2, 3 Aug., 2 Oct. 1933; Bowers, letter to Theodore Fred Kuper, 13 July 1933, Claude G. Bowers Collection, Henry E. Huntington Library, San Marino, Calif. (hereafter cited as BC); *New York Times*, 26 May 1933; *New York Evening World*, 13 May 1926; Bowers, letter to Wilbur Carr, 27 June 1933, 123 Bowers/38, NA; Bowers, letter to Frank Brubeck, 14 Dec. 1933; Bowers, "My Mission to Spain," 1945 MSS, 44, BC; Bowers, "Reminiscences of Claude Bowers," interview by Louis Starr, 24, 30 Aug. 1954 (Oral History Research Office, Columbia University, New York), 113; Bowers to Levenberg, 23 Nov. 1933.

3. Bowers to Levenberg, 23 Nov. 1933; Bowers to Kuper, 11 June 1933, BC; Bowers, *My Life: The Memoirs of Claude Bowers* (New York: Simon and Schuster, 1962), 173, 68; "Spanish Diary," 2 June 1933, 1 Nov. 1934, 20 May 1935; *My Mission*, 66–67, 291;

Horton Schoellkopf, interview with Holman Hamilton, 27 Apr. 1963; Kuper to Hamilton, 25 Oct. 1975; Bowers to Brubeck, 14 Dec. 1933.

4. "Spanish Diary," 31 May, 10 Nov. 1933, 12 Apr., 23 Dec. 1934, 10 Feb., 22 Dec. 1935; Bowers, letter to Breckinridge Long, 26 July 1935, Breckinridge Long Papers, Library of Congress, Washington, D.C.; Bowers to Levenberg, 6 Feb., 31 July 1935; Bowers, letters to Homer C. Cummings, 6 Dec. 1933, 11 Apr., 2 May 1934, Homer C. Cummings Collection, Manuscript Department, University of Virginia, Charlottesville (hereafter cited as HCC); Bowers, letter to Sybil [Bowers], 26 May 1936; Bowers, letter to Franklin D. Roosevelt, 13 Dec. 1933; Sybil Bowers, "Diary of Sybil Bowers," 15 June 1933, Claude G. Bowers Manuscripts, Lilly Library, Indiana University, Bloomington (hereafter cited as BM).

5. Kuper to Hamilton, 25 Oct. 1975; "Spanish Diary," 10, 11, 23 Aug., 22 Oct. 1933, 22 Feb., 29 May, 15–16 June, 14 Dec. 1934, 11–12 Jan., 13 Apr., 22 Dec. 1935, 17 Aug., 21 Sept. 1936; Sybil to Jessie, 7 May 1934; John Dos Passos, interview with Hamilton, 23 Feb. 1965; James M. Minifie, interview with Hamilton, 16 Feb. 1965; Lester Ziffren, interview with Hamilton, 16 May 1964; My Mission, 6, 43, 205, 239, 72; Bowers, "My Mission to Spain," 32, 33; Bowers to Monahan, 31 Oct. 1933, 20, 21 Sept. 1934, MC; Bowers, My Life, 320; Bowers to Kuper, 14 Jan. 1935, BC; Frank Oliver, interview with Hamilton, 26 Apr. 1963.

6. Bowers to Levenberg, 23 Nov. 1933, 31 July 1935; Theodore Dreiser, letter to Bowers, 26 Feb. 1936; Claude [Bowers], letter to Pat [Bowers], 6 Feb. 1934; Bowers to Monahan, 10 Oct., 28 Nov. 1933, 3 Jan., 7 Mar., 4, 18 Apr., 6 Sept., 3 Oct. 1934, MC; "Spanish Diary," 8, 25 Nov., 20 Dec. 1933, 23 May 1934, 8 Nov. 1935; Sybil to Jessie, 18 June 1933, 10 Jan., 7 May 1934, [1936]; Sybil Bowers, "Diary," 1:68–69; Theodore Fred Kuper, interview with Hamilton, 30 Aug. 1962; Ziffren interview; Eric C. Wendelin, interview with Hamilton, 18 Aug. 1965; Gustave Weigel, interview with Hamilton, 28 Apr. 1963; José "Pepe" Torres Rueda, interview with Hamilton, 12 Nov. 1966. This "bright young fellow" was Holman Hamilton.

7. Bowers, letter to Florence [Dinnen], 29 Dec. 1935, copy, Holman Hamilton Papers (hereafter cited as HP); Bowers to Allie [Alice C. Wolverton], 3 Feb. 1939, copy, ibid.; Sybil [Bowers] to Ruth [Kuper], [summer 1933], BC; Bowers to Brubeck, 18 July 1938; Bowers to Kuper, 6 Aug., 4 Dec. 1935, BC; "Spanish Diary," 8 Aug.–1 Sept. 1934, 15, 22 July 1935; My Mission, 89–90.

8. Schoellkopf, Wendelin, and Ziffren interviews; Bowers, letter to William E. Dodd, 9 Dec. 1934, copy, HP; Bowers to Brubeck, 14 Dec. 1935; "Spanish Diary," 2 Aug. 1933; Theodore Mariner quoted in Hallett Johnson, Diplomatic Memoirs: Serious and Frivolous (New York: Vantage Press, 1963), 106; Hugh Millard, letter to Bowers, 7 Mar. 1934; Bowers to Kuper, 31 Oct. 1934, BC.

9. Indianapolis Sentinel, 14 Apr. 1901; New York Evening World, 13 Nov. 1924, 28 Sept. 1926, 10 Feb. 1931; Manuel Azaña, 14 Feb. 1933, quoted in Antonio Ramos Oliveira, Politics, Economics and Men of Modern Spain: 1808–1946 (London: Arno Press, 1946), 472. On the Spanish Republic, 1933–36, see Gabriel Jackson, The Spanish Republic and the Civil War, 1931–1939 (Princeton, N.J.: Princeton University Press, 1965); Paul Preston, The Coming of the Spanish Civil War: Reform, Reaction and Revolution in the Second Republic, 1931–1939 (New York: Harper and Row, 1978); Manuel Tuñón de Lara, La España del siglo XX, vol. 2, De la Segunda República a la guerra civil (1931–1936) (Barcelona: Laia, 1974).

10. The abbreviations for organizations conform to their Spanish-language initials.

11. Bowers, "Reminiscences," 98, 101, 104; "Spanish Diary," 18 Oct. 1933, 6 Mar., 12 Apr., 5–8 Oct. 1934, 13 Nov. 1935; Bowers, My Life, 279.

12. "Spanish Diary," 8 Oct. 1934, 7 Jan. 1936; Paul Preston, "The Creation of the Popular Front in Spain," in *The Popular Front in Europe*, eds. Helen Graham and Paul Preston (New York: St. Martin's Press, 1987), 84–105; Santos Juliá Díaz, *Orígenes del frente popular en España (1931–1936)* (Madrid: Siglo Veintiuno Editores, 1979), 134–63; Stanley G. Payne, *The Spanish Revolution* (New York: W. W. Norton and Co., 1970), 156–84.

13. "Spanish Diary," 8 Oct. 1934, 13 Sept. 1935, 20, 24 Jan., 10, 17, 14, 22 Feb., 5, 7 Apr., 11, 17 Mar., 5, 17 May, 3, 5, 12 June 1936; Bowers to Levenberg, 4 Apr. 1936; Bowers to Kuper, 6 Apr. 1936, BC; Bowers, "Reminiscences," 108; *My Mission*, 188–89, 209, 215; Bowers to Hull, 14 Mar. 1935, 1, 7 Apr., 20 May 1936, 852.00/2143, 2153, 2156, 2166, NA.

14. Peter J. Sehlinger, "Personality, Politics, and Diplomacy: Claude G. Bowers and the State Department, 1933–1939," *Proceedings of the Indiana Academy of the Social Sciences*, 3d ser., 36 (1991): 10–19; Douglas Little, "Claude Bowers and His Mission to Spain: The Diplomacy of a Jeffersonian Democrat," *U.S. Diplomats in Europe, 1919–1941*, ed. Kenneth Paul Jones (Santa Barbara, Calif.: ABC-Clio, 1981), 127–46; Raymond Moley, *After Seven Years* (New York: Harper and Brothers, 1939), 131–32; "Spanish Diary," 11, 28 Apr., 31 May 1933; Jay Pierrepont Moffat, "Diary," 21 Dec., 1 Nov. 1933, 3 Feb. 1934, Jay Pierrepont Moffat Papers and Diaries, Houghton Library, Harvard University, Cambridge, Mass.; Hull, letter to James Farley, 25 Jan. 1933, BM; Martin Weil, *A Pretty Good Club: The Founding Fathers of the U.S. Foreign Service* (New York: W. W. Norton, 1978), 76–77; Carr to Bowers, 31 Mar., 9 July 1934; Moore to Bowers, 23 May, 9 July 1934; Bowers, letter to [Arthur M.] Schlesinger [Jr.], 12 Apr. 1951, copy, BM; *New York World Telegram*, 27 Nov. 1935; Bowers to Dodd, 25 July 1933, 9 Dec. 1935, copies, HP; Bowers to Daniels, 3 July 1933, copy, ibid.; Bowers to Moore, 27 June 1934, R. Walton Moore Papers, Franklin D. Roosevelt Library, Hyde Park, New York (hereafter cited as MP).

15. Graham H. Stuart, *The Department of State: A History of Its Organization, Procedure, and Personnel* (New York: Macmillan, 1949), 326; Bowers to Dodd, 12 Sept. 1933, 26 Feb. 1934, copies, HP; Dodd to Bowers, 20 July 1933, 17 Feb. 1934; Hugh R. Wilson, letter to Bowers, 22 Feb. 1934; Robert L. Owen, letter to Bowers, 17 Nov. 1933; Bowers, letter to Daniel C. Roper, 7 Dec. 1933, copy, HP; Roosevelt to Bowers, 5 Feb. 1934; Roper to Bowers, 18 Jan. 1934; Robert F. Wagner, letter to Bowers, 29 Mar. 1934; Carr to Bowers, 31 Mar. 1934; Frances H. Langlois, letter to Bowers, 11 June 1934; Millard to Bowers, 7 Mar. 1934; Bowers to Monahan, 27 Feb. 1934, MC.

16. Johnson, *Diplomatic Memoirs*, 117, 80–81; Bowers to Moore, 27 June, 18 July 1934, MP; Pat Bowers, letter to Hamilton, 3 Feb. 1961; Schoellkopf interview; ABC (Madrid), 22 Oct. 1935; Carr to Bowers, 30 Mar. 1935; "Spanish Diary," 20 Oct. 1934, 31 Mar. 1937; *My Mission*, 123; Bowers to Monahan, 27 Sept. 1933, MC; Bowers to Wagner, 25 June 1949, Robert F. Wagner Papers, Georgetown University, Washington, D.C.; Ziffren interview; Biddle Garrison, letter to Bowers, 10 July 1934.

17. Wendelin interview; Bowers to Kuper, 31 Oct. 1934, BC; Bowers to Hull, 10 Dec. 1935, 25 Feb., 7 Apr. 1936, 852.00/2122, 2142, 2156, NA; "Spanish Diary," 11 Oct. 1934; Laughlin quoted in Douglas Little, *Malevolent Neutrality: The United States, Great Britain, and the Origins of the Spanish Civil War* (Ithaca, N.Y.: Cornell University Press, 1985), 58–90, 184–220; Bowers to Roosevelt, 28 June 1933, copy, HP; Bowers, "Reminiscences," 110; Hallett Johnson, letter to Hull, 5 Mar. 1936, 852.00/2144, NA; William Phillips, "Journals," 2 June 1936, William Phillips Papers and Journals, Houghton Library.

18. "Spanish Diary," 11, 17, 27 Mar., 7 Apr., 5 May, 3, 12, 22 June, 13 July 1936; *My Mission*, 209, 206, 200; Bowers to Hull, 14 Mar. 1935, 24 Feb. 1936, 852.00/2143, 2136,

NA; *El Sol*, 2 June 1936; Bowers, "Reminiscences," 113, 114; Bowers to Monahan, 13 Apr. 1936, MC; Bowers to Levenberg, 4 Apr. 1936; Jackson, *Spanish Republic and the Civil War*, 198; Hugh Thomas, *The Spanish Civil War* (New York: Harper and Brothers, 1961), 98–108; Manuel Tuñón de Lara, "Orígines lejanos y próximos," *La guerra civil española 50 años después*, ed. Manuel Tuñón de Lara et al. (Barcelona: Editorial Labor, 1985), 38–41; Pierre Broué and Emile Témime, *The Revolution and the Civil War in Spain* (Cambridge, Mass.: MIT Press, 1972), 80–81, 93; Tuñón de Lara, *De la Segunda República*, 509–20; Raymond Carr, *The Spanish Tragedy: The Civil War in Perspective* (London: Weidenfeld and Nicholson, 1977), 69–70; Bowers, introduction to *The United States and the Spanish Civil War*, by F. Jay Taylor (New York: Bookman Associates, 1956), 17.

19. Bowers to Hull, 1, 7 Apr., 20 May 1936, 852.00/2153, 2156, 2166, 6, 13 July 1936, 852.00 PR/455, 456, 15 July 1936, 852.00/2297, NA.

20. Bowers, "Reminiscences," 95; Kelly, "Ambassador as Democrat," 220; Bowers to Kuper, 31 Oct. 1934, 11 June 1933, BC; Bowers to Cummings, 9 Dec. 1933, HCC; Bowers to Dodd, 9 Dec. 1934, copy, HP; Carlos de Miranda, memorandum, 2 May 1933, Estados Unidos, legajo 345, exp. 24576, Archivo del Ministerio de Asuntos Exteriores, Madrid, Spain (hereafter cited as AMAE); *My Mission*, 5; "Spanish Diary," 1, 16 June 1933; *El Sol*, 2 June 1933; Fernando de los Ríos, letter to Bowers, 23 June 1933; Bowers to Roosevelt, 28 June 1933, OF:303.1, Franklin D. Roosevelt: Papers as President, Franklin D. Roosevelt Library (hereafter cited as FDR); Roosevelt to Bowers, 11 July 1933.

21. Bowers, *My Life*, 44; "Spanish Diary," 3 Nov. 1935; Bowers to Roosevelt, 27 Mar. 1935, OF:303, FDR; Roosevelt to Asst. Sec. of the Navy [H. L. Roosevelt], 15 Apr. 1935, OF:422, ibid.; Roosevelt to Bowers, 22 Apr. 1935, with copy attached from H. L. Roosevelt to F. D. Roosevelt, 18 Apr. 1935; Bowers to Daniels, 26 July 1933, copy, HP; William Phillips to Consul, 15 June 1933, 352.1121, Blodgett, Walton/1, NA; Phillips to Foreign Service Administration, 28 June 1933, 352.1121, Blodgett/4, ibid.; *New York Times*, 11, 12 July, *Baltimore Sun*, 11 July, *New York Herald Tribune*, 18 July 1933; Bowers to Hull, 18 July 1933, D77 352.1121, Blodgett/78, 15 Nov. 1933, D206 352.1121, Blodgett/150, 20 Oct. 1933, T63 352.1121, Blodgett/131, NA; Hull to Bowers, 8 Sept. 1933, BM, 1 Mar. 1934, 352.1121, Blodgett/192, NA; Bowers to Hamilton, 20 Apr. 1952; Roosevelt to Bowers, 22 Aug. 1933; Owen to Bowers, 9 Oct. 1934; Moore to Bowers, 2 Mar. 1934.

22. "Spanish Diary," 11, 28 Apr., 2 May, 9, 10 Nov., 21 Dec. 1933, 2 Feb. 1934, 10, 14 Feb., 30 May 1936; Douglas Little, "Twenty Years of Turmoil: ITT, the State Department, and Spain, 1924–1944," *Business History Review* 53 (winter 1979): 449–72; Phillips, "Journals," 17 July, 15 Oct. 1934, 7 June 1935, 30 Jan. 1936; Moffat, "Diary," 21, 27 Dec. 1933, 11, 12 Jan., 2, 3 Feb. 1934; *My Mission*, 319; Bowers to Hull, 1 June 1936, 852.75 NTC/208, NA; Sosthenes Behn to Logan Rock, 2 June 1936, copy, HP.

23. "Spanish Diary," 28 Apr., 1 May 1933; Bowers to Roosevelt, 28 June 1933, OF:303, FDR; Emilio Zapico, "Memoria Trimestral," Estados Unidos, legajo 298, exp. 8, AMAE; Roosevelt to Bowers, 11 June 1933; Bowers to Roosevelt, 2 Aug. 1933, *Foreign Relations of the United States*, 1933 (Washington, D.C.: Government Printing Office, 1949), 1:342–43; Bowers to Hull, 8 May 1935, copy, BM; Roper to Bowers, 3 July 1933, 18 Oct. 1934. See Sabine Jessner, "Claude G. Bowers: New Deal Advocate of Spanish-American Commerce, 1933–39," *Proceedings of the Indiana Academy of the Social Sciences*, 3d ser., 20 (1985): 98–104, and Little, *Malevolent Neutrality*, 164–75.

24. Phillips, "Journals," 26 Dec. 1933; "Spanish Diary," 21 Dec. 1933, 17 Sept., 14 May 1934; Moffat, "Diary," 11, 18 Jan. 1934; Bowers to Roosevelt, 10 Jan. 1934, PSF:Spain, FDR; Edgar B. Nixon, ed., *Franklin D. Roosevelt and Foreign Affairs*, 3 vols. (Cambridge,

Mass.: Belknap Press of Harvard University, 1969), 1:587; Phillips to Roosevelt, 29 Jan. 1934, enclosed with Roosevelt to Bowers, 5 Feb. 1934; Moffat to Bowers, 7 May 1934; Moffat to Francis B. Sayre, 20 Apr. 1934, copy, HP.

25. Hull, memos, 6, 20 Apr. 1933, Cordell Hull Papers, Library of Congress; Roosevelt proclamation, 21 Aug. 1934, 611.5231/1019, NA; Moffat, "Diary," 6 Sept. 1934; Phillips, "Journals," 18 Sept. 1934; "Spanish Diary," 17 Sept. 1934; H. F. [Herbert Feis], memo, 30 Jan. 1936, Appendix D, 611.5231/1127½, NA; Zapico to Ministro de Estado, 15 June 1933, Estados Unidos, legajo 298, exp. 8, AMAE; Hull to Bowers, 12 July 1935.

26. Sayre to Bowers, 24 July 1935; Hull to Bowers, 12 July 1935, copy, HP, 8 Aug. 1934, 611.5231/1012A, NA, 26 Nov. 1935, 611.5231/1048, NA; Bowers to Hull, 18 July, 17, 21 Aug. 1935, 5, 20 Feb. 1936, 611.5231/994, 1061, 1020, 1131, 1135, 5 Mar. 1936, 852.51/325, NA; Bowers to Sayre, 27 June 1935, 611.5231/987, NA; Phillips to Roosevelt, 26 July 1935, OF:422, FDR; Roosevelt to Phillips, 27 July 1935, 611.5231/1011, NA; "Spanish Diary," 2 Oct., 12 Dec., 30 Sept. 1935, 6 Apr. 1936; Phillips, "Journals," 30 Jan., 2 Apr. 1936; Feis memo; Moffat, "Diary," 4 Apr. 1934; Little, *Malevolent Neutrality*, 193; Little, "Claude Bowers and His Mission to Spain," 136-37; Hull, 25 Mar. 1936, 611.5231/1150, NA.

27. Phillips, "Journals," 2 Apr. 1936; Hull memo, 11 May 1936, 611.5231/1162, NA; Moffat to John C. Wiley, [Aug. 1937], John C. Wiley Papers, Franklin D. Roosevelt Presidential Library; Moffat, "Diary," 12 Jan. 1934; "Spanish Diary," 21 Dec. 1933, 13, 14 Jan. 1934; Phillips to Bowers, 12 Jan. 1934, 625.116/34, NA.

28. Bowers to Long, 9 Dec. 1935, 24 Nov., 20 July 1933, copies, HP; Bowers to Cummings, 6 Dec. 1933, 2 May 1934, HCC; Roosevelt to Bowers, 5 Feb. 1934; Bowers to Kuper, 12 Dec. 1933, BC; Bowers to Daniels, 15 Oct. 1936, copy, HP.

29. "Spanish Diary," 18 May 1934; Bowers to Kuper, 31 Oct. 1934, BC; Barry Bingham, letter to Farley, n.d., copy, included in Farley to Bowers, 18 Oct. 1935; James A. Farley, interview with Hamilton, 25 Sept. 1967; James A. Farley, *Jim Farley's Story: The Roosevelt Years* (New York: Whittlesey House, 1948), 290; Harold L. Ickes, *The Secret Diary of Harold L. Ickes*, 3 vols. (New York: Simon and Schuster, 1953–54), 1:517; Thomas T. Spencer, "'Old Democrats' and New Deal Politics: Claude G. Bowers, James A. Farley, and the Changing Democratic Party, 1933–1940," *Indiana Magazine of History* 91 (Mar. 1996): 31–34; Bowers, letter to Joseph F. Guffey, 21 Oct. 1934, copy, BM; Guffey to Bowers, 21 Oct. 1934.

30. Bowers to Dodd, 23 July, 9 Dec. 1935, copies, HP; Bowers to Kuper, 29 June 1935, BC; "Spanish Diary," 29 June 1935; Bowers to [Dinnen], 29 Dec. 1935, copy, HP; Bowers to Daniels, 27 Nov. 1935, copy, ibid.; Bowers to Levenberg, 31 July 1935; Guffey to Bowers, 26 Mar., 25 Feb. 1935; Hull to Bowers, 26 Mar. 1935, 18 June 1936; Roosevelt to Bowers, 22 Aug. 1935; Roper to Bowers, 8 Nov. 1935; Dreiser to Bowers, 26 Feb. 1936.

31. [Bowers], letter to Jessie [Moore], 7 June 1936, HP; Bowers to Brubeck, 18 July 1938; "Spanish Diary," 7, 8, 10, 11, 13 July 1936; [Bowers] to Sybil , 27 May 1936; Farley to Bowers, 13 July 1936; Sybil to Jessie, [early 1936]; Bowers to Kuper, [May 1936], BC.

## 8. The Spanish Civil War

1. Claude Bowers, letter to Josephus Daniels, 16 Aug. 1938, copy; Bowers, "My Spanish Diary," 18, 19, 24 July, 21 Aug. 1936 (hereafter cited as "Spanish Diary"); Bowers, letter to Franklin D. Roosevelt, 6 Aug. 1936, PSF:Spain, Franklin D. Roosevelt: Papers as President, Franklin D. Roosevelt Library, Hyde Park, New York (hereafter cited as FDR); Bowers, letter to Holman Hamilton, 1 Apr. 1937.

2. Bowers, letter to Nell [Sights], 12 Dec. 1937, copy, Holman Hamilton Papers, Division of Special Collections and Archives of the Margaret I. King Library, University of Kentucky, Lexington (hereafter cited as HP); *New York Sun*, 27 July 1936; *New York Times*, 30 July 1936; Bowers, *My Mission to Spain: Watching the Rehearsal for World War II* (New York: Simon and Schuster, 1954), 249–50 (hereafter cited as *My Mission*); *Baltimore Evening Sun*, 24 July 1936; Bowers, letter to Hallett Johnson, n.d., in Hallett Johnson, *Diplomatic Memoirs: Serious and Frivolous* (New York: Vantage Press, 1963), 111–12; "Spanish Diary," 27 July 1937; Cordell Hull, letter to Paris Embassy, 26 July 1936, 123 Bowers/75, U.S. Department of State, RG 59, National Archives, Washington, D.C. (hereafter cited as NA).

3. "Spanish Diary," 27 July–5 Aug., 20 Aug., 30 Nov. 1936; *New York Evening World*, 31 July 1936; Bowers to Hull, 2 Aug. 1936, 852.00/2377, NA; Bowers, letter to Lawrence Levenberg, 15 June 1937; *Memphis Commercial Appeal*, 18 Aug. 1936; *Boston Globe*, 24 Aug. 1936; Adam B. Siegel, "The Tip of the Spear: The U.S. Navy and the Spanish Civil War" (MSS, 1992), 11–13, 20–27, copy, HP; Hull to Bowers, 9 Mar. 1937, 852.00/4947, NA; Bowers to Hull, 18 Feb., 1 July 1937, 852.00/4736, 5892, ibid.

4. Bowers to Hull, [5 Aug. 1939], 352.1115/447, 20 Dec. 1936, 123 Bowers/118, NA; Bowers, letter to Theodore Fred Kuper, 7 Oct. 1936, Claude G. Bowers Collection, Henry E. Huntington Library, San Marino, Calif. (hereafter cited as BC); "Spanish Diary," 14 Aug. 1936; William Phillips, "Journals," 5, 21 Aug. 1936, William Phillips Papers and Journals, Houghton Library, Harvard University, Cambridge, Mass.; *Chicago Tribune*, 16 Aug. 1936; Richard Norton Smith, *The Colonel: The Life and Legend of Robert R. McCormick, 1880–1955* (Boston: Houghton Mifflin, 1997), xx, 60; *Louisville Courier-Journal*, 19 Aug. 1936; R. Walton Moore, letter to Bowers, 7 Jan. 1937; Roosevelt to Bowers, 15 Jan. 1937, copy, HP.

5. Eric C. Wendelin, interview with Holman Hamilton, 18 Aug. 1965; Stephen Fuqua, letter to Bowers, 13 Aug. 1939, 852.00/2386, NA; Bowers to Hull, 8 June 1937, copy; Wendelin, letter to Bowers, 2 Sept. 1936; Bowers, letter to Wilbur Carr, 13 Nov. 1936, copy, HP; "Spanish Diary," 17 Sept., 19 Oct. 1936; Sybil [Bowers], letter to Jessie [Moore], [Nov. 1936].

6. See Raymond Carr, *The Spanish Tragedy: The Civil War in Perspective* (London: Weidenfeld and Nicholson, 1977); Paul Preston, *The Coming of the Spanish Civil War: Reform, Reaction and Revolution in the Second Republic, 1931–1939* (New York: Harper and Row, 1978); Hugh Thomas, *The Spanish Civil War* (New York: Harper and Brothers, 1961); Gabriel Jackson, *The Spanish Republic and the Civil War, 1931–1939* (Princeton, N.J.: Princeton University Press, 1965); Manuel Aznar, *Historia militar de la guerra civil en España*, 3 vols. (Madrid: Editora Nacional, 1958–63); Gabriel Jackson, *Historian's Quest* (New York: Alfred A. Knopf, 1969), 192–95.

7. "Spanish Diary," 27 Aug., 4, 28 Sept. 1936; Bowers to Hull, 11 Aug., copy, HP, 25 Aug., 852.00/3011, NA, 6 Oct. 1936, copy; *My Mission*, 283–85; Bowers to Hull, 7 Sept. 1936, copy, PSP:Spain, FDR.

8. For foreign relations see Dante A. Puzzo, *Spain and the Great Powers, 1936–1941* (New York: Columbia University Press, 1962); Robert H. Whealey, *Hitler and Spain: The Nazi Role in the Spanish Civil War, 1936–1939* (Lexington: University Press of Kentucky, 1989); John F. Coverdale, *Italian Intervention in the Spanish Civil War* (Princeton, N.J.: Princeton University Press, 1972); David T. Cattell, *Soviet Diplomacy and the Spanish Civil War* (Berkeley: University of California Press, 1957); E. H. Carr, *The Comintern and the Spanish Civil War* (New York: Pantheon Books, 1984); Bowers to Hull, 17 Aug. 852.00/2629, NA, 6 Oct. 1936, copy, HP; Lawrence T. Sondhaus, "The Non-Intervention Committee and the Spanish Civil War" (M.A. thesis, University of

Virginia, Charlottesville, 1982), 23–27; "Spanish Diary," 16, 22 Sept., 15 Oct. 1936; *My Mission*, 325; Bowers, letter to William E. Dodd, 1 Oct. 1936, copy, HP; Bowers, letter to Roosevelt, 29 Oct. 1936, PSF:Spain, FDR.

9. For the International Brigades see R. Dan Richardson, *Comintern Army: The International Brigades and the Spanish Civil War* (Lexington: University Press of Kentucky, 1982); Arthur H. Landis, *The Abraham Lincoln Brigade* (New York: Citadel Press, 1967); Peter N. Carroll, *The Odyssey of the Abraham Lincoln Brigade: Americans in the Spanish Civil War* (Stanford, Calif.: Stanford University Press, 1994); *My Mission*, 394.

10. "Spanish Diary," 18 Oct., 20 Nov. 1936, 21 Apr., 20 June 1937. For the Falange, see Stanley G. Payne, *Falange: A History of Spanish Fascism* (Stanford, Calif.: Stanford University Press, 1961). Stalin quoted in Burnett Bolloten, *The Spanish Civil War: Revolution and Counterrevolution* (Chapel Hill: University of North Carolina Press, 1991), 166.

11. "Spanish Diary," 22 Nov. 1936; Bowers to Hull, 1 Nov., 20 July 1937, 852.00/6903, 6132, NA; Roosevelt to Bowers, 16 Sept. 1936, PSF: Spain, FDR. For the Communists' role see Burnett Bolloten, *The Grand Camouflage: The Communist Conspiracy in the Spanish Civil War* (New York: Praeger, 1968) and *Spanish Civil War*; David T. Cattell, *Communism and the Spanish Civil War* (Berkeley: University of California Press, 1955). On Anarchists and POUM see George Orwell, *Homage to Catalonia* (New York: Harcourt, Brace, 1952). Bowers to Hull, 27 Apr., 11, 12, 18 May, 2 Dec. 1937, 852.00/5378, 5486, 5386, 5380, 5464, NA.

12. "Spanish Diary," 30 Sept., 2 Nov. 1938, 26 Jan., 2 Feb. 1939; Frank Sedwick, *The Tragedy of Manuel Azaña and the Fate of the Spanish Republic* (Columbus: Ohio State University Press, 1963), 174–76, 199–204; Bolloten, *Spanish Civil War*, 163–67, 572–81; Indalecio Prieto, letter to Juan Negrín, 23 June 1939, copy, HP; Bowers to Hull, 10 Apr. 1938, copy; Bowers, letters to Roosevelt, Hull, 9 May 1938, copies; Bowers to Kuper, 11 Jan. 1939, BC.

13. Bowers to Kuper, 14 Apr., 20 Aug. 1937, 5 May 1938, BC; Bowers to Hamilton, 1 Apr. 1937; "Spanish Diary," 6 Sept. 1938, 20 Feb. 1939; James A. Farley, letter to Bowers, 1 Feb. 1937; Joseph F. Guffey, letter to Bowers, 3 Oct. 1938; Daniel C. Roper, letter to Bowers, 19 Nov. 1936; Roosevelt to Bowers, 7 Mar. 1938; Bowers to Kuper, 20 Aug. 1937, BC.

14. "Spanish Diary," 28 Nov., 11 Dec. 1936, 30 Dec. 1937, 21 Aug. 1938; Bowers, letter to Frank Brubeck, 18 July 1938; Bowers to Hamilton, 1 Apr. 1937; Bowers to Levenberg, 15 July 1937; Sybil to Jessie, [Sept. 1938].

15. Bowers to Kuper, 12 Oct. 1937, BC; William B. Liebmann, interview with Peter J. Sehlinger, 23 Mar. 1982; Horton Schoellkopf, interview with Hamilton, 27 Apr. 1963; Bowers, draft of a letter to Arthur M. Schlesinger, Jr., 12 Apr. 1951, copy; Hallett Johnson, *Diplomatic Memoirs: Serious and Frivolous* (New York: Vantage Press, 1963), 106; Bowers to Roosevelt, 26 Aug. 1936, PSF:Spain, FDR; Bowers to Carr, 14 Nov. 1936, 123 Bowers/144, NA; Sybil to Jessie, [Nov. 1936]; Bowers, letter to Malin Craig, 31 Mar. 1937, copy, HP; "Spanish Diary," 19 Oct. 1938; Bowers to Hull, 25 Aug. 1937, 852.00/6392, NA; Jay Pierrepont Moffat, letter to Bowers, 4 Oct. 1937, copy, HP.

16. *My Mission*, 290, 285, 291; "Spanish Diary," 8 Sept., 12, 16, 25 Oct. 1936; Bowers to Brubeck, 18 July 1938; Holman Hamilton and Gayle Thornbrough, eds., *Indianapolis in the "Gay Nineties": High School Diaries of Claude G. Bowers* (Indianapolis: Indiana Historical Society, 1964), 220; William Stevenson, *A Man Called Intrepid: The Secret War* (New York: Harcourt Brace Jovanovich, 1976), 341–44.

17. Bowers to Hull, 15 Jan. 1937, 29 Aug. 1938, copies, HP; Angel Viñas, "Los condicionantes internacionales," in *La guerra civil española 50 años después*, ed. Manuel Tuñón de Lara et al. (Barcelona: Editorial Labor, 1985), 176–79, 191; Jackson, *Spanish Republic*

*and the Civil War*, 428–29, 494; Preston, *Coming of the Spanish Civil War*, 77, 68; "Spanish Diary," 31 Aug. 1939; *My Mission*, 305–8, 343–45; Bowers to Hull, 21 Nov. 1937, 852.00/7007, NA; Thomas, *Spanish Civil War*, 176–79; Stanley G. Payne, *The Spanish Revolution* (New York: W. W. Norton and Co., 1970), 225–26.

18. Bowers to Hull, 6 Oct. 1936, copy; ibid., 2 Feb. 1937, copy, HP; Bowers to Roosevelt, 16 Feb. 1937, 3 Oct. 1938, copies, HP; Paul Preston, *Franco: A Biography* (New York: Basic Books, 1994), 198, 300; Bowers to Roosevelt, 3 Oct. 1938, copy; Salvador de Madariaga, letter to Hamilton, 8 Mar. 1961; Bolloten, *Spanish Civil War*, 141; *The New Leader*, 5 July 1954.

19. Division of Western European Affairs, memo, 19 Jan. 1937, 852.4419½, NA; Bowers to Hull, 5 Feb. 1938, copy, HP, 11, 13 Dec. 1937, 701.5552/1, NA; Jay Pierrepont Moffat, "Diary," 30 Dec. 1937, 20, 31 Jan., 1 Feb. 1938, Jay Pierrepont Moffat Papers and Diaries, Houghton Libary; Juan F. de Cárdenas y Rodríguez de Rivas, letters to José Antonio Sangróniz y Castro, 2, 7 Jan. 1938, Estados Unidos, legajo R 1050, exp. 19, Archivo del Ministerio Asuntos Exteriores, Madrid, Spain (hereafter cited as AMAE); "Spanish Diary," 24, 29 Jan., 6, 8 Feb. 1938; New York Times, 22 Jan. 1938.

20. Bowers to Hull, 17 May 1938, copy; "Spanish Diary," 21 May, 16–21 June, 6, 4, 19 Aug., 2, 20 Sept., 8 Oct. 1938; Richard P. Traina, *American Diplomacy and the Spanish Civil War* (Bloomington: Indiana University Press, 1968), 176; Bowers to Roosevelt, 18 Aug. 1938, copy; Friends of the Lincoln Brigade, letter to Bowers, [8 Oct. 1938]; Norman Thomas, letter to Bowers, 9 Aug. 1938; Guido Viola di Campalto, letter to Bowers, 13 Dec. 1938.

21. "Spanish Diary," 21 Jan. 1937, 23 May, 4 July, 7, 9, 13, 14 Nov. 1938, 11 Feb. 1939; Bowers to Hull, 23 Feb. 1937, copy; Hull to Bowers, 12 Nov. 1937; Eleanor Roosevelt, letter to Bowers, 9 Feb. 1938; Bowers to Roosevelt, 17 Nov. 1938, copy, HP; Roosevelt to Bowers, 11 Nov. 1938; Moffat, "Diary," 3 Aug., 19 Oct. 1938; Roosevelt, letter to George MacDonald, 19 Dec. 1938, copy, HP; Traina, *American Diplomacy and the Spanish Civil War*, 188–202.

22. William Phillips, memorandum, 7 Aug. 1936, 852.00/2510a, NA; *New York Times*, 15 Aug. 1936; Cordell Hull, *The Memoirs of Cordell Hull*, 2 vols. (New York: Macmillan, 1948), 1:477; *Congressional Record*, 75th Cong., 1st sess., 1937, 81, pt. 1:84, 90; Bowers to Roosevelt, 11 Aug. 1936, 11 Aug. 1937, copies, HP; Roosevelt to Bowers, 16 Sept. 1936; Bowers to Hull, 21, 23 Sept. 1936, copy, HP, 20 July 1937, 852.00/6132, NA; Hull to Bowers, 2 Nov. 1936; "Spanish Diary," 24 June 1937.

23. Franklin D. Roosevelt, *The Public Papers and Addresses of Franklin D. Roosevelt*, 13 vols. (New York: Russell and Russell, 1969), 6:407–10; Basil Rauch, *Roosevelt from Munich to Pearl Harbor: A Study in the Creation of a Forign Policy* (New York: Creative Age Press, 1950), 47–48; Sumner Welles, *The Time for Decision* (New York: Harper and Brothers, 1944), 61; "Spanish Diary," 6 Oct. 1937, 28 Mar. 1938; Bowers to Roosevelt, 20, 26 Feb. 1938, copy; Roosevelt, *Public Papers and Addresses of Franklin D. Roosevelt*, 7:286.

24. Arthur Krock, interview with Hamilton, 16 Nov. 1965; *New York Times*, 20 Mar. 1938; Moffat, "Diary," 31 Mar. 1938; Jay [Allen], cable to Bowers, 23 Apr. 1938; Traina, *American Diplomacy and the Spanish Civil War*, 214–25; F. Jay Taylor, *The United States and the Spanish Civil War* (New York: Bookman Associates, 1956), 172–74; Robert Dallek, *Franklin D. Roosevelt and American Foreign Policy, 1932–1945* (New York: Oxford University Press, 1979), 158–61.

25. Bowers to Hull, 10 June 1938, 852.00/8133, NA, 7 Dec. 1938, 7 Jan. 1939, copies, HP; Bowers to Roosevelt, 18 Aug. 1938, OF:303, FDR, 5 Dec. 1938, copy, HP; Bowers, letter to Alvarez del Vayo, 7 Oct. 1938, copy, HP; Moffat, "Diary," 19 Nov. 1938; Hull to

Roosevelt, 22 Dec. 1938, 852.00/8746, NA; Roosevelt, *Public Papers and Addresses of Franklin D. Roosevelt*, 8:3–4; Bowers to Kuper, 11 Jan. 1939, BC.

26. Moffat, "Diary," 19–25 Jan. 1939; [Hull] to the President [Roosevelt], 23 Feb. 1939, 123 Bowers/155, NA; Hull, *Memoirs of Cordell Hull*, 1:616; "Spanish Diary," 10, 11 Mar. 1939; Harold L. Ickes, *Secret Diary of Harold L. Ickes*, 3 vols. (New York: Simon and Schuster, 1953–54), 2:562–70.

27. [Bowers], letter to Sybil and Pat, 9 Mar. 1939; "Spanish Diary," 14, 30 Mar. 1939; Moffat, "Diary," 1 Apr. 1939; My Mission, 419–20, 417; Traina, *American Diplomacy and the Spanish Civil War*, 230–35; Bowers to Hamilton, 8 July 1937; Bowers to Schlesinger, 14 Apr. 1951, copy, HP; Bowers, letter to James MacGregor Burns, 14 June 1955, copy, ibid.; Bowers, *My Life*, 283; Harold L. Ickes, letter to Bowers, 11 Jan. 1939; Ickes, *Secret Diary of Harold L. Ickes*, 3:217; Eleanor Roosevelt, *This I Remember* (New York: Harper, 1949), 162, 275; Claude D. Pepper, letter to Bowers, 2 Jan. 1948; Guffey to Hull, 4 Apr. 1939, copy, HP; Guffey to Bowers, 5 Apr. 1939; Felix Frankfurter, letter to Guffey, 22 Mar. 1939, Claude G. Bowers Manuscripts, Lilly Library, Indiana University, Bloomington; Dodd to Bowers, 29 Mar. 1939; Daniels to Bowers, 7 Aug. 1939; Welles, *Time for Decision*, 61.

28. Hull, "Draft Memoirs," 31 July, 19 Aug. 1946, microfilm reel 40, Cordell Hull Papers, Library of Congress, Washington, D.C.; Hull, *Memoirs of Cordell Hull*, 1:483–85, 617. See the three drafts of Bowers's "My Mission to Spain," BC. *My Mission*, 417, 420; Bowers to Hamilton, 11 July 1948; Bowers to Schlesinger, 12 Apr. 1951, copy; "Spanish Diary," 30 Mar., 15 May 1939; Bowers, letter to John Dos Passos, 1 May 1959, John Dos Passos Papers, Manuscripts Department, University of Virginia, Charlottesville; Hull to Count Jordana, 1 Apr. 1939, Estados Unidos, legajo R1050, exp. 19, AMAE; Bowers, *My Life: The Memoirs of Claude Bowers* (New York: Simon and Schuster, 1962), 293; Sumner Welles, letter to Bowers, 29 Jan. 1948; Stanley G. Payne, *Franco's Spain* (New York: Thomas Y. Crowell Co., 1967), 100–111.

29. Bowers, "Reminiscences of Claude Bowers," interview by Louis Starr, 24, 30 Aug. 1954 (Oral History Research Office, Columbia University, New York), 126–27; "Spanish Diary," 30 Mar., 5 Apr., 22 May 1939; *Indianapolis News*, 2 Sept. 1968; Bowers to Hull, 15 Apr. 1939, 123 Bowers/172, NA.

30. Bowers, "Reminiscences," 127; Bowers to Kuper, 28 May 1939, BC; "Spanish Diary," 22 May 1939; Bowers, *My Life*, 297; José "Pepe" Torres Rueda, interview with Hamilton, 12 Nov. 1966; Bowers, "Diary on Leaving Spain," 13 June 1939; *My Mission*, 422.

31. Bowers, *The Spanish Adventures of Washington Irving* (Boston: Houghton Mifflin, 1940); Bowers to Dodd, 2 Oct., 7 May 1935, 1 Oct. 1936, copies, HP; Bowers, *Jefferson in Power: The Death Struggle of the Federalists* (Boston: Houghton Mifflin, 1936), 168, vi, v, 452, 258, 502–3, vii, 10, 5; R. M. La Follette, Jr., letter to Bowers, 12 May 1936; Dodd to Bowers, 17 Oct. 1936; Daniels to Bowers, 28 Sept. 1936, copy, HP; Bowers, letters to Ferris Greenslet, 22, 26 May, 22, 29 June 1936, Houghton Mifflin Company Papers, Houghton Library (hereafter cited as HMP); Bowers, letter to Robert N. Linscott, 26 June 1936, ibid.; Bowers to Kuper, 15 Nov. 1937, BC.

32. Gilbert Chinard review, *American Historical Review* 38 (Jan. 1937): 413–15; Louis Martin Sears review, *Mississippi Valley Historical Review* 23 (Dec. 1936): 408–9; Henry H. Simms review, *Journal of Southern History* 3 (Feb. 1937): 106; Henry Steele Commager review, *New York Herald Tribune Books*, 6 Sept. 1936; Dumas Malone, "The Perennial Jefferson," *The Yale Review* 26 (Dec. 1936): 383–85; Matthew Josephson, "Whose Jefferson," *The Nation* 143 (19 Sept. 1936): 338–39; Daniels to Bowers, 28 Sept. 1936; Daniel C. Roper, letter to Bowers, 31 Mar. 1937; Roosevelt to Bowers, 16 Sept. 1936,

PSF:Spain, FDR; Greenslet to Bowers, 21 Aug., 2 Sept. 1936; Bowers to Kuper, 14 Apr. 1937, BC; Bowers to Hamilton, 1 Apr. 1937.

33. Greenslet to Bowers, 23 Feb. 1937; Bowers, *Spanish Adventures of Washington Irving*, xv-xvii, 16–17, 12, 276–78, 225.

34. Houghton Mifflin, memo to Hamilton, 3 Jan. 1961; Elliot Paul, "When Washington Irving Roamed in Spain," *New York Herald Tribune Books*, 10 Mar. 1940; *Indianapolis Star*, 31 Mar. 1940; Robert E. Spiller, "Dilettante Bachelor in a Spanish Town," *Saturday Review of Literature*, 23 Mar. 1940, p. 6; T. R. Ybarra, "A Return to the Spanish Past," *New York Times Book Review*, 17 Mar. 1940; S. C. C., "Washington Irving in Spain," *Christian Science Monitor*, 13 Apr. 1940; *Boston Evening Transcript*, 25 Mar. 1940; *The New Yorker*, 6 Apr. 1940, p. 75; *Time*, 11 Mar. 1940, pp. 85–87.

35. Bowers, *Las aventuras españolas de Washington Irving* (Santiago: Zig-Zag, 1946); *La Nación* (Santiago), 21 Apr. 1946; *Arriba* (Madrid), 11 Mar. 1947; Bowers to Kuper, 27 July 1947, BC.

36. Bowers to Kuper, 15 Nov. 1937, 28 May 1936, 11 Nov. 1940, 27 Nov. 1945, 8 Apr., 23 May 1946, BC; Bowers to Greenslet, 5 Mar. 1938, HMP; Bowers, "My Mission to Spain," 1939 MSS, 13–19, 238, 408, 380, 347; Truman quoted in Bowers to Kuper, 26 Jan. [1946], BC; *My Mission*, v, 411–22; Bowers, *Mi misión en España* (Mexico City: Editorial Grijalbo, 1955); *Ma mission en Espagne, 1933–1939* (Paris: Flammarion, 1957); *Missione in Spagna, 1933–1939: Prova generale della seconda guerra mondiale* (Milan: Feltrinelli Editore, 1958).

37. Gordon A. Craig, "Our Former Ambassador Sets the Spanish Story in Perspective," *New York Herald Tribune Book Reviews*, 13 June 1954, p. 3; *Manchester Guardian*, 16 Nov. 1956; *New York Times*, 13 June 1954; *New York Post*, 13 June 1954; *Le Figaro Littéraire* (Paris), 8 Sept. 1956; *Le Canard Enchaîné* (Paris), 19 Sept. 1956; Alvarez del Vayo to Bowers, 18 June 1954; Prieto to Bowers, 12 June 1957; Diego Martínez Barrio, letter to Bowers, 20 Dec. 1954.

38. Thomas J. Hamilton, "He Was Right All Along," *The Nation* 179 (24 July 1954): 74; Anthony West, "Years of Shame," *The New Yorker*, 14 Aug. 1954, pp. 80–81; Victor Alba and Stephen Schwartz, *Spanish Marxism versus Soviet Communism: A History of the P.O.U.M.* (New Brunswick, N.J.: Rutgers University Press, 1988), 198; *El Mercurio* (Santiago), 22 Nov. 1956; *Indianapolis News*, 5 June 1954; M. A. Fitzsimmons, "Partisan Memory," *Commonweal* 60 (23 July 1954): 397; Bowers, letter to Fernando de los Ríos, 27 Nov. 1945, BC; *My Mission*, 357.

39. Bowers, "Diary on Leaving Spain," 14 July 1939; Bowers, *My Life*, 294–96.

## 9. Chile

1. Only George P. Marsh and Edwin V. Morgan, ministers to Italy (1860–82) and Brazil (1912–33), served longer.

2. Claude G. Bowers, *Chile through Embassy Windows, 1939–1953* (New York: Simon and Schuster, 1958), 365, 3, 5–7 (hereafter cited as *Chile*); Bowers, "Chilean Diary," 29 Aug. 1939 (hereafter cited as "Chilean Diary").

3. Descriptions of the residence are from Carlos Griffin Garat, interview with Holman Hamilton, 15 Nov. 1966, and Lawrence Kerr, interview with Peter J. Sehlinger, 8 Apr. 1991; *Chile*, 7; "Chilean Diary," 30 Aug. 1939; Sybil Bowers, letter to Jessie Moore, 24 Oct. 1939.

4. *Terre Haute Star*, 1 Sept. 1906; *New York Evening World*, 26 Feb. 1924, 29 Nov. 1926, 24 Oct. 1930; Bowers, "Address at Chilean-American Luncheon," 31 Oct. 1939,

Holman Hamilton Papers, Division of Special Collections and Archives of the Margaret I. King Library, University of Kentucky, Lexington (hereafter cited as HP).

5. *Chile*, 33; Robert J. Alexander, *The Tragedy of Chile* (Westport, Conn.: Greenwood Press, 1978), 12–13; *New York Evening World*, 12 Sept. 1924; Bowers, "My Spanish Diary," 1 Dec. 1938. For overviews of Chilean politics in the 1920s and 1930s, see Mariana Aylwin Oyarzún et al., *Chile en el siglo XX* (Santiago: Editorial Emisión, [1985]), 114–25, 149–75; Luis Galdames, *A History of Chile*, trans. Isaac Joslin Cox (New York: Russell and Russell, 1964), 371–97; Fredrick B. Pike, *Chile and the United States, 1880–1962: The Emergence of Chile's Social Crisis and the Challenge to United States Diplomacy* (Notre Dame, Ind.: University of Notre Dame Press, 1963), 170–213; Brian Loveman, *Chile: The Legacy of Hispanic Capitalism* (New York: Oxford University Press, 1979), 241–55; John Reese Stevenson, *The Chilean Popular Front* (Philadelphia: University of Pennsylvania Press, 1942), 59–77; Simon Collier and William F. Sater, *A History of Chile, 1808–1994* (Cambridge: University of Cambridge Press, 1996), 233; Joaquín Fermandois, *Abismo y cimiento: Gustavo Ross y las relaciones entre Chile y Estados Unidos, 1932–1938* (Santiago: Ediciones Universidad Católica de Chile, 1996), 30–58.

6. "Chilean Diary," 1, 7, 8 Sept. 1939, 4 May 1940, 28 Aug. 1943; Bowers, letter to Cordell Hull, 7 Sept. 1939, 123 Bowers/219, U.S. Department of State, RG 59, National Archives, Washington, D.C. (hereafter cited as NA); *Chile*, 88; Bowers, letter to Theodore Fred Kuper, 28 Aug. 1941, Claude G. Bowers Collection, Henry E. Huntington Library, San Marino, Calif. (hereafter cited as BC); Eleanor Shields, interview with Hamilton, 29 Aug. 1963; Bowers, letter to Breckinridge Long, 28 Nov. 1940, copy, HP; Eric C. Wendelin, interview with Hamilton, 18 Aug. 1965; Griffin interview; Ellis O. Briggs, *Proud Servant: The Memoirs of a Career Ambassador* (Kent, Ohio: Kent State University Press, 1998), 146–47, 152–53; Hull to Bowers, 13 Jan. 1941, 11 Jan. 1944; Sumner Welles, letter to Bowers, 6 Dec. 1941, 825.00/1488, NA; Franklin D. Roosevelt, letter to Bowers, 25 Apr. 1944; Bowers, draft of a letter to Arthur M. Schlesinger, Jr., 12 Apr. 1951, copy; Welles, letter to Laurence Duggan, 2 Dec. 1941, 825.00/1599, NA; Welles, letters to [Roosevelt], 27 Nov. 1939, 6 Sept. 1940, OF:303, Franklin D. Roosevelt: Papers as President, Franklin D. Roosevelt Library, Hyde Park, New York (hereafter cited as FDR); LD [Laurence Duggan], letter to Josephus Daniels, 21 Nov. 1941, attached to Bowers to Roosevelt, 13 Nov. 1941, 825.00/1494, NA.

7. Bowers, "Reminiscences of Claude Bowers," interview by Louis Starr, 24, 30 Aug. 1954 (Oral History Research Office, Columbia University, New York), 146; Clarence C. Brooks, interview with Hamilton, 7 Apr. 1965; Lucy Richmond Lentz, interview with Hamilton, 11 Nov. 1967; Bowers to Kuper, 28 Aug. 1941, BC; Shields interview; Cecil Lyon, *The Lyon's Share* (New York: Vantage Press, 1973), 151–52; Sheldon T. Mills, interview with Hamilton, 18 Aug. 1965; "Chilean Diary," 20 July 1943; Cecil Lyon, letter to Bowers, 15 Aug. [1943]; Donald Heath, letter to Philip W. Bonsal, 24 Oct. 1942, 711.25/10-2422, to Duggan, 7 Jan. 1943, 711.25/254, NA; see Jack Thomas, "United States Ambassador to Chile Claude Bowers and the State Department during World War II," n.d., copy, HP; Donald Heath, interview with Hamilton, 5 Oct. 1965; Heath to Bowers, 8 Aug. 1944; Hugh Millard, letter to Bowers, 11 July 1947.

8. "Chilean Diary," 19 June 1944, 3 Feb., 4, 7 May, 7 Sept. 1940, 9 Dec. 1939; Bowers, letter to Dean Acheson, 10 Sept. 1945, 123/Bowers, NA; Welles to Bowers, 7 July 1939; Biddle [Garrison], letter to Bowers, 3 July 1950; Lester Ziffren, interview with Hamilton, 16 May 1964; Griffin interview; Bowers to Breck [Long], 15 Feb. 1940, copy, HP; Mills interview; F. Nieto del Río, letter to Ministerio de Relaciones Exteriores, 6 June 1949, Archivo del Ministerio de Relaciones Exteriores, Santiago, Chile (hereafter cited as AMRE).

9. Anthony F. O'Brien, "The Politics of Dependency: A Case Study of Dependency—Chile 1938–45" (Ph.D. diss., University of Notre Dame, 1977), 196; Michael J. Francis, *The Limits of Hegemony: United States Relations with Argentina and Chile during World War II* (Notre Dame, Ind.: University of Notre Dame Press, 1977), 184; Hugo Medina, letter to Ministerio de Relaciones Exteriores, 22 Sept. 1939, v. 1788, AMRE; P. T. Ellsworth, *Chile: An Economy in Transition* (New York: Macmillan, 1945), 122; Jon V. Kofas, "Developmentalism and Hemispheric Integration during World War II: U.S. Foreign Economic Policy and Chile's Development Corporation," *International Third World Studies Journal and Review* 6 (1994): 23–26; see Kalman Silvert, "The Chilean Development Corporation" (Ph.D. diss., University of Pennsylvania, 1948); Bowers to Roosevelt, 2 Nov. 1939, OF:303, FDR, 9 Oct. 1940, 825.00/1262½, NA; Frank Freidel, *Franklin D. Roosevelt: A Rendezvous with Destiny* (Boston: Little, Brown, 1990), 316; Roosevelt to Bowers, 7 May 1940, 12 May 1941; ibid., 21 Oct. 1940, copy, 825.00/1261, NA; Stevenson, *Chilean Popular Front*, 132, 124; Marcial Mora, letter to Manuel Bianchi, 12 Oct. 1940, v. 1832, AMRE; *South Pacific Mail* (Santiago), 4 July 1940; Joaquín Fermandois H., "Cobre, guerra e industrialización en Chile, 1939–1945," in "Colección Estudios Históricos" of the Comisión Chilena del Cobre (Santiago, 1992), 33–49.

10. Bowers to Hamilton, 17 Oct. 1940; John T. Whitaker, *Americas to the South* (New York: Macmillan, 1939), 114–15; Edwin Lieuwen, *U.S. Policy in Latin America: A Short History* (New York: Frederick A. Praeger, 1965), 78; see Michael Potashnik, "Nacismo: National Socialism in Chile, 1932–1938" (Ph.D. diss., UCLA, 1974); Joaquín Fermandois H., "Guerra y hegemonía 1939–1943: Un aspecto de las relaciones chileno-norteamericanas," Estudios Históricos No. 10, Instituto de Historia, Universidad Católica de Chile (Santiago, 1989), fn. 20, 12; Irwin F. Gellman, *Good Neighbor Diplomacy: United States Policies in Latin America, 1933–1945* (Baltimore, Md.: Johns Hopkins University Press, 1979), 112; Cordell Hull, *The Memoirs of Cordell Hull*, 2 vols. (New York: Macmillan, 1948), 2:1146, 1148; Roosevelt to Bowers, [June 1940], 825.00/1366½, NA; Fredrick B. Pike, *FDR's Good Neighbor Policy: Sixty Years of Generally Gentle Chaos* (Austin: University of Texas Press, 1995), 229; Robert Dallek, *Franklin D. Roosevelt and American Foreign Policy, 1932–1945* (New York: Oxford University Press, 1979), 233, 236.

11. Roosevelt to Bowers, 7 May 1940, copy, HP; *Chile*, 61–62; Bowers, "Reminiscences," 131; "Chilean Diary," 19 Aug., 8 July 1940; Welles to Bowers, 18 June, 15 July 1940, copies, HP; Bowers to Roosevelt, 23 Apr. 1941, PSF:Chile, FDR; Acting Secretary of State, letter to Bowers, 28 Mar. 1941, *Foreign Relations of the United States, 1941* (Washington, D.C.: Government Printing Office), 6:571 (hereafter cited as *FRUS*); Francis, *Limits of Hegemony*, 39.

12. Bowers to Roosevelt, 31 July 1941, PSF:Chile, FDR; *Chile*, 62–64, 70, 158; Bowers to Welles, 25 May, 7 July 1941, copies, HP; "Chilean Diary," 18 Aug. 1941; Paul W. Drake, "The Chilean Socialist Party and Coalition Politics, 1932–1946," *Hispanic American Historical Review* 53 (Nov. 1973): 630–35; Ernst Halperin, *Nationalism and Communism in Chile* (Cambridge, Mass.: MIT Press, 1965), 42–53; Stevenson, *Chilean Popular Front*, 107–12; Volodia Teitelboim, interview with Sehlinger, 4 Apr. 1991.

13. *Time*, 17 Nov. 1941, p. 28; Press Conference #786, FDR; William F. Sater, *Chile and the United States: Empires in Conflict* (Athens: University of Georgia Press, 1990), 116–17; Bowers to Hull, 18 Dec. 1941, 740.00 11/755, NA; Bowers to Welles, 7 July 1941, copy, HP.

14. Freidel, *Franklin D. Roosevelt*, 219; Hull, *Memoirs of Cordell Hull*, 2:1150, 1149; Benjamin Welles, *Sumner Welles: FDR's Global Strategist* (New York: St. Martin's Press, 1997), 320; *Chile*, 324–25; "Chilean Diary," 28 Sept. 1945, 24, 26 Feb., 27 Mar., 19 Apr.,

5, 18 May 1942; Heath to Hull, 27 Aug. 1943, 825.00/1973, NA; Rodolfo Michels to Ernesto Barros Jarpa, 19 July 1942, AMRE.

15. Bowers to Welles, 15 Apr. 1942, copy, HP; *Chile*, 99–100; see Laurence Duggan, *The Americas: The Search for Hemispheric Security* (New York: Holt, 1949); *La Opinión* (Santiago), 4 June; *El Siglo* (Santiago), 27 July 1942; "Chilean Diary," 15 May 1942; Bowers to Roosevelt, 29 Apr. 1942, 825.00/1680, NA, 18 July 1942, OF:303, FDR; Roosevelt to Bowers, 15 May 1942, 825.00/1678, NA, 11 Aug. 1942, OF:303, FDR.

16. "Chilean Diary," 6, 10 June, 16 Dec. 1942, 20 Nov. 1943, 28 Sept. 1945; Welles and Hull, letter to Bowers, 20 June 1942, 825.00/1687, NA; Duggan, memo, 1 Apr. 1943, 825.00/1860, NA; Oscar Bermúdez Miral, *El drama político de Chile* (Santiago: Editorial Tegualda, 1947), 144–45; Tobías Barros Ortiz, *Recogiendo los pasos: Testigo militar y político del siglo XX* (Santiago: Editorial Planeta Chilena, 1988), 418, 423; Fermandois, "Guerra," 19.

17. Bowers to Welles, 16 May 1942, 825.00/1686, 23 May 1942, 825.00/1681, NA, 7 July 1942, OF:303, FDR; *Topaze*, 7 Aug. 1942; U.S. Federal Bureau of Investigation, *Chile Today: March 1943* (Washington: Government Printing Office, 1943), 154, 143; "Chilean Diary," 18 May, 20 June 1942; Stanley E. Hilton, *Hitler's Secret War in South America, 1939–1945: German Military Espionage and Allied Counterespionage in Brazil* (Baton Rouge: Louisiana State University Press, 1981), 290–91; Barros Jarpa to Bowers, 25 May 1942, copy, HP; Ernesto Barros Jarpa, "Historia para olvidar: Ruptura con el Eje (1942–1943)," in *Homenaje a Guillermo Feliú Cruz*, ed. Neville Blanc Renard (Santiago: Editorial Andrés Bello, 1973), 55; U.S. Federal Communications Commission, "German Espionage Agents in Chile," v. 1970, AMRE.

18. Welles to Hull, 25 Jan. 1942, *FRUS*, 1942, p. 5:40; "Chilean Diary," 20, 10 June, 8, 14, 28 July 1942; Bowers, memo, 11 June 1942, 825.51/1453, NA; Bowers to Hull, 22 July 1942, 711.25/104, ibid.; Barros Jarpa, "Historia para olvidar," 63, 66; *Chile*, 109; Bowers to Roosevelt, 8 July, 1942, OF:303, FDR.

19. C. H. [Cordell Hull], memo, 14 Sept. 1942, copy, HP; Welles, memo, 1 Sept. 1942, *FRUS*, 1942, p. 5:33; Barros Jarpa to Michels, 16 Sept. 1942, v. 2019, AMRE; Barros Jarpa, "Historia para olvidar," 65–71; "Chilean Diary," 6, 3 Oct., 26 Sept. 1942.

20. "Chilean Diary," 25, 27, 30 June 1942; Michels to Barros Jarpa, 13, 20 June 1942, v. 2019, AMRE; Sumner Welles, speech, "Twenty-Ninth National Foreign Trade Convention," *Department of State Bulletin*, 10 Oct. 1942, p. 810; J. Edgar Hoover, letter to Adolf A. Berle, Jr., 1 Jan. 1943, 711.25/320, NA; Bowers, "Reminiscences," 128–29; Fermandois, "Guerra," 29; *La Nación* (Santiago), 11, 10, 12 Oct. 1942; *Chile*, 111; Ríos to Roosevelt, 11 Oct. 1942, copy, HP.

21. "Chilean Diary," 8, 11 Oct. 1942; *Chile*, 112; Irwin F. Gellman, *Secret Affairs: Franklin Roosevelt, Cordell Hull, and Sumner Welles* (Baltimore, Md.: Johns Hopkins University Press, 1995), 307; Fred L. Israel, ed., *The War Diary of Breckinridge Long* (Lincoln: University of Nebraska Press, 1966), 286; Jaime Eyzaguirre, interview with Hamilton, 14 Nov. 1966; Bermúdez, *El drama político de Chile*, 146; *Topaze*, 6 Nov. 1942; J. Lloyd Mecham, *The United States and Inter-American Security, 1899–1960* (Austin: University of Texas Press, 1961), 230; Samuel Flagg Bemis, *The Latin American Policy of the United States: An Historical Interpretation* (New York: Harcourt, Brace, 1943), 380; Ernesto Barros Jarpa, interview with Sehlinger, 28 Aug. 1970; see Senator Gregorio Amunátegui Jordán's remarks, Senate Session, 22 Dec. 1942, v. 2091, AMRE.

22. *Chile*, 114; Joaquín Fernández Fernández to Michels, 12 Nov. 1942, v. 2020, AMRE; Edgar [Hoover], letter to Harry L. Hopkins, 2 Nov. 1942, box 141, Harry L. Hopkins Papers, Franklin D. Roosevelt Presidential Library; "Chilean Diary," 9 Nov., 11 Dec. 1942; *Memoria del Ministerio de Relaciones Exteriores y Comercio correspondiente al año*

*1942* (Santiago), 116; Fernández to Senate, 2 Dec. 1942, v. 2091, AMRE; R. Morales to Ríos, 7 Jan. 1943, v. 2091, ibid.; Ríos to Roosevelt, 20 Jan. 1943, *FRUS*, 1943, pp. 5:803–4; *El Mercurio* (Santiago), 21 Jan. 1943.

23. Roosevelt to Bowers, 10 Feb. 1943, OF:303, FDR; Bowers to Hamilton, 8 July 1947; *Chile*, 119–20; Welles to Roosevelt, 6 Feb. 1943, OF:303, FDR; Michels to Fernández, 20 Jan. 1943, v. 2136, AMRE; Francis, *Limits of Hegemony*, 23, 115; O'Brien, "Politics of Dependency," 260; Barros Jarpa interview; Barros Ortiz, *Recogiendo los pasos*, 420; Philip W. Bonsal, interview with Hamilton, 27 July 1967.

24. Fernández to Michels, 4 Mar. 1943, AMRE; Graham H. Stuart and James L. Tigner, *Latin America and the United States*, 6th ed. (Englewood Cliffs, N.J.: Prentice-Hall, 1975), 638; Francis, *Limits of Hegemony*, 133, 135; O'Brien, "Politics of Dependency," 316; *Chile*, 125; Bowers to Welles, 2 Feb., 29 Apr. 1943, 825.00/1840, 1863, NA; Hilton, *Hitler's Secret War in South America*, 290–91.

25. Joaquín Fernández Fernández, interview with Hamilton, 16 Nov. 1966; Harry S. Truman quoted in "Oficios recibidos de la embajada de Chile en EE.UU.," 8 Nov. 1945, no. 1416/447, AMRE; *Chile*, 326, 128–30; *Memoria del Ministerio . . . 1945*, p. 1:424; Bowers to Hamilton, 18 Feb. 1942; Bonsal to Lyon, 9 Mar. 1944, 711.25/289, NA; "Chilean Diary," 29 May, 10 Dec. 1944; Ríos to Roosevelt, 14 Feb. 1945, *FRUS*, 1945, pp. 9:768–70; Francis, *Limits of Hegemony*, 144.

26. *Chile*, 158–59; Paul W. Drake, *Socialism and Populism in Chile, 1932–52* (Urbana: University of Illinois Press, 1978), 278, 281; "Chilean Diary," 4, 11, 17 Feb., 24 July, 5, 31 Aug. 1946.

27. "Chilean Diary," 10, 24, 31 Aug., 11 Sept. 1946; Bowers, "Reminiscences," 136; Roger S. Abbott, "The Role of Contemporary Political Parties in Chile," *American Political Science Review* 45 (June 1951): 456; Drake, *Socialism and Populism in Chile*, 282–83; Teitelboim interview.

28. S. Cole Blasier, "Chile: A Communist Battleground," *Political Science Quarterly* 65 (Sept. 1950): 353; Walter La Feber, *America, Russia, and the Cold War, 1945–1975*, 3d ed. (New York: Wiley, 1976), 43; "Chilean Diary," 4, 5 June, 15, 21 Sept., 28 Nov. 1946; Bowers to Martha [Dodd], 5 Nov. 1947, copy, HP.

29. "Chilean Diary," 11, 24 Sept., 2 Nov. 1946; Gabriel González Videla, interview with Hamilton, 20 Oct. 1966; Enrique Bernstein Carabantes, *Recuerdos de un diplomático: Haciendo camino 1933–1957* (Santiago: Editorial Andrés Bello, 1984), 97–98.

30. "Chilean Diary," 6 Sept. 1946; Drake, *Socialism and Populism in Chile*, 283, 289; James Petras, *Politics and Social Forces in Chilean Development* (Berkeley: University of California Press, 1969), 130–31.

31. Alexander Schnee, memo, 27 Sept. 1946, 825.51/9-2746, NA; Bowers, letter to James F. Byrnes, 6 Sept. 1946, 825.34/9-646:Tel., NA; Embassy, Washington, to Minister of Foreign Relations, 26 Nov. 1946, 3040/682, AMRE; Welles, memo, 12 Nov. 1946, 825.5045/11-1246, NA; "Chilean Diary," 28 Nov., 2 Dec. 1946.

32. Bowers to Byrnes, 12 Nov. 1946, 825.5045/11-1246:Tel., NA; Acheson to Bowers, 9 Nov. 1946, 825.5045/11-946:Tel., ibid.; Andreas Barnard, "Chilean Communists, Radical Presidents and Chilean Relations with the United States, 1940–1947," *Journal of Latin American Studies* 13 (1981): 360–61; "Chilean Diary," 28 Nov., 4, 31 Dec. 1946.

33. La Feber, *America, Russia, and the Cold War*, 39; John Lewis Gaddis, *Strategies of Containment: A Critical Appraisal of Postwar American National Security Policy* (New York: Oxford University Press, 1982), 18–22; Communist Party of Chile, *Ricardo Fonseca: Combatiente ejemplar* (Santiago, [1952]), 130–40; Halperin, *Nationalism and Communism in Chile*, 54; El Mercurio, 3 Dec. 1946; "Chilean Diary," 5 Dec. 1946.

34. "Chilean Diary," 27 Mar., 13 Aug. 1947; Drake, *Socialism and Populism in Chile*, 287; Federico G. Gil, *The Political System of Chile* (Boston: Houghton Mifflin, 1966), 72–73.

35. W. E. Dunn, letter to Bowers, 12 Feb. 1947, 825.50/2-1247, NA; Acheson to Bowers, 20 Feb. 1947, 825.51/2-2047, NA; "Chilean Diary," 2 June, 11 Aug. 1947; Harry Truman, letter to Bowers, 5 Aug. 1947; Brundage to Espy and Miller, 15 June 1947, 711.25/8-2847, NA; Brundage to Welles, 9 June 1947, 711.25/6-947, ibid.

36. Gabriel González Videla, *Memorias*, 2 vols. (Santiago: Editora Gabriela Mistral, 1975), 1:707–9; "Chilean Diary," 17 Apr., 8, 19 Aug., 7 Sept., 6 Oct. 1947; *El Mercurio*, 20 Aug. 1947; *El Siglo*, 5 Sept., 12 Oct. 1947; Alexander, *Tragedy of Chile*, 33–34; Halperin, *Nationalism and Communism in Chile*, 55; Germán Vergara Donoso, interview with Hamilton, 9 Nov. 1966; Bernstein Carabantes, *Recuerdos de un diplomático*, 119–25.

37. "Chilean Diary," 19 Aug. 1947, 21 Apr. 1948; Bowers to Martha [Dodd], 16 Dec. 1947, copy, HP; Bowers to Ziffren, 13 July 1953, Lester Ziffren letters, Holman Hamilton Papers (hereafter cited as LZ); Bowers to Marshall, 14 Sept. 1948, 825.00/9-1448, NA; Teitelboim interview; Collier and Sater, *History of Chile*, 248.

38. Jon V. Kofas, "The Politics of Foreign Debt: The IMF, the World Bank, and U.S. Foreign Policy in Chile, 1946–1952," *Journal of Developing Areas* 31 (winter 1997): 166–68; Andrew Barnard, "Chile," in *Latin America between the Second World War and the Cold War, 1944–1948*, ed. Leslie Bethell and Ian Roxborough (Cambridge: Cambridge University Press, 1992), 67–91, 368–73; Loveman, *Chile*, 290; Espy memo, 29 Jan. 1949, 825.51/1-2948, NA; Jon V. Kofas, "Latin American Foreign Debt and Dependent Capitalism during the Cold War," *Proceedings of the Indiana Academy of the Social Sciences*, 3d series, 50 (1996): 46–57; Sater, *Chile and the United States*, 123; Time, 17 Oct. 1949, p. 40; State Department, "Policy Statement: Chile," 27 Feb. 1951, p. 6, 611.25/2-2751, NA; "Chilean Diary," 28 Feb. 1948; Truman to Bowers, 25 July 1950, copy, HP; Adolf A. Berle, *Latin America—Diplomacy and Reality* (New York: Published for the Council on Foreign Relations by Harper and Row, 1962), 32–33; Gilbert J. Butland, *Chile: An Outline of Its Geography, Economics, and Politics* (London: Royal Institute of International Affairs, 1951), 81.

39. "Chilean Diary," 30 Oct., 31 Dec. 1939, 11 Dec. 1940, 11 Apr. 1951, 4 Nov. 1952; Francis Harrison, letter to Bowers, 4 Mar. 1940; Bowers to Marshall, 10 Aug. 1948, 825.5017/8 1048, NA; Bowers to Hull, 27 July 1943, 825.50/129, ibid.; Daniel E. Ellis, letter to Bowers, 29 Dec. 1947; Michels to Fernández, 22 Mar. 1943, v. 2136, AMRE; Theodore I. Gandy, interview with Hamilton, 10, 11 Aug. 1964; IIAA, "The Program of the Institute of Inter-American Affairs" (Washington, D.C., n.d.), 4, 14–16, copy, HP; State Department, "Policy Statement," 9; *South Pacific Mail*, 7 Aug. 1947.

40. Point IV, 16 Jan. 1951, FRUS, 1951, p. 1238; Bowers, letter to Edward Miller, 6 Apr. 1951, 725.00/4-651, NA; H. G. Smith to State Dept., 6 July 1951, 825.00/7-651, ibid.; Carlos C. Hall to State Dept., 22 July 1953, 725.00 (W)/7-2253, ibid.; Gandy to Bowers, 23 Jan. 1956; *El Imparcial* (Santiago), 4 July 1951; *South Pacific Mail*, 30 Oct. 1947; Salvador Allende Gossens, letter to Bowers, 9 Sept. 1949; *El Mercurio*, 24 Nov. 1974.

41. La Feber, *America, Russia, and the Cold War*, 68; Gaddis, *Strategies of Containment*, 30, 60; Bowers, letter to Spruille Braden, 9 Jan. 1946, 825.30 Missions/1-946, NA; "Chilean Diary," 21 June 1948; Acheson to Bowers, 11 Jan. 1946, 825.248/1-1146, NA; Truman to Bowers, 31 Aug. 1950; Hall to State Dept., 25 Jan. 1951, 725.00 (W)/a-2551, NA; Lieuwen, *U.S. Policy in Latin America*, 91; Bowers to Acheson, 22 Dec. 1951, 725.5-MSP/12-2551; González Videla interview; H. Gerald Smith to State Dept., 10 Apr. 1952, 725.00 (W)/4-1052; Eduardo Yrarrázaval Concha, interview with Hamilton, 8 Oct. 1966;

Emilio Meneses Ciuffardi, *El factor naval en las relaciones entre Chile y los Estados Unidos (1881-1951)* (Santiago: Ediciones Pedagógicas Chilenas, 1989), 215.

42. Salvador Allende Gossens, interview with Hamilton, 22 Nov. 1966; Bowers, letter to Charles W. McCarthy, 14 Apr. 1952; Francisco José Moreno, *Legitimacy and Stability in Latin America: A Study of Chilean Political Culture* (New York: New York University Press, 1969), 165; Gil, *Political System of Chile*, 77, 197; Bowers to Ziffren, 5 Oct., 26 Nov. 1952, LZ; Truman to Bowers, 12 Sept. 1952; "Chilean Diary," 13 Sept. 1952; Milton Barall, memo to Mann and Miller, 17 Nov. 1952, 825.00/11-1752, NA; Carlos Ibáñez del Campo to Dwight D. Eisenhower, 22 Aug. 1953, 611.25/9-1552, ibid.

43. Eduardo Yrarrázaval Concha, *América Latina en la guerra fría* (Santiago: Nascimento, 1959), 209; Bryce Wood, *The Making of the Good Neighbor Policy* (New York: Columbia University Press, 1961), 322; "Chilean Diary," 23 June 1948; *New York Times*, 27 Apr. 1957; Peter J. Grace, "The Private Investor in Latin America Today," in "Economics and Political Trends in Latin America," ed. Sigmund Diamond, *Proceedings of the Academy of Political Science* 27 (May 1964): 42–51; Gaddis Smith, *The Last Years of the Monroe Doctrine, 1945–1993* (New York: Hill and Wang, 1994), 44.

## 10. Don Claudio of Santiago

1. Claude Bowers, "Chilean Diary," 30 Aug. 1940, 15 Aug., 28 Nov. 1941, 29 Dec. 1943, 25 July 1944, 2 July 1948, 10 Sept., 4, 10 Nov., 11 Dec. 1949, 15 Dec. 1952 (hereafter cited as "Chilean Diary"); Juana Aguirre de Aguirre Cerda, letter to Bowers, 30 Dec. 1939.

2. *La Nación* (Santiago), 14 Dec. 1943; Eugenio Pereira Salas, "Recuerdos de veinte años," *Instituto Chileno-Norteamericano de Cultura* (Santiago, 1958), 6–16; Bowers, letters to Cordell Hull, 5, 10 July 1940, 9 Apr. 1942, 123 Bowers/247, 248, 127, U.S. Department of State, RG 59, National Archives, Washington, D.C. (hereafter cited as NA); *El Diario Ilustrado* (Santiago), 13 July, 3 Oct. 1951; "Chilean Diary," 9 June 1941, 20 July 1943; *El Imparcial* (Santiago), 29 Aug. 1942; Bowers, letters to Theodore Fred Kuper, 11 Nov., 17 June 1940, 18 Nov. 1944, Claude G. Bowers Collection, Henry E. Huntington Library, San Marino, Calif. (hereafter cited as BC).

3. Franklin D. Roosevelt to Bowers, 19 May 1943; Lucy Richmond Lentz, interview with Holman Hamilton, 11 Nov. 1967; "Chilean Diary," 11, 12 Aug., 4, 9 Apr. 1941, 28 Aug. 1942; Philip W. Bonsal, interview with Hamilton, 27 July 1967.

4. "Chilean Diary," 4 July 1941, 5 Apr. 1952, 24 Nov. 1944, 15 Aug. 1942; Bowers, letters to Holman Hamilton, 24 June, 28 Feb. 1949; Roosevelt to Bowers, 20 Dec. 1944; Bowers, *Chile through Embassy Windows, 1939–1953* (New York: Simon and Schuster, 1958), 259–68, 154 (hereafter cited as *Chile*); Bowers, letter to John Gunther, 26 Sept. 1941, copy, Holman Hamilton Papers, Division of Special Collections and Archives of the Margaret I. King Library, University of Kentucky, Lexington (hereafter cited as HP); Gunther to Bowers, 16 Sept., 23 Oct. 1941; *Indianapolis News*, 20 Feb. 1946; Herman B Wells, interview with Peter J. Sehlinger, 28 Sept. 1990.

5. "Chilean Diary," 4, 5 June 1946, 11 June 1941; Herbert Hoover, letter to Bowers, 8 June 1946; M. [Milton] and D. [Dwight] Eisenhower, letters to Bowers, 5, 19 Aug. 1953.

6. *Memoria del Ministerio de Relaciones Exteriores . . . 1943* (Santiago), 858; Bowers, *My Life: The Memoirs of Claude Bowers* (New York: Simon and Schuster, 1962), 198; "Chilean Diary," 26 Mar.–2 Apr. 1943; *Chile*, 263–66.

7. Bowers, letter to Joseph F. Guffey, 17 Jan. 1953; Bowers to State Department, 5 Dec. 1952, copy, HP; Joseph P. Lash, *Eleanor: The Years Alone* (New York: W. W. Norton, 1972),

204–5; *Chile*, 344; "Chilean Diary," 4, 18 Nov. 1952; Bowers, letter to Eleanor Roosevelt, 10 Nov. 1952, Eleanor Roosevelt Papers, Franklin D. Roosevelt Library, Hyde Park, New York; Eleanor Roosevelt to Bowers, 6 Nov. 1952; *Washington Daily News*, 11 Nov. 1952.

8. Joaquín Edwards Bello, "Espionaje en Chile," *La Nación*, 29 Aug. 1957; "Chilean Diary," 11 Sept., 6 Nov. 1939; Betty Pack, letter to Bowers, 9 Nov. 1939.

9. *Chile*, 298; Bowers to Roosevelt, 31 July 1941, PSF:Chile, 17 Sept. 1941, OF, Franklin D. Roosevelt: Papers as President, Franklin D. Roosevelt Library (hereafter cited as FDR); Edward G. Miller, Jr., letter to Bowers, 7 May 1951, *Foreign Relations of the United States*, 1951 (Washington, D.C.: Government Printing Office, 1979), 2:1280 (hereafter cited as *FRUS*); *Indianapolis Star*, 28 Dec. 1950; Bowers, letter to Lawrence F. Levenberg, 31 Dec. 1949, copy, HP; Joseph Cussens, interview with Hamilton, 15 Nov. 1966.

10. Patrick W. Collins, *Gustave Weigel: A Pioneer of Reform* (Collegeville, Minn.: Liturgical Press, 1992), 86–87; "Chilean Diary," 22 Oct. 1941, 14 Apr. 1944, 18 Apr., 11 Nov. 1945; Bowers to Kuper, 27 July 1947, BC; *Chile*, 147, 254–55; Bowers to Hamilton, 12 May 1952.

11. "Interview with Amanda Labarca," 7 Sept. 1970, in Peter J. Sehlinger, "Chile visto por chilenos"/"Chile, a Self-Portrait" (University Library, Indiana University, Indianapolis); "Chilean Diary," 17 Aug. 1940, 13 May 1941, 15 June 1944, 4 Dec. 1952.

12. Bowers, letter to Ben Cherrington, 15 Nov. 1939, 123 Bowers/237, NA; "Chilean Diary," 17 Sept. 1949; "Interview with Ricardo Donoso," 11 Aug. 1970, in Sehlinger, "Chile"; Bowers, letter to Ernesto Barros Jarpa, 17 July 1942, copy, HP; "Gestión del Embajador de EE.UU.," [30 Aug. 1942], copy, HP; *Chile*, 45–46.

13. Bowers to Levenberg, 27 Jan. 1941, copy, HP; Bowers to Hamilton, 21 Jan. 1941; Bowers to Roosevelt, 23 Jan. 1941, copy, HP; Roosevelt to Bowers, 5 May 1941; Nicholas Murray Butler, letter to Bowers, 15 Jan. 1941; Wesley Frost, letter to Bowers, 2 Apr. 1941.

14. *La Opinión* (Santiago), 12 May 1942; *La Hora* (Santiago), 3 Oct. 1945; Gabriela Mistral, letter to Bowers, 11 Aug. 1948; Donald Heath, letter to Hull, 24 Feb. 1943, 123 Bowers/295, NA; Philip W. Bonsal, letter to Bowers, 31 May 1944; Bonsal interview; Roosevelt to Bowers, 2 Jan. 1941.

15. *El Mercurio* (Santiago), 8 Sept. 1949; *South Pacific Mail* (Santiago), 15 Sept. 1949; Salvador Allende Gossens, letter to Bowers, 9 Sept. 1949; "Chilean Diary," 7 Sept. 1949; Bowers to Hamilton, 20 Sept. 1949; Harry Truman, letter to Bowers, 15 Sept. 1949; Horace R. Graham, letter to Bowers, 21 Dec. 1950; *La Nación*, 4 Oct. 1951; Anthony F. O'Brien, "The Politics of Dependency: A Case Study of Dependency—Chile 1938–45" (Ph.D. diss., University of Notre Dame, 1977), 195.

16. Eduardo Frei Montalva, interview with Sehlinger, 5 Nov. 1971, in Sehlinger, "Chile"; *El Mercurio*, 29 July 1954, 24 Nov. 1974; Charles W. Cole, foreword to *Career Diplomat: A Career in the Foreign Service of the United States*, by Willard L. Beaulac (New York: Macmillan, 1964), viii, 107; Willard Beaulac, interview with Hamilton, 28 July 1965; Beaulac, interview with Sehlinger, 14 Apr. 1970.

17. James A. Farley, letter to Bowers, 15 May 1940; Bowers to Hull, 10 Apr. 1940, copy, HP; Roosevelt to Bowers, 14 Sept. 1940; Lentz interview; Sumner Welles, letter to Bowers, 25 Oct. 1940, 123 Bowers/245, NA; Bowers to Kuper, 11 Nov. 1940, BC; Bowers to Welles, 26 Oct. 1940, copy, HP; *New York Times*, 2 Nov. 1940.

18. "Chilean Diary," 6 Nov. 1940, 2 Sept. 1943; Bowers to Hamilton, 14 Nov. 1944; Guffey to Bowers, 6 Oct. 1941; Robert Huntington, "Hoosier Diplomat," *Indianapolis Star Magazine*, 14 Aug. 1949.

19. "Chilean Diary," 30 Nov. 1943, 7 Nov. 1944, 8–24 Oct. 1945, 2 Aug. 1948; Truman to Bowers, 26 Apr. 1945; Milton Barall, letter to Hamilton, 1 May 1963; Bowers

to Kuper, 26 Nov. 1946, BC; Bowers to Hamilton, 1 Aug. 1948; Bowers to Truman, 23 Nov. 1948, copy, HP.

20. Bowers to Hamilton, 16 June 1950; *Chile*, 317; "Chilean Diary," 8, 18 May 1950; Bowers, letter to J. Edith Monahan, 18 June 1950, copy, HP; Bowers to Hamilton, 12 May 1952; Bowers, "My Life," typed MSS, [1953], BC; Frank E. McKinney, letter to Bowers, 15 Apr. 1952; Adlai E. Stevenson to Bowers, 21 Aug. 1952; Farley to Bowers, 15 Sept. 1952; Bowers, letter to Lester Ziffren, 17 Nov. 1952, Lester Ziffren letters, HP; Truman to Bowers, 17 Nov. 1952.

21. Bowers to Roosevelt, 10 June 1940, copy, HP, 3 Nov. 1941, 825.00/1452, NA, 15 Nov. 1940, OF:303, FDR; "Chilean Diary," 18 July 1940; Bowers to Kuper, 11 Nov. 1940, BC; Bowers, letter to Dolores Rivas de Azaña, 5 June 1945, copy, HP; Cipriano de Rivas Cherif, interview with Hamilton, 12 Aug. 1965; Roosevelt to Bowers, 9 Dec. 1940.

22. Lentz interview; Sybil Bowers, letter to Jessie Moore, 4 Dec. 1941; Bowers to Kuper, 30 May 1945, BC; "Chilean Diary," 22 Dec. 1940, 16 Dec. 1943, 20 Oct. 1944; Bowers, letter to Nellie [Sights], 10 June 1943, copy, HP.

23. Sybil Bowers to Jessie Moore, 25 June 1944, 22 Nov. 1939; "Chilean Diary," 22 Jan. 1940, 3 Jan. 1941, 24 Mar., 28 Feb. 1951; Bowers to Hamilton, 22 Jan. 1941; Carlos Griffin Garat, interview with Hamilton, 15 Nov. 1966.

24. Welles to Roosevelt, 1 Mar. 1943, 123 Bowers/293, NA; Eleanor Shields, interview with Hamilton, 29 Aug. 1963; "Chilean Diary," 20 Jan., 7 Mar. 1940, 24 Jan. 1941, 15 Jan. 1945, 13 Jan. 1946; *Time*, 20 Mar. 1944, p. 19; telegrams and letters from John White and the heads of several U.S. organizations, Mar. 1944, 123 Bowers/334, NA; Roosevelt and Hull to Bowers, 7, 8 Apr. 1944, 123 Bowers/334, 337, ibid.

25. William E. Dodd, *Ambassador Dodd's Diary, 1933–1938*, eds. William E. Dodd, Jr., and Martha Dodd (New York: Harcourt, Brace, 1941); *New York Times Book Review*, 2 Mar. 1941, p. 1; *Virginia Historical Quarterly* 21 (spring 1945): 219–33; Bowers to Kuper, 30 Apr. 1945, BC; Bowers, *The Young Jefferson, 1743–1789* (Boston: Houghton Mifflin, 1945); Archibald MacLeish, letters to Bowers, 30 Jan. 1940, 9 Dec. 1941; Bowers, *Young Jefferson*, ix.

26. Bowers to Kuper, 18 Nov. 1944, 27 Mar., 14 May, 12 June 1945, 18 Oct. 1948, BC; *The Nation* 160 (17 Mar. 1945): 307–8; Bowers, *Young Jefferson*, viii; *Newsweek*, 19 Mar. 1945; John Dos Passos, letter to Bowers, 27 June 1945; Butler to Bowers, 8 May 1945.

27. Bowers to Hamilton, 1 Aug. 1946; Thomas P. Abernethy, "Mr. Jefferson in Technicolor," *Virginia Quarterly Review* 22 (winter 1946): 159; Carl Bridenbaugh review, *Mississippi Valley Historical Review* 32 (Sept. 1945): 287; Marie Kimball review, *American Historical Review* 50 (July 1945): 810.

28. Arthur Ochs Sulzberger, letter to Bowers, 3 Oct. 1939; Holman Hamilton and Gayle Thornbrough, eds., *Indianapolis in the "Gay Nineties": High School Diaries of Claude G. Bowers* (Indianapolis: Indiana Historical Society, 1964), 190; Bowers, *Pierre Vergniaud: Voice of the French Revolution* (New York: Macmillan, 1950), viii–ix, 334; Bowers to Hamilton, 2 Oct. 1950, 11 Nov. 1951; Bowers to Kuper, 21 Dec. 1947.

29. André Maurois, "He Trusted the People and Overlooked the Mob," *New York Times Book Review*, 19 Nov. 1950, p. 5; "Girondin Leader," *Times Literary Supplement*, 28 Dec. 1950; Corbin Patrick review, *Indianapolis Star*, 19 Nov. 1950; Truman to Bowers, 15 Nov. 1950; *El Mercurio*, 14 Jan. 1951; Ricardo Donoso, letter to Sehlinger, 6 Mar. 1982, HP; Bowers to Kuper, 12 Dec. 1950, BC; R. R. Palmer review, *Saturday Review of Literature* 33 (9 Dec. 1950): 17–18; Crane Brinton review, *William and Mary Quarterly*, 3d ser., 8 (Apr. 1951): 274.

30. *Chile* and *Mi misión en Chile* (Santiago: Editorial del Pacífico, 1957); *Indianapolis Star*, 30 Mar. 1958; *Chile*, 319–30, 113; "Chilean Diary," 6 Apr. 1945, 16 Oct. 1942; Edwards Bello, letter to Bowers, [Sept. 1957]; *El Mercurio*, 19 Aug. 1957; Eulogio Rojas Mery, letter to Bowers, 16 Aug. 1957.

31. *Indianapolis Star*, 30 Mar. 1958; *Christian Science Monitor*, 27 Mar. 1958; *San Francisco Chronicle*, 26 Feb. 1958; Arthur A. Ageton review, *Saturday Review* 41 (22 Mar. 1958): 48; Herbert L. Matthews, "Assignment to a Lovely Land," *New York Times Book Review*, 9 Mar. 1958, pp. 6–7; Carleton Beals review, *The Nation* 186 (22 Mar. 1958): 259; Arthur P. Whitaker review, *Annals of the American Academy of Political and Social Sciences* 318 (July 1958): 165; Donald E. Worcester review, *American Historical Review* 63 (July 1958): 1083; *Chicago Tribune*, 2 Mar. 1958; *New York Herald Tribune Book Review*, 9 Mar. 1958.

32. Fredrick B. Pike, *Chile and the United States, 1880–1962: The Emergence of Chile's Social Crisis and the Challenge to United States Diplomacy* (Notre Dame, Ind.: University of Notre Dame Press, 1963), 272; Gonzalo Vial, "Fredrick B. Pike's *Chile and the United States 1880–1962*: A Dissenting View," *Hispanic American Historical Review* 46 (Aug. 1966): 283–85; O'Brien, "Politics of Dependency," 195–96.

33. "Chilean Diary," 21 Feb. 1940, 13 Nov. 1943, 14 June 1953; Bowers to Roosevelt, 23 Oct. 1941, 825.00/1478, NA; *Chile*, 354, 363; Dwight D. Eisenhower to Bowers, 3 Aug. 1953; Bowers to Levenberg, 16 Aug. 1953; Bowers, letter to Frank Brubeck, 16 Mar. 1942.

## 11. Retirement

1. Claude Bowers, "Diary," 14 Oct. 1953, 27 July, 19 Mar. 1954, 31 Mar., 1 Nov. 1955, 17 Feb. 1956 (hereafter cited as "Diary"); Bowers, letters to Lester Ziffren, 15 Apr. 1956, 18 Oct. 1955, Lester Ziffren letters, Holman Hamilton Papers, Division of Special Collections and Archives of the Margaret I. King Library, University of Kentucky, Lexington (hereafter cited as LZ); Bowers quoted by Lawrence Levenberg in Lawrence Levenberg, interview with Holman Hamilton, 30 Dec. 1961; Myla Jo Closser, letter to Bowers, 13 July 1955; Bowers, letter to Herbert H. Lehman, 13 Feb. 1954, Herbert H. Lehman Papers, School of International Affairs, Columbia University, New York.

2. "Diary," 26 Feb., 4 Aug. 1954; Milton Barall to Bowers, 10 Dec. 1953; Bowers to Ziffren, 26 Nov. 1953, 4 May 1954, LZ.

3. "Diary," 3 Dec., 21 Nov. 1953, 3, 2 Dec. 1954; Bowers to Eleanor Roosevelt, 29 Sept. 1954, Eleanor Roosevelt Papers, Franklin D. Roosevelt Library, Hyde Park, New York (hereafter cited as ER).

4. "Diary," 5 Apr. 1954; Gretchen Witt, letter to Bowers, 10 Feb. 1954; Bowers, *My Life: The Memoirs of Claude Bowers* (New York: Simon and Schuster, 1962), 325; *Washington Post*, 6 Apr. 1954.

5. "Diary," 9 Feb., 23 Oct. 1954, 16 Apr. 1956, 29 June 1957, 31 Oct. 1955; Harry Truman, letter to Bowers, 5 Dec. 1957; Dean Acheson, letter to Bowers, 18 Jan. 1957.

6. "Diary," 22 Oct. 1953, 16 Nov. 1955, 10 Mar. 1954; Robert F. Wagner, Jr., letter to Bowers, 26 Sept. 1956; Paul H. Douglas, letter to Bowers, 2 June 1955; Sam Rayburn, letter to Bowers, 21 Jan. 1955; Thomas T. Connally, letter to Bowers, 27 Nov. 1954; Lehman to Bowers, 24 Jan. 1956; Bowers to Ziffren, 18 Oct. 1955, LZ; Adlai E. Stevenson, letter to Bowers, 15 Dec. 1953.

7. Stevenson to Bowers, 7 Nov. 1955; "Diary," 28 Feb., 29 Jan., 25 Apr., 7 Sept., 8 Nov. 1956; Bowers, letters to Holman Hamilton, 11 Nov. 1955, 9 Dec. 1956; Bowers to

Ziffren, 13 Nov. 1955, 15 Apr. 1956, LZ; Eduardo Schijman, "Una Visita a Claude Bowers," *El Mercurio* (Santiago), 7 Oct. 1956.

8. "Diary," 11, 13 Aug. 1956; Bowers to Hamilton, 19 Mar. 1956; Bowers to Ziffren, 7 Nov. 1954, LZ.

9. "Diary," 27 Dec. 1940, 29 May 1951, 18 May 1954, 12 Mar. 1956; Bowers to Hamilton, 19 Mar. 1956, 24 July 1957.

10. Bowers to Hamilton, 11 Nov. 1955; Bowers to Ziffren, 27 Feb., 26 May 1956, LZ; Bowers to Mrs. Wilson, 8 Apr. 1956, copy, Holman Hamilton Papers (hereafter cited as HP); Truman to Bowers, 23 Mar. 1956; Richard E. Byrd to Bowers, 15 May 1956; James M. Cox to Bowers, 16 May 1956; "Diary," 3 May, 10 Feb. 1956; E. Walton Opie, letter to Bowers, 8 May 1957.

11. Bowers to Ziffren, 1 Dec. 1956, LZ; Arthur Schlesinger, letter to Bowers, 2 Dec. 1954; Moe Fishman, letter to Bowers, 26 Feb. 1957; "Diary," 18 Sept. 1954, 31 Mar., 25 Sept. 1955; Angel del Río, letter to Bowers, 3 Dec. 1954; Aníbal Jara, letter to Bowers, 25 Feb. 1955; Bowers, letter to Elizabeth Mason, 16 Jan. 1957, copy, HP.

12. "List of Speeches by C. Bowers, Oct. 26, 1953–Apr. 7, 1957," HP; "Diary," 26, 29 Oct., 12 Dec. 1953, 24 Jan., 15 Nov. 1954, 27 Apr., 13 Oct. 1955, 16, 19 Apr., 22 May, 13 June, 17 Nov. 1956; Bowers to Eleanor Roosevelt, 25 Feb. 1955, ER; Bowers to Ziffren, 11 Apr. 1957, LZ.

13. Allan Nevins, letters to Bowers, 21 Mar., 4 May, 21 June 1954, 31 Dec. 1955; Bowers to Hamilton, 20 Apr. 1954; "Diary," 27 Oct. 1954; *Fort Wayne Journal-Gazette*, 13 Dec. 1953; Gonzalo Figueroa Tagle, "Claude Bowers, Amigo de Chile," *El Mercurio*, 22 Sept. 1957.

14. "Diary," 12, 13 Dec. 1953, 14 Oct. 1955; Herman B Wells, interview with Peter J. Sehlinger, 28 Sept. 1990.

15. "Diary," 21 Jan., 21 May 1956; Bowers, *Twenty Years of New Deal and Fair Deal Achievement—And This They Call Treason!*, Special Bulletin No. 4 (New York: New York State C.I.O. Council, 1954); Truman to Bowers, 7 June 1954.

16. "Diary," 20 Nov. 1956; "List of C. Bowers's Retirement Publications," HP; Bowers, *Making Democracy a Reality: Jefferson, Jackson, and Polk* (Memphis: Memphis State Press, 1954); Bowers to Hamilton, 23 Feb. 1956; Bowers to Ziffren, 23 Dec. 1956, LZ.

17. Bowers to Ziffren, 15 Feb. 1955, LZ; Bowers to Eleanor Roosevelt, 12 May 1954, 27 Oct. 1957, ER; "Diary," 11 Aug. 1956, 16 May 1957; Truman to Bowers, 9 June 1954; Gabriel González Videla to Bowers, 11 Oct. 1957; *La Nación* (Santiago), 29 Sept. 1957; Bowers to J. Edith Monahan, [10 Oct. 1957], J. Edith Monahan Collection, HP. Bowers memorials were proposed but never implemented, see "Fundación 'Claude G. Bowers' . . . ," *El Mercurio*, 4 Dec. 1959; *Entretelones* (Santiago), 13 Sept. 1957.

18. Bowers, letter to Theodore Fred Kuper, 9 Sept. 1950, Claude G. Bowers Collection, Henry E. Huntington Library, San Marino, Calif. (hereafter cited as BC); Hamilton to Kuper, 26 Dec. 1962, copy, HP.

19. Allan Nevins review, *New York Times Book Review*, 7 Apr. 1963, p. 43; *Indianapolis News*, 29 Dec. 1963; *The New Yorker*, 9 Feb. 1963, p. 145; *Virginia Quarterly Review* 39 (spring 1963): 319; *Christian Science Monitor*, 5 Jan. 1963.

20. Bernard Kalb, "The Author," *Saturday Review of Literature* 37 (12 June 1954): 13–14; "Diary," 27 June 1954, 14 Apr. 1956; Bowers to Ziffren, 10 Oct., 26 Nov. 1953, LZ; Bowers to Mason, 16 Jan. 1957, copy, HP; Pat Bowers, letter to Mother and Dad, [2 Oct. 1954].

21. C. Edwards to Bowers, 24 Oct. 1954; "Diary," 17 Nov. 1953, 28 Oct. 1955, 5 Apr., 16 Dec., 20 Nov., 4 Dec. 1956, 26 June 1957; Bowers to Mason, 16 Jan. 1957, copy, HP;

Bowers to Ziffren, 23 Dec. 1956, 8 Jan. 1955, LZ; Elinor [Dillon], letter to Bowers, 9 Apr. 1956; Closser to Bowers, 26 Feb. 1956; Louis Starr, "Bowers," in Bowers, "Reminiscences of Claude Bowers," interview by Louis Starr, 24, 30 Aug. 1954 (Oral History Research Office, Columbia University, New York); Kuper to Hamilton, 2 May 1977.

22. Bowers to Ziffren, 3, 23 Sept., 3 Nov. 1957, LZ.

23. Ibid., 10 Dec. 1957; Santiago del Campo, letter to Bowers, 7 Oct. 1957; *El Mercurio, La Nación, El Diario Ilustrado* (Santiago), 14 Oct. 1957; *South Pacific Mail* (Santiago), 18 Oct. 1957; Cecil Lyon, letter to Bowers, 29 Oct. 1957; José María Caro Rodríguez, letter to Bowers, 29 Oct. 1957; *Terre Haute Tribune-Star,* 26, 28 Jan. 1958; Archibaldo Frugone Risso, interview with Hamilton, 6 Nov. 1966; Ramón Alliende, interview with Hamilton, 2 Nov. 1966; *New York Times,* 22 Jan., *Washington Post,* 25 Jan., *Indianapolis Times,* 26 Jan., *Indianapolis Star,* 26 Jan. 1958; *Indianapolis News,* 2 Sept. 1968; Kuper to Hamilton, 25 Oct. 1975.

24. *Fort Wayne Journal-Gazette,* 6 Dec. 1964; Pat Bowers to Hamilton, [7? Oct. 1963]; *Indianapolis News,* 2 Sept. 1968; Nevins to Bowers, 25 Apr. 1952; Truman to Bowers, 24 Oct. 1953; Sybil Bowers to Hamilton, 5 Feb. 1953; "Plat Book for Section 3 of Highland Lawn Cemetery," Highland Lawn Cemetery, Terre Haute, Ind.

25. Bowers, "Keynote," *The Political News* 10 (July 1928): 1–4; *Raleigh* (N.C.) *News and Observer,* 15 Jan. 1928.

26. Bowers, letter to Oswald Garrison Villard, 4 Jan. 1927, copy, HP; Bowers, letter to Louis Hollander, 28 Nov. 1957, copy, HP; Arthur A. Eckrich, *The Decline of American Liberalism* (New York: Citadel Press, 1955), 269–72; Joseph J. Ellis, *American Sphinx: The Character of Thomas Jefferson* (New York: Alfred A. Knopf, 1997), 292.

27. Dumas Malone quoted in Karl Schriftgiesser, letter to Bowers, 28 May 1948; Merrill Peterson, letter to Bowers, 7 Sept. 1954.

28. Bowers to Kuper, 18 June 1950, BC; Allan Nevins, "What's the Matter with History," *Saturday Review of Literature* 19 (4 Feb. 1939): 3–4, 16; *New York Times,* 11 Dec. 1987; Oliver Knight, "Claude G. Bowers," *Indiana Magazine of History* 52 (Sept. 1956): 268.

29. Quoted in Bowers, *My Life,* 264.

30. Bowers to Kuper, 20 Sept. 1945, BC; Bowers to Hamilton, 24 Oct. 1939; "Diary," 15 Mar. 1950; Bowers to Ziffren, 14 July 1957, LZ.

31. Fred L. Kelly, "Ambassador as Democrat," *Esquire* (Apr. 1937): 62; Starr, "Bowers," 1.

# Bibliography

## Manuscript Collections

Archivo del Ministerio de Asuntos Exteriores, Madrid, Spain.
  Estados Unidos.
Archivo del Ministerio de Relaciones Exteriores, Santiago, Chile.
Archivo Nacional, Santiago, Chile.
  Volúmenes Relativos a Estados Unidos.
DePauw University, Greencastle, Indiana.
  Max Ehrmann Papers.
Franklin D. Roosevelt Presidential Library, Hyde Park, New York.
  Eleanor Roosevelt Papers.
  Franklin D. Roosevelt: Papers as President.
  Harry L. Hopkins Papers.
  R. Walton Moore Papers.
  John C. Wiley Papers.
Georgetown University, Washington, D.C.
  Robert F. Wagner Papers.
Henry E. Huntington Library, San Marino, California.
  Claude G. Bowers Collection.
Hoover Institution, Stanford, California.
  Joaquín Maurín Collection.
Houghton Library, Harvard University, Cambridge, Massachusetts.
  Houghton Mifflin Company Papers.
  Jay Pierrepont Moffat Papers and Diaries.
  William Phillips Papers and Journals.

Indiana Historical Society, Indianapolis.
  James A. Stuart Collection.
  Sara Messing Harding, "Random Notes about Claude Bowers."
  Jessie Moore Collection.
Library of Congress, Washington, D.C.
  Albert J. Beveridge Papers.
  Breckinridge Long Papers.
  Cordell Hull Papers.
  Carl Schurz Papers.
Lilly Library, Indiana University, Bloomington.
  Claude G. Bowers Manuscripts.
Margaret I. King Library, University of Kentucky, Lexington.
  Holman Hamilton Papers including:
    George S. Messersmith Papers.
    J. Edith Monahan Collection.
    Lester Ziffren Letters.
Massachusetts Historical Society, Boston.
  William Everett Papers.
Minnesota Historical Society, St. Paul.
  Ignatius Donnelly Papers.
National Archives, Washington, D.C.
  United States Coast Guard, Record Group 26.
  United States Department of State, Record Group 59.
  United States Office of the Chief of Naval Operations, Record
    Group 38.
School of International Affairs, Columbia University, New York.
  Herbert H. Lehman Papers.
University of North Carolina, Chapel Hill.
  J. G. de R. Hamilton Papers.
University of Virginia, Charlottesville.
  Homer C. Cummings Collection.
  John Dos Passos Papers.

*Interviews*

The notes for these interviews are in the Holman Hamilton Papers, Division of Special Collections and Archives of the Margaret I. King Library, University of Kentucky, Lexington.

Holman Hamilton interviews with:

Alcalá Zamora, Niceto. 11 Aug. 1965. Mexico City.

Allende Gossens, Salvador. 22 Nov. 1966. Santiago, Chile.

Alliende, Ramón. 2 Nov. 1966. Santiago, Chile.

Azaña, Dolores Rivas Cherif de. 13 Aug. 1965. Mexico City.

Baer, James A., Jr. 9 Nov. 1972. Washington, D.C.

Beaulac, Willard L. 28 July 1965. Washington, D.C.

Beeman, Larkin L. 19 July 1963. Lebanon, Indiana.

Bittler, George. 3 Dec. 1960. Fort Wayne, Indiana.

Bonsal, Philip W. 27 July 1967. Washington, D.C.

Bowers, Claude G. 22 May 1956. Lexington, Kentucky.

Bowers, Patricia. 23 Nov. 1960. New York City.

Brooks, Clarence C. 7 Apr. 1965. Tampa, Florida.

Brubeck, Frank. 29 Dec. 1961. Washington, D.C.

Crawford, Jean. 23 Oct. 1963. Terre Haute, Indiana.

Cussens, Joseph. 15 Nov. 1966. Santiago, Chile.

Daggy, Maynard Lee. 25 Apr. 1963. Washington, D.C.

Dos Passos, John. 20 Feb. 1965. Baltimore, Maryland.

Eyzaguirre, Jaime. 14 Nov. 1966. Santiago, Chile.

Farley, James A. 25 Sept. 1967. New York City.

Fernández Fernández, Joaquín. 16 Nov. 1966. Santiago, Chile.

Frugone Risso, Archibaldo. 6 Nov. 1966. Santiago, Chile.

Gandy, Theodore I. 15 June, 10, 11 Aug. 1964. Milwaukee, Wisconsin.

Gilmore, W. Steele. 31 Dec. 1965. La Jolla, California.

González Videla, Gabriel. 20 Oct. 1966. Santiago, Chile.

Griffin Garat, Carlos. 15 Nov. 1966. Santiago, Chile.

Harrison, Joseph. 29 Dec. 1965. San Francisco, California.

Heath, Donald. 5 Oct. 1965. Lexington, Kentucky.

Krock, Arthur. 16 Nov. 1965. Washington, D.C.
Kuper, Theodore Fred. 30 Aug. 1962. Whittier, California.
Lentz, Lucy Richmond. 11 Nov. 1967. New York City.
Levenberg, Lawrence. 30 Dec. 1961. Washington, D.C.
Mills, Sheldon T. 18 Aug. 1965. Washington, D.C.
Minifie, James M. 16 Feb. 1965. Washington, D.C.
Norman, Martha Hawkins. 6 Aug. 1970. Indianapolis, Indiana.
O'Brien, John F. 24 Oct. 1962. Terre Haute, Indiana.
Oliver, Frank. 26 Apr. 1963. New York City.
Rivas Cherif, Cipriano de. 13 Aug. 1965. Mexico City.
Schoellkopf, Horton. 27 Apr. 1963. Washington, D.C.
Schooler, C. Walter. 8 June 1963. Whitestown, Indiana.
Shields, Eleanor. 29 Aug. 1963. La Jolla, California.
Sortor, Claude. 8 June 1963. Whitestown, Indiana.
Thomas, Lela. 11 June 1963. Hamilton Co., Indiana.
Tomlinson, Ben. 11 June 1963. Lebanon, Indiana.
Torres Rueda, José "Pepe." 12 Nov. 1966. Santiago, Chile.
Vergara Donoso, Germán. 9 Nov. 1966. Santiago, Chile.
Weigel, Gustave. 28 Apr. 1963. Washington, D.C.
Wendelin, Eric C. 18 Aug. 1965. Santa Barbara, California.
Yrarrázaval Concha, Eduardo. 8 Oct. 1966. Santiago, Chile.
Ziffren, Lester. 16 May 1964. New York City.

Peter J. Sehlinger interviews with:

Barros Jarpa, Ernesto. 28 Aug. 1970. Santiago, Chile.
Beaulac, Willard L. 14 Apr. 1970. Indianapolis, Indiana.
Frei Montalva, Eduardo. 5 Nov. 1971. Dayton, Ohio.
Godet, Chantal. 20 July 1990. St. Jean de Luz, France.
Kerr, Lawrence. 8 Apr. 1991. Santiago, Chile.
Liebmann, William B. 23 Mar. 1982. New York City.
Teitelboim, Volodia. 9 Apr. 1991. Santiago, Chile.
Wells, Herman B. 28 Sept. 1990. Bloomington, Indiana.

## Oral Histories

Bowers, Claude. "Reminiscences of Claude Bowers." Interview by Louis Starr. 24, 30 Aug. 1954. Oral History Research Office, Columbia University, New York City.

Phillips, William. "Reminiscences of William Phillips." Interview by Wendell H. Link. July 1951. Oral History Research Office, Columbia University, New York City.

Sehlinger, Peter J. "Chile visto por chilenos/Chile: A Self-Portrait." Interviews with Jacques Chonchol, Ricardo Donoso, Eduardo Frei Montalva, Amanda Labarca, Benjamín Matte, and Volodia Teitelboim. Aug. 1970–Nov. 1971. University Library, Indiana University, Indianapolis.

## Books

Adams, Henry. *History of the United States during the Administrations of Jefferson and Madison*. 9 vols. New York: C. Scribner's, 1889–91.

Alba, Víctor, and Stephen Schwartz. *Spanish Marxism versus Soviet Communism: A History of the P.O.U.M.* New Brunswick, N.J.: Rutgers University Press, 1988.

Alexander, Robert J. *The Tragedy of Chile*. Westport, Conn.: Greenwood Press, 1978.

*The Annual: Indianapolis High School*. 1897, 1898. Indianapolis, 1897–98.

Aylwin Oyarzún, Mariana, et al. *Chile en el siglo XX*. Santiago: Editorial Emisión, [1985].

Aznar, Manuel. *Historia militar de la guerra civil en España*. 3 vols. Madrid: Editora Nacional, 1958–63.

Bancroft, George. *History of the Formation of the Constitution of the United States of America*. 2 vols. New York: Appleton and Co., 1882.

Barnard, Andrew. "Chile." In *Latin America between the Second World War and the Cold War, 1944–1948*, edited by Leslie

Bethell and Ian Roxborough, 66–91. Cambridge: Cambridge University Press, 1992.

Barrett, James W. *Joseph Pulitzer and His World*. New York: The Vanguard Press, 1941.

Barros Jarpa, Ernesto. "Historia para olvidar: Ruptura con el Eje (1942–1943)." In *Homenaje a Guillermo Feliú Cruz*, edited by Neville Blanc Renard, 31–96. Santiago: Editorial Andrés Bello, 1973.

Barros Ortiz, Tobías. *Recogiendo los pasos: Testigo militar y político del siglo XX*. Santiago: Editorial Planeta Chilena, 1988.

Beale, Howard K. "Charles Beard: Historian." In *Charles A. Beard: An Appraisal*, edited by Howard K. Beale, 115–59. Lexington: University of Kentucky Press, 1954.

Beaulac, Willard L. *Career Diplomat: A Career in the Foreign Service of the United States*. New York: Macmillan, 1964.

Bemis, Samuel Flagg. *The Latin American Policy of the United States: An Historical Interpretation*. New York: Harcourt, Brace, 1943.

Bender, Thomas. *New York Intellect: A History of Intellectual Life in New York City, from 1750 to the Beginning of Our Own Time*. New York: Knopf, distributed by Random House, 1987.

Benson, Lee. *The Concept of Jacksonian Democracy: New York as a Test Case*. Princeton, N.J.: Princeton University Press, 1961.

Berle, Adolf A. *Latin America—Diplomacy and Reality*. New York: Published for the Council on Foreign Relations by Harper and Row, 1962.

Bermúdez Miral, Oscar. *El drama político de Chile*. Santiago: Editorial Tegualda, 1947.

Bernstein Carabantes, Enrique. *Recuerdos de un diplomático: Haciendo camino 1933–1957*. Santiago: Editorial Andrés Bello, 1984.

Berwick, Keith B. *The Federal Age, 1789–1829: America in the Process of Becoming*. Washington, D.C.: Service Center for Teachers of History, 1961.

*Biennial Report . . . Secretary of the State of Indiana for the Two Years Ending October 31, 1904 and 1906*. Indianapolis: Wm. B. Burford, 1904, 1906.

Bolloten, Burnett. *The Grand Camouflage: The Communist Conspiracy in the Spanish Civil War.* New York: Praeger, 1968.

_____. *The Spanish Civil War: Revolution and Counterrevolution.* Chapel Hill: University of North Carolina Press, 1991.

Boomhower, Ray E. *Jacob Piatt Dunn, Jr.: A Life in History and Politics, 1855–1924.* Indianapolis: Indiana Historical Society, 1997.

Bowers, Claude G. *Las aventuras españolas de Washington Irving.* Santiago: Zig-Zag, 1946.

_____. *Beveridge and the Progressive Era.* Boston: Houghton Mifflin, 1932.

_____. *Chile through Embassy Windows, 1939–1953.* New York: Simon and Schuster, 1958.

_____. Introduction to *The United States and the Spanish Civil War*, by F. Jay Taylor. New York: Bookman Associates, 1956.

_____. Introduction to *Zachary Taylor: Soldier of the Republic*, by Holman Hamilton. Indianapolis and New York: Bobbs-Merrill, 1941

_____. *The Irish Orators: A History of Ireland's Fight for Freedom.* Indianapolis: Bobbs-Merrill, 1916.

_____. *Jefferson and Hamilton: The Struggle for Democracy in America.* Boston: Houghton Mifflin, 1925.

_____. *Jefferson in Power: The Death Struggle of the Federalists.* Boston: Houghton Mifflin, 1936.

_____. *The Life of John Worth Kern.* Indianapolis: Hollenbeck Press, 1918.

_____. *Ma mission en Espagne, 1933–1939.* Paris: Flammarion, 1956.

_____. *Mi misión en Chile.* Santiago: Editorial del Pacífico, 1957.

_____. *Mi misión en España.* Mexico City: Editorial Grijalbo, 1955.

_____. *Missione in Spagna, 1933–1939: Prova generale della seconda guerre mondiale.* Milan: Feltrinelli Editore, 1958.

_____. *My Life: The Memoirs of Claude Bowers.* New York: Simon and Schuster, 1962.

_____. *My Mission to Spain: Watching the Rehearsal for World War II.* New York: Simon and Schuster, 1954.

_____. *The Party Battles of the Jackson Period*. Boston: Houghton Mifflin, 1922.

_____. *Pierre Vergniaud: Voice of the French Revolution*. New York: Macmillan, 1950.

_____. *The Spanish Adventures of Washington Irving*. Boston: Houghton Mifflin, 1940.

_____. *The Tragic Era: The Revolution after Lincoln*. Boston: Houghton Mifflin, 1929.

_____. *The Young Jefferson, 1743–1789*. Boston: Houghton Mifflin, 1945.

Braeman, John. *Albert J. Beveridge: American Nationalist*. Chicago: University of Chicago Press, 1971.

Briggs, Ellis O. *Proud Servant: The Memoirs of a Career Ambassador*. Kent, Ohio: Kent State University Press, 1998.

Broué, Pierre, and Emile Témime. *The Revolution and the Civil War in Spain*. Cambridge, Mass.: MIT Press, 1972.

Bullitt, William C. *The Bullitt Mission to Moscow*. New York: B. W. Huebsch, 1919.

Butland, Gilbert J. *Chile: An Outline of Its Geography, Economics, and Politics*. London: Royal Institute of International Affairs, 1951.

Butler, Nicholas Murray. *Across the Busy Years: Recollections and Reflections*. New York: C. Scribner's Sons, 1939.

_____. *Why Should We Change Our Form of Government?: Studies in Practical Politics*. New York: Charles Scribner's Sons, 1912.

Carr, E. H. *The Comintern and the Spanish Civil War*. New York: Pantheon Books, 1984.

Carr, Raymond. *The Spanish Tragedy: The Civil War in Perspective*. London: Weidenfeld and Nicholson, 1977.

Carroll, Peter N. *The Odyssey of the Abraham Lincoln Brigade: Americans in the Spanish Civil War*. Stanford, Calif.: Stanford University Press, 1994.

Cattell, David T. *Communism and the Spanish Civil War*. Berkeley: University of California Press, 1955.

_____. *Soviet Diplomacy and the Spanish Civil War*. Berkeley: University of California Press, 1957.

Caulfield, Max. *The Easter Rebellion.* New York: Holt Rinehart and Winston, 1963.

Chile. Ministerio de Relaciones Exteriores. *Memoria del Ministerio de Relaciones Exteriores.* . . . 1942, 1943, 1945, 1947. Santiago.

Clark, Thomas D. Introduction to *Kentucky Profiles: Biographies in Honor of Holman Hamilton,* edited by James C. Klotter and Peter J. Sehlinger. Frankfort: Kentucky Historical Society, 1982.

Coletta, Paolo E. *William Jennings Bryan.* 3 vols. Lincoln: University of Nebraska Press, 1964–69.

Collier, Simon, and William F. Sater. *A History of Chile, 1808–1994.* Cambridge: Cambridge University Press, 1996.

Collins, Patrick W. *Gustave Weigel: A Pioneer of Reform.* Collegeville, Minn.: Liturgical Press, 1992.

Communist Party of Chile. *Ricardo Fonseca: Combatiente ejemplar.* Santiago: N.p., [1952].

Coverdale, John F. *Italian Intervention in the Spanish Civil War.* Princeton, N.J.: Princeton University Press, 1972.

Cox, James M. *Journey through My Years.* New York: Simon and Schuster, 1946.

Croly, Herbert D. *The Promise of American Life.* Indianapolis: Bobbs-Merrill, 1965.

Cummins, Cedric S. *Indiana Public Opinion and the World War, 1914–1917. Indiana Historical Collections,* vol. 28. Indianapolis: Indiana Historical Bureau, 1945.

Dallek, Robert. *Franklin D. Roosevelt and American Foreign Policy, 1932–1945.* New York: Oxford University Press, 1979.

Daniels, Jonathan. *They Will Be Heard: America's Crusading Newspaper Editors.* New York: McGraw-Hill, 1965.

Democratic National Committee. *Official Report of the Proceedings of the Democratic National Convention . . . 1908.* Chicago: Press of the Western Newspaper Union, 1908.

Dodd, William E. *Ambassador Dodd's Diary, 1933–1938.* Edited by William E. Dodd, Jr., and Martha Dodd. New York: Harcourt, Brace, 1941.

Douglas, Ann. *Terrible Honesty: Mongrel Manhattan in the 1920's.* New York: Farrar, Straus, and Giroux, 1995.

Drake, Paul W. *Socialism and Populism in Chile, 1932–52.* Urbana: University of Illinois Press, 1978.

Dreiser, Theodore. *A Hoosier Holiday.* New York: John Lane Co., 1916.

Du Bois, W. E. B. *Black Reconstruction in America: An Essay toward a History of the Part Which Black Folk Played in the Attempt to Reconstruct Democracy in America, 1860–1880.* New York: Russell and Russell, 1935.

Duggan, Laurence. *The Americas: The Search for Hemispheric Security.* New York: Holt, 1949.

Dunning, William A. *Reconstruction: Political and Economic, 1865–1877.* New York: Harper Brothers, 1907.

Eckrich, Arthur A. *The Decline of American Liberalism.* New York: Citadel Press, 1955.

Eldot, Paula. *Governor Alfred E. Smith: The Politician as Reformer.* New York: Garland, 1983.

Elkins, Stanley, and Eric McKitrick. *The Age of Federalism.* New York: Oxford University Press, 1993.

Ellis, Joseph J. *American Sphinx: The Character of Thomas Jefferson.* New York: Alfred A. Knopf, 1997.

Ellsworth, P. T. *Chile: An Economy in Transition.* New York: Macmillan, 1945.

Emery, Edwin E., and Henry Ladd Smith. *The Press and America.* Englewood Cliffs, N.J.: Prentice-Hall, 1954.

Fadely, James P. *Thomas Taggart: Public Servant, Political Boss, 1856–1929.* Indianapolis: Indiana Historical Society, 1997.

Farley, James A. *Jim Farley's Story: The Roosevelt Years.* New York: Whittlesey House, 1948.

Fermandois H., Joaquín. *Abismo y cemiento: Gustavo Ross y las relaciones entre Chile y Estados Unidos, 1932–1938.* Santiago: Ediciones Universidad Católica de Chile, 1996.

Fischer, Louis. *The Life of Lenin.* New York: Harper and Row, 1964.

Flynn, Edward J. *You're the Boss.* New York: Viking Press, 1947.

Foner, Eric. *Reconstruction: America's Unfinished Revolution, 1863–1877.* New York: Harper and Row, 1988.

Francis, Michael J. *The Limits of Hegemony: United States Relations with Argentina and Chile during World War II*. Notre Dame, Ind.: University of Notre Dame Press, 1977.

Franklin, John Hope. *Reconstruction: After the Civil War*. Chicago: University of Chicago Press, 1961.

Freidel, Frank. *Franklin D. Roosevelt: A Rendezvous with Destiny*. Boston: Little, Brown, 1990.

Gaddis, John Lewis. *Strategies of Containment: A Critical Appraisal of Postwar American Security Policy*. New York: Oxford University Press, 1982.

Galdames, Luis. *A History of Chile*. Trans. Isaac Joslin Cox. New York: Russell and Russell, 1964.

Gellman, Irwin F. *Good Neighbor Diplomacy: United States Policies in Latin America*. Baltimore: Johns Hopkins University Press, 1979.

_____. *Secret Affairs: Franklin Roosevelt, Cordell Hull and Sumner Welles*. Baltimore: Johns Hopkins University Press, 1995.

Gil, Federico G. *The Political System of Chile*. Boston: Houghton Mifflin, 1966.

González Videla, Gabriel. *Memorias*. 2 vols. Santiago: Editora Gabriela Mistral, 1975.

Goodrich, Chauncey A. *Select British Eloquence. . . .* New York: Harper and Brothers, 1852.

Haines, John F. *History of Hamilton County, Indiana: Her People, Industries and Institutions*. Indianapolis: B. F. Bowen, 1915.

Halperin, Ernst. *Nationalism and Communism in Chile*. Cambridge: MIT Press, 1965.

Hamilton, Holman, and Gayle Thornbrough, eds. *Indianapolis in the "Gay Nineties": High School Diaries of Claude G. Bowers*. Indianapolis: Indiana Historical Society, 1964.

Harbaugh, William H. *Lawyer's Lawyer: The Life of John W. Davis*. New York: Oxford University Press, 1973.

_____. *Power and Responsibility: The Life and Times of Theodore Roosevelt*. New York: Farrar, Straus, and Cudahy, 1961.

Hilton, Stanley E. *Hitler's Secret War in South America, 1939–1945: German Military Espionage and Allied Counterespionage in Brazil*. Baton Rouge: Louisiana State University Press, 1981.

Hoehling, A. A., and Mary Hoehling. *The Last Voyage of the Lusitania*. New York: Holt, 1956.

Hofstadter, Richard. *The Progressive Historians: Turner, Beard, Parrington*. New York: Alfred A. Knopf, 1968.

Hosmer, Charles B., Jr. *Presence of the Past: A History of the Preservation Movement in the United States before Williamsburg*. New York: G. P. Putnam's Sons, 1965.

Hull, Cordell. *The Memoirs of Cordell Hull*. 2 vols. New York: Macmillan, 1948.

Hutchinson, Louise Daniel. *Anna Cooper: A Voice from the South*. Washington: Published for the Anacostia Neighborhood Museum of the Smithsonian Institution by the Smithsonian Institution Press, 1981.

[Hyman, Max R., ed.]. *Hyman's Hand Book of Indianapolis*. Indianapolis: M. R. Hyman Co., 1897.

Ickes, Harold L. *The Autobiography of a Curmudgeon*. New York: Reynal and Hitchcock, 1943.

_____. *The Secret Diary of Harold L. Ickes*. 3 vols. New York: Simon and Schuster, 1953–54.

*Indianapolis Directory for 1892–1898*. Indianapolis, 1892–98.

Israel, Fred L. *Nevada's Key Pittman*. Lincoln: University of Nebraska Press, 1963.

Jackson, Gabriel. *Historian's Quest*. New York: Alfred A. Knopf, 1969.

_____. *The Spanish Republic and the Civil War, 1931–1939*. Princeton, N.J.: Princeton University Press, 1965.

Johnson, Hallett. *Diplomatic Memoirs: Serious and Frivolous*. New York: Vantage Press, 1963.

*Journal of the House of Representatives of the State of Indiana during the Sixty-Seventh Session of the General Assembly*. Indianapolis: Wm. Burford, 1911.

Juliá Díaz, Santos. *Orígines del frente popular en España (1934–1936)*. Madrid: Siglo Veintiuno Editores, 1979.

Kirby, Jack Temple. *Media-Made Dixie: The South in the American Imagination*. Athens: University of Georgia Press, 1986.

Klotter, James C. *William Goebel: The Politics of Wrath*. Lexington: University Press of Kentucky, 1977.

La Feber, Walter. *America, Russia, and the Cold War, 1945–1975.* 3d ed. New York: Wiley, 1976.

Landis, Arthur H. *The Abraham Lincoln Brigade.* New York: Citadel Press, 1967.

Lash, Joseph P. *Eleanor: The Years Alone.* New York: W. W. Norton, 1972.

Lichtman, Allan J. *Prejudice and the Old Politics: The Presidential Election of 1928.* Chapel Hill: University of North Carolina Press, 1979.

Lieuwen, Edwin. *U.S. Policy in Latin America: A Short History.* New York: Frederick A. Praeger, 1965.

Lingeman, Richard. *Theodore Dreiser: An American Journey, 1908–1945.* New York: G. P. Putnam's Sons, 1990.

Link, Arthur S. *Wilson.* 5 vols. Princeton, N.J.: Princeton University Press, 1947–65.

Little, Douglas. "Claude Bowers and his Mission to Spain: The Diplomacy of a Jeffersonian Democrat." In *U.S. Diplomats in Europe, 1919–1941*, edited by Kenneth Paul Jones, 127–46. Santa Barbara, Calif.: ABC-Clio, 1981.

————. *Malevolent Neutrality: The United States, Great Britain, and the Origins of the Spanish Civil War.* Ithaca, N.Y.: Cornell University Press, 1985.

Lodge, Henry Cabot. *Alexander Hamilton.* Boston: Houghton Mifflin, 1882.

Long, Breckinridge. *The War Diary of Breckinridge Long.* Edited by Fred L. Israel. Lincoln: University of Nebraska Press, 1966.

Loveman, Brian. *Chile: The Legacy of Hispanic Capitalism.* New York: Oxford University Press, 1979.

Lyon, Cecil. *The Lyon's Share.* New York: Vantage Press, 1973.

McDonald, Forrest. *Alexander Hamilton: A Biography.* New York: W. W. Norton, 1979.

McMaster, John Bach. *History of the People of the United States: From the Revolution to the Civil War.* 8 vols. New York: D. Appleton, 1883–1913.

Mecham, J. Lloyd. *The United States and Inter-American Security, 1899–1960.* Austin: University of Texas Press, 1961.

Meneses Ciuffardi, Emilio. *El factor naval en la relaciones entre Chile y los Estados Unidos (1881–1951)*. Santiago: Ediciones Pedagógicas Chilenas, 1989.

Miller, John C. *The Federalist Era, 1789–1801*. New York: Harper and Row, 1960.

Moley, Raymond. *After Seven Years*. New York: Harper and Brothers, 1939.

Moreno, Francisco José. *Legitimacy and Stability in Latin America: A Study of Chilean Political Culture*. New York: New York University Press, 1969.

Morison, Samuel Eliot. *Three Centuries of Harvard, 1636–1936*. Cambridge, Mass.: Harvard University Press, 1936.

Mott, Frank L. *American Journalism: A History, 1690–1960*. New York: Macmillan, 1962.

O'Connor, Richard. *The First Hurrah: A Biography of Alfred E. Smith*. New York: G. P. Putnam's Sons, 1970.

Oleszek, Walter J. "John W. Kern: Portrait of a Floor Leader." In *First Among Equals: Outstanding Senate Leaders in the Twentieth Century*, edited by Richard A. Barker and Roger H. Davidson, 7–37. Washington, D.C.: Congressional Quarterly, 1991.

Orwell, George. *Homage to Catalonia*. New York: Harcourt, Brace, 1952.

Payne, Stanley G. *Falange: A History of Spanish Fascism*. Stanford, Calif.: Stanford University Press, 1961.

_____. *Franco's Spain*. New York: Thomas Y. Crowell, 1967.

_____. *The Spanish Revolution*. New York: W. W. Norton, 1970.

Pereira Salas, Eugenio. "Recuerdos de veinte años." In *Instituto Chileno-Norteamericano de Cultura, 1938–1958*, pp. 6–16. Santiago: N.p., 1958.

Perry, Elisabeth I. *Belle Moskowitz: Feminine Politics and the Exercise of Power in the Age of Alfred E. Smith*. New York: Oxford University Press, 1987.

Pessen, Edward. *Jacksonian America: Society, Personality, and Politics*. Homewood, Ill.: Dorsey Press, 1969.

Peterson, Merrill. *The Jefferson Image in the American Mind*. New York: Oxford University Press, 1960.

Petras, James. *Politics and Social Forces in Chilean Development.* Berkeley: University of California Press, 1970.

Phillips, Clifton J. *Indiana in Transition, 1880–1920: The Emergence of an Industrial Commonwealth. The History of Indiana,* vol. 4. Indianapolis: Indiana Historical Society and Indiana Historical Bureau, 1968.

Pike, Fredrick B. *Chile and the United States, 1880–1962: The Emergence of Chile's Social Crisis and the Challenge to United States Diplomacy.* Notre Dame, Ind.: University of Notre Dame Press, 1963.

_____. *FDR's Good Neighbor Policy: Sixty Years of Generally Gentle Chaos.* Austin: University of Texas Press, 1995.

Preston, Paul. *The Coming of the Spanish Civil War: Reform, Reaction and Revolution in the Second Republic, 1931–1939.* New York: Harper and Row, 1978.

_____. "The Creation of the Popular Front in Spain." In *The Popular Front in Europe,* edited by Helen Graham and Paul Preston, 84–105. New York: St. Martin's Press, 1978.

_____. *Franco: A Biography.* New York: Basic Books, 1994.

_____. *The Spanish Civil War, 1936–1939.* Chicago: Dorsey Press, 1986.

Puzzo, Dante A. *Spain and the Great Powers, 1936–1941.* New York: Columbia University Press, 1962.

Ramos Oliveira, Antonio. *Politics, Economics and Men of Modern Spain: 1808–1946.* London: Arno Press, 1946.

Rauch, Basil. *Roosevelt from Munich to Pearl Harbor: A Study in the Creation of a Foreign Policy.* New York: Creative Age Press, 1950.

Richardson, R. Dan. *Comintern Army: The International Brigades and the Spanish Civil War.* Lexington: University Press of Kentucky, 1982.

Roosevelt, Eleanor. *This I Remember.* New York: Harper, 1949.

Roosevelt, Franklin D. *Franklin D. Roosevelt and Foreign Affairs.* Edited by Edgar B. Nixon. 3 vols. Cambridge, Mass.: Belknap Press of Harvard University, 1969.

_____. *The Public Papers and Addresses of Franklin D. Roosevelt.* 13 vols. New York: Russell and Russell, 1969.

Rose, Ernestine Bradford. *The Circle: "The Center of Our Universe."* Indiana Historical Society Publications, vol. 18, no. 4. Indianapolis: Indiana Historical Society, 1957.

Sater, William F. *Chile and the United States: Empires in Conflict.* Athens: University of Georgia Press, 1990.

Schapsmeier, Edward L., and Frederick H. Schapsmeier. *Walter Lippmann: Philosopher-Journalist.* Washington, D.C.: Public Affairs Press, 1969.

Schlesinger, Arthur M., Jr. *The Age of Roosevelt: The Crisis of the Old Order, 1919–1933.* Boston: Houghton Mifflin, 1957.

Sedwick, Frank. *The Tragedy of Manuel Azaña and the Fate of the Spanish Republic.* Columbus: Ohio State University Press, 1963

Sehlinger, Peter J. "John W. Kern: A Hoosier Progressive." In *Gentlemen from Indiana: National Party Candidates, 1836–1940*, edited by Ralph D. Gray, 189–217. *Indiana Historical Collections*, vol. 50. Indianapolis: Indiana Historical Bureau, 1977.

Seldon, Mary E. "George Julian: A Political Independent." In *Gentlemen from Indiana: National Party Candidates, 1836–1940*, edited by Ralph D. Gray, 29–54. *Indiana Historical Collections*, vol. 50. Indianapolis: Indiana Historical Bureau, 1977.

Shoemaker, Rebecca Shepherd. "James D. Williams: Indiana's Farmer Governor." In *Their Infinite Variety: Essays on Indiana Politicians*, edited by Robert G. Barrows, 193–221. Indianapolis: Indiana Historical Bureau, 1981.

Sievers, Harry J. *Benjamin Harrison.* 3 vols. Chicago: H. Regnery Co., 1952–68.

Smith, Gaddis. *The Last Years of the Monroe Doctrine, 1945–1993.* New York: Hill and Wang, 1994.

Smith, Richard Norton. *The Colonel: The Life and Legend of Robert R. McCormick, 1880–1955.* Boston: Houghton Mifflin, 1997.

Stampp, Kenneth. *The Era of Reconstruction, 1865–1877.* New York: Knopf, 1965.

Steel, Ronald. *Walter Lippmann and the American Century.* Boston: Little, Brown, 1980.

Stevenson, John Reese. *The Chilean Popular Front.* Philadelphia: University of Pennsylvania Press, 1942.

Stevenson, William. *A Man Called Intrepid: The Secret War*. New York: Harcourt Brace Jovanovich, 1976.

Stuart, Graham H. *The Department of State: A History of Its Organization, Procedure, and Personnel*. New York: Macmillan, 1949.

_____, and James L. Tigner. *Latin America and the United States*. 6th ed. Englewood Cliffs, N.J.: Prentice-Hall, 1975.

Stuckey, W. J. *The Pulitzer Prize Novels: A Critical Backward Look*. Norman: University of Oklahoma Press, 1966.

Swanberg, W. A. *Citizen Hearst: A Biography of William Randolph Hearst*. New York: Charles Scribner's Sons, 1962.

_____. *Dreiser*. New York: Charles Scribner's Sons, 1965.

Taylor, F. Jay. *The United States and the Spanish Civil War*. New York: Bookman Associates, 1956.

Terre Haute, Ind. *City of Terre Haute . . . : An Index to the Common Council from January 1, 1908 to 1909 and . . . from January 1, 1910 to January 1911*. Terre Haute, 1909, 1911.

_____. *The General Ordinances of the City of Terre Haute . . . Revision of 1906*. Terre Haute, 1906.

*Terre Haute City Directory*. Terre Haute, 1906.

Thalheimer, M. E. *The Eclectic History of the United States*. Cincinnati: Van Antwerp, Bragg and Co., 1881.

Thomas, Charles M. *Thomas R. Marshall: Hoosier Statesman*. Oxford, Ohio: Mississippi Valley Press, 1939.

Thomas, Hugh. *The Spanish Civil War*. New York: Harper and Brothers, 1961.

Traina, Richard P. *American Diplomacy and the Spanish Civil War*. Bloomington: Indiana University Press, 1968.

Tuñón de Lara, Manuel. *La España del siglo XX*. Vol. 2. *De la Segunda República a la guerra civil (1931–1936)*. Barcelona: Laia, 1974.

_____. "Orígenes lejanos y próximos." In *La guerra civil española 50 años después*, edited by Manuel Tuñón de Lara et al., 7–44. Barcelona: Editorial Labor, 1985.

United States Census Office. *Compendium of the Eleventh Census: 1890*. Washington, D.C.: Government Printing Office, 1892.

_____. *Twelfth Census of the United States . . . 1900. Population*. Part 1. Washington, D.C.: Government Printing Office, 1901.

United States Congress. *Congressional Record.* 1911, 1913, 1916, 1937. Washington, D.C.: Government Printing Office.

United States Department of State. *Foreign Relations of the United States.* 1933 (1949), 1943 (1965), 1945 (1969), 1951 (1979). Washington, D.C.: Government Printing Office.

United States Federal Bureau of Investigation. *Chile Today: March 1943.* Washington, D.C.: Government Printing Office, 1943.

Vandenberg, Arthur H. *The Greatest American: Alexander Hamilton.* New York: G. P. Putnam's Sons, 1921.

Viñas, Angel. "Los condicionantes internacionales." In *La guerra civil española 50 años después*, edited by Manuel Tuñón de Lara et al., 176–91. Barcelona: Editorial Labor, 1985.

Ward, Geoffrey C. *A First-Class Temperament: The Emergence of Franklin Roosevelt.* New York: Harper and Row, 1989.

Warren, Harris G. *Hoover and the Great Depression.* New York: Oxford University Press, 1967.

Weil, Martin. *A Pretty Good Club: The Founding Fathers of the U.S. Foreign Service.* New York: W. W. Norton, 1978.

Welles, Benjamin. *Sumner Welles: FDR's Global Strategist.* New York: St. Martin's Press, 1997.

Welles, Sumner. *The Time for Decision.* New York: Harper and Brothers, 1944.

Whealey, Robert H. *Hitler and Spain: The Nazi Role in the Spanish Civil War, 1936–1939.* Lexington: University Press of Kentucky, 1989.

Whitaker, John T. *Americas to the South.* New York: Macmillan, 1939.

White, Graham J. *FDR and the Press.* Chicago: University of Chicago Press, 1979.

Wittke, Carl. *German Americans and the World War: With Special Emphasis on Ohio's German-Language Press. Ohio Historical Collections*, vol. 5. Columbus: The Ohio State Archaeological and Historical Society, 1936. Reprint, Englewood, N.J.: J. S. Ozer, 1974.

Wood, Bryce. *The Making of the Good Neighbor Policy.* New York: Columbia University Press, 1961.

Woodward, C. Vann. *The Strange Career of Jim Crow.* 3d rev. ed. New York: Oxford University Press, 1974.

Yrarrázaval Concha, Eduardo. *América Latina en la guerra fría.* Santiago: Nascimento, 1959.

## Articles, Pamphlets, and Speeches

Abbott, Roger S. "The Role of Contemporary Political Parties in Chile." *American Political Science Review* 45 (June 1951): 450–63.

Barnard, Andreas. "Chilean Communists, Radical Presidents and Chilean Relations with the United States, 1940–1947." *Journal of Latin American Studies* 13 (1981): 347–74.

Blasier, Cole. "Chile: A Communist Battleground." *Political Science Quarterly* 65 (Sept. 1950): 353–75.

Bowers, Claude G. *The Democracy of Woodrow Wilson: An Address.* Washington: Benedict Printing, [1913].

————. *Jeffersonian Democracy.* Indianapolis: Branford Press, [1901].

————. *John Tyler: Address by Hon. Claude G. Bowers.* Richmond, Va.: Richmond Press, 1932.

————. "Keynote." *The Political News* 10 (July 1928): 1–4.

————. *Making Democracy a Reality: Jefferson, Jackson, and Polk.* Memphis: Memphis State Press, 1954.

————. "Republicanism vs. the People." *The Jeffersonian Democrat* (Washington, D.C.) 2 (Mar. 1900): 710–20.

————. *A Truce to Negro Colonization.* Indianapolis: Bradford Press, [1913].

————. *Twenty Years of New Deal and Fair Deal Achievements— And This They Call Treason!* Special Bulletin No. 4. New York State C.I.O. Council. New York, 1954.

————. "What Is Republicanism?" *The Jeffersonian Democrat* (Washington, D.C.) 2 (Jan. 1900): 549–62.

Coles, Harry L. "Some Recent Interpretations of Jeffersonian America." In *Lectures, 1969–1970,* pp. 62–89. Indianapolis: Indiana Historical Society, 1970.

Drake, Paul W. "The Chilean Socialist Party and Coalition Politics, 1932–1946." *Hispanic American Historical Review* 53 (Nov. 1973): 619–43.

Grace, Peter J. "The Private Investor in Latin America Today." In "Economics and Political Trends," edited by Sigmund Diamond. *Proceedings of the Academy of Political Science* 27 (May 1964): 42–51.

Hamilton, Holman. "Before 'The Tragic Era': Claude Bowers's Earlier Attitudes toward Reconstruction." *Mid-America* 55 (Oct. 1973): 235–44.

_____. "Clio with Style." *Journal of Southern History* 46 (Feb. 1980): 3–16.

Jessner, Sabine. "Claude G. Bowers: New Deal Advocate of Spanish-American Commerce, 1933–1939." *Proceedings of the Indiana Academy of the Social Sciences*, 3d ser., 20 (1985): 98–104.

_____, and Peter J. Sehlinger. "Claude G. Bowers: A Partisan Hoosier." *Indiana Magazine of History* 83 (Sept. 1987): 217–43.

Kelly, Fred L. "Ambassador as Democrat." *Esquire* (Apr. 1937): 62, 219–20.

Knight, Oliver. "Claude G. Bowers, Historian." *Indiana Magazine of History* 52 (Sept. 1956): 247–68.

Kofas, Jon V. "Developmentalism and Hemispheric Integration during World War II: U.S. Foreign Economic Policy and Chile's Development Corporation." *International Third World Studies Journal and Review* 6 (1994): 20–36.

_____. "Latin American Foreign Debt and Dependent Capitalism during the Cold War." *Proceedings of the Indiana Academy of the Social Sciences*, 3d ser., 50 (1960): 46–57.

_____. "The Politics of Foreign Debt: The IMF, the World Bank, and U.S. Foreign Policy in Chile, 1946–1952." *Journal of Developing Areas* 31 (winter 1997): 157–82.

Kuper, Theodore Fred. "Collecting Monticello." *Manuscripts* 7 (summer 1955): 215–26.

Kyvig, David E. "History as Present Politics: Claude Bowers' *The Tragic Era*." *Indiana Magazine of History* 73 (Mar. 1977): 17–31.

Little, Douglas. "Twenty Years of Turmoil: ITT, the State Department, and Spain, 1924–1944." *Business History Review* 53 (winter 1979): 449–72.

Miles, Edwin A. "The Keynote Speech at National Conventions." *Quarterly Journal of Speech* 46 (Feb. 1960): 26–31.

Montgomery, Keith S. "Thomas R. Marshall's Victory in the Election of 1908." *Indiana Magazine of History* 53 (June 1957): 147–66.

Peterson, Merrill. "Bowers, Roosevelt, and the 'New Jefferson.'" *The Virginia Quarterly Review* 34 (autumn 1958): 530–43.

Ramage, James A. *Holman Hamilton: A Biographical Sketch.* Pamphlet published on the occasion of his retirement. Lexington, Ky., 1975.

Rice, J. M. "The Public Schools of St. Louis and Indianapolis." *The Forum* 14 (Dec. 1892): 437–51.

Roberts, George C. "Claude G. Bowers: Hoosier Historian and the Politics of Yesterday, Today, and Tomorrow." *Proceedings of the Indiana Academy of the Social Sciences*, 3d ser., 17 (1982): 61–69.

_____. "Woodrow Wilson, John W. Kern and the 1916 Indiana Election: Defeat of the Senate Majority Leader." *Presidential Studies Quarterly* 10 (winter 1980): 63–73.

Scharlotti, Bradford W. "The Hoosier Journalist and the Hooded Order: Indiana Press Reaction to the Ku Klux Klan in Indiana in the 1920s." *Journalism History* 15 (winter 1988): 122–31.

Sehlinger, Peter J. "Personality, Politics, and Diplomacy: Claude G. Bowers and the State Department, 1933–1939." *Proceedings of the Indiana Academy of the Social Sciences*, 3d ser., 36 (1991): 10–19.

Spencer, Thomas T. "'Old Democrats' and New Deal Politics: Claude G. Bowers, James A. Farley, and the Changing Democratic Party, 1933–1940." *Indiana Magazine of History* 91 (Mar. 1996): 26–45.

Welles, Sumner. "Twenty-Ninth National Foreign Trade Convention." *Department of State Bulletin.* 10 Oct. 1943.

Wise, Gene. "Political 'Reality' in Recent American Scholarship: Progressives versus Symbolists." *American Quarterly* 19 (summer 1967): 303–28.

## Unpublished Works

Fermandois H., Joaquín. "Cobre, guerra e industrialización en Chile, 1939–1945." In "Colección Estudios Históricos" of the Comisión Chilena del Cobre. Santiago, 1992.

————. "Guerra y hegemonía 1939–1943: Un aspecto de las relaciones chileno-norteamericanas." "Estudios Históricos" 10, Instituto de Historia, Universidad Católica de Chile, Santiago, 1989.

Haughton, Virginia F. "John Worth Kern and Wilson's New Freedom: A Study of a Senate Majority Leader." Ph.D. diss., University of Kentucky, 1973.

Moore, Leonard Joseph. "White Protestant Nationalism in the 1920's: The Ku Klux Klan in Indiana." Ph.D. diss., UCLA, 1986.

Mosher, Rollo E. "Tom Marshall's Term as Governor." M.A. thesis, Indiana University, Bloomington, 1932.

O'Brien, Anthony F. "The Politics of Dependency: A Case Study of Dependency—Chile, 1938–45." Ph.D. diss. University of Notre Dame, 1977.

Potashnik, Michael. "Nacismo: National Socialism in Chile, 1932–1938." Ph.D. diss., UCLA, 1974.

Rissler, Herbert J. "Charles Warren Fairbanks: Conservative Hoosier." Ph.D. diss., Indiana University, Bloomington, 1961.

Siegel, Adam B. "The Tip of the Spear: The U.S. Navy and the Spanish Civil War." Unpublished MSS, 1992. Copy, Holman Hamilton Papers, Division of Special Collections and Archives of the Margaret I. King Library, University of Kentucky, Lexington.

Silvert, Kalman. "The Chilean Development Corporation." Ph.D. diss., University of Pennsylvania, 1948.

Sondhaus, Lawrence T. "The Non-Intervention Committee and the Spanish Civil War." M.A. thesis, University of Virginia, Charlottesville, 1982.

Thomas, Jack. "United States Ambassador to Chile Claude Bowers and the State Department during World War II." Unpublished MSS, n.d. Copy, Holman Hamilton Papers, Division of Special Collections and Archives of the Margaret I. King Library, University of Kentucky, Lexington.


### Newspapers, Magazines, and Journals

*ABC* (Madrid), 1935.
*American Historical Review.*
*The American Review of Reviews*, 1916.
*Annals of the American Academy of Political and Social Sciences.*
*Arriba* (Madrid), 1947.
*The Atlantic Monthly*, 1927.
*Baltimore Evening Sun*, 1936.
*Baltimore Sun*, 1933.
*Boston Evening Transcript*, 1916, 1929.
*Boston Globe*, 1936.
*Boston Herald*, 1927.
*Le Canard Enchaîné* (Paris), 1956.
*Catholic World*, 1916.
*Chicago Evening Post*, 1923.
*Chicago Tribune*, 1916, 1928, 1958.
*Christian Science Monitor* (Boston), 1940, 1958, 1963.
*Commonweal*, 1954.
*Current History*, 1929.
*The Dial*, 1916.
*El Diario Ilustrado* (Santiago), 1951, 1957.
*Entretelones* (Santiago), 1957.
*Le Figaro Littéraire* (Paris), 1956.
*Fort Wayne Journal-Gazette*, 1917–23, 1926, 1953, 1958.
*Greencastle Star and Democrat*, 1904.

*Hispanic American Historical Review.*

*Historical Outlook,* 1929.

*La Hora* (Santiago), 1945.

*El Imparcial* (Santiago), 1942, 1951.

*The Independent,* 1915.

*Indiana Daily Times* (Indianapolis), 1916.

*Indiana Magazine of History.*

*Indianapolis Journal,* 1900–1901.

*Indianapolis News,* 1900–1902, 1910, 1954, 1963.

*Indianapolis Press,* 1900–1901.

*Indianapolis Sentinel,* 1900–1902.

*Indianapolis Star,* 1922, 1929, 1931, 1949–50, 1958.

*Indianapolis Sun,* 1901–1902.

*Indianapolis Times,* 1958.

*Journal of Negro History.*

*Journal of Southern History.*

*Lebanon Patriot,* 1889–95.

*Lebanon Pioneer,* 1888, 1902.

*Literary Digest,* 1915.

*London Times,* 1950.

*Louisville Courier-Journal,* 1936.

*Manchester Guardian,* 1956.

*Memphis Commercial Appeal,* 1936.

*El Mercurio* (Santiago), 1946–47, 1949, 1954, 1956–57, 1974.

*Mississippi Valley Historical Review.*

*La Nación* (Santiago), 1936, 1943, 1946, 1951, 1957.

*The Nation,* 1929, 1945–46, 1958.

*The New Republic,* 1929.

*Newsweek,* 1945.

*New York Evening Journal,* 1931–33.

*New York Evening Post,* 1929.

*New York Evening World,* 1923–31.

*New York Herald Tribune,* 1929, 1932–33, 1936, 1940, 1954, 1958.

*New York Journal,* 1924.

*New York Times,* 1916, 1928–29, 1932–33, 1940–41, 1950, 1954,
    1957–58, 1987.

*New York Tribune*, 1922.
*New York World Telegram*, 1935.
*The New Yorker*, 1954, 1956.
*La Opinión* (Santiago), 1942.
*The Outlook*, 1908, 1915.
*The Outlook and Independent*, 1929.
*The Political News*, 1928.
*Raleigh (N.C.) News and Observer*, 1923, 1928.
*Richmond (Ind.) Evening Item*, 1898.
*Rockville Republican*, 1906.
*Rockville Tribune*, 1904, 1906.
*St. Louis Post Dispatch*, 1926.
*San Francisco Chronicle*, 1958.
*Saturday Review of Literature*, 1929, 1939–40, 1950, 1954, 1958.
*El Siglo* (Santiago), 1942.
*El Sol* (Madrid), 1933, 1936.
*South Pacific Mail* (Santiago), 1947, 1949, 1957.
*Terre Haute Gazette*, 1904.
*Terre Haute Saturday Spectator*, 1906, 1908.
*Terre Haute Star*, 1904–6, 1911.
*Terre Haute Tribune*, 1905, 1908, 1911–17, 1922.
*Terre Haute Tribune-Star*, 1958.
*Time*, 1940, 1944, 1949.
*Virginia Historical Quarterly*.
*Washington Daily News*, 1952.
*Washington Post*, 1958.
*William and Mary Quarterly*.
*Yale Review*.

# Index

275; clerks for Bobbs-Merrill, 38; reads
law, 38; moves to Terre Haute, 38, 53;
salary and finances, 38, 52, 54, 99, 102,
144, 157, 254; adherent of progressive
ideas, 42–43, 46, 172–73, 177, 271,
275; political ideals, 42–43, 46, 138,
172–73; as raconteur, 45, 58, 150, 159,
163; as graceful loser, 48; writes articles
on literature, 49; and newspaper colleagues, 49, 160; and Eugene V. Debs,
50; and Roman Catholic Church, 50;
writes speeches for others, 52, 56,
128–29, 177; works for Board of Public
Works, 52–53, 54, 58; courtship of
Sybil McCaslin, 53–54, 55; correspon-
dence with Sybil, 54; attends 1908
Democratic National Convention
(Denver), 55–56, 57; and Thomas R.
Marshall, 59; secretary to John W.
Kern, 59, 60–82; lives in Washington,
D.C., 59, 63, 65; moves to Washington,
D.C., 61; elected to National Press
Club, 64; writes column "Washington
Side-Lights" for *Terre Haute Tribune*,
64, 70; marriage, 65; speaks at Irish-
American meeting, 67; addresses Irish-
Americans in Rhode Island, 72; praises
Wilson's foreign policy, 73; speaks in
Boston, 74; spends summer in
Indianapolis, 75; writes *The Irish
Orators: A History of Ireland's Fight for
Freedom*, 75; birth of daughter, 76;
remains anti-British and pro-German,
76; publishes *The Irish Orators*, 77;
campaigns in Indiana, 80; duties as
Kern's secretary end, 81; clerk of
Committee on Privileges and Elections,
81; returns to Fort Wayne to work at
*Fort Wayne Journal-Gazette*, 83; writes
*The Life of John Worth Kern*, 83, 92–93;
writes *The Party Battles of the Jackson
Period*, 83, 93–94; and Winston
Churchill, 85; and the Russian
Revolution, 85; and Vladimir Lenin,
86; and League of Nations, 86; and
William C. Bullitt, 87; and Raymond
Robins, 87–88; and Theodore
Roosevelt, Jr., 89; praises Charles Evans
Hughes, 90; attacks Ku Klux Klan, 90,

92, 109; and Warren G. Harding, 91;
begins research on Thomas Jefferson
and Alexander Hamilton, 95; offered
Democratic secretary of state nomina-
tion, 96; declines chairmanship of
Indiana Democratic party, 96; addresses
Indiana Democratic Editorial
Association, 97; death of mother, 99;
disenchantment with *Journal-Gazette*,
101; and Theodore Dreiser, 101, 127,
146, 149; moves to New York, 102; editorials for *New York Evening World*,
105–6, 129, 134, 137, 140; attacks
Herbert Hoover, 112, 137; writes
*Jefferson and Hamilton: The Struggle for
Democracy in America*, 114–17; receives
Jefferson Medal, 118; writes *The Tragic
Era: The Revolution after Lincoln*,
119–20; degrees and honors, 124, 248,
266, 270; writes *Beveridge and the
Progressive Era*, 125, 126; and Arthur
Krock, 127; 1928 keynote address, 127,
132, 133, 134–36, 137, 142, 177; political connections, 127, 133–34, 142–43,
150, 151, 167, 168, 262–63, 271–72;
and William G. McAdoo, 127, 146;
associations with intellectually and
socially prominent, 127–28, 146,
147–48, 149–50; lives in New York,
127–53, 268–69, 270; delegate to 1924
Democratic National  Convention
(New York), 128; involvement with
Robert F. Wagner's Senate bid, 128–29;
speech compared to William Jennings
Bryan's "Cross of Gold," 132, 136; noti-
fies Joseph T. Robinson of his selection
as Alfred E. Smith's running mate, 136;
writes pro-Smith editorials, 137; and
Franklin D. Roosevelt, 139, 140, 141,
142, 143, 151, 152, 178, 256; delegate
to 1932 Democratic National
Convention (Chicago), 142; speeches
over radio, 143; comments on effects of
depression, 144, 176; family travels and
vacations, 145–46, 163, 254; defends
Paxton Hibben's Henry Ward Beecher
biography, 148, 149; effects of New
York years on, 150–51; and ITT and
Spanish government, 151–52, 169, 172,